AMERICAN POETRY AND POETICS

Daniel G. Hoffman is a poet, critic, and associate professor of English literature at Swarthmore College. He is the author of two books of verse, *A Little Geste* and *An Armada of Thirty Whales;* his critical studies include *Form and Fable in American Fiction* and *The Poetry of Stephen Crane.* He has taught at Columbia University, as visiting professor of American literature at Dijon, and at the School of Letters in Indiana University; and he has held a research fellowship from the American Council of Learned Societies.

Daniel G. Hoffman is a poet, critic, and associate professor of English literature at Swarthmore College. He is the author of two books of verse, A Little Geste and An Armada of Thirty Whales, has critical studies behind them and Indian in American Fiction, and The Poetry of Stephen Crane. He has taught at Columbia University as visiting professor of American literature at Dijon, and at the School of Letters in Indiana University, and he has held a research fellowship from the American Council of Learned Societies.

AMERICAN POETRY AND POETICS

POEMS AND CRITICAL
DOCUMENTS
FROM THE PURITANS TO
ROBERT FROST

Edited by DANIEL G. HOFFMAN

ANCHOR BOOKS
DOUBLEDAY & COMPANY, INC., GARDEN CITY, NEW YORK

The Anchor Books edition is the first publication of *American Poetry and Poetics*.

Anchor Books edition: 1962

ACKNOWLEDGMENTS:

STEPHEN CRANE: "A man adrift on a slim spar" (No. 1 from "Three Poems") reprinted from *Collected Poems of Stephen Crane*, copyright 1929, 1930, by permission of Alfred A. Knopf, Inc.; "The patent of a lord" and "Bottles and bottles and bottles" from *The Poetry of Stephen Crane* by Daniel G. Hoffman, copyright 1957 by Columbia University Press, by permission of the Press, of Alfred A. Knopf, Inc., and of Butler Library, Columbia University, owner of the manuscripts.

EMILY DICKINSON: "I dwell in possibility" and "In winter, in my room" are reprinted from *The Complete Poems of Emily Dickinson*, copyright 1914, 1929, 1942, by Martha Dickinson Bianchi, copyright © 1957 by Mary L. Hampson; and "After great pain a formal feeling comes" from *The Complete Poems of Emily Dickinson*, copyright 1929 by Martha Dickinson Bianchi, copyright © 1957 by Mary L. Hampson, by permission of Little, Brown & Co.; and the following poems are reprinted by permission of the publishers from *The Poems of Emily Dickinson*, edited by Thomas H. Johnson (Cambridge, Mass.: The Belknap Press of Harvard University Press, copyright 1951, 1955, by The President and Fellows of Harvard College): Nos. 258, 280, 341, 465, 650, 712, 1068, 1304.

ROBERT FROST: All selections are from *Complete Poems of Robert Frost*, copyright 1930, 1947, copyright renewed 1949 by Holt, Rinehart and Winston, Inc.; reprinted by permission of Holt, Rinehart and Winston, Inc.

EDWIN ARLINGTON ROBINSON: The following poems are reprinted with the permission of Charles Scribner's Sons from *The Town Down the River* by Edwin Arlington Robinson: "How Annandale Went Out" and "For a Dead Lady" (copyright 1910 Charles Scribner's Sons; renewal copyright 1938 Ruth Niveson); "Miniver Cheevy" (Copyright 1907 Charles Scribner's Sons, renewal copyright 1935).

EDWARD TAYLOR: "Meditation Thirty-two" is reprinted by permission of author and publisher from "Poems of Edward Taylor" by Barbara Damon Simison, *Yale University Library Gazette*, XXVIII (1954), with the consent of Yale University Library, owner of the manuscript; all other selections are reprinted by permission of Princeton University Press from *Poetical Works of Edward Taylor*, edited by Thomas H. Johnson, copyright 1943, Princeton University Press.

HENRY TIMROD: "A Theory of Poetry" is reprinted from *The Essays of Henry Timrod*, edited by Edd Winfield Parks, copyright 1942, by permission of the University of Georgia Press, Athens, Georgia.

CONTENTS*

* Poems printed in full in the critical essays in Part II are
listed here. Dates of composition are given when earlier than
dates of first publication.

* This poem is called Proem to "Waif" in Poe's essay "The
Poetic Principle;" but in Longfellow's *Collected Poems* it is
titled "The Day Is Done."

PART II. CRITICAL THEORY: SELECTED DOCUMENTS

TRADITION AND INVENTION IN AMERICAN POETRY

American poetry is riddled with contradictions. Much of our best poetry has been written against the grain of American life, yet much of our best poetry has proclaimed that America is its subject and our life its theme. At the beginning of the Republic Freneau defined the opportunities for lyricism:

On these bleak climes by Fortune thrown,
Where rigid Reason reigns alone,
Where lovely Fancy has no sway,
Nor magic forms about us play—
Nor nature takes her summer hue
Tell me, what has the muse to do?

Half a century later Whitman could find the muse everywhere:

I speak the pass-word primeval—I give the sign of
    democracy;
By God! I will accept nothing which all cannot have
    their counterpart of on the same terms.

      .   .

I believe a leaf of grass is no less than the journey-
    work of the stars,
And the pismire is equally perfect, and a grain of
    sand, and the egg of the wren,
And the tree-toad is a chef-d'oeuvre for the highest,
And the running blackberry would adorn the parlors
    of heaven,
And the narrowest hinge in my hand puts to scorn all
    machinery,
And the cow crunching with depress'd head surpasses
    any statue,

And a mouse is miracle enough to stagger sextillions
    of infidels,
And I could come every afternoon of my life to look
    at the farmer's girl boiling her tea-kettle and
    baking short-cake.

But Emily Dickinson who, though a lawyer's girl, boiled
her own kettle and baked short-cake herself, finds her muse
in isolation rather than in the "En-Masse":

Much madness is divinest sense
To a discerning eye;
Much sense the starkest madness.
'Tis the majority
In this, as all, prevails.
Assent, and you are sane;
Demur,—you're straightway dangerous
And handled with a chain.

Emerson, for his part, found the muse, or said he did,
equally in the materialistic life as in introspection:

Justice is the rhyme of things;
Trade and counting use
The self-same tuneful muse;
And Nemesis,
Who with even matches odd,
Who athwart space redresses
The partial wrong,
Fills the just period,
And finishes the song.

Melville's song finishes differently:

And, flung to kiln, Apollo's bust
Makes lime for Mammon's tower.

And Poe's muse has nothing to do with trade, counting,
or kiln:

Ah, Psyche, from the regions which
Are Holy-Land!

It is a peculiar characteristic of American writing that
its outstanding achievements seem a series of new beginnings rather than a continuous development from one to
another. Nevertheless in the years between the Puritan
settlement and the beginnings of the modernist movement
of the present century there are several continuing concerns which the writings chosen here reflect. These can
best be described as opposing tendencies whose contradictions complement one another; the tensions between them
give our best poetry its strength. Insofar as we have had
poetic theories, they have posed the contradictory bases
from which American poetry could be conceived.

Our poets have been both traditionalists and revolution-
aries. They have sought to perpetuate the values of English literature and its styles and forms; and they have tried
to repudiate those values in order to discover the inherent
nature of their own experience on a new continent, under
a new conception of government and of human nature,
using a new language and new forms of expression. Yet
even our traditionalists cannot be considered in the main-
stream of the English literature that nurtured them, for
they worked in provincial isolation long after the values
they conserved had become obsolete. Or they interpreted
the work of their British contemporaries in the terms im-
posed by their contemporary America, a culture that surrounded them with institutions and attitudes rather different from those with which the Romantic and Victorian
British poets contended. At the same time our revolution-
aries were deeply influenced by the traditions they sought
to escape; the most radical statements of aesthetic aims
by Poe and Emerson and Whitman would be almost inconceivable without the prior influence upon them of
Coleridge.

The most salient fact of the situation of our poets has
been the difficulties that their culture placed between the
poet and his language, between the poet and his subjects,
between the poet and his audience. What Emerson says

of the poet is probably true of the creative artist everywhere: "He is isolated among his contemporaries by truth and by his art"; yet in America there were historically valid reasons why this isolation was felt with special intensity and contributed much to the discontinuity that has been mentioned.

2

Let us begin by acknowledging early limitations, narrowness of scope, penury of achievement, the almost effective discouragement of a whole set of conditions antipathetic to the emergence of a major poetry. Most obvious of these is the brevity of our history. "The flower of art blooms only where the soil is deep. . . . it takes a great deal of history to produce a literature. . . . it needs a complex social machinery to set a writer in motion," Henry James observed. It might fancifully be proposed that the "Preface" to *The Bay Psalm Book* should stand in the development of American poetry in a role similar to that of Sidney's "Defense of Poetry" in England; we must inevitably compare Edward Taylor to his master, George Herbert; Anne Bradstreet, to hers, Joshua Sylvester; and find Philip Freneau at his best a colonial Cowper who strangely anticipates Coleridge's Gothicism. Bryant, hailed in his own time as our greatest bard, seems limited, bland, and monotonous beside Wordsworth.

These authors are included here not only to show their limitations but because each, in a few poems, has so successfully overcome the difficulties placed in his way, whether by temperament or by his fate as an American poet, that his lines deserve the continuing life of being read by those who value poetic excellence. Compared to the English poetry of the seventeenth, eighteenth, and early nineteenth centuries we have not very much to show. Perhaps it was impossible that a small population in a raw land could have produced or nurtured a Donne, a Milton, a Dryden, a Pope, a Keats, a Shelley, a Coleridge—but the best poets in these colonies and States have excellences of their own with which no work by their greater English contemporaries quite corresponds.

When we come to Poe, Emerson, Whitman, and Dickinson, we discover originality of style and distinctiveness of thought which makes obvious their claims for major consideration. The power of their achievements is so great as to persuade us that their work creates a world; yet the dimensions of the universe within which their imaginations could operate are circumscribed by the culture around them, a culture profoundly inimical to any exercise of the literary imagination at all. Their successes are won by the engagement of their deepest psychic energies in heroic acts of repudiation and evasion, by their faith in the power of the imagination to discover the structure and the language of truth.

What were these obstacles that made necessary such radical rejections or adaptations of tradition as our best poets had to devise?

The three chief intellectual currents which together form the foreground to their achievements were Puritanism, pragmatic utilitarianism, and egalitarianism. In these movements a set of assumptions about the nature of language, of knowledge, of man, and of art became fixed. It can scarcely be claimed that any of these is a solely American phenomenon, yet the circumstances which obtained in their confluence made the poetic environment of our early nineteenth century significantly distinctive.

Puritanism, for us, was the dominating theological and intellectual tradition of our culturally most influential region. In England, Puritanism was a sectarian faith that never had the hold on the national sensibility which in America it had on the colonial. When we assess its influence upon later American poetry we find that the tendencies most strongly perpetuated were restrictive upon what the Romantic era conceived of as the role of the imagination. Puritanism had assumed the primary function of art to be, not the discovery of truth, but the elaboration of doctrines already known. The virtue of the plain style which the Puritans preferred was that it encouraged the widest possible comprehension, where the complex

rhetoric of Anglican preaching and the complicated metaphors of metaphysical verse were fully understood only by
an elite few. Their didactic aim reinforced the Puritans'
conception of language as a monistic medium in which
one word had one proper signification, and of allegory in
which a direct correspondence was demonstrated between
the events of this life and spiritual experience. It is true
that these bequests to the nineteenth century hardly do
justice to either the range of ideas or the literary ambition
of the Puritans themselves. Despite their commitment to
plain style they could hardly keep from employing the
poetic conceits of their Anglican contemporaries; and they
found it no contradiction to their piety to write, as Mistress
Bradstreet did, elegies to Sir Philip Sidney or long allegories on "The Four Elements," "The Four Ages of Man,"
the seasons, or "The Four Humours in Man's Constitution." But it was not such imitations of late Elizabethan
writings that made Puritan literary ideals influential on a
later age, nor is it their imitative and mediocre versifying
to which the modern reader turns for pleasure. Neither do
we find poetic merit in the verse that the Puritans themselves most highly valued, their poems on doctrinal subjects and on historical subjects doctrinally interpreted. Of
the Puritan poets, those chosen here are represented by
verses that served no public function in their own time.
Mistress Bradstreet is most appealing—and universally so
—in a few poems to her husband and children and in a
devout and touching allegory of a domestic tragedy, the
burning of her house. Edward Taylor was known to his
fellows only as the minister of Westfield, Massachusetts;
his poetry was his private indulgence. Since he wrote for
fifty years in the ornamented metaphysical style he had
learned from the Anglican poet George Herbert before
emigrating to the colonies in his early twenties, Taylor
knew that his poems contradicted the stylistic tenets of his
church. His manuscript was not found until 1937, when it
was discovered that America had had a metaphysical religious poet after all. Taylor cannot have influenced anyone who came after him; he requires inclusion here because some of his meditations are the most distinguished

verse written on this continent in colonial times, and because his work reveals the deep undercurrent of sympathy in the New England sensibility for the quality of ingeniously intellectualized passion which characterizes the metaphysical style. This quality comes into play again in the concern with language and metaphor in the essays of Emerson and in the poems of Dickinson, both of whom read the seventeenth century poets (as did Thoreau) at a time when what T. S. Eliot calls their union of sensibility and intellect was not generally admired.

Puritan America inevitably assimilated the changing attitudes toward poetry of the English eighteenth century. Cotton Mather's treatise for ministerial candidates advises the writing of poetry as a rhetorical accomplishment, and acknowledges a plurality of styles to accord with the individual "gait" of the authors. In the succeeding era we had many Men of the Enlightenment, but no Enlightenment Poet. The practice of letters in the later eighteenth century was a gentlemanly accomplishment which, like the writing of theatricals and the composing of music, was pursued for the most part in unquestioning obeisance to the English models of the preceding generation. Our Hartford wits—Timothy Dwight, Jonathan Trumbull, Joel Barlow—dutifully heeded ambition's call and succumbed in the wonted way to that devourer of small talents, the Heroic Poem. In this genre Barlow's huge failure, *The Columbiad*, became the jape of later generations although his mock epic "The Hasty Pudding" remains a minor classic.

One might hazard the difficulties of producing a neoclassical literature (which assumes the background of a stable society) in a remote colony torn by oppression, rebellion, and the establishment of a new political order. Also operative upon our poets was the condition of their language. I allude not only to the decadent diction which Wordsworth and Coleridge found inadequate to the occasions of passion, but to assumptions as to the nature of words. From Dennie to Tocqueville, commentators on America stress the intolerance in a mercantile culture for any conceptions of language that did not reinforce the prosaic

virtues of unambiguous diction, of the progress of thought
from the known to the unknown, of the obligation of literature to improve the reader's virtue or his knowledge. These
are exemplary dicta for expository writing; Benjamin
Franklin, replying to a query on style, had set them forth
with his customary clarity and force. In these widely held
conceptions, secular utilitarian thought, like theological
sanction earlier, operated to reduce language to a monistic
medium best fitted for allegory and rational exposition.

The career of Philip Freneau is testamentary to the discouragement that Euterpe found in our democratic land.
The only muse who can flourish here, Freneau laments in
"To an Author," is satire, the muse of reason turned against
its own pretension; how else speak to men who scorn the
realm of "Fancy's sway"? Perhaps, in a more receptive
culture, Freneau would have developed the most original
aspects of his talent: before Wordsworth he already responded to nature with accurate observation and sympathy; before Coleridge he brought into his long poem "The
House of Night" a sense of supernal terror; and his poems
giving somber dignity to the Indian place him among our
earliest romantic primitivists. Ultimately the victim of the
situation Joseph Dennie described in reviewing his work,
Freneau expended his considerable powers in topical satire
and versified political journalism. Of course it is possible
that his lyric impulse simply failed after 1799; we do
know that his slight poems, which alone of the verse written here in the eighteenth century still have poetic merit,
brought him neither renown nor security. Freneau's language indicates his uneasy transitional position. Like his
contemporaries Gray and Cowper he had been reared on
the decorous artificiality of Augustan diction, a linguistic
mold which his incipient romanticism had to break.

3

It is at this point in the development of our poetry that
Tocqueville made his celebrated analysis of the effects
of democracy upon language, thought, and literature. In
Democracy in America he defines these effects by present-

ing a series of dialectical contrasts between the operations of an aristocratic society and those of an egalitarian culture. Tocqueville's conception of these two societies was based on his experience in France and his observations during a tour of the United States in 1831. Yet they are more accurate as definitions of tendencies than as portraits of contemporary reality. Like Plato's Republic, and like all typologies based on intellectual constructs, Tocqueville's states are completely articulated and consistent versions of human possibilities. What makes his fictive democracy so valuable is his identification of the one synergizing principle of American society—indeed of all modern, democratic Western societies since the industrial revolution. Taking the conception of equality seriously, to a degree far exceeding its enactment in our popular culture and political institutions, Tocqueville posits the effects of such a total commitment on all of the institutions, attitudes, and mores of the culture. With respect to language and literature, the principles underlying the traditions of aristocratic nations would seem at every point to be subverted and denied. It may be suggested that Tocqueville's definitions of an aristocratic literature disclose his own rationalistic bias for the productions of the Enlightenment, rather than for such Romantic writings as had been appearing for almost half a century in England and France before his visit to America. Yet he might argue that Romanticism itself, rejecting authority, decorum, traditional diction, and traditional forms, seeking in nature and in man alone the sources of poetical inspiration, was almost as much a product of egalitarian tendencies as was the hypothetical literature of the future which he predicted for America.

It is interesting to compare to Tocqueville's brilliantly reasoned discourse the views of Bryant in "On Poetry in its Relation to Our Age and Country." Bryant himself might be taken as that type of intermediate bard whom Tocqueville describes. Writing after the decline of credence in the hierarchy of spiritual beings which aristocratic ages interpose between the Deity and human affairs, Bryant found his chief subject in Nature. But, Tocqueville argues, this is only a preparatory stage to the discovery of the only possible subject for a viable literature in an egalitarian state: Man himself, who, by being just like every other individual, is both unable to conceive of the aristocratic hero and is fated to celebrate his own universality. Bryant, however, sees no such implications in his own position; instead he exalts America's freedom from the superstitions of the past, and, far from finding our own lack of traditions a bar to conventional poetry, he takes this condition as warrant to ransack the traditions of every other land and age. Even our native locutions seem suited for the creation of a poetry "of beauty and grandeur, intellectual greatness and moral truth." But Bryant conceives of all of these qualities for American verse as being in no way different from what they were in English poetry. Himself an example of the effect of democracy on poetic possibilities, he was still too rooted in the past to realize the extent of the repudiations his situation made possible; nor did Bryant have the radical independence of mind to penetrate to the true spiritual center of American life.

Tocqueville's chapter is often taken as a telepathic anticipation of a poem the first version of which appeared fifteen years after *Democracy in America*. There is no reason to suppose that the author of *Leaves of Grass* had read—or needed to have read—the Frenchman's work (although it had been translated almost immediately). But Whitman had read Emerson—"I was simmering, simmering, simmering," he once said, "and Emerson brought me to a boil." It is Whitman whose poetry most fully realizes the radical promises of democratic literature, but it is Emerson's aesthetic theory which most fully defines in what that promise may consist. Emerson's original assumption resembles Tocqueville's, but he begins from an entirely different point of view. Tocqueville had conceived of equality as primarily a political condition; for Emerson, on the contrary, "Society is everywhere in a conspiracy against the manhood of each of its members." The members are superior in their identity as individuals to the ethically compromised, corporate creatures their surrender to each other would require them to become. Emerson begins with the conviction of spiritual egalitarianism: we are equals because each of us partakes of the Oversoul, contains within himself Divinity. The free man is he who heeds the true nature of his own spirit and defies the inheritance of error which our institutions perpetuate.

Language, too, is "perverted to stand for things which are not . . . and words lose all power to stimulate the understanding or the affections. . . . But wise men pierce this rotten diction and fasten words again to visible things." Emerson continues the purification of language begun by Wordsworth's "Preface" to *Lyrical Ballads* and by Coleridge in *Biographia Literaria,* a task that each generation requires to be performed anew. The succession leads from Emerson toward Frost, Eliot, and Pound.

For Emerson, language must be both concretely fastened to visible things and at the same time metaphors of unseen but imminent truths. "Parts of speech are metaphors because the whole of nature is a metaphor of the human mind." The Poet is the true hero who "names the thing because he sees it, or comes one step nearer to it than any other. This expression or naming is not art, but a second nature, grown out of the first, as a leaf out of a tree." In such organic images Emerson expresses his conviction of the Poet as Seer, and of art as the discovery of the form of truth:

For it is not metres, but a metre-making argument that makes a poem—a thought so passionate and alive that like the spirit of a plant or an animal it has an architecture of its own, and adorns nature with a new thing.

In the making of such new things the poet will tap the joyous metamorphic powers inherent in words themselves. "The use of symbols has a certain power of emancipation and exhilaration in all men," and the poets who bring this joy to others "are thus liberating gods."

Emerson's conception of art is profoundly ethical. The poet "is the sayer, the namer, and represents beauty," and for Emerson, "the love of truth, the love of good, the love of beauty—are equal—each of these three has the power of the others latent in him." Coleridge had proposed that a poem has "for its immediate object pleasure, not truth," a distinction Poe would seize upon; Emerson, reflecting the moral concern of his Puritan-Unitarian heritage, refuses to separate joy from morality. In this he is true to the mystical side of his nature—Lowell characterized him as "a Plotinus-Montaigne"—for how can knowledge of the good be other than beautiful and joyous?

At the same time Emerson's radical egalitarianism led his aesthetics toward conceptions of new possibilities for poetry in American life. Not, perhaps, so much because it was American as because American life was *the present:* since for Emerson each age must have its own Homer as well as its own miracles and its own Revelations. "I look in vain for the poet whom I describe. . . . Our log-rolling, our stumps and their politics, our fisheries, our Negroes and Indians, our boats and our repudiations, the wrath of rogues and the pusillanimity of honest men, the northern trade, the southern planting, the western clearing, Oregon and Texas, are yet unsung. Yet America is a poem in our eyes; its ample geography dazzles the imagination, and it will not wait long for metres." After *Leaves of Grass* Emerson did not look in vain for such a poet.

In his own verse, despite moments of genuine power, Emerson seems unable to bring about the poetry for whose advent his prose so eloquently called. The best of his poems so differ from one another as to give the impression of the discontinuous achievement of an experimenter who never fully realized his own distinctive qualities of mind and feeling in a characteristic poetic diction and form. The best of Whitman's poems, on the contrary, are so marked by the same qualities of language and feeling as to convince us that an original master knew exactly what were the sources and materials of his own mastery. We may regard Whitman as an idiosyncratic embodiment of the Emersonian Poet. (Any embodiment of Emerson's ideas would have had to be idiosyncratic, but they did not obligate such a poet to share Whitman's rather diffused sexuality or his purposed confusion between "amativeness" and egalitarian brotherhood.)

Emerson had written, "We are symbols and inhabit

symbols," but it was Whitman who discovered—we should say, created—the master-symbol inherent in the Emersonian aesthetic. This is the Self, which, as Tocqueville had foretold, proves the inevitable and all-encompassing theme and subject of a literature founded on the principle of democracy.

Radical though it is, Whitman's revolutionary poetics has, as Emerson observed in his letter of congratulation to the author of *Leaves of Grass,* "a long foreground somewhere." Whitman exemplifies the extreme expression of certain intellectual currents and dispositions of feeling that were widespread in the early nineteenth century: besides egalitarianism, Whitman expresses an absolute humanitarianism; complete free will; Romantic empathy with nature; an incandescent sense of the immediacy of spiritual transfiguration. Added to these is Whitman's capacity to take in joy through each of his five senses. These conceptions make no logical program of thought or action, but in the extraordinary poetic forms Whitman achieved for them they are combined in a consequent, intuitively coordinated accommodation of the individual consciousness to the mystery, the terror, the joy, and the wonder of living and dying.

To achieve his unexampled largeness of feeling Whitman had to make unparalleled rejections of proprieties, decorum, and established modes of response to experience which the culture of the past had, as he would say, "promulged" upon the present. Emerson's heroic vision of the poet is doubtless too much encumbered with the traditional—that is to say, late Augustan and low-pressure Romantic—aspects of vatic dignity. Despite such daring as he shows in the opening section of "Hamatreya," Emerson cannot make Whitman's thorough-going repudiations of the traditional bases of poetic form, structure, and meter. Whitman attributes these technical aspects to the same disease of society which he holds responsible for the traditional subjects of poetry. It is aristocracy which leads equally to rhyme and pentameter, and to the celebration of privilege and immorality. He warns against "the hiatus of singular eminence," and sets out to celebrate the most common, knowing that "the great master . . . sees health for himself in being one of the mass." "The genius of the United States is . . . always most in the common people." The Self that annunciates truth in his poems differs from his readers only in that he has found tongue for the truths which their souls acknowledge as their own. This Self must be taken not as Walt Whitman's own egoistic person (although it is that too) but as the radical poetic device by which his sensibility encompasses reality. The transcendant power of the Self is to be larger than any of the single aspects of reality with which it merges; in this way ugliness, disease, defeat, and death are accommodated to Whitman's dynamic conception of life as process. They are subordinated to the "procreant urge" which is the Self's source of strength, its triumph over all that threatens it. Whitman thus absorbs into his verse the subjects that his contemporaries avoided. He makes levies from them into contributions to his own affirmations. Considering the Self as a master-symbol in his poems, we find it equated with, and sometimes interchangeable with, other master-symbols: the leaves of grass sprouting everywhere; the sea; the earth; and particularly, America. Whitman's vision of the vatic role makes him urge his "Song of Myself" upon us as a democratic equivalent of the "Song of Songs"; as he says, "the known universe has one complete lover and that is the greatest poet." His song of himself is both a "Song of America" and a hymn of devotion to the world.

4

Consistent as are the theory of Emerson and the poetry of Whitman with Tocqueville's analysis of democracy, America has also nurtured a body of poetry and its poetics that countervenes that of the Transcendental-egalitarian movement at every point. Tocqueville's dialectic excluded from his view any notion of American culture other than the completely egalitarian. This conception had little applicability to the society of Richmond, Virginia, in which the orphaned son of itinerant actors had been brought up by a plantation-owning tobacco factor. Edgar Poe was never legally adopted by James Allan, with whom he quarreled, and by the age of twenty he found his hopes of an inheritance permanently dashed. Poe represents not Tocqueville's pure aristocrat, but a distinctive American subspecies: the disinherited gentleman. (Hawthorne, Melville, and Mark Twain envisaged themselves in this role.) With egalitarian sentiment he had nothing to do. If Whitman's poetic program is the aesthetic of democracy, of the poet who identifies himself with his countrymen, Poe's is that of the artist of the beautiful whose private vision is opposed to the vulgar materialism of the masses. It is indicative of Whitman's generosity of spirit that when a tomb to Poe was belatedly dedicated in 1880, Whitman was the only poet in the United States who cared to attend. His recollection of this occasion tells us how deep he recognized the chasm to be between Poe's intentions and his own; yet in the dream he records we can infer a subcurrent of kinship with the poet of "nocturnal themes" and "demoniac undertones"; as indeed a comparison of Whitman's "The Sleepers" with Poe's "Dream-Land" and "The City in the Sea" makes manifest.

Where Whitman takes all life as the province of his poems, Poe decrees that poetry has only one subject, Beauty, and that the subject most fitting for poetry is the one most melancholy and therefore most beautiful, the death of a beautiful woman. Whitman affirms the moral function of art; Poe, led on by Coleridge's distinction that poetry has as its object pleasure rather than truth, denies that poetry has any concern with either truth or virtue. This takes Poe far toward his conception of poetry as divorced from quotidian reality—which he identifies with rationalism and materialism; poetry seeks beauty alone, subject only to the laws of its own autonomous existence. The poet, like "Israfel," aims to speak in the tongues of angels, of beauties beyond human knowledge, beyond the capacity of language to describe. Poe opposes Whitman on the grounds of diction, rhythm, and structure, as well as on those of poetic intention. Whitman repudiates all the customary techniques of verse and invents new principles of organization for his poems; Poe commits his verse to an hypnotic regularity of meter, a mnemonically insistent rhyme, and, usually, a strict and arbitrary stanzaic arrangement. Whitman conceives of all of his verse as a single poem, which he spends his whole life enlarging; Poe maintains that a long poem is a contradiction in terms, and posits a limit of 100 lines as the maximum allowable. Whitman is concerned with what his poems are about, Poe with how his may produce a preconceived effect upon the reader. Whitman wants to break down the reader's rational consciousness, to enlarge it to include his own vision of equality in which the differences between sexes, stations, life and death, comedy and tragedy, the present and the past and the future, mortality and immortality, are all subsumed in the act of becoming one with the knowledge he proffers—the knowledge of the power of the Self to participate in reality. Poe wants to break down the reader's conscious rationality, to exclude the material life of causation and suffering by his insistence upon a realm of spiritual ecstasy so different from ordinary life that he cannot describe it. Whitman exults in the "democratic concretes" of which reality is made; Poe exults in a vagueness that leads his soul beyond the limitations of the material world. In both poets there is an implacable derangement of reason and of language, pursued to opposite ends. Poe's end is an escape from life, from language, from humanity. He focuses his attention exclusively on his own imaginative processes, identifying them with the operation of the soul. Confusing what should be an aspect of treatment with subject (as Mr. Yvor Winters has observed), in his quest for beauty beyond human experience Poe reduces poetry to serve a mechanistic conception of psychology and denies himself almost all the materials of which literature can be made. In his tales he can avoid the insoluble problems his theory of verse posed for his poems. His fictional allegories show the dissolution of the rational self; the only subject of his poems is the journey of the spiritual half of his divided soul into a condition of otherness, or nonlife. Whether he calls this the region of Auber, a city in the sea, or a Holy Land, it is "Out of SPACE, out of TIME." Even given such a subject, Poe's means of dealing with it

—his metronomic rhythms, his incantatory refrains, the subjection of meanings to sounds, and the lack of tactile reality
or perception—seem often as mechanical as the calculated
devices for producing *frissons* which he describes in "The
Philosophy of Composition." The subject of that essay,
however, is Poe's theory of his verse, which he would hoax
us into thinking the same as his practice.

Poe felt himself shut out from literary recognition by
the cabal of New Englanders who controlled the major
periodicals and puffed each other's reputations. It is true
that except for Lowell's early praise, he was not taken
seriously by his Northern contemporaries. Although the
conception of poetry as an expression of ideality was a
commonplace among later nineteenth-century poets, none
was willing, as he had been, to repudiate "the heresy of
the didactic." Poe's theory of poetry was influential only
in his native region, and there, fourteen years after his
death, its limitations were firmly analyzed by another poet
who could recognize the importance of Poe's aims without
endorsing them. Henry Timrod, whose death was hastened
by his sufferings in the Civil War, had a talent nourished
on Wordsworth's Romanticism and disciplined by his love
of Latin literature. He wrote with a clarity and precision
distinctive in an age and culture in which rhetoric was
so often mistaken for eloquence. Timrod recognized that
Poe had tried to make universal laws of his own limitations;
as they were the limitations of genius, they deserve to be
refuted where they have no application, and acknowledged
where they do. Timrod's sensitive analysis of *Paradise Lost*
asserts the principle of unity in diversity which modern
criticism recognizes as the cumulative effect of controlled
variety in texture.

In the halfway house between Poe's isolate castle and
Whitman's thronged bivouac live most of the lesser poets
of the American Romantic movement. While Whitman
celebrated the senses, Lowell followed Bryant in avoiding
the antipoetic native bias by modeling his poems on those
of the sanctioned masters. Bryant and Longfellow between
them translated the two greatest poems of Western culture, *The Iliad* and *The Divine Comedy*, respectively.

Longfellow and Lowell were both professors at Harvard, fluent in other languages, widely traveled and widely read. Not subscribing to the aesthetic consequences of political equality, they never deviated from traditional versification and rarely from decorous poetic diction, save in the satiric or humorous ballads by which they remain best known. Their view of nature was unfailingly to find in each contemplated object a demonstration of the great divine design. Their responses to native life took the forms of dialect verse, the retelling of regional folktale, and historical narrative. Regarding literature as a continuum with the great works of the past, they took those for their guides and wrote as though they were Englishmen resident in Cambridge, Massachusetts. Their pieties are outdated, their verses often relaxed and prolix, yet, as Whitman finally concedes in *Specimen Days*, they brought a much-needed note of cultivation and reverence for the past into the literature of a raw land. Although they were its most honored bards, the poems most expressive of the major tendencies of American culture were written by the neglected Poe and Whitman and by two other poets who had no visible audience during their lifetimes: Herman Melville and Emily Dickinson.

5

Melville's poems are sometimes taken as the mere by-blows of his imaginative life. Of course *Moby-Dick* is the great achievement among his heroic efforts to weave the "linked analogies" of the world of experience on the loom of divine truth. Melville turned to poetry after *Pierre* and *The Confidence-Man* (1852, 1857) had alienated what readers his whaling story and the earlier South Seas romances had won. He had written light verse as early as in *Mardi* (1849), but now, in *Battle Pieces* (1866) he composed almost a day-by-day commentary on the Civil War. These poems are, with Whitman's *Drum Taps* and Timrod's Confederate elegies the major poetic expression of the war. In Melville's poems, "War is now placed / Where War belongs— / Among the trades and artisans."

His imagery is drawn with the boldness of metaphysical poetry from mechanics and law courts—he writes of "Contemned foreclosures of surprise," of battle where "all went on by crank, / Pivot, and screw, / And calculations of caloric." What banners fly in Melville's poems are singed by irony; his conception of war is modern, though the verse is often trammeled by conventions uncomfortably worn. In the same poems that have such extraordinary images as those just cited there are also archaisms and clumsy rhymes. Yet his best poems have an authority and a precision of image unparalleled by any American poet of the time save Emily Dickinson. The first line of "A Utilitarian View of the Monitor's Fight" describes his poetry at its best: "Plain be the phrase, yet apt the verse." The techniques Melville never quite mastered were designed for gentler, more genteel sensibilities than his; for a Longfellow, of whom Lowell wrote that his "rare, tender, virgin-like" poems take their place

> . . . apart
> Where time has no sway, in the realm of pure Art,
> 'Tis a shrine of retreat from Earth's hubbub and
> strife. . . .

Melville's *materia poetica*, the reality he worked with, is on the contrary taken determinedly from the realm in which time has sway: the history of the present moment, the sufferings and ineluctable tragedies of the life around him. (Lowell was describing Longfellow's *Evangeline*, in which the strife and hubbub were subdued because long ago, and in another country.) Melville knew what contrarieties must

> fuse with Jacob's mystic heart,
> To wrestle with the Angel—Art.

He romanticizes nothing and cannot accept Poe's consolation, "To seek a shelter in some happier star"; Melville must endure the fated suffering of the life he knows. In

"The Aeolian Harp," he proposes the unavoidable subject of song for Nature's instrument:

> Listen: less a strain ideal
> Than Ariel's rendering of the real.

This reality encompasses, in the war poems, disaster, defeat, riot, death; in his succeeding collection, *John Marr and Other Sailors*, Melville returns to the sea for subjects, and unlike any other American poet of the element, he had dealt with "the inhuman sea" and knew that reality must include the wreck in "The Aeolian Harp," the dreamlike rammed and sinking ship in "The Berg." Melville's sea nurtures creatures like "The Maldive Shark"—"Pale ravener of horrible meat." His last book of poems, *Timoleon*, strikes a new note of poignance (as in the "Monody" to Hawthorne) and a lapidary delicacy of expression. Some have compared these poems to Landor's. His most successful single poem may well be "The House-Top," a meditation on the draft riots in New York. Here the blank verse rhythms are superbly controlled, alliteration harshly gongs the emphases, and the imagery projects catastrophe across the spaces of heaven in the constellations, thence into mythology and back through time to the present. The experience of riot and civil chaos is made comprehensible by the form in which the language, rhythms, and images of this poem embody it. This is how Ariel renders the Real.

Melville had sought to publish his verses, although after the Harper's edition of *Battle-Pieces* sold only 525 copies in ten years he conceded the futility of seeking, or speaking to, a national audience and brought out his last collection in a private edition of twenty-five copies for his friends. Emily Dickinson conceded the impossibility of finding readers from the beginning; of the 1,750 poems known to have been written by the Amherst recluse, only seven appeared while she was alive, and most of these without her consent and with extensive editorial revision of her text. It has been conjectured that after a conventional girlhood and a year at the Mount Holyoke Female Seminary she withdrew from the world into the house of her austere father because of a blighted love affair. Whether or not this is true hardly matters. The important fact is her choosing to live a life that accords with Thoreau's advice to "Simplify, simplify, simplify," to reach down through the mire of custom to touch the bedrock of reality on which we stand. Like Thoreau, who said he had "travelled much in Concord," Emily Dickinson traveled much in Amherst. Her poems show the effects of her reading, especially of the dictionary, the Bible, and Shakespeare, as well as such metaphysical poets as Donne, Vaughan, and Marvell, and the prose of Sir Thomas Browne. Like Whitman, she seems, after a few conventional and sentimental verses, suddenly to have devised a style of unexampled originality. In her case too the achievement of a style both made possible the delineation of a personal vision of fate and required the rejection of many extant conceptions of poetic technique. Although her basic meter and stanza are directly derived from the "fourteeners" quatrain of the hymnal—womanly, she conserves this most traditional of forms, but adapts it to her own extraordinary uses—her off-rhymes, her rhythmic syncopations and grammatical elisions, and the intensity of her view of life were too unconventional to please readers accustomed to Longfellow and the English Victorians. Emily Dickinson's instinct for privacy in her life and her avoidance of publication of her work were right. Yet she did not wish to be entirely cut off from the world around her. Its ideas, as she found them in Emerson's essays, she admitted freely into her solitude. She even sought literary advice from one of the mediators of genteel taste of the time, Thomas Wentworth Higginson. His account of her poetry, published after her death (see p. 416) indicates how right she was to follow the eccentric bent of her own genius. The alternative was trying to conform to the age's ideas of what a lady poet should be and how her work should scan, rhyme, address itself to narratives, and present uplifting sentiments in decorous language.

Where Whitman is all amplitude, Dickinson is economy itself; where Poe seeks beauty in ineffable vagueness, Dickinson creates it from the precision with which she delineates suffering; where Melville's images are masculine, of war, machinery, and shipwreck, Dickinson's imagery is from the woman's world of her house, her callers, her village landscape, and especially her religion. It has been proposed by Mr. Allen Tate that Emily Dickinson inherited the vocabulary of the Puritan faith at a time when the absolute quality of Puritan belief was of the past, a circumstance which gave her leave to make imaginative, and even sportive, use of conceptions which had in earlier New England been parts of a sacred machinery, exempt from poetic manipulation. Such conditions have obtained equally for other nineteenth-century poets. Yet it is true that Emily Dickinson confronts the immensity of death with an intensity and an acceptance of Calvinism that recalls Jonathan Edwards and the seventeenth century Puritans. With Whitman's pantheistic merging of consciousness or with Bryant's Roman stoicism in "Thanatopsis" she has nothing to do. Like Melville, she is a poet of the inscrutable necessity which we endure. In her best poems she is in absolute command of her own powers, which she creates out of the common language. Mr. Richard Chase has observed a crucial distinction between her uses of language: in some poems she is playful, and sentimentally descriptive in a manner he describes as "rococo." In her best poems, those that deal directly and boldly with suffering and death, her style is governed by the "sublime." It is her special gift to create sublimity not by the "elevated," abstract diction of Augustan pomp, but by such tropes as this:

> There's a certain Slant of light,
> Winter Afternoons—
> That oppresses, like the Heft
> Of Cathedral Tunes—

where one is struck equally by the muscular colloquialism of "Heft" (which Higginson primly improved to "weight"), and by the extraordinary image in which it occurs. What has made Emily Dickinson seem as much a poet of our time as of her own is not merely the accidents of her belated publication but the poetic conviction from which she writes. Her poems create the forms of the feelings they embody, and those feelings are conceived with an immediacy of language that responds to passion in disregard of the clichés of emotion and of speech with which we usually protect ourselves from the "Heavenly Hurt" of suffering. Emily Dickinson acknowledges her "imperial affliction," and transcends it, "Magnanimous as Bird / By Boy descried— / Singing unto the Stone / Of which it died." She deals directly with dying, with transfiguration, regarding Death as a courtly gentleman, a judge or lawgiver, and dying as the conferral upon her soul of status, of bridehood. In her best poems there is a mingling of the high diction of theology with the low diction of the kitchen commonplace. It was this impurity of idiom which seemed both crude and unpoetic to conventional editors and readers in the 1890's, when her verse began posthumously to appear. Tocqueville would have recognized in her mixed diction a distinctively American poetic style. But there was no theorist of poetry to prepare the public for Emily Dickinson's originality; her verse had to win its own readers. It has forced them to redefine their notions of poetry to include her poems. "I dwell in Possibility / A fairer house than Prose," she tells them, and confesses that her occupation's this:

> The spreading wide my narrow hands
> To gather Paradise.

6

No poet in the generation after the four just discussed built directly on their achievements; in fact it was not until after the modernist movement began in 1912 that their work had important consequences for American poetry. The years between the Civil War and the turn of the century have been called the twilight era of American verse. Perhaps its characteristic note of gentility and imitative idealism was struck by such a versifier as Richard Watson Gilder, whom T. S. Eliot succinctly characterized as "nimbly dull." Except he be an historian of Victorian America, the modern reader will find little reward in the writings of Gilder, Edmund Clarence Stedman, Bayard Taylor or Bliss Carman. Their work exhibits the interests of a class for whom literature was a decorous pastime, an escape from the business of life. Their intricate stanzas of *vers de societé* and rhetorical and sentimental poems on medieval themes dominated the magazines. Even such better poets than they as Sidney Lanier and William Vaughan Moody seem fatally trapped by their commitments to outmoded diction, poeticizing gestures, and rhetoric. This was the era in which the masters of modern poetry grew up: E. A. Robinson, Robert Frost, Wallace Stevens, Ezra Pound, T. S. Eliot passed their boyhoods in the '90's, when the language of poetry in English had come to a dead end, just as it had a century earlier. The live voices of Whitman and Melville were scarcely heard; Emily Dickinson's poems were a craze in the early years of the decade, but they influenced hardly anyone save Stephen Crane until the verse traditions which she avoided and which Crane defied were swept away in the revolution of language and poetic method that the founding of the magazine *Poetry* in 1912 and the first publications by the poets named above inaugurate.

Crane refused to call his verses "poems," lest he be called a "Poet" at a time when that epithet linked one in the public mind with a Gilder. His "lines" repudiate everything the '90's held dear: stanza, rhyme, meter, and especially piety. Crane is not a great poet—he did not take sufficient pains with his impressionistic notations—but he had an acute sense of the isolation and despair man feels in a universe where there is no rule but that of force. And he had what his contemporaries for the most part lacked, an absolute aesthetic honesty. His "lines" seemed to come from nowhere, they were so unlike any other poetry the age had seen. They do of course have derivations—in the ironic prose of Ambrose Bierce, in the parables of the Bible, and the sermons preached by Crane's family of Methodist ministers. Working all by himself—he did not know a single poet or author when he published *The Black*

Riders at twenty-four—Crane devised his own gawky ironic style in which to defy the false gods and fake emotions of the time. His later poems allow some of the devices of conventional verse; their taut honesty remains inimitable. "Do not weep, maiden, for war is kind" and "A man adrift on a slim spar" are worthy of the author of *The Red Badge of Courage*. But Crane's "lines" were mercilessly parodied in the press and in the polite magazines. Twenty years later, Sandburg would address his "Letter to Dead Imagists" to Crane and Dickinson. Crane's repudiations were made all over again after 1912 by poets of broader sensibilities than his intense but narrow view of fate permitted him. They would not be as antitheoretical as he; in place of his inferrable homemade poetics, the moderns would assimilate all the unrecognized masters of 19th century American verse—especially Poe, Whitman, and Emily Dickinson.

Robinson and Santayana, the two other major figures of the generation before the "Little Renaissance," were less iconoclastic than Crane, but both had a more direct and lasting influence upon the poetry of the twentieth century. Edwin Arlington Robinson published his first book in 1896, his last in 1935, and in the last decade of his life won wide popular recognition. By then however, he was writing an almost yearly long poem, often on the most Victorian of subjects, the legends from Malory's *Morte d'Arthur*. In retrospect it seems that Robinson's considerable talent expressed itself most strongly in his short lyrics on particular persons. His great gift was to define an entire personality in a single dramatic, representative gesture. His more ambitious philosophical poems, such as "The Man Against the Sky," are abstract and ill-defined. But in the character studies of the fictive New England village he called Tilbury Town, and in several other short poems of incomparable ironic delicacy, Robinson struck a note of complete honesty which he wrung within the extant traditions of versification. What is remarkable is the individual uses to which he put such conventional forms as the sonnet and the ballad. Robinson is deeply rooted in New England; his character studies are often of quirky individualists, eccentrics mastered by a single passion or idea. He is the heir of Emerson's philosophy, but it is a gift he cannot find usable in the world about him, a world that he renders in vignettes of ambitions defeated, talents half-realized, promises unfulfilled. Robinson feels "the black and awful chaos of the night" which so many others besides Crane of his generation felt—Henry Adams, Mark Twain, and Dreiser among them. Although he tries to affirm "the coming of the light," the images that we remember are those of hopeless Luke Havergal and his ghostly lover, Cliff Klingenhagen's draught of wormwood, the futile irony of Miniver Cheevy, the inconsolable loss in "For a Dead Lady." During half a century of radical experiments in poetic diction, meters, and forms, the best work of Robinson has remained a reminder of the conserving force of tradition, and of the subtle and personal idiom an original poet can create within established conventions.

George Santayana's sonnets and odes lack Robinson's ironies. In diction and meters modeled on two ancient traditions—the Petrarchan sonnet and the Sapphic ode— they reflect the platonizing tendency of much of the verse of the time. Santayana's platonism, however, is the intellectually rigorous commitment of a great mind to a mode of apprehending experience, not, as for instance in the case of Stedman, the avoidance of the unpleasant by a mind essentially shallow. His best poems pose the problem that he designed his philosophy to solve: how to confront "this great disaster of our birth" so that "We can be happy and forget our doom." His poems propose that we transcend the quotidian to apprehend the eternal truths of nature. "Beauty" Santayana identifies with the rational structure of the universe, and its apprehension is, in the end, the participation of our intellect in the intelligence that orders the world. The materials of poetry, however, are those of our experience, which the great poet reconstructs to accord with a new order. "As verse breaks up the prosaic order of syllables and subjects them to a recognizable and pleasing meter, so poetry breaks up the whole prosaic picture of experience to introduce into it a rhythm more congenial and intelligible to the mind." The "poetry of the creative reason," motivated by the principle of Beauty, reconstitutes experience to conform "to the deeper innate cravings of the mind. The highest ideality is the comprehension of the real. . . . Poetry at its best . . . initiates us, by feigning something which as an experience is impossible, into the meaning of the experience which we have actually had."

Like the aesthetic of the French symbolist movement, that of Santayana defines the experience of poetry as an autonomous imaginative construct. Better than other kinds of experience or other modes of knowledge, poetry creates the reality of the ideal which the appearances of the real obscure. Such a theory provides a much broader base for poetry than did Poe's ideality, since Santayana's idealism avoids the fanatical rejection of life which Poe demanded. At a time when religious certitude has been widely questioned, a Romantic-Symbolist aesthetic such as Santayana's has proved particularly attractive and viable. Santayana makes of poetry a secularist's sacrament. In its highest function, poetry operates in "the sphere of significant imagination, of relevant fiction, of idealism become the interpretation of the reality it leaves behind." This might be intimated from Santayana's own poems, but, as was true for Emerson half a century earlier, the poetic consequences of Santayana's aesthetic were best expressed by another —in this case by Wallace Stevens, who had studied in Santayana's course at Harvard in the '90's, when the philosopher formulated the position expressed in *Interpretations of Poetry and Religion* (1900). The conception of poetry Stevens gives in his "Notes Toward a Supreme Fiction" and elsewhere derives obviously from Santayana's teaching. This debt the later poet has generously acknowledged in another poem, "To an Old Philosopher in Rome," where, "On the threshold of heaven, the figures in the street / Become the figures of heaven."

7

The poet who brings to a culmination many of the tendencies of our nineteenth-century masters is Robert Frost. When he approaches the figures of heaven he is careful to return to earth; he leaves his ladder in the apple-tree, pointing "Toward heaven still," but he comes down. Frost once reported a conversation with "A fellow" who "said to me the trouble with you is that you write on subjects. I replied, the trouble with you is that you write on small bric-a-brac." The "fellow" was Wallace Stevens. Frost's "subjects" are usually characters, events, or creatures of rural New England; they give his work popular antiquarian appeal, as though the poems were Currier & Ives prints capturing the vanished joys of agrarian America. But there is as much of Theocritus as of Currier & Ives (or their literary equivalent, Whittier) in Frost's bucolics. Interspersed among them are a goodly number of the most distinguished poems of the century. Most of these make us "Acquainted with the Night," when "the time was neither wrong nor right," when the world's design is "of darkness to appall." At a time when most poetry has been lyrical in mode Frost has kept verse narrative a fresh and living art; the stories he tells are often Gothic and grotesque. If "The Witch of Coös" has antecedents in American writing, they are in Poe's short stories.

"The proof of a poet is that his country absorbs him as affectionately as he has absorbed it," wrote Whitman in the year when the country was absorbing *Hiawatha*. In our day the country's affection has absorbed only one great poet. Frost is Longfellow's successor as household bard. His books have sold over half a million copies. Such popularity is no accident. Although the tale of the early neglect of his verse and his having to go to England at almost forty to find a publisher is often cited to show America's disdain for poetry, the fact is that Frost early conceived of a style and a method that would have great appeal. He had only to await the overthrow of the mellifluous, imprecise diction of the late Victorians to step into Longfellow's place. He has said, "I wouldn't want for anyone to be listening to a poem of mine who had to prepare for it then, or afterwards. . . . You know it says in the Bible that things are said in parables so that the wrong people won't understand them and so get saved. But it says in the same Bible, 'Except ye are as little children ye shall not be saved.'" Even as he promises simplicity he speaks of (and in) parables. His remarks may gloss and be glossed by his poem "Directive"; there, salvation is vouchsafed only to the isolated pilgrim who returns to find the grail cup hidden in his childhood—after he has blocked the road behind him so the wrong ones won't get saved. Like this traveler, Frost too goes back behind the disordered present into a remembered valley, haunted by primal forces, to seek his destination and his destiny.

His first book took its title, *A Boy's Will,* from the refrain of Longfellow's poem "My Lost Youth"; his next, *North of Boston,* announced his tenacious loyalty to a particular part of the land. Most striking about these lyrics and narrative dialogues is their language: seemingly colloquial, homely, un-"poetic" yet a sensitive literary idiom. More successfully than any other American poet Frost has fulfilled Wordsworth's aim of using common speech heightened by passion. In his diction there is none of the humorous condescension of Lowell's Yankee dialect; it is never assumed in a Frost poem that either the poet or the reader is superior to the speakers. This is a democratic attitude which only Mark Twain among stylists of the colloquial has held as consistently. Frost's interest in his characters is not in their eccentricities but in their humanity. He has justly said, "I am not a regionalist. I am a realist. I write about realms of democracy and realms of the spirit."

Frost's poetry, deeply rooted in the nineteenth century, yet complements and parallels many tendencies in the work of T. S. Eliot, Ezra Pound, Stevens, and poets of younger generations. As he explicitly says in "The Figure a Poem Makes," Frost is by intention a symbolist who takes his symbols from the public domain. His method owes nothing to Laforgue or Verlaine, just as the world of reference in his poems owes nothing to Dante or Cavalcanti and the means of presentation have nothing to do with fertility cults or Chinese ideographs. Frost's symbolism, like his means of presentation, owe most to Emerson's and Thoreau's examples. He realizes in a contemporary idiom the potentialities latent in Emerson's ideas of poetry and language. When Pound reviewed *A Boy's Will* in 1913 he wrote, "This man has the good sense to speak naturally and to paint the thing, the thing as he sees it." Frost, without ever submitting to the Imagist dogma of "no ideas but in things," worked out his own brand of directness, economy, and functional metrics which paralleled the Imagist program. In method he combines Down East pragmatism with Roman rationality (Horace and Juvenal are among his favorite poets). He is not tempted to make irrational means the architectural principle of his poems. If Frost has a tale to tell he tells it, not repressing everything in the story save the moments of epiphany or self-realization. Yet he delights, within the structure of plot or ideas, to make his poems move by intuitive and subtle connections: by the interlinkages of metaphor (as in "Design"); or the deepening of self-revelation ("The Witch of Coös"). He can make the fantastic logic of a dream seem matter-of-fact and yet not lose its mystery (in "After Apple-Picking"). Frost's view of life is austere and tragic, yet his capacity for finding joy is poignantly ever ready. His spirit is torn by our dubieties; his best poems offer queries, not affirmations. The salvation he seeks seems hard to come by. It demands great renunciations. His sensibility is deeply marked by the Puritan heritage of his ancestors. In many ways he is the counterpart to our only other twentieth-century poet of comparable stature, T. S. Eliot.

8

F. O. Matthiessen has proposed that "in the broadest terms, most of our later poets could be described as descendants of Whitman or as descendants of Poe." It might be more accurate to say that together Poe and Whitman continue to define possibilities for American poetry. Some poets have been influenced by both, and have even sought to reconcile their contradictions. At the same time modern poetry, like modern life, has become international; Pound and Eliot have long since fulfilled Bryant's prediction that in a land without stable traditions poets would ransack those from other nations and ages. Yet their very effort demonstrates their isolation from the society whose lacunae they attempt to fill by individual assertion. The situation of the poet has not changed nearly so much since Poe's or Whitman's time as has the range of materials he is likely to work with. (Paradoxically, Frost, with his half-million readers, uses language they can understand but speaks as though they weren't listening.) What options do Poe and Whitman define for the modern poet? He may follow Whitman and turn the materialism of his country against itself by asserting the spiritual primacy of the commonplace, the dignity of the meanest twitch of life, the "divine equality" of all mankind. This course leads in several directions; most promisingly, toward William Carlos Williams' symbolist-epic *Paterson,* the only poem based on similar materials worthy to be compared to "Song of Myself." Whitman remains a potent liberating influence because of his amplitude of feeling, his inventive language, his replacement of rational argument by intuitive movement as a structural principle. Yet those who have most blatantly imitated Whitman's rejections of traditional prosody have conspicuously failed to make discoveries comparable to his of the forms of feelings. His influence, like his poetry, has moved most successfully by indirection: in the attempts of Williams and Hart Crane to comprehend communal experience, in the democratic sensibility of Williams and Marianne Moore, in her and E. E. Cummings' linguistic and metrical boldness; most pervasively in Ezra Pound. However reluctantly, Pound has made "A Pact" with Walt Whitman: "It was you that broke the new wood. . . . / We have one sap and one root." Surely *The Cantos* are more reasonably comparable to *Leaves of Grass* than to the poems of Homer and Ovid which Pound once claimed were their models. Yet Pound resembles Poe in his fractious antagonism to modern life and in the insistence of his polemical essays on the technique of writing, on measuring poetry by poetic standards alone. But it is Longfellow whom Pound most resembles in his attempt to bring into poetry in English the forms and effects of the verse of ancient China, Renaissance Italy, and Provence—a Longfellow with the sensibility of a Pound.

Poe's influence has come into American literature in large part through the intercession of T. S. Eliot. One would think Eliot has little in common with a poet who spurned the role of the intellect in his verse, denied that art is moral, detached himself from history, and is the exemplar of the writer without access to a community or a shared tradition. "And yet one cannot be sure that one's own writing has *not* been influenced by Poe," wrote Eliot in an essay in 1949 that made explicit the influences he had been instrumental in spreading a generation earlier. Eliot quotes Baudelaire's remark that Poe believed "that the goal of poetry is of the same nature as its principle, and that it should have nothing in view but itself." Poe provides also "the notion that the composition of a poem should be as conscious and deliberate as possible, that the poet should observe himself in the act of composition." Yet even without Eliot's intercession, an aesthetic similar to that of Poe's French disciples would have taken hold here. We have seen that Santayana had expressed the symbolist rationale by 1900 and that Wallace Stevens became the American poet most concerned with making the poetic process the poetic subject. Yet Stevens is akin to Whitman in his secular humanism, in his avoidance of tragedy as a mode of interpreting experience, and in his acceptance of the *materia poetica* in the "banal suburb."

Emily Dickinson's bequest to modern verse is all-pervading. Her intense economy, her manipulation of the metaphoric nature of words, her syncopations that create the rhythms of her emotions, and especially her refining the primary tones of rhyme to the infinite chromatics of assonance have influenced every poet who has been alive to the sounds and rhythms of our language in the present century. Perhaps even more than Whitman she has made hopelessly obsolete the slack lines and limpid argument of the American Victorians. With Poe and Whitman she has reformed the technique and style of American poetry. Behind our contemporaries looms Emerson's conviction that the world is metaphor, that language is the symbol of nature and nature the symbol of spirit. The possibilities these forebears formulate for poetry have not been exhausted by the examples of their own writings or those of their successors. Modified by influences already absorbed from other traditions or yet to be discovered, American poets now and in the future will continue to explore and fulfill them.

PART I

POETRY

ANNE BRADSTREET

1612?–1672

Born in England before the death of Shakespeare,
Anne Dudley Bradstreet emigrated in 1630 to Massachusetts Bay with her father and husband, both of whom later
served as governors of the colony. By 1632 her activity as
an author had begun. Her poetry owes allegiances to that
of Joshua Sylvester, translator of Du Bartas; and to Sidney, Spenser, and Donne. Her work first appeared in London in 1650 as *The Tenth Muse Lately Sprung Up in
America . . . By a Gentlewoman of Those Parts,* in an edition published without her consent by her brother-in-law.
This book of doctrinal and historical poems arranged in
"Quaternions," or groups of four, offered "The Four Elements," "The Four Seasons," "The Four Humours," and
other conventional exercises of the time. Far more interesting to later readers were the poems she wrote after 1650
on domestic subjects. These may be taken as the first examples of poetry written about the circumstances of life
in the New World.

TEXT: *The Works of Anne Bradstreet in Prose and Verse,*
edited by John H. Ellis (1867, reprinted 1932).

FROM TO THE MEMORY OF MY DEAR AND EVER HONOURED FATHER THOMAS DUDLEY ESQ; WHO DECEASED, JULY 31. 1653. AND OF HIS AGE, 77.

HIS EPITAPH

Within this Tomb a Patriot lyes
That was both pious, just and wise,
To Truth a shield, to right a Wall,
To Sectaryes a whip and Maul,

A Magazine of History,
A Prizer of good Company
In manners pleasant and severe
The Good him lov'd, the bad did fear,
And when his time with years was spent
If some rejoyc'd, more did lament.

UPON THE BURNING OF OUR HOUSE, JULY 10th, 1666.

In silent night when rest I took,
For sorrow neer I did not look,
I waken'd was with thundring nois
And Piteous shreiks of dreadfull voice.
That fearfull sound of fire and fire,
Let no man know is my Desire.

I, starting up, the light did spye,
And to my God my heart did cry
To strengthen me in my Distresse
And not to leave me succourlesse.
Then coming out beheld a space,
The flame consume my dwelling place.

And, when I could no longer look,
I blest his Name that gave and took,
That layd my goods now in the dust:
Yea so it was, and so 'twas just.
It was his own: it was not mine;
Far be it that I should repine.

He might of All justly bereft,
But yet sufficient for us left.
When by the Ruines oft I past,
My sorrowing eyes aside did cast,
And here and there the places spye
Where oft I sate, and long did lye.

Here stood that Trunk, and there that chest;
There lay that store I counted best:
My pleasant things in ashes lye,
And them behold no more shall I.
Under thy roof no guest shall sitt,
Nor at thy Table eat a bitt.

No pleasant tale shall 'ere be told,
Nor things recounted done of old.
No Candle 'ere shall shine in Thee,
Nor bridegroom's verse ere heard shall bee.
In silence ever shalt thou lye;
Adeiu, Adeiu; All's vanity.

Then streight I gin my heart to chide,
And did thy wealth on earth abide?
Didst fix thy hope on mouldring dust,
The arm of flesh didst make thy trust?
Raise up thy thoughts above the skye
That dunghill mists away may flie.

Thou hast an house on high erect,
Fram'd by that mighty Architect,
With glory richly furnished,
Stands permanent tho' this bee fled.
It's purchaséd, and paid for too
By him who hath enough to doe.

A Prize so vast as is unknown,
Yet, by his Gift, is made thine own.
Ther's wealth enough, I need no more;
Farewell my Pelf, farewell my Store.
The world no longer let me Love,
My hope and Treasure lyes Above.

ON MY DEAR GRAND-CHILD SIMON BRADSTREET,

WHO DYED ON 16. NOVEMB. 1669, BEING BUT A MONETH, AND ONE DAY OLD.

No sooner come, but gone, and fal'n asleep,
Acquaintance short, yet parting caus'd us weep,
Three flours, two scarcely blown, the last i'th' bud,
Cropt by th' Almighties hand; yet is he good,
With dreadful awe before him let's be mute,
Such was his will, but why, let's not dispute,
With humble hearts and mouths put in the dust,
Let's say he's merciful as well as just.
He will return, and make up all our losses,
And smile again, after our bitter crosses.
Go pretty babe, go rest with Sisters twain
Among the blest in endless joyes remain.

TO MY DEAR AND LOVING HUSBAND

If ever two were one, then surely we.
If ever man were lov'd by wife, then thee;
If ever wife was happy in a man,
Compare with me ye women if you can.
I prize thy love more then whole Mines of gold,
Or all the riches that the East doth hold.
My love is such that Rivers cannot quench,
Nor ought but love from thee, give recompence.
Thy love is such I can no way repay,
The heavens reward thee manifold I pray.
Then while we live, in love lets so persever,
That when we live no more, we may live ever.

EDWARD TAYLOR

1645?–1729

Taylor came to Boston from his home in Coventry, England, in 1668, and immediately attended Harvard. On graduation in 1671 he became Congregational pastor at the isolated village of Westfield, Massachusetts, in the Connecticut Valley, a charge he held for fifty-eight years. He published nothing during his lifetime, indeed instructed his heirs not to issue his poems. They were held in the family until 1883, when a descendant presented them to the Yale Library, where Thomas H. Johnson found them, undisturbed and as yet unread, over two centuries after the poet's death. Taylor's writings include "God's Determinations Touching His Elect," a long series of dialogues on the drama of sin and redemption; "Sacramental Meditations" (the major part of his work), written between 1682–1722; and a dozen miscellaneous poems. Writing a generation after Milton, Taylor maintained his unwavering allegiance to the metaphysical poetry of conceit which he knew from the work of Donne, Quarles, Crashaw, and particularly Herbert, a mode already out of fashion in England. Deeply committed to orthodox Puritan theology, Taylor wrote with such an ingenuity of metaphor, such delight in language, and so intermingled divine passion with sensuous ecstasy—in short, wrote so firmly in the poetic tradition of his Anglican and Catholic models—that he never felt free to expose his verse to the view of his Puritan contemporaries whose aesthetic did not permit language in poetry to be used for its own sake rather than exclusively as a means to knowledge of grace.

TEXT: *The Poetical Works of Edward Taylor*, edited by Thomas H. Johnson (1939); Barbara Damon Simison, "Poems of Edward Taylor," *Yale University Library Gazette*, XXVIII (1954); *The Poems of Edward Taylor*, edited by Donald E. Sanford (1960).

FROM THE PREFACE TO GOD'S DETERMINATIONS TOUCHING HIS ELECT

Infinity, when all things it beheld
In Nothing, and of Nothing all did build,
Upon what Base was fixt the Lath, wherein
He turn'd this Globe, and riggalld it so trim?
Who blew the Bellows of his Furnace Vast?
Or held the Mould wherein the world was Cast?
Who laid its Corner Stone? Or whose Commands?
Where stand the Pillars upon which it stands?
Who Lac'de and Fillitted the earth so fine,
With Rivers like green Ribbons Smaragdine?
Who made the Sea's its Selvedge, and it locks
Like a Quilt Ball within a Silver Box?
Who Spread its Canopy? Or Curtains Spun?
Who in this Bowling Alley bowld the Sun?

MEDITATION EIGHT

JOHN VI: 51. I AM THE LIVING BREAD.

I ken[n]ing through Astronomy Divine
   The Worlds bright Battlement, wherein I spy
A Golden Path my Pensill cannot line
   From that bright Throne unto my Threshold ly.
     And while my puzzled thoughts about it pore,
     I find the Bread of Life in't at my doore.

When that this Bird of Paradise put in
   The Wicker Cage (my Corps) to tweedle praise
Had peckt the Fruit forbad: and so did fling
   Away its Food, and lost its golden dayes;
     It fell into Celestiall Famine sore:
     And never could attain a morsell more.

Alas! alas! Poore Bird, what wilt thou doe?
  This Creatures field no food for Souls e're gave:
And if thou knock at Angells dores they show
  An Empty Barrell: they no soul bread have.
  Alas! Poore Bird, the Worlds White Loafe is done.
  And cannot yield thee here the smallest Crumb.

In this sad state, Gods Tender Bowells run
  Out streams of Grace: And he to end all strife
The Purest Wheate in Heaven, his deare-dear Son
  Grinds, and kneads up into this Bread of Life:
  Which Bread of Life from Heaven down came and
    stands
  Disht on thy Table up by Angells Hands.

Did God mould up this Bread in Heaven, and bake,
  Which from his Table came, and to thine goeth?
Doth he bespeake thee thus, This Soule Bread take.
  Come Eate thy fill of this thy Gods White Loafe?
  Its Food too fine for Angells, yet come, take
  And Eate thy fill. Its Heavens Sugar Cake.

What Grace is this knead in this Loafe? This thing
  Souls are but petty things it to admire.
Yee Angells, help: This fill would to the brim
  Heav'ns whelm'd-down Chrystall meele Bowle, yea
    and higher.
  This Bread of Life dropt in thy mouth doth Cry.
  Eate, Eate me, Soul, and thou shalt never dy.

MEDITATION THIRTY-TWO

1. COR. 3. 22. WHETHER PAUL OR APPOLLOS, OR CEPHAS
[*or the world, or life, or death, or things present, or
things to come; all are yours; and ye are Christ's;
and Christ is God's.*]

Thy Grace, Dear Lord's my golden Wrack, I finde
   Screwing my Phancy into ragged Rhimes,
Tuning thy Praises in my feeble minde
   Untill I come to strike them on my Chimes.
   Were I an Angell bright, and borrow could
   King David's Harp, I would them play on gold.

But plung'd I am, my mind is puzzled,
   When I would spin my Phancy thus unspun,
In finest Twine of Praise I'm muzzled.
   My tazzled Thoughts twirld into Snick-Snarls run.
   Thy Grace, my Lord, is such a glorious thing,
   It doth Confound me when I would it sing.

Eternall Love an Object mean did smite
   Which by the Prince of Darkness was beguilde,
That from this Love it ran and sweld with spite
   And in the way with filth was all defilde
   Yet must be reconcild, cleansd, and begrac'te
   Or from the fruits of Gods first Love displac'te.

Then Grace, my Lord, wrought in thy Heart a vent,
   Thy Soft Soft hand to this hard worke did goe,
And to the Milke White Throne of Justice went
   And entred bond that Grace might overflow.
   Hence did thy Person to my Nature ty
   And bleed through humane Veans to satisfy.

Oh! Grace, Grace, Grace! this Wealthy Grace doth lay
   Her Golden Channells from thy Fathers throne,
Into our Earthen Pitchers to Convay
   Heavens Aqua Vitae to us for our own.

O! let thy Golden Gutters run into
My Cup this Liquour till it overflow.

Thine Ordinances, Graces, Wine-fats where
   Thy Spirits Walkes, and Graces runs doe ly
And Angells waiting stand with holy Cheere
   From Graces Conduite Head, with all Supply.
These Vessells full of Grace are, and the Bowls
In which their Taps do run, are pretious Souls.

Thou to the Cup dost say (that Catch this Wine,)
   This Liquour, Golden Pipes, and Wine-fats plain,
Whether Paul, Apollos, Cephas, all are thine.
   Oh Golden Word! Lord speake it ore again.
Lord speake it home to me, say these are mine.
My Bells shall then thy Praises bravely chime.

UPON A SPIDER CATCHING A FLY

Thou sorrow, venom Elfe.
   Is this thy play,
To spin a web out of thyselfe
   To Catch a Fly?
     For why?

I saw a pettish wasp
   Fall foule therein:
Whom yet thy Whorle pins did not clasp
   Lest he should fling
     His sting.

But as afraid, remote
   Didst stand hereat,
And with thy little fingers stroke
   And gently tap
     His back.

Thus gently him didst treate
  Lest he should pet,
And in a froppish, aspish heate
  Should greatly fret
    Thy net.

Whereas the silly Fly,
  Caught by its leg
Thou by the throate tookst hastily,
  And 'hinde the head
    Bite Dead.

This goes to pot, that not
  Nature doth call.
Strive not above what strength hath got,
  Lest in the brawle
    Thou fall.

This Frey seems thus to us:
  Hells Spider gets
His intrails spun to whip Cords thus,
  And wove to nets
    And sets.

To tangle Adams race
  In's stratagems
To their Destructions, spoil'd, made base
  By venom things,
    Damn'd Sins.

But mighty, Gracious Lord,
  Communicate
Thy Grace to breake the Cord; afford
  Us Glorys Gate
    And State.

We'l Nightingaile sing like,
  When pearcht on high
In Glories Cage, thy glory, bright,
  And thankfully,
    For joy.

HUSWIFERY

Make me, O Lord, thy Spin[n]ing Wheele compleat.
  Thy Holy Worde my Distaff make for mee.
Make mine Affections thy Swift Flyers neate
  And make my Soule thy holy Spoole to bee.
  My Conversation make to be thy Reele
  And reele the yarn thereon spun of thy Wheele.

Make me thy Loome then, knit therein this Twine:
  And make thy Holy Spirit, Lord, winde quills:
Then weave the Web thyselfe. The yarn is fine.
  Thine Ordinances make my Fulling Mills.
  Then dy the same in Heavenly Colours Choice,
  All pinkt with Varnish't Flowers of Paradise.

Then cloath therewith mine Understanding, Will,
  Affections, Judgment, Conscience, Memory
My Words and Actions, that their shine may fill
  My wayes with glory and thee glorify.
  Then mine apparell shall display before yee
  That I am Cloathd in Holy robes for glory.

PHILIP FRENEAU

1752–1832

Freneau attended Princeton College, where he was a friend of James Madison and of the novelist H. H. Brackenridge. His training was neoclassical but his sensibility had a strong Romantic strain. As his times were devoted to political questions, Freneau the Romantic poet was not acclaimed as was Freneau the topical satirist. He wrote vigorous, plebeian satire voluminously, first against the British, later as a Jeffersonian partisan, earning the ire of George Washington, who referred to him as "That rascal, Freneau." He edited newspapers in New York, Philadelphia, and New Jersey, and published his verse in *The Poems of Philip Freneau Written Chiefly During the Late War* (1786); *Poems Written Between the Years 1768 & 1794* (1795); and later collections in 1809 and 1815. See the critique of Freneau's work by his contemporary Joseph Dennie, reprinted in this volume on p. 258.

TEXT: *Poems of Philip Freneau*, edited by F. L. Pattee, 3 vols. (1902–1907). See also Harry Hayden Clark, "Introduction" to *Poems of Freneau* (1929); and Lewis Leary, *That Rascal Freneau: A Study in Literary Failure* (1941).

TO THE MEMORY OF THE BRAVE AMERICANS

UNDER GENERAL GREENE, IN SOUTH CAROLINA, WHO FELL IN THE ACTION OF SEPTEMBER 8, 1781

At Eutaw Springs the valiant died;
   Their limbs with dust are covered o'er—
Weep on, ye springs, your tearful tide:
   How many heroes are no more!

If in this wreck of ruin, they
  Can yet be thought to claim a tear,
O smite your gentle breast, and say
  The friends of freedom slumber here!

Thou, who shalt trace this bloody plain,
  If goodness rules thy generous breast,
Sigh for the wasted rural reign;
  Sigh for the shepherds, sunk to rest!

Stranger, their humble graves adorn;
  You too may fall, and ask a tear;
'Tis not the beauty of the morn
  That proves the evening shall be clear.—

They saw their injured country's woe;
  The flaming town, the wasted field;
Then rushed to meet the insulting foe;
  They took the spear—but left the shield.

Led by thy conquering genius, Greene,
  The Britons they compelled to fly;
None distant viewed the fatal plain,
  None grieved, in such a cause to die—

But, like the Parthian, famed of old,
  Who, flying, still their arrows threw,
These routed Britons, full as bold,
  Retreated, and retreating slew.

Now rest in peace, our patriot band;
  Though far from nature's limits thrown,
We trust they find a happier land,
  A brighter sunshine of their own.

THE VANITY OF EXISTENCE

TO THYRSIS

In youth, gay scenes attract our eyes,
　　And not suspecting their decay
Life's flowery fields before us rise,
　　Regardless of its winter day.

But vain pursuits and joys as vain
　　Convince us life is but a dream.
Death is to wake, to rise again
　　To that true life you best esteem.

So nightly on some shallow tide,
　　Oft have I seen a splendid show;
Reflected stars on either side,
　　And glittering moons were seen below.

But when the tide had ebbed away,
　　The scene fantastic with it fled,
A bank of mud around me lay,
　　And sea-weed on the river's bed.

THE WILD HONEY SUCKLE

Fair flower, that dost so comely grow,
Hid in this silent, dull retreat,
Untouched thy honied blossoms blow,
Unseen thy little branches greet:
　　No roving foot shall crush thee here,
　　No busy hand provoke a tear.

By Nature's self in white arrayed,
She bade thee shun the vulgar eye,
And planted here the guardian shade,
And sent soft waters murmuring by;

Thus quietly thy summer goes,
Thy days declining to repose.

Smit with those charms, that must decay,
I grieve to see your future doom;
They died—nor were those flowers more gay,
The flowers that did in Eden bloom;
  Unpitying frosts, and Autumn's power
  Shall leave no vestige of this flower.

From morning suns and evening dews
At first thy little being came:
If nothing once, you nothing lose,
For when you die you are the same;
  The space between, is but an hour,
  The frail duration of a flower.

THE INDIAN BURYING GROUND

In spite of all the learned have said,
  I still my old opinion keep;
The posture, that we give the dead,
  Points out the soul's eternal sleep.

Not so the ancients of these lands—
  The Indian, when from life released,
Again is seated with his friends,
  And shares again the joyous feast.

His imaged birds, and painted bowl,
  And venison, for a journey dressed,
Bespeak the nature of the soul,
  Activity, that knows no rest.

His bow, for action ready bent,
  And arrows, with a head of stone,
Can only mean that life is spent,
  And not the old ideas gone.

Thou, stranger, that shalt come this way,
   No fraud upon the dead commit—
Observe the swelling turf, and say
   They do not lie, but here they sit.

Here still a lofty rock remains,
   On which the curious eye may trace
(Now wasted, half, by wearing rains)
   The fancies of a ruder race.

Here still an aged elm aspires,
   Beneath whose far-projecting shade
And which the shepherd still admires
   The children of the forest played!

There oft a restless Indian queen
   (Pale Shebah, with her braided hair)
And many a barbarous form is seen
   To chide the man that lingers there.

By midnight moons, o'er moistening dews;
   In habit for the chase arrayed,
The hunter still the deer pursues,
   The hunter and the deer, a shade!

And long shall timorous fancy see
   The painted chief, and pointed spear,
And Reason's self shall bend the knee
   To shadows and delusions here.

TO AN AUTHOR

Your leaves bound up compact and fair,
In neat array at length prepare,
To pass their hour on learning's stage,
To meet the surly critic's rage;
The statesman's slight, the smatterer's sneer—
Were these, indeed, your only fear,

You might be tranquil and resigned:
What most should touch your fluttering mind;
Is that, few critics will be found
To sift your works, and deal the wound.

Thus, when one fleeting year is past
On some bye-shelf your book is cast—
Another comes, with something new,
And drives you fairly out of view:
With some to praise, but more to blame,
The mind returns to—whence it came;
And some alive, who scarce could read
Will publish satires on the dead.

Thrice happy Dryden, who could meet
Some rival bard in every street!
When all were bent on writing well
It was some credit to excel:—

Thrice happy Dryden, who could find
A Milbourne for his sport designed—
And Pope, who saw the harmless rage
Of Dennis bursting o'er his page
Might justly spurn the critic's aim,
Who only helped to swell his fame.

On these bleak climes by Fortune thrown,
Where rigid Reason reigns alone,
Where lovely Fancy has no sway,
Nor magic forms about us play—
Nor nature takes her summer hue
Tell me, what has the muse to do?—

An age employed in edging steel
Can no poetic raptures feel;
No solitude's attracting power,
No leisure of the noon day hour,
No shaded stream, no quiet grove
Can this fantastic century move;

The muse of love in no request—
Go—try your fortune with the rest,
One of the nine you should engage,
To meet the follies of the age:—

On one, we fear, your choice must fall—
The least engaging of them all—
Her visage stern—an angry style—
A clouded brow—malicious smile—
A mind on murdered victims placed—
She, only she, can please the taste!

EPISTLE

FROM DR. FRANKLIN [DECEASED] TO HIS POETICAL PANEGYRISTS, ON SOME OF THEIR ABSURD COMPLIMENTS

"Good Poets, why so full of pain,
Are you sincere—or do you feign?
Love for your tribe I never had,
Nor penned three stanzas, good or bad.

At funerals, sometimes, grief appears,
Where legacies have purchased tears:
'Tis folly to be sad for nought,
From me you never gained a groat.

To better trades I turned my views,
And never meddled with the muse;
Great things I did for rising States,
And kept the lightning from some pates.

This grand discovery, you adore it,
But ne'er will be the better for it:
You are still subject to those fires,
For poets' houses have no spires.

Philosophers are famed for pride;
But, pray, be modest—when I died,
No 'sighs disturbed old ocean's bed,'
No 'Nature wept' for Franklin dead!

That day, on which I left the coast,
A beggar-man was also lost:
If 'Nature wept,' you must agree
She wept for him—as well as me.

There's reason even in telling lies—
In such profusion of her 'sighs,'
She was too sparing of a tear—
In Carolina, all was clear:

And if there fell some snow and sleet,
Why must it be my winding sheet?
Snows oft have cloathed the April plain,
Have melted, and will melt again.

Poets, I pray you, say no more,
Or say what Nature said before;
That reason should your pens direct,
Or else you pay me no respect.

Let reason be your constant rule,
And Nature, trust me, is no fool—
When to the dust great men she brings,
Make her do—some uncommon things."

WILLIAM CULLEN BRYANT

1794–1878

Bryant grew up in Cummington, Massachusetts, influenced by both his Calvinist maternal grandfather and his Unitarian father, a physician who stocked his library with the late eighteenth-century Romantics. Young Bryant attended Williams College, but after a year had to drop out and continue his studies in a nearby law office. He read Wordsworth at this time. His early religious liberalism is apparent in "Thanatopsis," written when he was only seventeen. This poem shows, too, how far Bryant had already come in freeing his meters from the Augustan regularity then prevalent. Although he was America's first nationally-recognized poet, he spent his life in liberal journalism. In 1825 he gave up his Great Barrington law practice to become editor of the *New-York Review and Atheneum Magazine;* soon he was editor, then part-owner of the New York *Post,* which his editorials on the rights of labor, abolition, and free speech, free trade and political liberty made a national organ of opinion. His verse reiterates a set of uncomplicated ideas. He identifies God with love and truth, liberty and justice. He believes in human progress. Nature is a temple of joy and health. His emotional range is not wide; he writes of reverence, attacks injustice, shows pity for the suffering and sympathy with his natural surroundings. He describes American scenes, but his style is Anglo-American rather than a native idiom. Although somewhat overshadowed by the later popularity of Longfellow, Holmes, and Lowell, Bryant was universally respected until the end of his long life. In his last years he translated *The Iliad* and *The Odyssey.* His observations on the effects of American conditions upon the poetic imagination appear on p. 269.

THANATOPSIS

To him who in the love of Nature holds
Communion with her visible forms, she speaks
A various language; for his gayer hours
She has a voice of gladness, and a smile
And eloquence of beauty, and she glides
Into his darker musings, with a mild
And healing sympathy, that steals away
Their sharpness, ere he is aware. When thoughts
Of the last bitter hour come like a blight
Over thy spirit, and sad images
Of the stern agony, and shroud, and pall,
And breathless darkness, and the narrow house,
Make thee to shudder, and grow sick at heart,—
Go forth, under the open sky, and list
To Nature's teachings, while from all around—
Earth and her waters, and the depths of air,—
Comes a still voice—Yet a few days, and thee
The all-beholding sun shall see no more
In all his course; nor yet in the cold ground,
Where thy pale form was laid, with many tears,
Nor in the embrace of ocean, shall exist
Thy image. Earth, that nourished thee, shall claim
Thy growth, to be resolved to earth again,
And, lost each human trace, surrendering up
Thine individual being, shalt thou go
To mix forever with the elements,
To be a brother to the insensible rock
And to the sluggish clod, which the rude swain
Turns with his share, and treads upon. The oak
Shall send his roots abroad, and pierce thy mould.

Yet not to thine eternal resting-place
Shalt thou retire alone, nor couldst thou wish
Couch more magnificent. Thou shalt lie down

With patriarchs of the infant world—with kings,
The powerful of the earth—the wise, the good,
Fair forms, and hoary seers of ages past,
All in one mighty sepulchre. The hills
Rock-ribbed and ancient as the sun,—the vales
Stretching in pensive quietness between;
The venerable woods—rivers that move
In majesty, and the complaining brooks
That make the meadows green; and, poured round all,
Old Ocean's gray and melancholy waste,—
Are but the solemn decorations all
Of the great tomb of man. The golden sun,
The planets, all the infinite host of heaven,
Are shining on the sad abodes of death,
Through the still lapse of ages. All that tread
The globe are but a handful to the tribes
That slumber in its bosom.—Take the wings
Of morning, pierce the Barcan wilderness,
Or lose thyself in the continuous woods
Where rolls the Oregon, and hears no sound,
Save his own dashings—yet the dead are there:
And millions in those solitudes, since first
The flight of years began, have laid them down
In their last sleep—the dead reign there alone.
So shalt thou rest, and what if thou withdraw
In silence from the living, and no friend
Take note of thy departure? All that breathe
Will share thy destiny. The gay will laugh
When thou art gone, the solemn brood of care
Plod on, and each one as before will chase
His favorite phantom; yet all these shall leave
Their mirth and their employments, and shall come
And make their bed with thee. As the long train
Of ages glide away, the sons of men,
The youth in life's green spring, and he who goes
In the full strength of years, matron and maid,
The speechless babe, and the gray-headed man—
Shall one by one be gathered to thy side,
By those, who in their turn shall follow them.

So live, that when thy summons comes to join
The innumerable caravan, which moves
To that mysterious realm, where each shall take
His chamber in the silent halls of death,
Thou go not, like the quarry-slave at night,
Scourged to his dungeon, but, sustained and soothed
By an unfaltering trust, approach thy grave,
Like one who wraps the drapery of his couch
About him, and lies down to pleasant dreams.

INSCRIPTION FOR THE ENTRANCE TO A WOOD

Stranger, if thou hast learned a truth which needs
No school of long experience, that the world
Is full of guilt and misery, and hast seen
Enough of all its sorrows, crimes, and cares
To tire thee of it, enter this wild wood
And view the haunts of Nature. The calm shade
Shall bring a kindred calm, and the sweet breeze,
That makes the green leaves dance, shall waft a balm
To thy sick heart. Thou wilt find nothing here
Of all that pained thee in the haunts of men
And made thee loathe thy life. The primal curse
Fell, it is true, upon the unsinning earth,
But not in vengeance. God hath yoked to guilt
Her pale tormentor, misery. Hence, these shades
Are still the abodes of gladness; the thick roof
Of green and stirring branches is alive
And musical with birds, that sing and sport
In wantonness of spirit; while, below,
The squirrel, with raised paws and form erect,
Chirps merrily. Throngs of insects in the shade
Try their thin wings and dance in the warm beam
That waked them into life. Even the green trees
Partake the deep contentment; as they bend
To the soft winds, the sun from the blue sky
Looks in and sheds a blessing on the scene.

Scarce less the cleft-born wild-flower seems to enjoy
Existence than the wingèd plunderer
That sucks its sweets. The mossy rocks themselves,
And the old and ponderous trunks of prostrate trees
That lead from knoll to knoll a causey rude
Or bridge the sunken brook, and their dark roots,
With all their earth upon them, twisting high,
Breathe fixed tranquillity. The rivulet
Sends forth glad sounds, and, tripping o'er its bed
Of pebbly sands or leaping down the rocks,
Seems with continuous laughter to rejoice
In its own being. Softly tread the marge,
Lest from her midway perch thou scare the wren
That dips her bill in water. The cool wind,
That stirs the stream in play, shall come to thee,
Like one that loves thee nor will let thee pass
Ungreeted, and shall give its light remembrance.

TO A WATERFOWL

Whither, midst falling dew,
While glow the heavens with the last steps of day,
Far, through their rosy depths, dost thou pursue
Thy solitary way?

Vainly the fowler's eye
Might mark thy distant flight to do thee wrong,
As, darkly seen against the crimson sky,
Thy figure floats along.

Seek'st thou the plashy brink
Of weedy lake, or marge of river wide,
Or where the rocking billows rise and sink
On the chafed ocean-side?

There is a Power whose care
Teaches thy way along that pathless coast—
The desert and illimitable air—
Lone wandering, but not lost.

All day thy wings have fanned,
At that far height, the cold, thin atmosphere,
Yet stoop not, weary, to the welcome land,
    Though the dark night is near.

And soon that toil shall end;
Soon shalt thou find a summer home, and rest,
And scream among thy fellows; reeds shall bend,
    Soon, o'er thy sheltered nest.

Thou 'rt gone, the abyss of heaven
Hath swallowed up thy form; yet, on my heart
Deeply has sunk the lesson thou hast given,
    And shall not soon depart.

He who, from zone to zone
Guides through the boundless sky thy certain flight,
In the long way that I must tread alone,
    Will lead my steps aright.

EDGAR ALLAN POE

1809–1849

Poe was the son of itinerant actors; his father abandoned his mother and disappeared, and the mother died while on tour in Richmond, Virginia, leaving her eighteen-month-old son. The infant became the ward of John Allan, a Scottish tobacco merchant of Richmond. Five of Poe's boyhood years were spent in Scotland and England, where he attended a classical preparatory school. In 1826 he entered the University of Virginia but left within a year because of gambling debts. Allan had never adopted Poe, and relations between them became increasingly strained. Poe refused to enter Allan's business, instead enlisting in the Army under an assumed name; in 1830 he entered West Point, but after eight months provoked his own dismissal. Poe had published *Tamerlane and Other Poems* (1827) and *Al Araaf, Tamerlane and Minor Poems* (1829), and in New York he issued *Poems* (1831). These slight books contain most of the forty-eight poems Poe wrote, yet they brought him neither recognition nor security. From 1831 to 1835 he lived in extreme poverty at the home of his aunt in Baltimore; later he married her young daughter Virginia Clemm. During these years he began publishing short stories; a prize for one of these led to his appointment as assistant editor of the *Southern Literary Messenger* (Richmond) from 1835–1837. From 1838–1844 he edited successively several magazines in Philadelphia, writing much of their contents himself, and developing his critical theories as he reviewed innumerable current books, most of them entirely lacking in intrinsic interest. In 1844 the Poes moved to New York, where Virginia died of tuberculosis. The apogee of Poe's fame came in 1845 with the publication of *The Raven and Other Poems,* his major volume. In 1849 Poe arranged to marry a childhood sweetheart then a widow in Richmond. But on his way north he was found unconscious on the streets in Baltimore and died in delirium.

Poe did not make friends for his own work, although Lowell, among others, recognized that there was at least "three fifths of him genius" along with the "two fifths sheer fudge." Posthumously his reputation suffered from unjust allegations of his depravity and from the grudging steward-ship of his writings by a hostile editor, the Reverend Rufus W. Griswold. Although several of his tales and such poems as "The Raven" have always been widely read, Poe's theory of verse and his poems were virtually without direct effect on American literature until T. S. Eliot and others rediscovered Poe's principles in the writings of his chief enthusiast, Baudelaire, and his later followers in the French symbolist movement.

TEXT: *The Complete Works of Edgar Allan Poe*, edited by James A. Harrison, 17 vols. (1902), vol. 7. For biographical and critical comment see: D. H. Lawrence, *Studies in Classic American Literature* (1923); Allen Tate, "Our Cousin, Mr. Poe," in *The Forlorn Demon* (1948); T. S. Eliot, "From Poe to Valéry," *Hudson Review*, III (1949), 327–43; E. H. David-son, *Poe: A Critical Study* (1957); Richard Wilbur, "Intro-duction" to *Poe* (1959).

SONNET—TO SCIENCE

Science! true daughter of Old Time thou art!
   Who alterest all things with thy peering eyes.
Why preyest thou thus upon the poet's heart,
   Vulture, whose wings are dull realities?
How should he love thee? or how deem thee wise,
   Who wouldst not leave him in his wandering
To seek for treasure in the jewelled skies,
   Albeit he soared with an undaunted wing?
Hast thou not dragged Diana from her car?
   And driven the Hamadryad from the wood
To seek a shelter in some happier star?
   Hast thou not torn the Naiad from her flood,
The Elfin from the green grass, and from me
The summer dream beneath the tamarind tree?

TO HELEN

Helen, thy beauty is to me
　Like those Nicéan barks of yore,
That gently, o'er a perfumed sea,
　The weary, way-worn wanderer bore
　To his own native shore.

On desperate seas long wont to roam,
　Thy hyacinth hair, thy classic face,
Thy Naiad airs have brought me home
　To the glory that was Greece,
　And the grandeur that was Rome.

Lo! in yon brilliant window-niche
　How statue-like I see thee stand,
The agate lamp within thy hand!
　Ah, Psyche, from the regions which
　Are Holy-Land!

ISRAFEL *

In Heaven a spirit doth dwell
　"Whose heart-strings are a lute;"
None sing so wildly well
As the angel Israfel,
And the giddy stars (so legends tell)
Ceasing their hymns, attend the spell
　Of his voice, all mute.

Tottering above
　In her highest noon,
　The enamoured moon
Blushes with love,

* And the angel Israfel, [whose heart-strings are a lute, and]
who has the sweetest voice of all God's creatures.—KORAN.
[Poe's note.]

While, to listen, the red levin
(With the rapid Pleiads, even,
  Which were seven,)
    Pauses in Heaven.

And they say (the starry choir
  And other listening things)
That Israfeli's fire
Is owing to that lyre
  By which he sits and sings—
The trembling living wire
  Of those unusual strings.

But the skies that angel trod,
  Where deep thoughts are a duty—
Where Love's a grown-up God—
  Where the Houri glances are
Imbued with all the beauty
  Which we worship in a star.

Therefore, thou are not wrong,
  Israfeli, who despisest
An unimpassioned song;
To thee the laurels belong,
  Best bard, because the wisest!
Merrily live and long!

The ecstasies above
  With thy burning measures suit—
Thy grief, thy joy, thy hate, thy love,
  With the fervour of thy lute—
Well may the stars be mute!

Yes, Heaven is thine; but this
  Is a world of sweets and sours;
  Our flowers are merely—flowers,
And the shadow of thy perfect bliss
  Is the sunshine of ours.

If I could dwell
Where Israfel
  Hath dwelt, and he where I,
He might not sing so wildly well
  A mortal melody,
While a bolder note than this might swell
  From my lyre within the sky.

TO ONE IN PARADISE

Thou wast that all to me, love,
  For which my soul did pine—
A green isle in the sea, love,
  A fountain and a shrine,
All wreathed with fairy fruits and flowers,
  And all the flowers were mine.

Ah, dream too bright to last!
  Ah, starry Hope! that didst arise
But to be overcast!
  A voice from out the Future cries,
"On! on!"—but o'er the Past
  (Dim gulf!) my spirit hovering lies
Mute, motionless, aghast!

For, alas! alas! with me
  The light of Life is o'er!
No more—no more—no more—
(Such language holds the solemn sea
  To the sands upon the shore)
Shall bloom the thunder-blasted tree,
  Or the stricken eagle soar!

And all my days are trances,
  And all my nightly dreams
Are where thy grey eye glances,
  And where thy footstep gleams—
In what ethereal dances,
  By what eternal streams.

THE HAUNTED PALACE

In the greenest of our valleys,
   By good angels tenanted,
Once a fair and stately palace—
   Radiant palace—reared its head.
In the monarch Thought's dominion—
   It stood there!
Never seraph spread a pinion
   Over fabric half so fair!

Banners yellow, glorious, golden,
   On its roof did float and flow,
(This—all this—was in the olden
   Time long ago,)
And every gentle air that dallied,
   In that sweet day,
Along the ramparts plumed and pallid,
   A wingéd odor went away.

Wanderers in that happy valley
   Through two luminous windows saw
Spirits moving musically
   To a lute's well-tuned law,
Round about a throne, where sitting
   Porphyrogene!
In state his glory well befitting,
   The ruler of the realm was seen.

And all with pearl and ruby glowing
   Was the fair palace door,
Through which came flowing, flowing, flowing
   And sparkling evermore,
A troop of Echoes whose sweet duty
   Was but to sing,
In voices of surpassing beauty,
   The wit and wisdom of their king.

But evil things, in robes of sorrow,
   Assailed the monarch's high estate.
(Ah, let us mourn, for never morrow
   Shall dawn upon him, desolate!)
And, round about his home, the glory
   That blushed and bloomed
Is but a dim-remembered story
   Of the old time entombed.

And travellers, now, within that valley,
   Through the red-litten windows see
Vast forms, that move fantastically
   To a discordant melody,
While, like a ghastly rapid river,
   Through the pale door,
A hideous throng rush out forever,
   And laugh—but smile no more.

THE CONQUEROR WORM

Lo! 'tis a gala night
   Within the lonesome latter years!
An angel throng, bewinged, bedight
   In veils, and drowned in tears,
Sit in a theatre, to see
   A play of hopes and fears,
While the orchestra breathes fitfully
   The music of the spheres.

Mimes, in the form of God on high,
   Mutter and mumble low,
And hither and thither fly—
   Mere puppets they, who come and go
At bidding of vast formless things
   That shift the scenery to and fro,
Flapping from out their Condor wings
   Invisible Wo!

That motley drama—oh, be sure
　　It shall not be forgot!
With its Phantom chased for evermore,
　　By a crowd that seize it not,
Through a circle that ever returneth in
　　To the self-same spot,
And much of Madness, and more of Sin,
　　And Horror the soul of the plot.

But see, amid the mimic rout
　　A crawling shape intrude!
A blood-red thing that writhes from out
　　The scenic solitude!
It writhes!—it writhes!—with mortal pangs
　　The mimes become its food,
And the seraphs sob at vermin fangs
　　In human gore imbued.

Out—out are the lights—out all!
　　And, over each quivering form,
The curtain, a funeral pall,
　　Comes down with the rush of a storm,
And the angels, all pallid and wan,
　　Uprising, unveiling, affirm
That the play is the tragedy, "Man,"
　　And its hero the Conqueror Worm.

DREAM-LAND

By a route obscure and lonely,
Haunted by ill angels only,
Where an Eidolon, named NIGHT,
On a black throne reigns upright,
I have reached these lands but newly
From an ultimate dim Thule—
From a wild weird clime that lieth, sublime,
　　Out of SPACE—out of TIME.

Bottomless vales and boundless floods,
And chasms, and caves and Titan woods,
With forms that no man can discover
For the tears that drip all over;
Mountains toppling evermore;
Into seas without a shore;
Seas that restlessly aspire,
Surging, unto skies of fire;
Lakes that endlessly outspread
Their lone waters—lone and dead,—
Their still waters—still and chilly
With the snows of the lolling lily.

By the lakes that thus outspread
Their lone waters, lone and dead,—
Their sad waters, sad and chilly
With the snows of the lolling lily,—
By the mountains—near the river
Murmuring lowly, murmuring ever,—
By the grey woods,—by the swamp
Where the toad and the newt encamp,—
By the dismal tarns and pools
     Where dwell the Ghouls,—
By each spot the most unholy—
In each nook most melancholy,—
There the traveller meets aghast
Sheeted Memories of the Past—
Shrouded forms that start and sigh
As they pass the wanderer by—
White-robed forms of friends long given,
In agony, to the Earth—and Heaven.

For the heart whose woes are legion
'Tis a peaceful, soothing region—
For the spirit that walks in shadow
'Tis—oh, 'tis an Eldorado!
But the traveller, travelling through it,
May not—dare not openly view it;
Never its mysteries are exposed
To the weak human eye unclosed;

So wills its King, who hath forbid
The uplifting of the fringéd lid;
And thus the sad Soul that here passes.
Beholds it but through darkened glasses.

By a route obscure and lonely,
Haunted by ill angels only,
Where an Eidolon, named NIGHT,
On a black throne reigns upright,
I have wandered home but newly
From this ultimate dim Thule.

THE CITY IN THE SEA

Lo! Death has reared himself a throne
In a strange city lying alone
Far down within the dim West,
Where the good and the bad and the worst and the
    best
Have gone to their eternal rest.
There shrines and palaces and towers
(Time-eaten towers that tremble not!)
Resemble nothing that is ours.
Around, by lifting winds forgot,
Resignedly beneath the sky
The melancholy waters lie.

No rays from the holy heaven come down
On the long night-time of that town;
But light from out the lurid sea
Streams up the turrets silently—
Gleams up the pinnacles far and free—
Up domes—up spires—up kingly halls—
Up fanes—up Babylon-like walls—
Up shadowy long-forgotten bowers
Of sculptured ivy and stone flowers—
Up many and many a marvellous shrine
Whose wreathéd friezes intertwine

The viol, the violet, and the vine.
Resignedly beneath the sky
The melancholy waters lie.
So blend the turrets and shadows there
That all seem pendulous in air,
While from a proud tower in the town
Death looks gigantically down.

There open fanes and gaping graves
Yawn level with the luminous waves
But not the riches there that lie
In each idol's diamond eye—
Not the gaily-jewelled dead
Tempt the waters from their bed;
For no ripples curl, alas!
Along that wilderness of glass—
No swellings tell that winds may be
Upon some far-off happier sea—
No heavings hint that winds have been
On seas less hideously serene.

But lo, a stir is in the air!
The wave—there is a movement there!
As if the towers had thrust aside,
In slightly sinking, the dull tide—
As if their tops had feebly given
A void within the filmy Heaven.
The waves have now a redder glow—
The hours are breathing faint and low—
And when, amid no earthly moans,
Down, down that town shall settle hence,
Hell, rising from a thousand thrones,
Shall do it reverence.

THE RAVEN

Once upon a midnight dreary, while I pondered, weak
and weary,
Over many a quaint and curious volume of forgotten
lore—
While I nodded, nearly napping, suddenly there came
a tapping,
As of some one gently rapping, rapping at my chamber door.
"'Tis some visitor," I muttered, "tapping at my chamber door—

        Only this and nothing more."

Ah, distinctly I remember it was in the bleak De-
cember;
And each separate dying ember wrought its ghost
upon the floor.
Eagerly I wished the morrow;—vainly I had sought to
borrow
From my books surcease of sorrow—sorrow for the lost
Lenore—
For the rare and radiant maiden whom the angels
name Lenore—

        Nameless *here* for evermore.

And the silken, sad, uncertain rustling of each purple
curtain
Thrilled me—filled me with fantastic terrors never felt
before;
So that now, to still the beating of my heart, I stood
repeating
"'Tis some visitor entreating entrance at my chamber
door—
Some late visitor entreating entrance at my chamber
door;—

        This it is and nothing more."

Presently my soul grew stronger; hesitating then no longer,

"Sir," said I, "or Madam, truly your forgiveness I implore;

But the fact is I was napping, and so gently you came rapping,

And so faintly you came tapping, tapping at my chamber door,

That I scarce was sure I heard you"—here I opened wide the door;——

Darkness there and nothing more.

Deep into that darkness peering, long I stood there wondering, fearing,

Doubting, dreaming dreams no mortal ever dared to dream before;

But the silence was unbroken, and the stillness gave no token,

And the only word there spoken was the whispered word, "Lenore?"

This I whispered, and an echo murmured back the word "Lenore!"

Merely this and nothing more.

Back into the chamber turning, all my soul within me burning,

Soon again I heard a tapping somewhat louder than before.

"Surely," said I, "surely that is something at my window lattice;

Let me see, then, what thereat is, and this mystery explore—

Let my heart be still a moment and this mystery explore;—

'Tis the wind and nothing more!"

Open here I flung the shutter, when, with many a flirt and flutter,

In there stepped a stately Raven of the saintly days of yore;

Not the least obeisance made he; not a minute
    stopped or stayed he;
But, with mien of lord or lady, perched above my
    chamber door—
Perched upon a bust of Pallas just above my chamber
    door—
        Perched, and sat, and nothing more.

Then this ebony bird beguiling my sad fancy into
    smiling,
By the grave and stern decorum of the countenance it
    wore,
"Though thy crest be shorn and shaven, thou," I said,
    "art sure no craven,
Ghastly grim and ancient Raven wandering from the
    Nightly shore—
Tell me what thy lordly name is on the Night's Plu-
    tonian shore!"
        Quoth the Raven "Nevermore."

Much I marvelled this ungainly fowl to hear discourse
    so plainly,
Though its answer little meaning—little relevancy
    bore;
For we cannot help agreeing that no living human
    being
Ever yet was blessed with seeing bird above his cham-
    ber door—
Bird or beast upon the sculptured bust above his
    chamber door,
        With such name as "Nevermore."

But the Raven, sitting lonely on the placid bust, spoke
    only
That one word, as if his soul in that one word he did
    outpour.
Nothing farther then he uttered—not a feather then
    he fluttered—
Till I scarcely more than muttered "Other friends
    have flown before—

On the morrow *he* will leave me, as my Hopes have
flown before."
>   Then the bird said "Nevermore."

Startled at the stillness broken by reply so aptly
spoken,
"Doubtless," said I, "what it utters is its only stock
and store
Caught from some unhappy master whom unmerciful
Disaster
Followed fast and followed faster till his songs one
burden bore—
Till the dirges of his Hope that melancholy burden
bore
>   Of 'Never—nevermore.'"

But the Raven still beguiling all my fancy into smiling,
Straight I wheeled a cushioned seat in front of bird,
and bust and door;
Then, upon the velvet sinking, I betook myself to
linking
Fancy unto fancy, thinking what this ominous bird of
yore—
What this grim, ungainly, ghastly, gaunt, and ominous bird of yore
>   Meant in croaking "Nevermore."

This I sat engaged in guessing, but no syllable expressing
To the fowl whose fiery eyes now burned into my
bosom's core;
This and more I sat divining, with my head at ease
reclining
On the cushion's velvet lining that the lamp-light
gloated o'er,
But whose velvet-violet lining with the lamp-light
gloating o'er,
>   *She* shall press, ah, nevermore!

Then, methought, the air grew denser, perfumed from
an unseen censer

Swung by Seraphim whose foot-falls tinkled on the
tufted floor.

"Wretch," I cried, "thy God hath lent thee—by these
angels he hath sent thee

Respite—respite and nepenthe from thy memories of
Lenore;

Quaff, oh quaff this kind nepenthe and forget this lost
Lenore!"

      Quoth the Raven "Nevermore."

"Prophet!" said I, "thing of evil!—prophet still, if bird
or devil!—

Whether Tempter sent, or whether tempest tossed
thee here ashore,

Desolate yet all undaunted, on this desert land enchanted—

On this home by Horror haunted—tell me truly, I
implore—

Is there—*is* there balm in Gilead?—tell me—tell me, I
implore!"

      Quoth the Raven "Nevermore."

"Prophet!" said I, "thing of evil!—prophet still, if bird
or devil!

By that Heaven that bends above us—by that God we
both adore—

Tell this soul with sorrow laden if, within the distant
Aidenn,

It shall clasp a sainted maiden whom the angels name
Lenore—

Clasp a rare and radiant maiden whom the angels
name Lenore."

      Quoth the Raven "Nevermore."

"Be that word our sign of parting, bird or fiend!" I
shrieked, upstarting—

"Get thee back into the tempest and the Night's Plu-
tonian shore!

Leave no black plume as a token of that lie thy soul
    hath spoken!
Leave my loneliness unbroken!—quit the bust above
    my door!
Take thy beak from out my heart, and take thy form
    from off my door!"
              Quoth the Raven "Nevermore."

And the Raven, never flitting, still is sitting, *still* is
    sitting
On the pallid bust of Pallas just above my chamber
    door;
And his eyes have all the seeming of a demon's that
    is dreaming,
And the lamp-light o'er him streaming throws his
    shadow on the floor;
And my soul from out that shadow that lies floating
    on the floor
              Shall be lifted—nevermore!

ULALUME

The skies they were ashen and sober;
    The leaves they were crisped and sere—
    The leaves they were withering and sere;
It was night in the lonesome October
    Of my most immemorial year;
It was hard by the dim lake of Auber,
    In the misty mid region of Weir—
It was down by the dank tarn of Auber,
    In the ghoul-haunted woodland of Weir.

Here once, through an alley Titanic,
    Of cypress, I roamed with my Soul—
    Of cypress, with Psyche, my Soul.
These were days when my heart was volcanic
    As the scoriac rivers that roll—
    As the lavas that restlessly roll

Their sulphurous currents down Yaanek
    In the ultimate climes of the pole—
That groan as they roll down Mount Yaanek
    In the realms of the boreal pole.

Our talk had been serious and sober,
    But our thoughts they were palsied and sere—
    Our memories were treacherous and sere—
For we knew not the month was October,
    And we marked not the night of the year—
    (Ah, night of all nights in the year!)
We noted not the dim lake of Auber—
    (Though once we had journeyed down here)—
We remembered not the dank tarn of Auber,
    Nor the ghoul-haunted woodland of Weir.

And now, as the night was senescent
    And star-dials pointed to morn—
    As the star-dials hinted of morn—
At the end of our path a liquescent
    And nebulous lustre was born,
Out of which a miraculous crescent
    Arose with a duplicate horn—
Astarte's bediamonded crescent
    Distinct with its duplicate horn.

And I said—"She is warmer than Dian:
    She rolls through an ether of sighs—
    She revels in a region of sighs:
She has seen that the tears are not dry on
    These cheeks, where the worm never dies
And has come past the stars of the Lion
    To point us the path to the skies—
    To the Lethean peace of the skies—
Come up, in despite of the Lion,
    To shine on us with her bright eyes—
Come up through the lair of the Lion,
    With love in her luminous eyes."

But Psyche, uplifting her finger,
    Said—"Sadly this star I mistrust—
    Her pallor I strangely mistrust:—
Oh, hasten!—oh, let us not linger!
    Oh, fly!—let us fly!—for we must."
In terror she spoke, letting sink her
    Wings until they trailed in the dust—
In agony sobbed, letting sink her
    Plumes till they trailed in the dust—
    Till they sorrowfully trailed in the dust.

I replied—"This is nothing but dreaming:
    Let us on by this tremulous light!
    Let us bathe in this crystalline light!
Its Sibyllic splendor is beaming
    With Hope and in Beauty to-night:—
    See!—it flickers up the sky through the night!
Ah, we safely may trust to its gleaming,
    And be sure it will lead us aright—
We safely may trust to a gleaming
    That cannot but guide us aright,
    Since it flickers up to Heaven through the night."

Thus I pacified Psyche and kissed her,
    And tempted her out of her gloom—
    And conquered her scruples and gloom;
And we passed to the end of the vista,
    But were stopped by the door of a tomb—
    By the door of a legended tomb;
And I said—"What is written, sweet sister,
    On the door of this legended tomb?"
    She replied—"Ulalume—Ulalume—
    'Tis the vault of thy lost Ulalume!"

Then my heart it grew ashen and sober
    As the leaves that were crisped and sere—
    As the leaves that were withering and sere,
And I cried—"It was surely October
    On *this* very night of last year
    That I journeyed—I journeyed down here—

That I brought a dread burden down here—
  On this night of all nights in the year,
  Ah, what demon has tempted me here?
Well I know, now, this dim lake of Auber—
  This misty mid region of Weir—
Well I know, now, this dank tarn of Auber,
  This ghoul-haunted woodland of Weir."

Said we then,—the two, then: "Ah, can it
  Have been that the woodlandish ghouls—
  The pitiful, the merciful ghouls—
To bar up our way and to ban it
  From the secret that lies in these wolds
  From the thing that lies hidden in these wolds—
Have drawn up the spectre of a planet
  From the limbo of lunary souls—
This sinfully scintillant planet
  From the Hell of the planetary souls?"

ANNABEL LEE

It was many and many a year ago,
  In a kingdom by the sea
That a maiden there lived whom you may know
  By the name of ANNABEL LEE;
And this maiden she lived with no other thought
  Than to love and be loved by me.

I was a child and *she* was a child,
  In this kingdom by the sea,
But we loved with a love that was more than love—
  I and my ANNABEL LEE—
With a love that the winged seraphs of heaven
  Coveted her and me.

And this was the reason that, long ago,
  In this kingdom by the sea,
A wind blew out of a cloud, chilling
  My beautiful ANNABEL LEE;

So that her highborn kinsmen came
    And bore her away from me,
To shut her up in a sepulchre
    In this kingdom by the sea.

The angels, not half so happy in heaven,
    Went envying her and me—
Yes!—that was the reason (as all men know,
    In this kingdom by the sea)
That the wind came out of the cloud by night,
    Chilling and killing my ANNABEL LEE.

But our love it was stronger by far than the love
    Of those who were older than we—
    Of many far wiser than we—
And neither the angels in heaven above,
    Nor the demons down under the sea,
Can ever dissever my soul from the soul
    Of the beautiful ANNABEL LEE:

For the moon never beams, without bringing me
        dreams
    Of the beautiful ANNABEL LEE;
And the stars never rise, but I feel the bright eyes
    Of the beautiful ANNABEL LEE:
And so, all the night-tide, I lie down by the side
Of my darling—my darling—my life and my bride,
    In the sepulchre there by the sea—
    In her tomb by the sounding sea.

RALPH WALDO EMERSON

1803–1882

"I am born a poet," Emerson wrote to his fiancée
Lydia Jackson in 1835, "of a low class without doubt, yet
a poet. That is my vocation. My singing, to be sure, is
very 'husky,' and is for the most part in prose. Still I am
a poet in the sense of a perceiver and dear lover of the
harmonies that are in the soul and in matter, and specially
of the correspondence between these and those." Emerson
conceived of the poet as such a perceiver, or seer, rather
than narrowly as a maker of verses. While he wrote verse
intermittently from his Harvard days as class poet, it is his
prose which gives most sustained expression to the cor-
respondences he found between matter and spirit. In his
essay "The Poet" he scorns meters in favor of meter-
making arguments, and in the poem "Merlin" he spurns
the "jingling serenader's art." (Emerson once called Poe
"the jingle-man.") Although he would "mount to paradise /
By the stairway of surprise," his surprises are expressed
in the modification of conventional meters rather than, as
in Whitman, by the invention of wholly new rhythms and
forms. Emerson can use traditional meters expertly ("Concord Hymn," "Brahma"); often he purposely roughens the
texture of his verse (as in the "Ode" to Channing), or
uses a variety of meters in the same poem ("Hamatreya").
At times he anticipates Emily Dickinson's bold modula-
tions of traditional forms, but without her consistency. The
poems chosen here illustrate several of Emerson's chief
themes. "Merlin" states his bardic ideal and makes interesting comparison to Poe's "Israfel" and to Melville's
"The Aeolian Harp." The ode inscribed to his former
teacher, a leading Unitarian minister and reformer, expresses both Emerson's concern against the materialism of
his time and his reluctance to endorse panaceas for society:
let man first "Live for friendship, live for love . . . The
state may follow how it can." "Hamatreya" shows the van-

ity of earthly ambition; the first part remarkably anticipates
Frost in diction, tone, and theme; only Emerson would
have thought it necessary to add a passage paraphrasing
the *Vishnu Parana* as a moral. "The Snow-Storm" enun-
ciates in flexible blank verse a conception of organic form
in nature which Art can only "mimic in slow structures,
stone on stone." Emerson's doctrine of the Oversoul is tan-
talizingly dramatized in "Brahma," another poem that
draws on the correspondence between his Transcendentalist
philosophy and his readings of Eastern religious thought.
Emerson's books of verse are *Poems* (1847); *May-Day and
Other Pieces* (1867); and *Selected Poems* (1876). For an
account of his life see p. 336.

CONCORD HYMN

SUNG   AT   THE   COMPLETION   OF   THE
BATTLE   MONUMENT,   APRIL   19,   1836

By the rude bridge that arched the flood,
   Their flag to April's breeze unfurled,
Here once the embattled farmers stood,
   And fired the shot heard round the world.

The foe long since in silence slept;
   Alike the conqueror silent sleeps;
And Time the ruined bridge has swept
   Down the dark stream which seaward creeps.

On this green bank, by this soft stream,
   We set today a votive stone;
That memory may their deed redeem,
   When, like our sires, our sons are gone.

Spirit, that made those heroes dare
   To die, and leave their children free,
Bid Time and Nature gently spare
   The shaft we raise to them and thee.

THE SNOW-STORM

Announced by all the trumpets of the sky,
Arrives the snow, and, driving o'er the fields,
Seems nowhere to alight: the whited air
Hides hills and woods, the river, and the heaven,
And veils the farm-house at the garden's end.
The sled and traveller stopped, the courier's feet
Delayed, all friends shut out, the housemates sit
Around the radiant fireplace, enclosed
In a tumultuous privacy of storm.

Come see the north wind's masonry.
Out of an unseen quarry evermore
Furnished with tile, the fierce artificer
Curves his white bastions with projected roof
Round every windward stake, or tree, or door.
Speeding, the myriad-handed, his wild work
So fanciful, so savage, nought cares he
For number or proportion. Mockingly,
On coop or kennel he hangs Parian wreaths;
A swan-like form invests the hidden thorn;
Fills up the farmer's lane from wall to wall,
Maugre the farmer's sighs; and at the gate
A tapering turret overtops the work.
And when his hours are numbered, and the world
Is all his own, retiring, as he were not,
Leaves, when the sun appears, astonished Art
To mimic in slow structures, stone by stone,
Built in an age, the mad wind's night-work,
The frolic architecture of the snow.

HAMATREYA

Bulkeley, Hunt, Willard, Hosmer, Meriam, Flint,
Possessed the land which rendered to their toil
Hay, corn, roots, hemp, flax, apples, wool and wood.
Each of these landlords walked amidst his farm,
Saying, "'Tis mine, my children's and my name's.
How sweet the west wind sounds in my own trees!
How graceful climb those shadows on my hill!
I fancy these pure waters and the flags
Know me, as does my dog: we sympathize;
And, I affirm, my actions smack of the soil."

Where are these men? Asleep beneath their grounds:
And strangers, fond as they, their furrows plough.
Earth laughs in flowers, to see her boastful boys
Earth-proud, proud of the earth which is not theirs;
Who steer the plough, but cannot steer their feet
Clear of the grave.
They added ridge to valley, brook to pond,
And sighed for all that bounded their domain;
"This suits me for a pasture; that's my park;
We must have clay, lime, gravel, granite-ledge,
And misty lowland, where to go for peat.
The land is well,—lies fairly to the south.
'Tis good, when you have crossed the sea and back,
To find the sitfast acres where you left them."
Ah! the hot owner sees not Death, who adds
Him to his land, a lump of mould the more.
Hear what the Earth says:—

EARTH-SONG

"Mine and yours;
Mine, not yours.
Earth endures;
Stars abide—

Shine down in the old sea;
Old are the shores;
But where are old men?
I who have seen much,
Such have I never seen.

"The lawyer's deed
Ran sure,
In tail,
To them, and to their heirs
Who shall succeed,
Without fail,
Forevermore.

"Here is the land,
Shaggy with wood,
With its old valley,
Mound and flood.
But the heritors?—
Fled like the flood's foam.
The lawyer, and the laws,
And the kingdom,
Clean swept herefrom.

"They called me theirs,
Who so controlled me;
Yet every one
Wished to stay, and is gone,
How am I theirs,
If they cannot hold me,
But I hold them?"

When I heard the Earth-song,
I was no longer brave;
My avarice cooled
Like lust in the chill of the grave.

ODE

INSCRIBED TO W. H. CHANNING

Though loath to grieve
The evil time's sole patriot,
I cannot leave
My honied thought
For the priest's cant,
Or statesman's rant.

If I refuse
My study for their politique,
Which at the best is trick,
The angry Muse
Puts confusion in my brain.

But who is he that prates
Of the culture of mankind,
Of better arts and life?
Go, blindworm, go,
Behold the famous States
Harrying Mexico
With rifle and with knife!

Or who, with accent bolder,
Dare praise the freedom-loving mountaineer?
I found by thee, O rushing Contoocook!
And in thy valleys, Agiochook!
The jackals of the Negro-holder.

The God who made New Hampshire
Taunted the lofty land
With little men;—
Small bat and wren
House in the oak:—
If earth-fire cleave
The upheaved land, and bury the folk,
The southern crocodile would grieve.

Virtue palters; Right is hence;
Freedom praised, but hid;
Funeral eloquence
Rattles the coffin-lid.

What boots thy zeal,
O glowing friend,
That would indignant rend
The northland from the south?
Wherefore? to what good end?
Boston Bay and Bunker Hill
Would serve things still;—
Things are of the snake.

The horseman serves the horse,
The neatherd serves the neat,
The merchant serves the purse,
The eater serves his meat;
'Tis the day of the chattel,
Web to weave, and corn to grind;
Things are in the saddle,
And ride mankind.

There are two laws discrete,
Not reconciled,—
Law for man, and law for thing;
The last builds town and fleet,
But it runs wild,
And doth the man unking.

'Tis fit the forest fall,
The steep be graded,
The mountain tunnelled,
The sand shaded,
The orchard planted,
The glebe tilled,
The prairie granted,
The steamer built.

Let man serve law for man;
Live for friendship, live for love,
For truth's and harmony's behoof;
The state may follow how it can,
As Olympus follows Jove.

Yet do not I implore
The wrinkled shopman to my sounding woods,
Nor bid the unwilling senator
Ask votes of thrushes in the solitudes.
Every one to his chosen work;—
Foolish hands may mix and mar;
Wise and sure the issues are.
Round they roll till dark is light,
Sex to sex, and even to odd;—
The over-god
Who marries Right to Might,
Who peoples, unpeoples,—
He who exterminates
Races by stronger races,
Black by white faces,—
Knows to bring honey
Out of the lion;
Grafts gentlest scion
On pirate and Turk.

The Cossack eats Poland
Like stolen fruit;
Her last noble is ruined,
Her last poet mute:
Straight, into double band
The victors divide;
Half for freedom strike and stand;—
The astonished Muse finds thousands at her side.

MERLIN

I

Thy trivial harp will never please
Or fill my craving ear;
Its chords should ring as blows the breeze,
Free, peremptory, clear.
No jingling serenader's art,
Nor tinkle of piano strings,
Can make the wild blood start
In its mystic springs.
The kingly bard
Must smite the chords rudely and hard,
As with hammer or with mace;
That they may render back
Artful thunder, which conveys
Secrets of the solar track,
Sparks of the supersolar blaze.
Merlin's blows are strokes of fate,
Chiming with the forest tone,
When boughs buffet boughs in the wood;
Chiming with the gasp and moan
Of the ice-imprisoned flood;
With the pulse of manly hearts;
With the voice of orators;
With the din of city arts;
With the cannonade of wars;
With the marches of the brave;
And prayers of might from martyrs' cave.

Great is the art,
Great be the manners, of the bard.
He shall not his brain encumber
With the coil of rhythm and number;
But, leaving rule and pale forethought,
He shall aye climb
For his rhyme.

"Pass in, pass in," the angels say,
"In to the upper doors,
Nor count compartments of the floors.
But mount to paradise
By the stairway of surprise."

Blameless master of the games,
King of sport that never shames,
He shall daily joy dispense
Hid in song's sweet influence.
Forms more cheerly live and go.
What time the subtle mind
Sings aloud the tune whereto
Their pulses beat,
And march their feet,
And their members are combined.

By Sybarites beguiled,
He shall no task decline;
Merlin's mighty line
Extremes of nature reconciled,—
Bereaved a tyrant of his will,
And made the lion mild.
Songs can the tempest still,
Scattered on the stormy air,
Mold the year to fair increase
And bring in poetic peace.

He shall not seek to weave,
In weak, unhappy times,
Efficacious rhymes;
Wait his returning strength.
Bird, that from the nadir's floor
To the zenith's top can soar,
The soaring orbit of the muse exceeds that journey's
        length.
Nor profane affect to hit
Or compass that, by meddling wit,
Which only the propitious mind
Publishes when 'tis inclined.

There are open hours
When the God's will sallies free,
And the dull idiot might see
The flowing fortunes of a thousand years;—
Sudden, at unawares,
Self-moved, fly-to the doors,
Nor sword of angels could reveal
What they conceal.

II

The rhyme of the poet
Modulates the king's affairs;
Balance-loving Nature
Made all things in pairs.
To every foot its antipode;
Each color with its counter glowed;
To every tone beat answering tones,
Higher or graver;
Flavor gladly blends with flavor;
Leaf answers leaf upon the bough;
And match the paired cotyledons.
Hands to hands, and feet to feet,
In one body grooms and brides;
Eldest rite, two married sides
In every mortal meet.
Light's far furnace shines,
Smelting balls and bars,
Forging double stars,
Glittering twins and trines.
The animals are sick with love,
Lovesick with rhyme;
Each with all propitious time
Into chorus wove.

Like the dancer's ordered band,
Thoughts come also hand in hand;
In equal couples mated,
Or else alternated;
Adding by their mutual gage,
One to other, health and age.

Solitary fancies go
Short-lived wandering to and fro,
Most like to bachelors,
Or an ungiven maid,
Not ancestors,
With no posterity to make the lie afraid,
Or keep truth undecayed.
Perfect-paired as eagle's wings,
Justice is the rhyme of things;
Trade and counting use
The self-same tuneful muse;
And Nemesis,
Who with even matches odd,
Who athwart space redresses
The partial wrong,
Fills the just period,
And finishes the song.

Subtle rhymes, with ruin rife,
Murmur in the house of life,
Sung by the Sisters as they spin;
In perfect time and measure they
Build and unbuild our echoing clay.
As the two twilights of the day
Fold us music-drunken in.

BRAHMA

If the red slayer think he slays,
  Or if the slain think he is slain,
They know not well the subtle ways
  I keep, and pass, and turn again.

Far or forgot to me is near;
  Shadow and sunlight are the same;
The vanished gods to me appear;
  And one to me are shame and fame.

They reckon ill who leave me out;
    When me they fly, I am the wings;
I am the doubter and the doubt,
    And I the hymn the Brahmin sings.

The strong gods pine for my abode,
    And pine in vain the sacred Seven;
But thou, meek lover of the good!
    Find me, and turn thy back on heaven.

DAYS

Daughters of Time, the hypocritic Days,
Muffled and dumb like barefoot dervishes,
And marching single in an endless file,
Bring diadems and fagots in their hands.
To each they offer gifts after his will,
Bread, kingdoms, stars, and sky that holds them all.
I, in my pleached garden, watched the pomp,
Forgot my morning wishes, hastily
Took a few herbs and apples, and the Day
Turned and departed silent. I, too late,
Under her solemn fillet saw the scorn.

JAMES RUSSELL LOWELL

1819–1891

"I shall never be a poet till I get out of the pulpit, and New England was all meeting house when I was growing up," Lowell wrote in 1865. By then he had been class poet at Harvard, '38; taken a law degree in 1840; edited several antislavery magazines; and been for a decade professor of French and Spanish Languages and Literatures and of belles-lettres at Harvard. He was a man of great wit and charm who wrote engagingly of his enthusiasms, and they included Dante, Spenser, Milton, Dryden, Wordsworth, and Keats, but he lacked discipline and intellectual force. His verse attempted a variety of things— lyricism, declamation, romantic narrative, local color, polemic—but only in the last two genres did he achieve something original and not even in these does he reach intensity. Although Lowell poeticized from a pulpit it was his own facility, more than the meeting house, which undid him. His nimble, often platitudinous, and ill-constructed verse was widely popular, but his reputation has rapidly diminished. *A Fable for Critics* is still an entertaining *jeu d'esprit*, a jumble of bad puns and impressionistic judgments, often shrewd, on his literary contemporaries. In *The Biglow Papers* he versified the vein of crackerbarrel political comment which such Yankee journalists as Seba Smith had been rendering in prose; Lowell's first series was written during the Mexican War (1848), the second during the Civil War (1867). He had a good ear, and worked out in his introduction to the 1867 volume a sound rationale for rendering literary dialect. Succeeding Longfellow to his Harvard chair, Lowell soon became also the first editor of *The Atlantic Monthly* (1857–1861) and later edited the *North American*, where he strongly influenced public taste in literature and opinion on social issues. He served as American Minister to Spain (1877–1880) and to Great Britain (1880–1885). Of his latter appointment Henry James remarked that "the true reward of an English style was to be sent to England."

FROM A FABLE FOR CRITICS

> There comes Emerson first, whose rich words,
>   every one,
> Are like gold nails in temples to hang trophies on,
> Whose prose is grand verse, while his verse, the Lord
>   knows,
> Is some of it pr— No, 'tis not even prose;
> I'm speaking of metres; some poems have welled
> From those rare depths of soul that have ne'er been
>   excelled;
> They're not epics, but that doesn't matter a pin,
> In creating, the only hard thing's to begin;
> A grass-blade's no easier to make than an oak;
> If you've once found the way, you've achieved the
>   grand stroke;
> In the worst of his poems are mines of rich matter,
> But thrown in a heap with a crash and a clatter;
> Now it is not one thing nor another alone
> Makes a poem, but rather the general tone,
> The something pervading, uniting the whole,
> The before unconceived, unconceivable soul,
> So that just in removing this trifle or that, you
> Take away, as it were, a chief limb of the statue;
> Roots, wood, bark, and leaves singly perfect may be,
> But, clapt hodge-podge together, they don't make a
>   tree.
>
> But to come back to Emerson (whom, by the
>   way
> I believe we left waiting),—his is, we may say,
> A Greek head on right Yankee shoulders, whose range
> Has Olympus for one pole, for t'other the Exchange;
> He seems, to my thinking (although I'm afraid
> The comparison must, long ere this, have been made),

A Plotinus-Montaigne, where the Egyptian's gold mist
And the Gascon's shrewd wit cheek-by-jowl coexist;
All admire, and yet scarcely six converts he's got
To I don't (nor they either) exactly know what;
For though he builds glorious temples, 'tis odd
He leaves never a doorway to get in a god.
'Tis refreshing to old-fashioned people like me
To meet such a primitive Pagan as he,
In whose mind all creation is duly respected
As parts of himself—just a little projected;
And who's willing to worship the stars and the sun,
A convert to—nothing but Emerson.
So perfect a balance there is in his head,
That he talks of things sometimes as if they were
    dead;
Life, nature, love, God, and affairs of that sort,
He looks at as merely ideas; in short,
As if they were fossils stuck round in a cabinet,
Of such vast extent that our earth's a mere dab in it;
Composed just as he is inclined to conjecture her,
Namely, one part pure earth, ninety-nine parts pure
    lecturer;
You are filled with delight at his clear demonstration,
Each figure, word, gesture, just fits the occasion,
With the quiet precision of science he'll sort 'em,
But you can't help suspecting the whole a *post
    mortem.*

There are persons, mole-blind to the soul's make
    and style,
Who insist on a likeness 'twixt him and Carlyle;
To compare him with Plato would be vastly fairer,
Carlyle's the more burly, but E. is the rarer;
He sees fewer objects, but clearlier, trulier,
If C.'s as original, E.'s more peculiar;
That he's more of a man you might say of the one,
Of the other he's more of an Emerson.
C.'s the Titan, as shaggy of mind as of limb,—
E. the clear-eyed Olympian, rapid and slim;

The one's two thirds Norseman, the other half Greek,
Where the one's most abounding, the other's to seek;
C.'s generals require to be seen in the mass,—
E.'s specialties gain if enlarged by the glass;
C. gives nature and God his own fits of the blues,
And rims common-sense things with mystical hues,—
E. sits in a mystery calm and intense,
And looks coolly around him with sharp common-
    sense;
C. shows you how every-day matters unite
With the dim transdiurnal recesses of night,—
While E., in a plain, preternatural way,
Makes mysteries matters of mere every day;
C. draws all his characters quite *à la* Fuseli,—
Not sketching their bundles of muscles and thews illy,
He paints with a brush so untamed and profuse,
They seem nothing but bundles of muscles and thews;
E. is rather like Flaxman, lines strait and severe,
And a colorless outline, but full, round, and clear;—
To the men he thinks worthy he frankly accords
The design of a white marble statue in words.
C. labors to get at the centre, and then
Take a reckoning from there of his actions and men;
E. calmly assumes the said centre as granted,
And, given himself, has whatever is wanted.

He has imitators in scores, who omit
No part of the man but his wisdom and wit,—
Who go carefully o'er the sky-blue of his brain,
And when he has skimmed it once, skim it again;
If at all they resemble him, you may be sure it is
Because their shoals mirror his mists and obscurities,
As a mud-puddle seems deep as heaven for a minute,
While a cloud that floats o'er is reflected within it.

. . . .

There is Bryant, as quiet, as cool, and as
    dignified,
As a smooth, silent iceberg, that never is ignified,

Save when by reflection, 'tis kindled o'nights
With a semblance of flame by the chill Northern
    Lights.
He may rank (Griswold says so) first bard of your
    nation
(There's no doubt that he stands in supreme ice-
    olation),
Your topmost Parnassus he may set his heel on,
But no warm applauses come, peal following peal
    on,—
He's too smooth and too polished to hang any zeal on:
Unqualified merits, I'll grant, if you choose, he has
    'em,
But he lacks the one merit of kindling enthusiasm;
If he stir you at all, it is just, on my soul,
Like being stirred up with the very North Pole.

He is very nice reading in summer, but *inter
Nos*, we don't want *extra* freezing in winter;
Take him up in the depth of July, my advice is,
When you feel an Egyptian devotion to ices,
But, deduct all you can, there's enough that's right
    good in him,
He has a true soul for field, river, and wood in him;
And his heart, in the midst of brick walls, or where'er
    it *is*,
Glows, softens, and thrills with the tenderest
    charities—
To you mortals that delve in this trade-ridden planet?
No, to old Berkshire's hills, with their limestone and
    granite.
If you're one who *in loco* (add *foco* here) *desipis*,
You will get of his outermost heart (as I guess) a
    piece;
But you'd get deeper down if you came as a precipice,
And would break the last seal of its inwardest
    fountain,
If you only could palm yourself off for a mountain.
Mr. Quivis, or somebody quite as discerning,
Some scholar who's hourly expecting his learning,

Calls B. the American Wordsworth; but Wordsworth
May be rated at more than your whole tuneful herd's
    worth.
No, don't be absurd, he's an excellent Bryant;
But, my friends, you'll endanger the life of your
    client,
By attempting to stretch him up into a giant:
If you choose to compare him I think there are two
    per-
-sons fit for a parallel—Thompson and Cowper;[1]
I don't mean exactly,—there's something of each,
There's T.'s love of nature, C.'s penchant to preach;
Just mix up their minds so that C.'s spice of craziness
Shall balance and neutralize T.'s turn for laziness,
And it gives you a brain cool, quite frictionless, quiet,
Whose internal police nips the buds of all riot,—
A brain like a permanent strait-jacket put on
The heart that strives vainly to burst off a button,—
A brain which, without being slow or mechanic,
Does more than a larger less drilled, more volcanic;
He's a Cowper condensed, with no craziness bitten
And the advantage that Wordsworth before him had
    written.

    But, my dear little Bardlings, don't prick up your
       ears
Nor suppose I would rank you and Bryant as peers;
If I call him an iceberg, I don't mean to say
There is nothing in that which is grand in its way;
He is almost the one of your poets that knows
How much grace, strength, and dignity lie in Repose;
If he sometimes falls short, he is too wise to mar
His thought's modest fulness by going too far;
'Twould be well if your authors should all make a
    trial
Of what virtue there is in severe self-denial

[1] To demonstrate quickly and easily how per-
  versely absurd 'tis to sound this name *Cowper,*
  As people in general call him named *super,*
I remark that he rhymes it himself with horse-trooper.
                  [Lowell's note.]

And measure their writings by Hesiod's staff,
Which teaches that all has less value than half.

. . . .

There comes Poe, whith his raven, like Barnaby
Rudge,
Three fifths of him genius and two fifths sheer fudge,
Who talks like a book of iambs and pentameters,
In a way to make people of common sense damn
metres,
Who has written some things quite the best of their
kind,
But the heart somehow seems all squeezed out by the
mind,
Who—But hey-day! What's this? Messieurs Mathews
and Poe,
You mustn't fling mud-balls at Longfellow so,
Does it make a man worse that his character's such
As to make his friends love him (as you think) too
much?
Why, there is not a bard at this moment alive
More willing than he that his fellows should thrive;
While you are abusing him thus, even now
He would help either one of you out of a slough;
You may say that he's smooth and all that till you're
hoarse,
But remember that elegance also is force;
After polishing granite as much as you will,
The heart keeps its tough old persistency still;
Deduct all you can, *that* still keeps you at bay;
Why, he'll live till men weary of Collins and Gray.
I'm not over-fond of Greek metres in English,
To me rhyme's a gain, so it be not too jinglish,
And your modern hexameter verses are no more
Like Greek ones than sleek Mr. Pope is like Homer;
As the roar of the sea to the coo of a pigeon is,
So, compared to your moderns, sounds old
Melesigenes;
I may be too partial, the reason, perhaps, o't is
That I've heard the old blind man recite his own
rhapsodies,

And my ear with that music impregnate may be,
Like the poor exiled shell with the soul of the sea,
Or as one can't bear Strauss when his nature is cloven
To its deeps within deeps by the stroke of Beethoven;
But, set that aside, and 'tis truth that I speak,
Had Theocritus written in English, not Greek,
I believe that his exquisite sense would scarce change
 a line
In that rare, tender, virgin-like pastoral Evangeline.
That's not ancient nor modern, its place is apart
Where time has no sway, in the realm of pure Art,
'Tis a shrine of retreat from Earth's hubbub and strife
As quiet and chaste as the author's own life.

. . . .

   There is Lowell, who's striving Parnassus to
     climb
With a whole bag of *isms* tied together with rhyme,
He might get on alone, spite of brambles and
     boulders,
But he can't with that bundle he has on his shoulders,
The top of the hill he will ne'er come nigh reaching
Till he learns the distinction 'twixt singing and
     preaching;
His lyre has some chords that would ring pretty well,
But he'd rather by half make a drum of the shell,
And rattle away till he's old as Methusalem,
At the head of a march to the last new Jerusalem.

THE COURTIN'

God makes sech nights, all white an' still
   Fur 'z you can look or listen,
Moonshine an' snow on field an' hill,
   All silence an' all glisten.

Zekle crep' up quite unbeknown
   An' peeked in thru' the winder,
An' there sot Huldy all alone,
   'ith no one nigh to hender.

A fireplace filled the room's one side
   With half a cord o' wood in—
There warn't no stoves (tell comfort died)
   To bake ye to a puddin'.

The wa'nut logs shot sparkles out
   Towards the pootiest, bless her,
An' leetle flames danced all about
   The chiny on the dresser.

Agin the chimbley crook-necks hung,
   An' in amongst 'em rusted
The ole queen's-arm that gran'ther Young
   Fetched back f'om Concord busted.

The very room, coz she was in,
   Seemed warm f'om floor to ceiln',
An' she looked full ez rosy agin
   Ez the apples she was peelin'.

'T was kin' o' kingdom-come to look
   On sech a blessed cretur,
A dogrose blushin' to a brook
   Ain't modester nor sweeter.

He was six foot o' man, A 1,
   Clear grit an' human natur',
None could n't quicker pitch a ton
   Nor dror a furrer straighter.

He 'd sparked it with full twenty gals,
   He'd squired 'em, danced 'em, druv 'em,
Fust this one, an' then thet, by spells—
   All is, he could n't love 'em.

But long o' her his veins 'ould run
   All crinkly like curled maple,
The side she breshed felt full o' sun
   Ez a south slope in Ap'il.

She thought no v'ice hed sech a swing
    Ez hisn in the choir;
My! when he made Ole Hundred ring,
    She *knowed* the Lord was nigher.

An' she'd blush scarlit, right in prayer,
    When her new meetin'-bunnet
Felt somehow thru' its crown a pair
    O' blue eyes sot upon it.

Thet night, I tell ye, she looked *some!*
    She seemed to've gut a new soul,
For she felt sartin-sure he'd come,
    Down to her very shoe-sole.

She heered a foot, an' knowed it tu,
    A-raspin' on the scraper,—
All ways to once her feelins flew
    Like sparks in burnt-up paper.

He kin' o' l'itered on the mat,
    Some doubtfle o' the sekle,
His heart kep' goin' pity-pat,
    But hern went pity Zekle.

An' yit she gin her cheer a jerk
    Ez though she wished him furder,
An' on her apples kep' to work,
    Parin' away like murder.

"You want to see my Pa, I s'pose?"
    "Wal . . . no . . . I come dasignin'"—
"To see my Ma? She's sprinklin' clo'es
    Agin to-morrer's i'nin'."

To say why gals acts so or so,
    Or don't, 'ould be presumin';
Mebby to mean *yes* an' say *no*
    Comes nateral to women.

He stood a spell on one foot fust,
  Then stood a spell on t'other,
An' on which one he felt the wust
  He could n't ha' told ye nuther.

Says he, "I'd better call agin":
  Says she, "Think likely, Mister";
Thet last word pricked him like a pin,
  An' . . . Wal, he up an' kist her.

When Ma bimeby upon 'em slips,
  Huldy sot pale ez ashes,
All kin' o' smily roun' the lips
  An' teary roun' the lashes.

For she was jes' the quiet kind
  Whose naturs never vary,
Like streams that keep a summer mind
  Snowhid in Jenooary.

The blood clost roun' her heart felt glued
  Too tight for all expressin',
Tell mother see how metters stood,
  An' gin 'em both her blessin'.

Then her red come back like the tide
  Down to the Bay o' Fundy,
An' all I know is they was cried
  In meetin' come nex' Sunday.

HENRY WADSWORTH LONGFELLOW

1807–1882

"I most eagerly aspire after eminence in literature," Longfellow wrote his father when a senior at Bowdoin College in 1825. He became the most widely read poet of his time in the English-speaking world. His first book of poems, *Voices of the Night* (1839), sold 43,000 copies, and many of his didactic and narrative poems became at once as familiar as proverbs. His seventy-fifth birthday was celebrated in every classroom in this country, and two years after his death a bust was unveiled in Poet's Corner at Westminster Abbey. Yet Longfellow's poetry rarely shows any originality of vision or execution, any intensity of feeling or expression. His bland blending of antiquarianism, sentimentality, and moral imperatives in mellifluous though prolix verse expressed the temper of his age, and its limitations. He regarded poetry as an escape from experience, and cast his poems, even on contemporary or native subjects, in the molds of antiquity. Yet through his mastery of poetic conventions and his love of the past he brought dignity to literature in the minds of his thousands of readers. In a few poems his customary themes—nostalgia in "My Lost Youth," the exotic past in "The Jewish Cemetery," his tribute in "Chaucer"—take memorable form. The great tragedy in Longfellow's otherwise serene life was the loss of his second wife, who was burned to death in 1862. Longfellow buried his grief by translating Dante's *Divine Comedy;* the series of six sonnets he wrote, two to preface each book, is among his most fortuitous work. After graduation he was offered a professorship of modern literatures on condition that he travel in France, Italy, Spain, and Germany to prepare himself for the charge; he served at Bowdoin from 1829–1835, and at Harvard from 1835–1854. Longfellow was virtually untouched by the Tran-

scendental movement; his Romanticism remained at the
stage exemplified by Washington Irving, a lasting influence on him. His verse reflects Goldsmith in its grace,
Bryant's purity of diction, and Keats's sensuous appeal;
Wordsworth and Goethe were among his enthusiasms. His
chief value is as an interpreter of the European past.

THE JEWISH CEMETERY AT NEWPORT

How strange it seems! These Hebrews in their graves,
   Close by the street of this fair seaport town,
Silent beside the never-silent waves,
   At rest in all this moving up and down!

The trees are white with dust, that o'er their sleep
   Wave their broad curtains in the southwind's
      breath,
While underneath these leafy tents they keep
   The long, mysterious Exodus of Death.

And these sepulchral stones, so old and brown,
   That pave with level flags their burial-place,
Seem like the tablets of the Law, thrown down
   And broken by Moses at the mountain's base.

The very names recorded here are strange,
   Of foreign accent, and of different climes;
Alvares and Rivera interchange
   With Abraham and Jacob of old times.

'Blessed be God! for he created Death!'
   The mourners said, 'and Death is rest and peace;'
Then added, in the certainty of faith,
   'And giveth Life that nevermore shall cease.'

Closed are the portals of their Synagogue,
   No Psalms of David now the silence break,
No Rabbi reads the ancient Decalogue
   In the grand dialect the Prophets spake.

Gone are the living, but the dead remain,
  And not neglected; for a hand unseen,
Scattering its bounty, like a summer rain,
  Still keeps their graves and their remembrance
    green.

How came they here? What burst of Christian hate,
  What persecution, merciless and blind,
Drove o'er the sea—that desert desolate—
  These Ishmaels and Hagars of mankind?

They lived in narrow streets and lanes obscure,
  Ghetto and Judenstrass, in mirk and mire;
Taught in the school of patience to endure
  The life of anguish and the death of fire.

All their lives long, with the unleavened bread
  And bitter herbs of exile and its fears,
The wasting famine of the heart they fed,
  And slaked its thirst with the marah of their tears.

Anathema marantha! was the cry
  That rang from town to town, from street to street;
At every gate the accused Mordecai
  Was mocked and jeered, and spurned by Christian
    feet.

Pride and humiliation hand in hand
  Walked with them through the world where'er
    they went;
Trampled and beaten were they as the sand,
  And yet unshaken as the continent.

For in the background figures vague and vast
  Of patriarchs and of prophets rose sublime,
And all the great traditions of the Past
  They saw reflected in the coming time.

And thus forever with reverted look
   The mystic volume of the world they read,
Spelling it backward, like a Hebrew book,
   Till life became a Legend of the Dead.

But ah! what once has been shall be no more!
   The groaning earth in travail and in pain
Brings forth its races, but does not restore,
   And the dead nations never rise again.

MY LOST YOUTH

Often I think of the beautiful town
   That is seated by the sea;
Often in thought go up and down
The pleasant streets of that dear old town,
   And my youth comes back to me.
     And a verse of a Lapland song
     Is haunting my memory still:
     'A boy's will is the wind's will,
And the thoughts of youth are long, long thoughts.'

I can see the shadowy lines of its trees,
   And catch, in sudden gleams,
The sheen of the far-surrounding seas,
And islands that were the Hesperides
   Of all my boyish dreams.
     And the burden of that old song,
     It murmurs and whispers still:
     'A boy's will is the wind's will,
And the thoughts of youth are long, long thoughts.'

I remember the black wharves and the slips,
   And the sea-tides tossing free;
And Spanish sailors with bearded lips,
And the beauty and mystery of the ships,
   And the magic of the sea.

And the voice of that wayward song
Is singing and saying still:
'A boy's will is the wind's will,
And the thoughts of youth are long, long thoughts.'

I remember the bulwarks by the shore,
And the fort upon the hill;
The sunrise gun, with its hollow roar,
The drum-beat repeated o'er and o'er,
And the bugle wild and shrill.
And the music of that old song
Throbs in my memory still:
'A boy's will is the wind's will,
And the thoughts of youth are long, long thoughts.'

I remember the sea-fight far away,
How it thundered o'er the tide!
And the dead captains, as they lay
In their graves, o'erlooking the tranquil bay,
Where they in battle died.
And the sound of that mournful song
Goes through me with a thrill:
'A boy's will is the wind's will,
And the thoughts of youth are long, long thoughts.'

I can see the breezy dome of groves,
The shadows of Deering's Woods;
And the friendships old and the early loves
Come back with a Sabbath sound, as of doves
In quiet neighborhoods.
And the verse of that sweet old song,
It flutters and murmurs still:
'A boy's will is the wind's will,
And the thoughts of youth are long, long thoughts.'

I remember the gleams and glooms that dart
Across the school-boy's brain;
The song and the silence in the heart,
That in part are prophecies, and in part
Are longings wild and vain.

And the voice of that fitful song
    Sings on, and is never still:
        'A boy's will is the wind's will,
And the thoughts of youth are long, long thoughts.'

There are things of which I may not speak;
    There are dreams that cannot die;
There are thoughts that make the strong heart weak,
And bring a pallor into the cheek,
    And a mist before the eye,
        And the words of that fatal song
        Come over me like a chill:
            'A boy's will is the wind's will,
And the thoughts of youth are long, long thoughts.'

Strange to me now are the forms I meet
    When I visit the dear old town;
But the native air is pure and sweet,
And the trees that o'ershadow each well-known street,
    As they balance up and down,
        Are singing the beautiful song,
        Are sighing and whispering still:
            'A boy's will is the wind's will,
And the thoughts of youth are long, long thoughts.'

And Deering's Woods are fresh and fair,
    And with joy that is almost pain
My heart goes back to wander there,
And among the dreams of the days that were,
    I find my lost youth again.
        And the strange and beautiful song,
        The groves are repeating it still:
            'A boy's will is the wind's will,
And the thoughts of youth are long, long thoughts.'

DIVINA COMMEDIA

I

Oft have I seen at some cathedral door
  A laborer, pausing in the dust and heat,
  Lay down his burden, and with reverent feet
  Enter, and cross himself, and on the floor
Kneel to repeat his paternoster o'er;
  Far off the noises of the world retreat;
  The loud vociferations of the street
  Become an undistinguishable roar.
So, as I enter here from day to day,
  And leave my burden at this minster gate,
  Kneeling in prayer, and not ashamed to pray,
The tumult of the time disconsolate
  To inarticulate murmurs dies away,
  While the eternal ages watch and wait.

II

How strange the sculptures that adorn these towers!
  This crowd of statues, in whose folded sleeves
  Birds build their nests; while canopied with leaves
  Parvis and portal bloom like trellised bowers,
And the vast minster seems a cross of flowers!
  But fiends and dragons on the gargoyled eaves
  Watch the dead Christ between the living thieves,
  And, underneath, the traitor Judas lowers!
Ah! from what agonies of heart and brain,
  What exultations trampling on despair,
  What tenderness, what tears, what hate of wrong,
What passionate outcry of a soul in pain,
  Uprose this poem of the earth and air,
  This mediæval miracle of song!

III

I enter, and I see thee in the gloom
  Of the long aisles, O poet saturnine!
  And strive to make my steps keep pace with thine.
  The air is filled with some unknown perfume;
The congregation of the dead make room
  For thee to pass; the votive tapers shine;
  Like rooks that haunt Ravenna's groves of pine
  The hovering echoes fly from tomb to tomb.
From the confessionals I hear arise
  Rehearsals of forgotten tragedies,
  And lamentations from the crypts below;
And then a voice celestial that begins
  With the pathetic words, "Although your sins
  As scarlet be," and ends with "as the snow."

IV

With snow-white veil and garments as of flame,
  She stands before thee, who so long ago
  Filled thy young heart with passion and the woe
  From which thy song and all its splendors came;
And while with stern rebuke she speaks thy name,
  The ice about thy heart melts as the snow
  On mountain heights, and in swift overflow
  Comes gushing from thy lips in sobs of shame.
Thou makest full confession; and a gleam,
  As of the dawn on some dark forest cast,
  Seems on thy lifted forehead to increase;
Lethe and Eunoë—the remembered dream
  And the forgotten sorrow—bring at last
  That perfect pardon which is perfect peace.

V

I lift mine eyes, and all the windows blaze
  With forms of Saints and holy men who died,
  Here martyred and hereafter glorified;
  And the great Rose upon its leaves displays

Christ's Triumph, and the angelic roundelays,
  With splendor upon splendor multiplied;
  And Beatrice again at Dante's side
  No more rebukes, but smiles her words of praise.
And then the organ sounds, and unseen choirs
  Sing the old Latin hymns of peace and love
  And benedictions of the Holy Ghost;
And the melodious bells among the spires
  O'er all the house-tops and through heaven above
  Proclaim the elevation of the Host!

VI

O star of morning and of liberty!
  O bringer of the light, whose splendor shines
  Above the darkness of the Apennines,
  Forerunner of the day that is to be!
The voices of the city and the sea,
  The voices of the mountains and the pines,
  Repeat thy song, till the familiar lines
  Are footpaths for the thought of Italy!
Thy flame is blown abroad from all the heights,
  Through all the nations, and a sound is heard,
  As of a mighty wind, and men devout,
Strangers of Rome, and the new proselytes,
  In their own language hear thy wondrous word,
  And many are amazed and many doubt.

CHAUCER

An old man in a lodge within a park;
  The chamber walls depicted all around
  With portraitures of huntsman, hawk, and hound
  And the hurt deer. He listeneth to the lark,
Whose song comes with the sunshine through the
    dark
  Of painted glass in leaden lattice bound;
  He listeneth and he laugheth at the sound,
  Then writeth in a book like any clerk.

He is the poet of the dawn, who wrote
  The Canterbury Tales, and his old age
  Made beautiful with song; and as I read
I hear the crowing cock, I hear the note
  Of lark and linnet, and from every page
  Rise odors of ploughed field or flowery mead.

THE TIDE RISES, THE TIDE FALLS

The tide rises, the tide falls,
The twilight darkens, the curlew calls,
Along the sea-sands damp and brown
The traveller hastens toward the town,
  And the tide rises, the tide falls.

Darkness settles on roofs and walls,
But the sea, the sea in the darkness calls;
The little waves, with their soft, white hands,
Efface the footprints in the sands,
  And the tide rises, the tide falls.

The morning breaks; the steeds in their stalls
Stamp and neigh, as the hostler calls;
The day returns, but nevermore
Returns the traveller to the shore,
  And the tide rises, the tide falls.

THE CROSS OF SNOW

In the long, sleepless watches of the night,
  A gentle face—the face of one long dead—
  Looks at me from the wall, where round its head
  The night-lamp casts a halo of pale light.
Here in this room she died; and soul more white
  Never through martyrdom of fire was led
  To its repose; nor can in books be read
  The legend of a life more benedight.

There is a mountain in the distant West
  That, sun-defying, in its deep ravines
  Displays a cross of snow upon its side.
Such is the cross I wear upon my breast
  These eighteen years, through all the changing
    scenes
  And seasons, changeless since the day she died.

WALT WHITMAN

1819–1892

Nothing in Whitman's background or early life makes probable his emergence in 1855, at the age of thirty-six, as one of the great original poets in the language. Born in Brooklyn, New York, to a plebeian Quaker family, Whitman grew up in a household where illiteracy, poverty, alcoholism, and insanity were familiars. Walter (as he was then called) drifted from country schoolteaching on Long Island into newspaper work and political stump speaking. He edited several papers in the 1840's, notably the Brooklyn *Eagle,* writing undistinguished editorials on liberal causes, occasional saccharine verses, and a melodramatic temperance novel. In 1848 he went to New Orleans to take over a paper but soon returned North after political differences with its owner. During these years the outwardly indolent and affectedly dandyish Whitman was gestating *Leaves of Grass.* In 1855 he set some of the type himself and had the book sold by a phrenological bookstore. (Walt was an enthusiast of that science which read human character in the contours of the skull.) He not only sent copies around to Emerson, Lowell, Whittier, et al., but himself wrote several congratulatory reviews.

Whitman was part *poseur,* and his latter-day admirers made him part myth. The poet Whitman was a complicated and evasive person, incomparably daring in his manipulation of language, in his repudiations of literary tradition, and in his reconstituting poetic form. His conceptions of love and of democracy seem curiously intermingled. Had he a political program it would have been based on "amativeness," comradely affection. His eroticism is so diffused that he can respond, as an infant can, with passionate identification to the stimulus of any object or person—even of an abstraction. Whatever else the effects of such a psychological disposition may be, it enabled Whitman to take "the known universe" as his lover.

During the Civil War, Whitman went to Washington to care for his brother in a Union Army hospital. There he found a new vocation. In tending the wounded boys and men of both armies he sublimated his conception of egalitarian brotherhood. But the war betrayed his dream of a healthy, affectionate America of equals. By the end of the war Whitman's work had attracted some adherents, one of whom arranged his appointment as a government clerk. But his book came to the notice of a member of the cabinet, who, scandalized by such indecencies, fired him. Whitman suffered a stroke in 1873 which left him partly paralyzed; he retired to his brother's house in Camden, N.J., where he wrote *Specimen Days* (his prose reminiscences) and revised and added to *Leaves of Grass*. He brought out nine editions of his book, pouring into it all the verse he ever published.

In "The Sleepers" Whitman delves into the subterranean reaches and sufferings of his own personality which, dreamlike, merges with those of sleepers everywhere. He dreams his own destruction as the heroic swimmer, who in turn becomes the many dead fallen in war—the American Revolution. The images move backward in time toward a primordial America as his mother describes the Indian squaw who mysteriously came, mysteriously departed. She represents a source of rejuvenative energy to Whitman, whose poem moves next through the sensuous vibrancy of remembered summer to encompass all humanity, finding beauty in even the deformed and diseased. The mother addressed at the end is the night, in whose bosom he has found the power to unify all threatening, conflicting, suffering dreams and wakings. The main strategies and devices of Whitman's poems are discernible in this one. The nightmarish descent into the sea and the return from death to affirmation establishes a cyclical movement, the characteristic rhythm of Whitman's feeling. In "There Was a Child Went Forth" the unifying voyage into experience is taken by daylight, into joyous sensations, the result of happy natural inclination rather than, as in "The Sleepers," subconscious compulsion.

"Song of Myself" is Whitman's most ambitious poem,

the only successful heroic poem in American literature. It invokes comparison with Wordsworth's *The Prelude;* where Wordsworth traces "The Growth of a Poet's Mind," Whitman celebrates its present powers. By unexpected turns lyrical, comic, rhetorical, delicate, assertive, "Song of Myself" undertakes (as D. H. Lawrence observed) to change morality by changing our capacity to feel. Now Whitman presents life as the journey of the Self through contradictions which it encompasses and transfigures into the joyous knowledge of its own infinite variety. Body and soul, defeat and victory, suffering and ecstasy, death and life, the single self and the democratic mass, the past and present are equally welcome. "Amused, complacent, compassionating, idle, unitary" stands "what I am." Bracing his exploration of these antinomies is a structure the main outline of which creates cyclical repetitions of the life processes; within these the poem moves, as Whitman says in his 1855 Preface, "by indirection" from one sense impression to another. Yet again patterns of sound and rhythm organize the parts, repeating in little the cyclical swing of the whole. "Song of Myself" cannot be truncated since its meaning is attained by the attempt of the Self to reconcile the contradictions it encounters.

"Out of the Cradle, Endlessly Rocking" is among Whitman's most poignant celebrations of death. Where death was welcomed in "Song of Myself" as the necessary prelude to rebirth, here Death is "the savage old mother," "that strong and delicious word which . . . the sea whisper'd to me." But this Death has lost the terror of the sea-death in "The Sleepers." Now death, the great bereavement, is the source of the bird's song, of the boy's tears, of poetry. The Civil War poems from *Drum Taps* show the compassion of "the solitary singer."

TEXT: *Leaves of Grass,* 9th edition (1891–1892). See also: Gay Wilson Allen, *Walt Whitman Handbook* (1946) and *The Solitary Singer* (1955); Roger Asselineau, *The Evolution of Walt Whitman* (1960); Richard Chase, *Walt Whitman Reconsidered* (1955); Randall Jarrell, *Poetry and the Age* (1953).

ONE'S SELF I SING

One's-Self I sing, a simple separate person,
Yet utter the word Democratic, the word En-Masse.

Of physiology from top to toe I sing,
Not physiognomy alone nor brain alone is worthy for
    the Muse, I say the Form complete is worthier
    far,
The Female equally with the Male I sing.

Of Life immense in passion, pulse, and power,
Cheerful, for freest action form'd under the laws
    divine,
The Modern Man I sing.

THE SLEEPERS

1

I wander all night in my vision,
Stepping with light feet, swiftly and noiselessly step-
    ping and stopping,
Bending with open eyes over the shut eyes of sleepers,
Wandering and confused, lost to myself, ill-assorted,
    contradictory,
Pausing, gazing, bending, and stopping.

How solemn they look there, stretch'd and still,
How quiet they breathe, the little children in their
    cradles.

The wretched features of ennuyés, the white features
    of corpses, the livid faces of drunkards, the sick-
    gray faces of onanists,

The gash'd bodies on battle-fields, the insane in their
strong-door'd rooms, the sacred idiots, the new-
born emerging from gates, and the dying emerging from gates,
The night pervades them and infolds them.

The married couple sleep calmly in their bed, he with
his palm on the hip of the wife, and she with
her palm on the hip of the husband,
The sisters sleep lovingly side by side in their bed,
The men sleep lovingly side by side in theirs,
And the mother sleeps with her little child carefully
wrapt.

The blind sleep, and the deaf and dumb sleep,
The prisoner sleeps well in the prison, the runaway
son sleeps,
The murderer that is to be hung next day, how does
he sleep?
And the murder'd person, how does he sleep?

The female that loves unrequited sleeps,
And the male that loves unrequited sleeps,
The head of the money-maker that plotted all day
sleeps,
And the enraged and treacherous dispositions, all, all
sleep.

I stand in the dark with drooping eyes by the worst-
suffering and the most restless,
I pass my hands soothingly to and fro a few inches
from them,
The restless sink in their beds, they fitfully sleep.

Now I pierce the darkness, new beings appear,
The earth recedes from me into the night,
I saw that it was beautiful, and I see that what is
not the earth is beautiful.

I go from bedside to bedside, I sleep close with the
other sleepers each in turn,
I dream in my dream all the dreams of the other
dreamers,
And I become the other dreamers.

I am a dance—play up there! the fit is whirling me
fast!

I am the ever-laughing—it is new moon and twilight,
I see the hiding of douceurs, I see nimble ghosts
whichever way I look,
Cache and cache again deep in the ground and sea,
and where it is neither ground nor sea.

Well do they do their jobs those journeymen divine,
Only from me can they hide nothing, and would not
if they could,
I reckon I am their boss and they make me a pet
besides,
And surround me and lead me and run ahead when
I walk,
To lift their cunning covers to signify me with
stretch'd arms, and resume the way;
Onward we move, a gay gang of blackguards! with
mirth-shouting music and wild-flapping pennants
of joy!

I am the actor, the actress, the voter, the politician,
The emigrant and the exile, the criminal that stood
in the box,
He who has been famous and he who shall be famous
after to-day,
The stammerer, the well-form'd person, the wasted
or feeble person.

I am she who adorn'd herself and folded her hair
expectantly,
My truant lover has come, and it is dark.

Double yourself and receive me darkness,
Receive me and my lover too, he will not let me go
    without him.

I roll myself upon you as upon a bed, I resign myself
    to the dusk.

He whom I call answers me and takes the place of
    my lover,
He rises with me silently from the bed.

Darkness, you are gentler than my lover, his flesh was
    sweaty and panting,
I feel the hot moisture yet that he left me.

My hands are spread forth, I pass them in all
    directions,
I would sound up the shadowy shore to which you
    are journeying.
Be careful darkness! already what was it touch'd
    me?
I thought my lover had gone, else darkness and he
    are one,
I hear the heart-beat, I follow, I fade away.

2

I descend my western course, my sinews are flaccid,
Perfume and youth course through me and I am
    their wake.

It is my face yellow and wrinkled instead of the old
    woman's,
I sit low in a straw-bottom chair and carefully darn
    my grandson's stockings.

It is I too, the sleepless widow looking out on the
    winter midnight,
I see the sparkles of starshine on the icy and pallid
    earth.

A shroud I see and I am the shroud, I wrap a body
and lie in the coffin,
It is dark here under ground, it is not evil or pain
here, it is blank here, for reasons.

(It seems to me that every thing in the light and
air ought to be happy,
Whoever is not in his coffin and the dark grave let
him know he has enough.)

3

I see a beautiful gigantic swimmer swimming naked
through the eddies of the sea,
His brown hair lies close and even to his head, he
strikes out with courageous arms, he urges himself with his legs,
I see his white body, I see his undaunted eyes,
I hate the swift-running eddies that would dash him
head-foremost on the rocks.

What are you doing you ruffianly red-trickled waves?
Will you kill the courageous giant? will you kill him
in the prime of his middle age?

Steady and long he struggles,
He is baffled, bang'd, bruis'd, he holds out while his
strength holds out,
The slapping eddies are spotted with his blood, they
bear him away, they roll him, swing him, turn
him,
His beautiful body is borne in the circling eddies, it
is continually bruis'd on rocks,
Swiftly and out of sight is borne the brave corpse.

4

I turn but do not extricate myself,
Confused, a past-reading, another, but with darkness
yet.

The beach is cut by the razory ice-wind, the wreck-
    guns sound,
The tempest lulls, the moon comes floundering
    through the drifts.

I look where the ship helplessly heads end on, I hear
    the burst as she strikes, I hear the howls of dis-
    may, they grow fainter and fainter.

I cannot aid with my wringing fingers,
I can but rush to the surf and let it drench me and
    freeze upon me.

I search with the crowd, not one of the company is
    wash'd to us alive,
In the morning I help pick up the dead and lay
    them in rows in a barn.

5

Now of the older war-days, the defeat at Brooklyn,
Washington stands inside the lines, he stands on the
    intrench'd hills amid a crowd of officers,
His face is cold and damp, he cannot repress the
    weeping drops,
He lifts the glass perpetually to his eyes, the color is
    blanch'd from his cheeks,
He sees the slaughter of the southern braves con-
    fided to him by their parents.

The same at last and at last when peace is declared,
He stands in the room of the old tavern, the well-
    belov'd soldiers all pass through,
The officers speechless and slow draw near in their
    turns,
The chief encircles their necks with his arm and kisses
    them on the cheek,
He kisses lightly the wet cheeks one after another,
    he shakes hands and bids good-by to the army.

6

Now what my mother told me one day as we sat
at dinner together,
Of when she was a nearly grown girl living home
with her parents on the old homestead.

A red squaw came one breakfast-time to the old
homestead,
On her back she carried a bundle of rushes for
rush-bottoming chairs,
Her hair, straight, shiny, coarse, black, profuse, half-
envelop'd her face,
Her step was free and elastic, and her voice sounded
exquisitely as she spoke.

My mother look'd in delight and amazement at the
stranger,
She look'd at the freshness of her tall-borne face and
full and pliant limbs,
The more she look'd upon her she loved her,
Never before had she seen such wonderful beauty and
purity,
She made her sit on a bench by the jamb of the fireplace, she cook'd food for her,
She had no work to give her, but she gave her remembrance and fondness.

The red squaw staid all the forenoon, and toward the
middle of the afternoon she went away,
O my mother was loth to have her go away,
All the week she thought of her, she watch'd for her
many a month,
She remember'd her many a winter and many a
summer,
But the red squaw never came nor was heard of there
again.

7

A show of the summer softness—a contact of some-
    thing unseen—an amour of the light and air,
I am jealous and overwhelm'd with friendliness,
And will go gallivant with the light and air myself.

O love and summer, you are in the dreams and in me,
Autumn and winter are in the dreams, the farmer
    goes with his thrift,
The droves and crops increase, the barns are well-fill'd.

Elements merge in the night, ships make tacks in the
    dreams,
The sailor sails, the exile returns home,
The fugitive returns unharm'd, the immigrant is back
    beyond months and years,
The poor Irishman lives in the simple house of his
    childhood with the well-known neighbors and
    faces,
They warmly welcome him, he is barefoot again, he
    forgets he is well off,
The Dutchman voyages home, and the Scotchman
    and Welshman voyage home, and the native of
    the Mediterranean voyages home,
To every port of England, France, Spain, enter well-
    fill'd ships,
The Swiss foots it toward his hills, the Prussian goes
    his way, the Hungarian his way, and the Pole
    his way,
The Swede returns, and the Dane and Norwegian
    return.

The homeward bound and the outward bound,
The beautiful lost swimmer, the ennuyé, the onanist,
    the female that loves unrequited, the money-
    maker,
The actor and actress, those through with their parts
    and those waiting to commence,

The affectionate boy, the husband and wife, the voter,
the nominee that is chosen and the nominee that
has fail'd,

The great already known and the great any time after
to-day,

The stammerer, the sick, the perfect-form'd, the
homely,

The criminal that stood in the box, the judge that
sat and sentenced him, the fluent lawyers, the
jury, the audience,

The laugher and weeper, the dancer, the midnight
widow, the red squaw,

The consumptive, the erysipalite, the idiot, he that is
wrong'd,

The antipodes, and every one between this and them
in the dark,

I swear they are averaged now—one is no better than
the other,

The night and sleep have liken'd them and restored
them.

I swear they are all beautiful,

Every one that sleeps is beautiful, every thing in the
dim light is beautiful,

The wildest and bloodiest is over, and all is peace.

Peace is always beautiful,

The myth of heaven indicates peace and night.

The myth of heaven indicates the soul,

The soul is always beautiful, it appears more or it
appears less, it comes or it lags behind,

It comes from its embower'd garden and looks pleas-
antly on itself and encloses the world,

Perfect and clean the genitals previously jetting, and
perfect and clean the womb cohering,

The head well-grown proportion'd and plumb, and
the bowels and joints proportion'd and plumb.

The soul is always beautiful,
The universe is duly in order, every thing is in its
place,
What has arrived is in its place and what waits shall
be in its place,
The twisted skull waits, the watery or rotten blood
waits,
The child of the glutton or venerealee waits long, and
the child of the drunkard waits long, and the
drunkard himself waits long,
The sleepers that lived and died wait, the far advanced are to go on in their turns, and the far
behind are to come on in their turns,
The diverse shall be no less diverse, but they shall
flow and unite—they unite now.

8

The sleepers are very beautiful as they lie unclothed,
They flow hand in hand over the whole earth from
east to west as they lie unclothed,
The Asiatic and African are hand in hand, the European and American are hand in hand,
Learn'd and unlearn'd are hand in hand, and male
and female are hand in hand,
The bare arm of the girl crosses the bare breast of
her lover, they press close without lust, his lips
press her neck,
The father holds his grown or ungrown son in his
arms with measureless love, and the son holds
the father in his arms with measureless love,
The white hair of the mother shines on the white
wrist of the daughter,
The breath of the boy goes with the breath of the
man, friend is inarm'd by friend,
The scholar kisses the teacher and the teacher kisses
the scholar, the wrong'd is made right,
The call of the slave is one with the master's call,
and the master salutes the slave,

The felon steps forth from the prison, the insane becomes sane, the suffering of sick persons is reliev'd,

The sweatings and fevers stop, the throat that was unsound is sound, the lungs of the consumptive are resumed, the poor distress'd head is free,

The joints of the rheumatic move as smoothly as ever, and smoother than ever,

Stiflings and passages open, the paralyzed become supple,

The swell'd and convuls'd and congested awake to themselves in condition,

They pass the invigoration of the night and the chemistry of the night, and awake.

I too pass from the night,

I stay a while away O night, but I return to you again and love you.

Why should I be afraid to trust myself to you?

I am not afraid, I have been well brought forward by you,

I love the rich running day, but I do not desert her in whom I lay so long,

I know not how I came of you and I know not where I go with you, but I know I came well and shall go well.

I will stop only a time with the night, and rise betimes,

I will duly pass the day O my mother, and duly return to you.

THERE WAS A CHILD WENT FORTH

There was a child went forth every day,

And the first object he look'd upon, that object he became,

And that object became part of him for the day or a
    certain part of the day,
Or for many years or stretching cycles of years.

The early lilacs became part of this child,
And grass and white and red morning-glories, and
    white and red clover, and the song of the phœbe-
    bird,
And the Third-month lambs and the sow's pink-faint
    litter, and the mare's foal and the cow's calf,
And the noisy brood of the barnyard or by the mire
    of the pond-side,
And the fish suspending themselves so curiously below
    there, and the beautiful curious liquid,
And the water-plants with their graceful flat heads,
    all became part of him.

The field-sprouts of Fourth-month and Fifth-month
    became part of him,
Winter-grain sprouts and those of the light-yellow
    corn, and the esculent roots of the garden,
And the apple-trees cover'd with blossoms and the
    fruit afterward, and wood-berries, and the com-
    monest weeds by the road,
And the old drunkard staggering home from the out-
    house of the tavern whence he had lately risen,
And the schoolmistress that pass'd on her way to
    the school,
And the friendly boys that pass'd and the quarrelsome
    boys,
And the tidy and fresh-cheek'd girls, and the barefoot
    negro boy and girl,
And all the changes of city and country wherever he
    went.

His own parents, he that had father'd him and she
    that had conceiv'd him in her womb and birth'd
    him,
They gave this child more of themselves than that,
They gave him afterward every day, they became
    part of him.

The mother at home quietly placing the dishes on the
    supper-table,

The mother with mild words, clean her cap and gown,
    a wholesome odor falling off her person and
    clothes as she walks by,

The father, strong, self-sufficient, manly, mean, an-
    ger'd, unjust,

The blow, the quick loud word, the tight bargain,
    the crafty lure,

The family usages, the language, the company, the
    furniture, the yearning and swelling heart,

Affection that will not be gainsay'd, the sense of what
    is real, the thought if after all it should prove
    unreal,

The doubts of day-time and the doubts of night-time,
    the curious whether and how,

Whether that which appears so is so, or is it all flashes
    and specks?

Men and women crowding fast in the streets, if they
    are not flashes and specks what are they?

The streets themselves and the façades of houses,
    and goods in the windows,

Vehicles, teams, the heavy-plank'd wharves, the huge
    crossing at the ferries,

The village on the highland seen from afar at sunset,
    the river between,

Shadows, aureola and mist, the light falling on roofs
    and gables of white or brown two miles off,

The schooner near by sleepily dropping down the
    tide, the little boat slack-tow'd astern,

The hurrying tumbling waves, quick-broken crests,
    slapping,

The strata of color'd clouds, the long bar of maroon-
    tint away solitary by itself, the spread of purity
    it lies motionless in,

The horizon's edge, the flying sea-crow, the fragrance
    of salt marsh and shore mud,

These became part of that child who went forth every
    day, and who now goes, and will always go
    forth every day.

SONG OF MYSELF

1

I celebrate myself, and sing myself,
And what I assume you shall assume,
For every atom belonging to me as good belongs to
    you.

I loafe and invite my soul,
I lean and loafe at my ease observing a spear of
    summer grass.

My tongue, every atom of my blood, form'd from this
    soil, this air,
Born here of parents born here from parents the same,
    and their parents the same,
I, now thirty-seven years old in perfect health begin,
Hoping to cease not till death.

Creeds and schools in abeyance,
Retiring back a while sufficed at what they are, but
    never forgotten,
I harbor for good or bad, I permit to speak at every
    hazard,
Nature without check with original energy.

2

Houses and rooms are full of perfumes, the shelves
    are crowded with perfumes,
I breathe the fragrance myself and know it and like it,
The distillation would intoxicate me also, but I shall
    not let it.

The atmosphere is not a perfume, it has no taste of
    the distillation, it is odorless,
It is for my mouth forever, I am in love with it,

I will go to the bank by the wood and become un-
    disguised and naked,
I am mad for it to be in contact with me.

The smoke of my own breath,
Echoes, ripples, buzz'd whispers, love-root, silk-
    thread, crotch and vine,
My respiration and inspiration, the beating of my
    heart, the passing of blood and air through my
    lungs,
The sniff of green leaves and dry leaves, and of the
    shore and dark-color'd sea-rocks, and of hay in
    the barn,
The sound of the belch'd words of my voice loos'd
    to the eddies of the wind,
A few light kisses, a few embraces, a reaching around
    of arms,
The play of shine and shade on the trees as the sup-
    ple boughs wag,
The delight alone or in the rush of the streets, or
    along the fields and hill-sides,
The feeling of health, the full-noon trill, the song of
    me rising from bed and meeting the sun.

Have you reckon'd a thousand acres much? have you
    reckon'd the earth much?
Have you practis'd so long to learn to read?
Have you felt so proud to get at the meaning of
    poems?

Stop this day and night with me and you shall possess
    the origin of all poems,
You shall possess the good of the earth and sun,
    (there are millions of suns left,)
You shall no longer take things at second or third
    hand, nor look through the eyes of the dead, nor
    feed on the spectres in books,
You shall not look through my eyes either, nor take
    things from me,
You shall listen to all sides and filter them from your
    self.

3

I have heard what the talkers were talking, the talk
    of the beginning and the end,
But I do not talk of the beginning or the end.

There was never any more inception than there is
    now,
Nor any more youth or age than there is now,
And will never be any more perfection than there is
    now,
Nor any more heaven or hell than there is now.

Urge and urge and urge,
Always the procreant urge of the world.

Out of the dimness opposite equals advance, always
    substance and increase, always sex,
Always a knit of identity, always distinction, always
    a breed of life.

To elaborate is no avail, learn'd and unlearn'd feel
    that it is so.

Sure as the most certain sure, plumb in the uprights,
    well entretied, braced in the beams,
Stout as a horse, affectionate, haughty, electrical,
I and this mystery here we stand.

Clear and sweet is my soul, and clear and sweet is
    all that is not my soul.
Lack one lacks both, and the unseen is proved by the
    seen,
Till that becomes unseen and receives proof in its
    turn.

Showing the best and dividing it from the worst age
    vexes age,
Knowing the perfect fitness and equanimity of things,
    while they discuss I am silent, and go bathe and
    admire myself.

Welcome is every organ and attribute of me, and of
    any man hearty and clean,
Not an inch nor a particle of an inch is vile, and
    none shall be less familiar than the rest.

I am satisfied—I see, dance, laugh, sing;
As the hugging and loving bed-fellow sleeps at my
    side through the night, and withdraws at the
    peep of the day with stealthy tread,
Leaving me baskets cover'd with white towels swell-
    ing the house with their plenty,
Shall I postpone my acceptation and realization and
    scream at my eyes,
That they turn from gazing after and down the road,
And forthwith cipher and show to me a cent,
Exactly the value of one and exactly the value of two,
    and which is ahead?

4

Trippers and askers surround me,
People I meet, the effect upon me of my early life
    or the ward and city I live in, or the nation,
The latest dates, discoveries, inventions, societies, au-
    thors old and new,
My dinner, dress, associates, looks, compliments, dues,
The real or fancied indifference of some man or
    woman I love,
The sickness of one of my folks or of myself, or ill-
    doing or loss or lack of money, or depressions or
    exaltations,
Battles, the horrors of fratricidal war, the fever of
    doubtful news, the fitful events;
These come to me days and nights and go from me
    again,
But they are not the Me myself.

Apart from the pulling and hauling stands what I am,
Stands amused, complacent, compassionating, idle,
    unitary,

Looks down, is erect, or bends an arm on an impalpable certain rest,

Looking with side-curved head curious what will
come next,

Both in and out of the game and watching and wondering at it.

Backward I see in my own days where I sweated
through fog with linguists and contenders,

I have no mockings or arguments, I witness and wait.

5

I believe in you my soul, the other I am must not
abase itself to you,

And you must not be abased to the other.

Loafe with me on the grass, loose the stop from your
throat,

Not words, not music or rhyme I want, not custom or
lecture, not even the best,

Only the lull I like, the hum of your valvèd voice.

I mind how once we lay such a transparent summer
morning,

How you settled your head athwart my hips and
gently turn'd over upon me,

And parted the shirt from my bosom-bone, and
plunged your tongue to my bare-stript heart,

And reach'd till you felt my beard, and reach'd till
you held my feet.

Swiftly arose and spread around me the peace and
knowledge that pass all the argument of the
earth,

And I know that the hand of God is the promise of
my own,

And I know that the spirit of God is the brother of
my own,

And that all the men ever born are also my brothers,
and the women my sisters and lovers,
And that a kelson of the creation is love,
And limitless are leaves stiff or drooping in the fields,
And brown ants in the little wells beneath them,
And mossy scabs of the worm fence, heap'd stones,
elder, mullein and poke-weed.

6

A child said *What is the grass?* fetching it to me with
full hands;
How could I answer the child? I do not know what it
is any more than he.

I guess it must be the flag of my disposition, out of
hopeful green stuff woven.
Or I guess it is the handkerchief of the Lord,
A scented gift and remembrancer designedly dropt,
Bearing the owner's name someway in the corners,
that we may see and remark, and say *Whose?*

Or I guess the grass is itself a child, the produced
babe of the vegetation.

Or I guess it is a uniform hieroglyphic,
And it means, Sprouting alike in broad zones and
narrow zones,
Growing among black folks as among white,
Kanuck, Tuckahoe, Congressman, Cuff, I give them
the same, I receive them the same.

And now it seems to me the beautiful uncut hair of
graves.

Tenderly will I use you curling grass,
It may be you transpire from the breasts of young
men,
It may be if I had known them I would have loved
them,

It may be you are from old people, or from offspring
    taken soon out of their mothers' laps,
And here you are the mothers' laps.

This grass is very dark to be from the white heads of
    old mothers,
Darker than the colorless beards of old men,
Dark to come from under the faint red roofs of
    mouths.

O I perceive after all so many uttering tongues,
And I perceive they do not come from the roofs of
    mouths for nothing.

I wish I could translate the hints about the dead
    young men and women,
And the hints about old men and mothers, and the
    offspring taken soon out of their laps.

What do you think has become of the young and
    old men?
And what do you think has become of the women
    and children?

They are alive and well somewhere,
The smallest sprout shows there is really no death,
And if ever there was it led forward life, and does
    not wait at the end to arrest it,
And ceas'd the moment life appear'd.

All goes onward and outward, nothing collapses,
And to die is different from what any one supposed,
    and luckier.

7

Has any one supposed it lucky to be born?
I hasten to inform him or her it is just as lucky to die,
    and I know it.

I pass death with the dying and birth with the new-
wash'd babe, and am not contain'd between my
hat and boots,
And peruse manifold objects, no two alike and every
one good,
The earth good and the stars good, and their adjuncts
all good.

I am not an earth nor an adjunct of an earth,
I am the mate and companion of people, all just as
immortal and fathomless as myself,
(They do not know how immortal, but I know.)

Every kind for itself and its own, for me mine male
and female,
For me those that have been boys and that love
women,
For me the man that is proud and feels how it stings
to be slighted,
For me the sweet-heart and the old maid, for me
mothers and the mothers of mothers,
For me lips that have smiled, eyes that have shed
tears,
For me children and the begetters of children.

Undrape! you are not guilty to me, nor stale nor discarded,
I see through the broadcloth and gingham whether
or no,
And am around, tenacious, acquisitive, tireless, and
cannot be shaken away.

8

The little one sleeps in its cradle,
I lift the gauze and look a long time, and silently
brush away flies with my hand.

The youngster and the red-faced girl turn aside up
the bushy hill,
I peeringly view them from the top.

The suicide sprawls on the bloody floor of the bedroom,
I witness the corpse with its dabbled hair, I note
where the pistol has fallen.

The blab of the pave, tires of carts, sluff of boot-
soles, talk of the promenaders,
The heavy omnibus, the driver with his interrogating
thumb, the clank of the shod horses on the granite
floor,
The snow-sleighs, clinking, shouted jokes, pelts of
snow-balls,
The hurrahs for popular favorites, the fury of rous'd
mobs,
The flap of the curtain'd litter, a sick man inside borne
to the hospital,
The meeting of enemies, the sudden oath, the blows
and fall,
The excited crowd, the policeman with his star
quickly working his passage to the centre of the
crowd,
The impassive stones that receive and return so many
echoes,
What groans of over-fed or half-starv'd who fall sun-
struck or in fits,
What exclamations of women taken suddenly who
hurry home and give birth to babes,
What living and buried speech is always vibrating
here, what howls restrain'd by decorum,
Arrests of criminals, slights, adulterous offers made,
acceptances, rejections with convex lips,
I mind them or the show or resonance of them—I
come and I depart.

9

The big doors of the country barn stand open and
ready,
The dried grass of the harvest-time loads the slow-
drawn wagon,

The clear light plays on the brown gray and green
    intertinged,
The armfuls are pack'd to the sagging mow.

I am there, I help, I came stretch'd atop of the load,
I felt its soft jolts, one leg reclined on the other,
I jump from the cross-beams and seize the clover and
    timothy,
And roll head over heels and tangle my hair full of
    wisps.

10

Alone far in the wilds and mountains I hunt,
Wandering amazed at my own lightness and glee,
In the late afternoon choosing a safe spot to pass the
    night,
Kindling a fire and broiling the fresh-kill'd game,
Falling asleep on the gather'd leaves with my dog and
    gun by my side.

The Yankee clipper is under her sky-sails, she cuts
    the sparkle and scud,
My eyes settle the land, I bend at her prow or shout
    joyously from the deck.

The boatmen and clam-diggers arose early and stopt
    for me,
I tuck'd my trowser-ends in my boots and went and
    had a good time;
You should have been with us that day round the
    chowder-kettle.

I saw the marriage of the trapper in the open air in
    the far west, the bride was a red girl,
Her father and his friends sat near cross-legged and
    dumbly smoking, they had moccasins to their
    feet and large thick blankets hanging from their
    shoulders,

On a bank lounged the trapper, he was drest mostly
    in skins, his luxuriant beard and curls protected
    his neck, he held his bride by the hand,
She had long eyelashes, her head was bare, her coarse
    straight locks descended upon her voluptuous
    limbs and reach'd to her feet.

The runaway slave came to my house and stopt out-
    side,
I heard his motions crackling the twigs of the wood-
    pile,
Through the swung half-door of the kitchen I saw
    him limpsy and weak,
And went where he sat on a log and led him in and
    assured him,
And brought water and fill'd a tub for his sweated
    body and bruis'd feet,
And gave him a room that enter'd from my own, and
    gave him some coarse clean clothes,
And remember perfectly well his revolving eyes and
    his awkwardness,
And remember putting plasters on the galls of his
    neck and ankles;
He staid with me a week before he was recuperated
    and pass'd north,
I had him sit next me at table, my fire-lock lean'd in
    the corner.

11

Twenty-eight young men bathe by the shore,
Twenty-eight young men and all so friendly;
Twenty-eight years of womanly life and all so lone-
    some.

She owns the fine house by the rise of the bank,
She hides handsome and richly drest aft the blinds
    of the window.

Which of the young men does she like the best?
Ah the homeliest of them is beautiful to her.

Where are you off to, lady? for I see you,
You splash in the water there, yet stay stock still in
your room.

Dancing and laughing along the beach came the
twenty-ninth bather,
The rest did not see her, but she saw them and loved
them.

The beards of the young men glisten'd with wet, it
ran from their long hair,
Little streams pass'd all over their bodies.

An unseen hand also pass'd over their bodies,
It descended tremblingly from their temples and ribs.

The young men float on their backs, their white bel-
lies bulge to the sun, they do not ask who seizes
fast to them,
They do not know who puffs and declines with pendant and bending arch,
They do not think whom they souse with spray.

12

The butcher-boy puts off his killing-clothes, or sharp-
ens his knife at the stall in the market,
I loiter enjoying his repartee and his shuffle and break-
down.

Blacksmiths with grimed and hairy chests environ the
anvil,
Each has his main-sledge, they are all out, there is
a great heat in the fire.

From the cinder-strew'd threshold I follow their movements,
The lithe sheer of their waists plays even with their
massive arms,

Overhand the hammers swing, overhand so slow,
    overhand so sure.
They do not hasten, each man hits in his place.

13

The negro holds firmly the reins of his four horses,
    the block swags underneath on its tied-over
    chain,
The negro that drives the long dray of the stone-yard,
    steady and tall he stands pois'd on one leg on the
    string-piece,
His blue shirt exposes his ample neck and breast and
    loosens over his hip-band,
His glance is calm and commanding, he tosses the
    slouch of his hat away from his forehead,
The sun falls on his crispy hair and mustache, falls
    on the black of his polish'd and perfect limbs.

I behold the picturesque giant and love him, and I
    do not stop there,
I go with the team also.

In me the caresser of life wherever moving, backward
    as well as forward sluing,
To niches aside and junior bending, not a person or
    object missing,
Absorbing all to myself and for this song.

Oxen that rattle the yoke and chain or halt in the
    leafy shade, what is that you express in your
    eyes?
It seems to me more than all the print I have read
    in my life.

My tread scares the wood-drake and wood-duck on
    my distant and day-long ramble,
They rise together, they slowly circle around.

I believe in those wing'd purposes,
And acknowledge red, yellow, white, playing within
　me,
And consider green and violet and the tufted crown
　intentional,
And do not call the tortoise unworthy because she is
　not something else,
And the jay in the woods never studied the gamut,
　yet trills pretty well to me,
And the look of the bay mare shames silliness out of
　me.

14

The wild gander leads his flock through the cool night,
Ya-honk he says, and sounds it down to me like an
　invitation,
The pert may suppose it meaningless, but I listening
　close,
Find its purpose and place up there toward the wintry
　sky.

The sharp-hoof'd moose of the north, the cat on the
　house-sill, the chickadee, the prairie-dog,
The litter of the grunting sow as they tug at her teats,
The brood of the turkey-hen and she with her half-
　spread wings,
I see in them and myself the same old law.

The press of my foot to the earth springs a hundred
　affections,
They scorn the best I can do to relate them.

I am enamour'd of growing out-doors,
Of men that live among cattle or taste of the ocean or
　woods,
Of the builders and steerers of ships and the wielders
　of axes and mauls, and the drivers of horses,
I can eat and sleep with them week in and week out.

What is commonest, cheapest, nearest, easiest, is Me,
Me going in for my chances, spending for vast returns,
Adorning myself to bestow myself on the first that will
    take me,
Not asking the sky to come down to my good will,
Scattering it freely forever.

15

The pure contralto sings in the organ loft,
The carpenter dresses his plank, the tongue of his
    foreplane whistles its wild ascending lisp,
The married and unmarried children ride home to
    their Thanksgiving dinner,
The pilot seizes the king-pin, he heaves down with a
    strong arm,
The mate stands braced in the whale-boat, lance and
    harpoon are ready,
The duck-shooter walks by silent and cautious
    stretches,
The deacons are ordain'd with cross'd hands at the
    altar,
The spinning-girl retreats and advances to the hum
    of the big wheel,
The farmer stops by the bars as he walks on a First-
    day loafe and looks at the oats and rye,
The lunatic is carried at last to the asylum a con-
    firm'd case,
(He will never sleep any more as he did in the cot
    in his mother's bed-room;)
The jour printer with gray head and gaunt jaws
    works at his case,
He turns his quid of tobacco while his eyes blurr with
    the manuscript;
The malform'd limbs are tied to the surgeon's table,
What is removed drops horribly in a pail;
The quadroon girl is sold at the auction-stand, the
    drunkard nods by the bar-room stove,
The machinist rolls up his sleeves, the policeman trav-
    els his beat, the gate-keeper marks who pass,

The young fellow drives the express-wagon, (I love him, though I do not know him;)

The half-breed straps on his light boots to compete in the race,

The western turkey-shooting draws old and young, some lean on their rifles, some sit on logs,

Out from the crowd steps the marksman, takes his position, levels his piece;

The groups of newly-come immigrants cover the wharf or levee,

As the woolly-pates hoe in the sugar-field, the overseer views them from his saddle,

The bugle calls in the ball-room, the gentlemen run for their partners, the dancers bow to each other,

The youth lies awake in the cedar-roof'd garret and harks to the musical rain,

The Wolverine sets traps on the creek that helps fill the Huron,

The squaw wrapt in her yellow-hemm'd cloth is offering moccasins and bead-bags for sale,

The connoisseur peers along the exhibition-gallery with half-shut eyes bent sideways,

As the deck-hands make fast the steamboat the plank is thrown for the shore-going passengers,

The young sister holds out the skein while the elder sister winds it off in a ball, and stops now and then for the knots,

The one-year wife is recovering and happy having a week ago borne her first child,

The clean-hair'd Yankee girl works with her sewing-machine or in the factory or mill,

The paving-man leans on his two-handed rammer, the reporter's lead flies swiftly over the note-book, the sign-painter is lettering with blue and gold,

The canal boy trots on the tow-path, the book-keeper counts at his desk, the shoemaker waxes his thread,

The conductor beats time for the band and all the performers follow him,

The child is baptized, the convert is making his first
professions,

The regatta is spread on the bay, the race is begun,
(how the white sails sparkle!)

The drover watching his drove sings out to them that
would stray,

The pedler sweats with his pack on his back, (the pur-
chaser higgling about the odd cent;)

The bride unrumples her white dress, the minute-
hand of the clock moves slowly,

The opium-eater reclines with rigid head and just-
open'd lips,

The prostitute draggles her shawl, her bonnet bobs on
her tipsy and pimpled neck,

The crowd laugh at her blackguard oaths, the men
jeer and wink to each other,

(Miserable! I do not laugh at your oaths nor jeer
you;)

The President holding a cabinet council is surrounded
by the great Secretaries,

On the piazza walk three matrons stately and friendly
with twined arms,

The crew of the fish-smack pack repeated layers of
halibut in the hold,

The Missourian crosses the plains toting his wares
and his cattle,

As the fare-collector goes through the train he gives
notice by the jingling of loose change,

The floor-men are laying the floor, the tinners are
tinning the roof, the masons are calling for
mortar,

In single file each shouldering his hod pass onward
the laborers;

Seasons pursuing each other the indescribable crowd
is gather'd, it is the fourth of Seventh-month,
(what salutes of cannon and small arms!)

Seasons pursuing each other the plougher ploughs,
the mower mows, and the winter-grain falls in
the ground;

Off on the lakes the pike-fisher watches and waits by
    the hole in the frozen surface,
The stumps stand thick round the clearing, the squat-
    ter strikes deep with his axe,
Flatboatmen make fast towards dusk near the cotton-
    wood or pecan-trees,
Coon-seekers go through the regions of the Red river
    or through those drain'd by the Tennessee, or
    through those of the Arkansas,
Torches shine in the dark that hangs on the Chatta-
    hooche or Altamahaw,
Patriarchs sit at supper with sons and grandsons and
    great-grandsons around them,
In walls of adobie, in canvas tents, rest hunters and
    trappers after their day's sport,
The city sleeps and the country sleeps,
The living sleep for their time, the dead sleep for their
    time,
The old husband sleeps by his wife and the young
    husband sleeps by his wife;
And these tend inward to me, and I tend outward to
    them,
And such as it is to be of these more or less I am,
And of these one and all I weave the song of myself.

16

I am of old and young, of the foolish as much as the
    wise,
Regardless of others, ever regardful of others,
Maternal as well as paternal, a child as well as a man,
Stuff'd with the stuff that is coarse and stuff'd with the
    stuff that is fine,
One of the Nation of many nations, the smallest the
    same and the largest the same,
A Southerner soon as a Northerner, a planter non-
    chalant and hospitable down by the Oconee I
    live,
A Yankee bound my own way ready for trade, my
    joints the limberest joints on earth and the stern-
    est joints on earth,

A Kentuckian walking the vale of the Elkhorn in my
    deer-skin leggings, a Louisianian or Georgian,
A boatman over lakes or bays or along coasts, a
    Hoosier, Badger, Buckeye;
At home on Kanadian snow-shoes or up in the bush,
    or with fishermen off Newfoundland,
At home in the fleet of ice-boats, sailing with the
    rest and tacking,
At home on the hills of Vermont or in the woods of
    Maine, or the Texan ranch,
Comrade of Californians, comrade of free North-
    Westerners, (loving their big proportions,)
Comrade of raftsmen and coalmen, comrade of all
    who shake hands and welcome to drink and
    meat,
A learner with the simplest, a teacher of the thought-
    fullest,
A novice beginning yet experient of myriads of sea-
    sons,
Of every hue and caste am I, of every rank and
    religion,
A farmer, mechanic, artist, gentleman, sailor, quaker,
Prisoner, fancy-man, rowdy, lawyer, physician, priest.

I resist any thing better than my own diversity,
Breathe the air but leave plenty after me,
And am not stuck up, and am in my place.

(The moth and the fish-eggs are in their place,
The bright suns I see and the dark suns I cannot see
    are in their place,
The palpable is in its place and the impalpable is in
    its place.)

17

These are really the thoughts of all men in all ages
    and lands, they are not original with me,
If they are not yours as much as mine they are noth-
    ing, or next to nothing,

If they are not the riddle and the untying of the riddle
    they are nothing,
If they are not just as close as they are distant they
    are nothing.

This is the grass that grows wherever the land is and
    the water is,
This the common air that bathes the globe.

18

With music strong I come, with my cornets and my
    drums,
I play not marches for accepted victors only, I play
    marches for conquer'd and slain persons.

Have you heard that it was good to gain the day?
I also say it is good to fall, battles are lost in the
    same spirit in which they are won.

I beat and pound for the dead,
I blow through my embouchures my loudest and
    gayest for them.

Vivas to those who have fail'd!
And to those whose war-vessels sank in the sea!
And to those themselves who sank in the sea!
And to all generals that lost engagements, and all
    overcome heroes!
And the numberless unknown heroes equal to the
    greatest heroes known!

19

This is the meal equally set, this the meat for natural
    hunger,
It is for the wicked just the same as the righteous,
    I make appointments with all,
I will not have a single person slighted or left away,
The kept-woman, sponger, thief, are hereby invited,

The heavy-lipp'd slave is invited, the venerealee is in-
     vited;
There shall be no difference between them and the
     rest.

This is the press of a bashful hand, this the float and
     odor of hair,
This the touch of my lips to yours, this the murmur
     of yearning,
This the far-off depth and height reflecting my own
     face,
This the thoughtful merge of myself, and the outlet
     again.

Do you guess I have some intricate purpose?
Well I have, for the Fourth-month showers have, and
     the mica on the side of a rock has.

Do you take it I would astonish?
Does the daylight astonish? does the early redstart
     twittering through the woods?
Do I astonish more than they?

This hour I tell things in confidence,
I might not tell everybody, but I will tell you.

20

Who goes there? hankering, gross, mystical, nude;
How is it I extract strength from the beef I eat?

What is a man anyhow? what am I? what are you?

All I mark as my own you shall offset it with your
     own,
Else it were time lost listening to me.

I do not snivel that snivel the world over,
That months are vacuums and the ground but wallow
     and filth.

Whimpering and truckling fold with powders for in-
 valids, conformity goes to the fourth-remov'd,
I wear my hat as I please indoors or out.

Why should I pray? why should I venerate and be
 ceremonious?

Having pried through the strata, analyzed to a hair,
 counsel'd with doctors and calculated close,
I find no sweeter fat than sticks to my own bones.

In all people I see myself, none more and not one a
 barley-corn less,
And the good or bad I say of myself I say of them.

I know I am solid and sound,
To me the converging objects of the universe perpetually flow,
All are written to me, and I must get what the writing means.

I know I am deathless,
I know this orbit of mine cannot be swept by a carpenter's compass,
I know I shall not pass like a child's carlacue cut with
 a burnt stick at night.

I know I am august,
I do not trouble my spirit to vindicate itself or be
 understood,
I see that the elementary laws never apologize,
(I reckon I behave no prouder than the level I plant
 my house by, after all.)

I exist as I am, that is enough,
If no other in the world be aware I sit content,
And if each and all be aware I sit content.

One world is aware and by far the largest to me, and
    that is myself,
And whether I come to my own to-day or in ten
    thousand or ten million years,
I can cheerfully take it now, or with equal cheerful-
    ness I can wait.

My foothold is tenon'd and mortis'd in granite,
I laugh at what you call dissolution,
And I know the amplitude of time.

21

I am the poet of the Body and I am the poet of the
    Soul,
The pleasures of heaven are with me and the pains
    of hell are with me,
The first I graft and increase upon myself, the latter
    I translate into a new tongue.

I am the poet of the woman the same as the man,
And I say it is as great to be a woman as to be a man,
And I say there is nothing greater than the mother of
    men.

I chant the chant of dilation or pride,
We have had ducking and deprecating about enough,
I show that size is only development.

Have you outstript the rest? are you the President?
It is a trifle, they will more than arrive there every
    one, and still pass on.

I am he that walks with the tender and growing night,
I call to the earth and sea half-held by the night.

Press close bare-bosom'd night—press close magnetic
    nourishing night!
Night of south winds—night of the large few stars!
Still nodding night—mad naked summer night.

Smile O voluptuous cool-breath'd earth!
Earth of the slumbering and liquid trees!
Earth of departed sunset—earth of the mountains misty-topt!
Earth of the vitreous pour of the full moon just tinged with blue!
Earth of shine and dark mottling the tide of the river!
Earth of the limpid gray of clouds brighter and clearer for my sake!
Far-swooping elbow'd earth—rich apple-blossom'd earth!
Smile, for your lover comes.

Prodigal, you have given me love—therefore I to you give love!
O unspeakable passionate love.

22

You sea! I resign myself to you also—I guess what you mean,
I behold from the beach your crooked inviting fingers,
I believe you refuse to go back without feeling of me,
We must have a turn together, I undress, hurry me out of sight of the land,
Cushion me soft, rock me in billowy drowse,
Dash me with amorous wet, I can repay you.

Sea of stretch'd ground-swells,
Sea breathing broad and convulsive breaths,
Sea of the brine of life and of unshovell'd yet always-ready graves,
Howler and scooper of storms, capricious and dainty sea,
I am integral with you, I too am of one phase and of all phases.

Partaker of influx and efflux I, extoller of hate and conciliation,
Extoller of amies and those that sleep in each others' arms.

I am he attesting sympathy,
(Shall I make my list of things in the house and skip
    the house that supports them?)
I am not the poet of goodness only, I do not decline
    to be the poet of wickedness also.

What blurt is this about virtue and about vice?
Evil propels me and reform of evil propels me, I
    stand indifferent,
My gait is no fault-finder's or rejecter's gait,
I moisten the roots of all that has grown.

Did you fear some scrofula out of the unflagging
    pregnancy?
Did you guess the celestial laws are yet to be work'd
    over and rectified?

I find one side a balance and the antipodal side a
    balance,
Soft doctrine as steady help as stable doctrine,
Thoughts and deeds of the present our rouse and
    early start.

This minute that comes to me over the past decillions,
There is no better than it and now.

What behaved well in the past or behaves well to-day
    is not such a wonder,
The wonder is always and always how there can be
    a mean man or an infidel.

23

Endless unfolding of words of ages!
And mine a word of the modern, the word En-Masse.

A word of the faith that never balks,
Here or henceforward it is all the same to me, I accept
    Time absolutely.

It alone is without flaw, it alone rounds and completes
all,
That mystic baffling wonder alone completes all.

I accept Reality and dare not question it,
Materialism first and last imbuing.

Hurrah for positive science! long live exact demonstration!
Fetch stonecrop mixt with cedar and branches of
lilac,
This is the lexicographer, this the chemist, this made
a grammar of the old cartouches,
These mariners put the ship through dangerous unknown seas,
This is the geologist, this works with the scalpel, and
this is a mathematician.

Gentlemen, to you the first honors always!
Your facts are useful, and yet they are not my
dwelling,
I but enter by them to an area of my dwelling.

Less the reminders of properties told my words,
And more the reminders they of life untold, and of
freedom and extrication,
And make short account of neuters and geldings, and
favor men and women fully equipt,
And beat the gong of revolt, and stop with fugitives
and them that plot and conspire.

24

Walt Whitman, a kosmos, of Manhattan the son,
Turbulent, fleshy, sensual, eating, drinking and breed-
ing,
No sentimentalist, no stander above men and women
or apart from them,
No more modest than immodest.

Unscrew the locks from the doors!
Unscrew the doors themselves from their jambs!

Whoever degrades another degrades me,
And whatever is done or said returns at last to me.

Through me the afflatus surging and surging, through
me the current and index.

I speak the pass-word primeval, I give the sign of
democracy,
By God! I will accept nothing which all cannot have
their counterpart of on the same terms.

Through me many long dumb voices,
Voices of the interminable generations of prisoners
and slaves,
Voices of the diseas'd and despairing and of thieves
and dwarfs,
Voices of cycles of preparation and accretion,
And of the threads that connect the stars, and of
wombs and of the father-stuff,
And of the rights of them the others are down upon,
Of the deform'd, trivial, flat, foolish, despised,
Fog in the air, beetles rolling balls of dung.

Through me forbidden voices,
Voices of sexes and lusts, voices veil'd and I remove
the veil,
Voices indecent by me clarified and transfigur'd.

I do not press my fingers across my mouth,
I keep as delicate around the bowels as around the
head and heart,
Copulation is no more rank to me than death is.
I believe in the flesh and the appetites,
Seeing, hearing, feeling, are miracles, and each part
and tag of me is a miracle.

Divine am I inside and out, and I make holy whatever
    I touch or am touch'd from,
The scent of these arm-pits aroma finer than prayer,
This head more than churches, bibles, and all the
    creeds.

If I worship one thing more than another it shall be
    the spread of my own body, or any part of it,
Translucent mould of me it shall be you!
Shaded ledges and rests it shall be you!
Firm masculine colter it shall be you!
Whatever goes to the tilth of me it shall be you!
You my rich blood! your milky stream pale strippings
    of my life!
Breast that presses against other breasts it shall be
    you!
My brain it shall be your occult convolutions!
Root of wash'd sweet-flag! timorous pond-snipe! nest
    of guarded duplicate eggs! it shall be you!
Mix'd tussled hay of head, beard, brawn, it shall be
    you!
Trickling sap of maple, fibre of manly wheat, it shall
    be you!
Sun so generous it shall be you!
Vapors lighting and shading my face it shall be you!
You sweaty brooks and dews it shall be you!
Winds whose soft-tickling genitals rub against me it
    shall be you!
Broad muscular fields, branches of live oak, loving
    lounger in my winding paths, it shall be you!
Hands I have taken, face I have kiss'd, mortal I have
    ever touch'd, it shall be you.

I dote on myself, there is that lot of me and all so
    luscious,
Each moment and whatever happens thrills me with
    joy,
I cannot tell how my ankles bend, nor whence the
    cause of my faintest wish,
Nor the cause of the friendship I emit, nor the cause
    of the friendship I take again.

That I walk up my stoop, I pause to consider if it
    really be,
A morning-glory at my window satisfies me more than
    the metaphysics of books.

To behold the day-break!
The little light fades the immense and diaphanous
    shadows,
The air tastes good to my palate.

Hefts of the moving world at innocent gambols si-
    lently rising, freshly exuding,
Scooting obliquely high and low.

Something I cannot see puts upward libidinous
    prongs,
Seas of bright juice suffuse heaven.

The earth by the sky staid with, the daily close of
    their junction,
The heav'd challenge from the east that moment over
    my head,
The mocking taunt, See then whether you shall be
    master!

25

Dazzling and tremendous how quick the sun-rise
    would kill me,
If I could not now and always send sun-rise out of me.

We also ascend dazzling and tremendous as the sun,
We found our own O my soul in the calm and cool
    of the day-break.

My voice goes after what my eyes cannot reach,
With the twirl of my tongue I encompass worlds and
    volumes of worlds.

Speech is the twin of my vision, it is unequal to
measure itself,
It provokes me forever, it says sarcastically,
*Walt you contain enough, why don't you let it out
then?*

Come now I will not be tantalized, you conceive too
much of articulation,
Do you not know O speech how the buds beneath
you are folded?
Waiting in gloom, protected by frost,
The dirt receding before my prophetical screams,
I underlying causes to balance them at last,
My knowledge my live parts, it keeping tally with
the meaning of all things,
Happiness, (which whoever hears me let him or her
set out in search of this day.)

My final merit I refuse you, I refuse putting from me
what I really am,
Encompass worlds, but never try to encompass me,
I crowd your sleekest and best by simply looking toward you.

Writing and talk do not prove me,
I carry the plenum of proof and every thing else in my
face,
With the hush of my lips I wholly confound the
skeptic.

26

Now I will do nothing but listen,
To accrue what I hear into this song, to let sounds
contribute toward it.

I hear bravuras of birds, bustle of growing wheat,
gossip of flames, clack of sticks cooking my meals,
I hear the sound I love, the sound of the human
voice,

I hear all sounds running together, combined, fused or
    following,
Sounds of the city and sounds out of the city, sounds
    of the day and night,
Talkative young ones to those that like them, the
    loud laugh of work-people at their meals,
The angry base of disjointed friendship, the faint tones
    of the sick,
The judge with hands tight to the desk, his pallid
    lips pronouncing a death-sentence,
The heave'e'yo of stevedores unlading ships by the
    wharves, the refrain of the anchor-lifters,
The ring of alarm-bells, the cry of fire, the whirr of
    swift-streaking engines and hose-carts with pre-
    monitory tinkles and color'd lights,
The steam-whistle, the solid roll of the train of ap-
    proaching cars,
The slow march play'd at the head of the association
    marching two and two,
(They go to guard some corpse, the flag-tops are
    draped with black muslin.)
I hear the violoncello, ('tis the young man's heart's
    complaint,)
I hear the key'd cornet, it glides quickly in through
    my ears,
It shakes mad-sweet pangs through my belly and
    breast.

I hear the chorus, it is a grand opera,
Ah this indeed is music—this suits me.

A tenor large and fresh as the creation fills me,
The orbic flex of his mouth is pouring and filling me
    full.

I hear the train'd soprano (what work with hers is
    this?)
The orchestra whirls me wider than Uranus flies,
It wrenches such ardors from me I did not know I
    possess'd them,

It sails me, I dab with bare feet, they are lick'd by the
    indolent waves,
I am cut by bitter and angry hail, I lose my breath,
Steep'd amid honey'd morphine, my windpipe throt-
    tled in fakes of death,
At length let up again to feel the puzzle of puzzles,
And that we call Being.

27

To be in any form, what is that?
(Round and round we go, all of us, and ever come
    back thither,)
If nothing lay more develop'd the quahaug in its cal-
    lous shell were enough.

Mine is no callous shell,
I have instant conductors all over me whether I pass
    or stop,
They seize every object and lead it harmlessly through
    me.

I merely stir, press, feel with my fingers, and am
    happy,
To touch my person to some one else's is about as
    much as I can stand.

28

Is this then a touch? quivering me to a new identity,
Flames and ether making a rush for my veins,
Treacherous tip of me reaching and crowding to
    help them,
My flesh and blood playing out lightning to strike
    what is hardly different from myself,
On all sides prurient provokers stiffening my limbs,
Straining the udder of my heart for its withheld drip,
Behaving licentious toward me, taking no denial,
Depriving me of my best as for a purpose,
Unbuttoning my clothes, holding me by the bare
    waist,

Deluding my confusion with the calm of the sunlight
    and pasture-fields,
Immodestly sliding the fellow-senses away,
They bribed to swap off with touch and go and graze
    at the edges of me,
No consideration, no regard for my draining strength
    or my anger,
Fetching the rest of the herd around to enjoy them
    a while,
Then all uniting to stand on a headland and worry me.

The sentries desert every other part of me,
They have left me helpless to a red marauder,
They all come to the headland to witness and assist
    against me.

I am given up by traitors,
I talk wildly, I have lost my wits, I and nobody else
    am the greatest traitor,
I went myself first to the headland, my own hands
    carried me there.

You villain touch! what are you doing? my breath is
    tight in its throat,
Unclench your floodgates, you are too much for me.

29

Blind loving wrestling touch, sheath'd hooded sharp-
    tooth'd touch!
Did it make you ache so, leaving me?

Parting track'd by arriving, perpetual payment of
    perpetual loan,
Rich showering rain, and recompense richer after-
    ward.

Sprouts take and accumulate, stand by the curb pro-
    lific and vital,
Landscapes projected masculine, full-sized and
    golden.

30

All truths wait in all things,
They neither hasten their own delivery nor resist it,
They do not need the obstetric forceps of the surgeon,
The insignificant is as big to me as any,
(What is less or more than a touch?)
Logic and sermons never convince,
The damp of the night drives deeper into my soul.

(Only what proves itself to every man and woman is
    so,
Only what nobody denies is so.)

A minute and a drop of me settle my brain,
I believe the soggy clods shall become lovers and
    lamps,
And a compend of compends is the meat of a man or
    woman,
And a summit and flower there is the feeling they
    have for each other,
And they are to branch boundlessly out of that lesson
    until it becomes omnific,
And until one and all shall delight us, and we them.

31

I believe a leaf of grass is no less than the journey-
    work of the stars,
And the pismire is equally perfect, and a grain of
    sand, and the egg of the wren,
And the tree-toad is a chef-d'œuvre for the highest,
And the running blackberry would adorn the parlors
    of heaven,
And the narrowest hinge in my hand puts to scorn all
    machinery,
And the cow crunching with depress'd head surpasses
    any statue,
And a mouse is miracle enough to stagger sextillions
    of infidels.

I find I incorporate gneiss, coal, long-threaded moss,
    fruits, grains, esculent roots,
And am stucco'd with quadrupeds and birds all over,
And have distanced what is behind me for good
    reasons,
But call any thing back again when I desire it.

In vain the speeding or shyness,
In vain the plutonic rocks send their old heat against
    my approach,
In vain the mastodon retreats beneath its own pow-
    der'd bones,
In vain objects stand leagues off and assume manifold
    shapes,
In vain the ocean settling in hollows and the great
    monsters lying low,
In vain the buzzard houses herself with the sky,
In vain the snake slides through the creepers and logs,
In vain the elk takes to the inner passes of the woods,
In vain the razor-bill'd auk sails far north to Labrador,
I follow quickly, I ascend to the nest in the fissure of
    the cliff.

32

I think I could turn, and live with animals, they are
    so placid and self-contain'd,
I stand and look at them long and long.

They do not sweat and whine about their condition,
They do not lie awake in the dark and weep for
    their sins,
They do not make me sick discussing their duty to
    God,
Not one is dissatisfied, not one is demented with the
    mania of owning things,
Not one kneels to another, nor to his kind that lived
    thousands of years ago,
Not one is respectable or unhappy over the whole
    earth.

So they show their relations to me and I accept them,
They bring me tokens of myself, they evince them
plainly in their possession.

I wonder where they get those tokens,
Did I pass that way huge times ago and negligently
drop them?
Myself moving forward then and now and forever,
Gathering and showing more always and with
velocity,
Infinite and omnigenous, and the like of these among
them,
Not too exclusive toward the reachers of my remem-
brancers,
Picking out here one that I love, and now go with
him on brotherly terms.

A gigantic beauty of a stallion, fresh and responsive
to my caresses,
Head high in the forehead, wide between the ears,
Limbs glossy and supple, tail dusting the ground,
Eyes full of sparkling wickedness, ears finely cut,
flexibly moving.

His nostrils dilate as my heels embrace him,
His well-built limbs tremble with pleasure as we race
around and return.

I but use you a minute, then I resign you, stallion,
Why do I need your paces when I myself out-gallop
them?
Even as I stand or sit passing faster than you.

33

Space and Time! now I see it is true, what I guessed
at,
What I guess'd when I loaf'd on the grass,
What I guess'd while I lay alone in my bed,
And again as I walk'd the beach under the paling
stars of the morning.

My ties and ballasts leave me, my elbows rest in sea-
gaps,
I skirt sierras, my palms cover continents,
I am afoot with my vision.

By the city's quadrangular houses—in log huts, camp-
ing with lumbermen,
Along the ruts of the turnpike, along the dry gulch
and rivulet bed,
Weeding my onion-patch or hoeing rows of carrots
and parsnips, crossing savannas, trailing in
forests,
Prospecting, gold-digging, girdling the trees of a new
purchase,
Scorch'd ankle-deep by the hot sand, hauling my boat
down the shallow river,
Where the panther walks to and fro on a limb overhead, where the buck turns furiously at the
hunter,
Where the rattlesnake suns his flabby length on a
rock, where the otter is feeding on fish,
Where the alligator in his tough pimples sleeps by
the bayou,
Where the black bear is searching for roots or honey,
where the beaver pats the mud with his paddle-
shaped tail;
Over the growing sugar, over the yellow-flower'd cotton plant, over the rice in its low moist field,
Over the sharp-peak'd farm house, with its scallop'd
scum and slender shoots from the gutters,
Over the western persimmon, over the long-leav'd
corn, over the delicate blue-flower flax,
Over the white and brown buckwheat, a hummer and
buzzer there with the rest,
Over the dusky green of the rye as it ripples and
shades in the breeze;
Scaling mountains, pulling myself cautiously up, holding on by low scragged limbs,
Walking the path worn in the grass and beat through
the leaves of the brush,

Where the quail is whistling betwixt the woods and
the wheat-lot,

Where the bat flies in the Seventh-month eve, where
the great gold-bug drops through the dark,

Where the brook puts out of the roots of the old tree
and flows to the meadow,

Where cattle stand and shake away flies with the
tremulous shuddering of their hides,

Where the cheese-cloth hangs in the kitchen, where
andirons straddle the hearth-slab, where cob-
webs fall in festoons from the rafters;

Where trip-hammers crash, where the press is whirling its cylinders,

Wherever the human heart beats with terrible throes
under its ribs,

Where the pear-shaped balloon is floating aloft, (floating in it myself and looking composedly down,)

Where the life-car is drawn on the slip-noose, where
the heat hatches pale-green eggs in the dented
sand,

Where the she-whale swims with her calf and never
forsakes it,

Where the steam-ship trails hind-ways its long pen-
nant of smoke,

Where the fin of the shark cuts like a black chip out
of the water,

Where the half-burn'd brig is riding on unknown
currents,

Where shells grow to her slimy deck, where the dead
are corrupting below;

Where the dense-starr'd flag is borne at the head of
the regiments,

Approaching Manhattan up by the long-stretching island,

Under Niagara, the cataract falling like a veil over
my countenance,

Upon a door-step, upon the horse-block of hard wood
outside,

Upon the race-course, or enjoying picnics or jigs or a
good game of base-ball,

At he-festivals, with blackguard gibes, ironical license,
bull-dances, drinking, laughter,

At the cider-mill tasting the sweets of the brown mash,
sucking the juice through a straw,

At apple-peelings wanting kisses for all the red fruit
I find,

At musters, beach-parties, friendly bees, huskings,
house-raisings;

Where the mocking-bird sounds his delicious gurgles,
cackles, screams, weeps,

Where the hay-rick stands in the barn-yard, where
the dry-stalks are scatter'd, where the brood-cow
waits in the hovel,

Where the bull advances to do his masculine work,
where the stud to the mare, where the cock is
treading the hen,

Where the heifers browse, where geese nip their food
with short jerks,

Where sun-down shadows lengthen over the limitless
and lonesome prairie,

Where herds of buffalo make a crawling spread of the
square miles far and near,

Where the humming-bird shimmers, where the neck
of the long-lived swan is curving and winding,

Where the laughing-gull scoots by the shore, where
she laughs her near-human laugh,

Where bee-hives range on a gray bench in the garden half hid by the high weeds,

Where band-neck'd partridges roost in a ring on the
ground with their heads out,

Where burial coaches enter the arch'd gates of a
cemetery,

Where winter wolves bark amid wastes of snow and
icicled trees,

Where the yellow-crown'd heron comes to the edge
of the marsh at night and feeds upon small crabs,

Where the splash of swimmers and divers cools the
warm noon,

Where the katy-did works her chromatic reed on the
walnut-tree over the well,

Through patches of citrons and cucumbers with silver-
wired leaves,

Through the salt-lick or orange glade, or under conical
firs,

Through the gymnasium, through the curtain'd sa-
loon, through the office or public hall;

Pleas'd with the native and pleas'd with the foreign,
pleas'd with the new and old,

Pleas'd with the homely woman as well as the handsome,

Pleas'd with the quakeress as she puts off her bonnet
and talks melodiously,

Pleas'd with the tune of the choir of the whitewash'd
church,

Pleas'd with the earnest words of the sweating Methodist preacher, impress'd seriously at the camp-
meeting;

Looking in at the shop-windows of Broadway the
whole forenoon, flatting the flesh of my nose on
the thick plate-glass,

Wandering the same afternoon with my face turn'd
up to the clouds, or down a lane or along the
beach,

My right and left arms round the sides of two friends,
and I in the middle;

Coming home with the silent and dark-cheek'd bush-
boy, (behind me he rides at the drape of the
day,)

Far from the settlements studying the print of animals'
feet, or the moccasin print,

By the cot in the hospital reaching lemonade to a
feverish patient,

Nigh the coffin'd corpse when all is still, examining
with a candle;

Voyaging to every port to dicker and adventure,

Hurrying with the modern crowd as eager and fickle
as any,

Hot toward one I hate, ready in my madness to knife
him,

Solitary at midnight in my back yard, my thoughts
    gone from me a long while,
Walking the old hills of Judæa with the beautiful
    gentle God by my side,
Speeding through space, speeding through heaven
    and the stars,
Speeding amid the seven satellites and the broad ring,
    and the diameter of eighty thousand miles,
Speeding with tail'd meteors, throwing fire-balls like
    the rest,
Carrying the crescent child that carries its own full
    mother in its belly,
Storming, enjoying, planning, loving, cautioning,
Backing and filling, appearing and disappearing,
I tread day and night such roads.

I visit the orchards of spheres and look at the product,
And look at quintillions ripen'd and look at quintillions
    green.

I fly those flights of a fluid and swallowing soul,
My course runs below the soundings of plummets.

I help myself to material and immaterial,
No guard can shut me off, no law prevent me.

I anchor my ship for a little while only,
My messengers continually cruise away or bring their
    returns to me.

I go hunting polar furs and the seal, leaping chasms
    with a pike-pointed staff, clinging to topples of
    brittle and blue.

I ascend to the foretruck,
I take my place late at night in the crow's-nest,
We sail the arctic sea, it is plenty light enough,
Through the clear atmosphere I stretch around on the
    wonderful beauty,
The enormous masses of ice pass me and I pass them,
    the scenery is plain in all directions,

The white-topt mountains show in the distance, I fling
    out my fancies toward them,
We are approaching some great battle-field in which
    we are soon to be engaged,
We pass the colossal outposts of the encampment, we
    pass with still feet and caution,
Or we are entering by the suburbs some vast and
    ruin'd city,
The blocks and fallen architecture more than all the
    living cities of the globe.
I am a free companion, I bivouac by invading watch-
    fires,
I turn the bridegroom out of bed and stay with the
    bride myself, I tighten her all night to my thighs
    and lips.

My voice is the wife's voice, the screech by the rail of
    the stairs,
They fetch my man's body up dripping and drown'd.

I understand the large hearts of heroes,
The courage of present times and all times,
How the skipper saw the crowded and rudderless
    wreck of the steam-ship, and Death chasing it
    up and down the storm,
How he knuckled tight and gave not back an inch,
    and was faithful of days and faithful of nights,
And chalk'd in large letters on a board, *Be of good
    cheer, we will not desert you;*
How he follow'd with them and tack'd with them
    three days and would not give it up,
How he saved the drifting company at last,
How the lank loose-gown'd women look'd when
    boated from the side of their prepared graves,
How the silent old-faced infants and the lifted sick,
    and the sharp-lipp'd unshaved men;
All this I swallow, it tastes good, I like it well, it be-
    comes mine,
I am the man, I suffer'd, I was there.

The disdain and calmness of martyrs,
The mother of old, condemn'd for a witch, burnt with
    dry wood, her children gazing on,
The hounded slave that flags in the race, leans by the
    fence, blowing, cover'd with sweat,
The twinges that sting like needles his legs and neck,
    the murderous buckshot and the bullets,
All these I feel or am.

I am the hounded slave, I wince at the bite of the
    dogs,
Hell and despair are upon me, crack and again crack
    the marksmen,
I clutch the rails of the fence, my gore dribs, thinn'd
    with the ooze of my skin,
I fall on the weeds and stones,
The riders spur their unwilling horses, haul close,
Taunt my dizzy ears and beat me violently over the
    head with whip-stocks.

Agonies are one of my changes of garments,
I do not ask the wounded person how he feels, I my-
    self become the wounded person,
My hurts turn livid upon me as I lean on a cane and
    observe.

I am the mash'd fireman with breast-bone broken,
Tumbling walls buried me in their debris,
Heat and smoke I inspired, I heard the yelling shouts
    of my comrades,
I heard the distant click of their picks and shovels,
They have clear'd the beams away, they tenderly lift
    me forth.

I lie in the night air in my red shirt, the pervading
    hush is for my sake,
Painless after all I lie exhausted but not so unhappy,
White and beautiful are the faces around me, the
    heads are bared of their fire-caps,
The kneeling crowd fades with the light of the
    torches.

Distant and dead resuscitate,
They show as the dial or move as the hands of me, I
    am the clock myself.

I am an old artillerist, I tell of my fort's bombardment,
I am there again.

Again the long roll of the drummers,
Again the attacking cannon, mortars,
Again to my listening ears the cannon responsive.

I take part, I see and hear the whole,
The cries, curses, roar, the plaudits for well-aim'd
    shots,
The ambulanza slowly passing trailing its red drip,
Workmen searching after damages, making indispen-
    sable repairs,
The fall of grenades through the rent roof, the fan-
    shaped explosion,
The whizz of limbs, heads, stone, wood, iron, high in
    the air.

Again gurgles the mouth of my dying general, he
    furiously waves with his hand,
He gasps through the clot *Mind not me—mind—the
    entrenchments.*

34

Now I tell what I knew in Texas in my early youth,
(I tell not the fall of Alamo,
Not one escaped to tell the fall of Alamo,
The hundred and fifty are dumb yet at Alamo,)
'Tis the tale of the murder in cold blood of four hun-
    dred and twelve young men.

Retreating they had form'd in a hollow square with
    their baggage for breastworks,
Nine hundred lives out of the surrounding enemy's,
    nine times their number, was the price they took
    in advance,

Their colonel was wounded and their ammunition gone,

They treated for an honorable capitulation, receiv'd writing and seal, gave up their arms and march'd back prisoners of war.

They were the glory of the race of rangers,

Matchless with horse, rifle, song, supper, courtship,

Large, turbulent, generous, handsome, proud, and affectionate,

Bearded, sunburnt, drest in the free costume of hunters,

Not a single one over thirty years of age.

The second First-day morning they were brought out in squads and massacred, it was beautiful early summer,

The work commenced about five o'clock and was over by eight.

None obey'd the command to kneel,

Some made a mad and helpless rush, some stood stark and straight,

A few fell at once, shot in the temple or heart, the living and dead lay together,

The maim'd and mangled dug in the dirt, the new-comers saw them there,

Some half-kill'd attempted to crawl away,

These were dispatch'd with bayonets or batter'd with the blunts of muskets,

A youth not seventeen years old seiz'd his assassin till two more came to release him,

The three were all torn and cover'd with the boy's blood.

At eleven o'clock began the burning of the bodies;

That is the tale of the murder of the four hundred and twelve young men.

35

Would you hear of an old-time sea-fight?
Would you learn who won by the light of the moon
    and stars?
List to the yarn, as my grandmother's father the sailor
    told it to me.

Our foe was no skulk in his ship I tell you, (said he,)
His was the surly English pluck, and there is no
    tougher or truer, and never was, and never
    will be;
Along the lower'd eve he came horribly raking us.

We closed with him, the yards entangled, the cannon
    touch'd,
My captain lash'd fast with his own hands.

We had receiv'd some eighteen pound shots under
    the water,
On our lower-gun-deck two large pieces had burst at
    the first fire, killing all around and blowing up
    overhead.

Fighting at sun-down, fighting at dark,
Ten o'clock at night, the full moon well up, our leaks
    on the gain, and five feet of water reported,
The master-at-arms loosing the prisoners confined in
    the after-hold to give them a chance for them-
    selves.

The transit to and from the magazine is now stopt by
    the sentinels,
They see so many strange faces they do not know
    whom to trust.

Our frigate takes fire,
The other asks if we demand quarter?
If our colors are struck and the fighting done?

Now I laugh content, for I hear the voice of my little captain,

We have not struck, he composedly cries, *we have just begun our part of the fighting*.

Only three guns are in use,

One is directed by the captain himself against the enemy's main-mast,

Two well serv'd with grape and canister silence his musketry and clear his decks.

The tops alone second the fire of this little battery, especially the main-top,

They hold out bravely during the whole of the action.

Not a moment's cease,

The leaks gain fast on the pumps, the fire eats toward the powder-magazine.

One of the pumps has been shot away, it is generally thought we are sinking.

Serene stands the little captain,

He is not hurried, his voice is neither high nor low,

His eyes give more light to us than our battle-lanterns.

Toward twelve there in the beams of the moon they surrender to us.

36

Stretch'd and still lies the midnight,

Two great hulls motionless on the breast of the darkness,

Our vessel riddled and slowly sinking, preparations to pass to the one we have conquer'd,

The captain on the quarter-deck coldly giving his orders through a countenance white as a sheet,

Near by the corpse of the child that serv'd in the cabin,

The dead face of an old salt with long white hair and carefully curl'd whiskers,

The flames spite of all that can be done flickering aloft
    and below,
The husky voices of the two or three officers yet fit
    for duty,
Formless stacks of bodies and bodies by themselves,
    dabs of flesh upon the masts and spars,
Cut of cordage, dangle of rigging, slight shock of the
    soothe of waves,
Black and impassive guns, litter of powder-parcels,
    strong scent,
A few large stars overhead, silent and mournful
    shining,
Delicate sniffs of sea-breeze, smells of sedgy grass and
    fields by the shore, death-messages given in
    charge to survivors,
The hiss of the surgeon's knife, the gnawing teeth of
    his saw
Wheeze, cluck, swash of falling blood, short wild
    scream, and long, dull, tapering groan,
These so, these irretrievable.

37

You laggards there on guard! look to your arms!
In at the conquer'd doors they crowd! I am possess'd!
Embody all presences outlaw'd or suffering,
See myself in prison shaped like another man,
And feel the dull unintermitted pain.

For me the keepers of convicts shoulder their carbines
    and keep watch,
It is I let out in the morning and barr'd at night.

Not a mutineer walks handcuff'd to jail but I am
    handcuff'd to him and walk by his side,
(I am less the jolly one there, and more the silent one
    with sweat on my twitching lips.)

Not a youngster is taken for larceny but I go up too,
    and am tried and sentenced.

Not a cholera patient lies at the last gasp but I also
    lie at the last gasp,
My face is ash-color'd, my sinews gnarl, away from
    me people retreat.

Askers embody themselves in me and I am embodied
    in them,
I project my hat, sit shame-faced, and beg.

38

Enough! enough! enough!
Somehow I have been stunn'd. Stand back!
Give me a little time beyond my cuff'd head, slum-
    bers, dreams, gaping,
I discover myself on the verge of a usual mistake.

That I could forget the mockers and insults!
That I could forget the trickling tears and the blows
    of the bludgeons and hammers!
That I could look with a separate look on my own
    crucifixion and bloody crowning.

I remember now,
I resume the overstaid fraction,
The grave of rock multiplies what has been confided
    to it, or to any graves,
Corpses rise, gashes heal, fastenings roll from me.

I troop forth replenish'd with supreme power, one of
    an average unending procession,
Inland and sea-coast we go, and pass all boundary
    lines,
Our swift ordinances on their way over the whole
    earth,
The blossoms we wear in our hats the growth of
    thousands of years.

Eleves, I salute you! come forward!
Continue your annotations, continue your ques-
    tionings.

39

The friendly and flowing savage, who is he?
Is he waiting for civilization, or past it and mastering
it?

Is he some Southwesterner rais'd out-doors? is he
Kanadian?
Is he from the Mississippi country? Iowa, Oregon,
California?
The mountains? prairie-life, bush-life? or sailor from
the sea?

Wherever he goes men and women accept and desire
him,
They desire he should like them, touch them, speak
to them, stay with them.

Behavior lawless as snow-flakes, words simple as grass,
uncomb'd head, laughter, and naiveté,
Slow-stepping feet, common features, common modes
and emanations,
They descend in new forms from the tips of his
fingers,
They are wafted with the odor of his body or breath,
they fly out of the glance of his eyes.

40

Flaunt of the sunshine I need not your bask—lie over!
You light surfaces only, I force surfaces and depths
also.

Earth! you seem to look for something at my hands,
Say, old top-knot, what do you want?

Man or woman, I might tell how I like you, but cannot,
And might tell what it is in me and what it is in you,
but cannot,
And might tell that pining I have, that pulse of my
nights and days.

Behold, I do not give lectures or a little charity,
When I give I give myself.

You there, impotent, loose in the knees,
Open your scarf'd chops till I blow grit within you,
Spread your palms and lift the flaps of your pockets,
I am not to be denied, I compel, I have stores plenty
    and to spare,
And any thing I have I bestow.

I do not ask who you are, that is not important to me,
You can do nothing and be nothing but what I will
    infold you.

To cotton-field drudge or cleaner of privies I lean,
On his right cheek I put the family kiss,
And in my soul I swear I never will deny him.

On women fit for conception I start bigger and nim-
    bler babes,
(This day I am jetting the stuff of far more arrogant
    republics.)

To any one dying, thither I speed and twist the knob
    of the door,
Turn the bed-clothes toward the foot of the bed,
Let the physician and the priest go home.

I seize the descending man and raise him with resist-
    less will,
O despairer, here is my neck,
By God, you shall not go down! hang your whole
    weight upon me.

I dilate you with tremendous breath, I buoy you up,
Every room of the house do I fill with an arm'd force,
Lovers of me, bafflers of graves.

Sleep—I and they keep guard all night,

Not doubt, not decease shall dare to lay finger upon
you,

I have embraced you, and henceforth possess you to
myself,

And when you rise in the morning you will find what
I tell you is so.

41

I am he bringing help for the sick as they pant on
their backs,

And for strong upright men I bring yet more needed
help.

I heard what was said of the universe,

Heard it and heard it of several thousand years;

It is middling well as far as it goes—but is that all?

Magnifying and applying come I,

Outbidding at the start the old cautious hucksters,

Taking myself the exact dimensions of Jehovah,

Lithographing Kronos, Zeus his son, and Hercules his
grandson,

Buying drafts of Osiris, Isis, Belus, Brahma, Buddha,

In my portfolio placing Manito loose, Allah on a leaf,
the crucifix engraved,

With Odin and the hideous-faced Mexitli and every
idol and image,

Taking them all for what they are worth and not a
cent more,

Admitting they were alive and did the work of their
days,

(They bore mites as for unfledg'd birds who have now
to rise and fly and sing for themselves,)

Accepting the rough deific sketches to fill out better
in myself, bestowing them freely on each man
and woman I see,

Discovering as much or more in a framer framing a
house,

Putting higher claims for him there with his roll'd-up
　　sleeves driving the mallet and chisel,
Not objecting to special revelations, considering a curl
　　of smoke or a hair on the back of my hand just as
　　curious as any revelation,
Lads ahold of fire-engines and hook-and-ladder ropes
　　no less to me than the gods of the antique wars,
Minding their voices peal through the crash of de-
　　struction,
Their brawny limbs passing safe over charr'd laths,
　　their white foreheads whole and unhurt out of
　　the flames;
By the mechanic's wife with her babe at her nipple
　　interceding for every person born,
Three scythes at harvest whizzing in a row from three
　　lusty angels with shirts bagg'd out at their waists,
The snag-tooth'd hostler with red hair redeeming sins
　　past and to come,
Selling all he possesses, traveling on foot to fee law-
　　yers for his brother and sit by him while he is
　　tried for forgery;
What was strewn in the amplest strewing the square
　　rod about me, and not filling the square rod
　　then,
The bull and the bug never worshipp'd half enough,
Dung and dirt more admirable than was dream'd,
The supernatural of no account, myself waiting my
　　time to be one of the supremes,
The day getting ready for me when I shall do as
　　much good as the best, and be as prodigious;
By my life-lumps! becoming already a creator,
Putting myself here and now to the ambush'd womb
　　of the shadows.

42

A call in the midst of the crowd,
My own voice, orotund sweeping and final.

Come my children,

Come my boys and girls, my women, household and
 intimates,

Now the performer launches his nerve, he has pass'd
 his prelude on the reeds within.

Easily written loose-finger'd chords—I feel the thrum
 of your climax and close.

My head slues round on my neck,

Music rolls, but not from the organ,

Folks are around me, but they are no household of
 mine.

Ever the hard unsunk ground,

Ever the eaters and drinkers, ever the upward and
 downward sun, ever the air and the ceaseless
 tides,

Ever myself and my neighbors, refreshing, wicked,
 real,

Ever the old inexplicable query, ever that thorn'd
 thumb, that breath of itches and thirsts,

Ever the vexer's *hoot! hoot!* till we find where the sly
 one hides and bring him forth,

Ever love, ever the sobbing liquid of life,

Ever the bandage under the chin, ever the trestles of
 death.

Here and there with dimes on the eyes walking,

To feed the greed of the belly the brains liberally
 spooning,

Tickets buying, taking, selling, but in to the feast
 never once going,

Many sweating, ploughing, thrashing, and then the
 chaff for payment receiving,

A few idly owning, and they the wheat continually
 claiming.

This is the city and I am one of the citizens,

Whatever interests the rest interests me, politics, wars,
 markets, newspapers, schools,

The mayor and councils, banks, tariffs, steamships,
  factories, stocks, stores, real estate and personal
  estate.

The little plentiful manikins skipping around in collars
  and tail'd coats,
I am aware who they are, (they are positively not
  worms or fleas,)
I acknowledge the duplicates of myself, the weakest
  and shallowest is deathless with me,
What I do and say the same waits for them,
Every thought that flounders in me the same flounders
  in them.

I know perfectly well my own egotism,
Know my omnivorous lines and must not write any
  less,
And would fetch you whoever you are flush with
  myself.

Not words of routine this song of mine,
But abruptly to question, to leap beyond yet nearer
  bring;
This printed and bound book—but the printer and the
  printing-office boy?
The well-taken photographs—but your wife or friend
  close and solid in your arms?
The black ship mail'd with iron, her mighty guns in
  her turrets—but the pluck of the captain and
  engineers?
In the houses the dishes and fare and furniture—but
  the host and hostess, and the look out of their
  eyes?
The sky up there—yet here or next door, or across the
  way?
The saints and sages in history—but you yourself?
Sermons, creeds, theology—but the fathomless human
  brain,
And what is reason? and what is love? and what is
  life?

43

I do not despise you priests, all time, the world over,
My faith is the greatest of faiths and the least of
faiths,
Enclosing worship ancient and modern and all be-
tween ancient and modern,
Believing I shall come again upon the earth after five
thousand years,
Waiting responses from oracles, honoring the gods,
saluting the sun,
Making a fetich of the first rock or stump, powowing
with sticks in the circle of obis,
Helping the lama or brahmin as he trims the lamps
of the idols,
Dancing yet through the streets in a phallic proces-
sion, rapt and austere in the woods a gymnoso-
phist,
Drinking mead from the skull-cup, to Shastas and
Vedas admirant, minding the Koran,
Walking the teokallis, spotted with gore from the
stone and knife, beating the serpent-skin drum,
Accepting the Gospels, accepting him that was cruci-
fied, knowing assuredly that he is divine,
To the mass kneeling or the puritan's prayer rising, or
sitting patiently in a pew,
Ranting and frothing in my insane crisis, or waiting
dead-like till my spirit arouses me,
Looking forth on pavement and land, or outside of
pavement and land,
Belonging to the winders of the circuit of circuits.

One of that centripetal and centrifugal gang I turn
and talk like a man leaving charges before a
journey.

Down-hearted doubters dull and excluded,
Frivolous, sullen, moping, angry, affected, disheart-
en'd, atheistical,
I know every one of you, I know the sea of torment,
doubt, despair and unbelief.

How the flukes splash!
How they contort rapid as lightning, with spasms and
    spouts of blood!

Be at peace bloody flukes of doubters and sullen
    mopers,
I take my place among you as much as among any,
The past is the push of you, me, all, precisely the
    same,
And what is yet untried and afterward is for you,
    me, all, precisely the same.

I do not know what is untried and afterward,
But I know it will in its turn prove sufficient, and
    cannot fail.

Each who passes is consider'd, each who stops is con-
    sider'd, not a single one can it fail.

It cannot fail the young man who died and was
    buried,
Nor the young woman who died and was put by his
    side,
Nor the little child that peep'd in at the door, and then
    drew back and was never seen again,
Nor the old man who has lived without purpose, and
    feels it with bitterness worse than gall,
Nor him in the poor house tubercled by rum and the
    bad disorder,
Nor the numberless slaughter'd and wreck'd, nor the
    brutish koboo call'd the ordure of humanity,
Nor the sacs merely floating with open mouths for
    food to slip in,
Nor any thing in the earth, or down in the oldest
    graves of the earth,
Nor any thing in the myriads of spheres, nor the
    myriads of myriads that inhabit them,
Nor the present, nor the least wisp that is known.

44

It is time to explain myself—let us stand up.

What is known I strip away,
I launch all men and women forward with me into
the Unknown.

The clock indicates the moment—but what does eternity indicate?

We have thus far exhausted trillions of winters and
summers,
There are trillions ahead, and trillions ahead of them.

Births have brought us richness and variety,
And other births will bring us richness and variety.

I do not call one greater and one smaller,
That which fills its period and place is equal to any.

Were mankind murderous or jealous upon you, my
brother, my sister?
I am sorry for you, they are not murderous or jealous
upon me,
All has been gentle with me, I keep no account with
lamentation,
(What have I to do with lamentation?)

I am an acme of things accomplish'd, and I an encloser of things to be.

My feet strike an apex of the apices of the stairs,
On every step bunches of ages, and larger bunches
between the steps,
All below duly travel'd, and still I mount and mount.

Rise after rise bow the phantoms behind me,
Afar down I see the huge first Nothing, I know I was
even there,

I waited unseen and always, and slept through the
    lethargic mist,
And took my time, and took no hurt from the fetid
    carbon.

Long I was hugg'd close—long and long.

Immense have been the preparations for me,
Faithful and friendly the arms that have help'd me.

Cycles ferried my cradle, rowing and rowing like
    cheerful boatmen,
For room to me stars kept aside in their own rings,
They sent influences to look after what was to hold
    me.

Before I was born out of my mother generations
    guided me,
My embryo has never been torpid, nothing could over-
    lay it.

For it the nebula cohered to an orb,
The long slow strata piled to rest it on,
Vast vegetables gave it sustenance,
Monstrous sauroids transported it in their mouths and
    deposited it with care.

All forces have been steadily employ'd to complete
    and delight me,
Now on this spot I stand with my robust soul.

45

O span of youth! ever-push'd elasticity!
O manhood, balanced, florid and full.

My lovers suffocate me,
Crowding my lips, thick in the pores of my skin,
Jostling me through streets and public halls, coming
    naked to me at night,

Crying by day *Ahoy!* from the rocks of the river,
    swinging and chirping over my head,
Calling my name from flower-beds, vines, tangled
    underbrush,
Lighting on every moment of my life,
Bussing my body with soft balsamic busses,
Noiselessly passing handfuls out of their hearts and
    giving them to be mine.

Old age superbly rising! O welcome, ineffable grace
    of dying days!

Every condition promulges not only itself, it promulges
    what grows after and out of itself,
And the dark hush promulges as much as any.

I open my scuttle at night and see the far-sprinkled
    systems,
And all I see multiplied as high as I can cipher edge
    but the rim of the farther systems.

Wider and wider they spread, expanding, always
    expanding,
Outward and outward and forever outward.

My sun has his sun and round him obediently wheels,
He joins with his partners a group of superior circuit,
And greater sets follow, making specks of the greatest
    inside them.

There is no stoppage and never can be stoppage,
If I, you, and the worlds, and all beneath or upon
    their surfaces, were this moment reduced back
    to a pallid float, it would not avail in the long
    run,
We should surely bring up again where we now stand,
And surely go as much farther, and then farther and
    farther.

A few quadrillions of eras, a few octillions of cubic
    leagues, do not hazard the span or make it im-
    patient,
They are but parts, any thing is but a part.

See ever so far, there is limitless space outside of that,
Count ever so much, there is limitless time around
    that.

My rendezvous is appointed, it is certain,
The Lord will be there and wait till I come on perfect
    terms,
The great Camerado, the lover true for whom I pine
    will be there.

46

I know I have the best of time and space, and was
    never measured and never will be measured.

I tramp a perpetual journey, (come listen all!)
My signs are a rain-proof coat, good shoes, and a staff
    cut from the woods,
No friend of mine takes his ease in my chair,
I have no chair, no church, no philosophy,
I lead no man to a dinner-table, library, exchange,
But each man and each woman of you I lead upon a
    knoll,
My left hand hooking you round the waist,
My right hand pointing to landscapes of continents
    and the public road.

Not I, not any one else can travel that road for you,
You must travel it for yourself.

It is not far, it is within reach,
Perhaps you have been on it since you were born and
    did not know,
Perhaps it is everywhere on water and on land.

Shoulder your duds dear son, and I will mine, and let
  us hasten forth,
Wonderful cities and free nations we shall fetch as we
  go.

If you tire, give me both burdens, and rest the chuff
  of your hand on my hip,
And in due time you shall repay the same service to
  me,
For after we start we never lie by again.

This day before dawn I ascended a hill and look'd at
  the crowded heaven,
And I said to my spirit *When we become the en-
  folders of those orbs, and the pleasure and knowledge of every thing in them, shall we be fill'd
  and satisfied then?*
And my spirit said *No, we but level that lift to pass
  and continue beyond.*

You are also asking me questions and I hear you,
I answer that I cannot answer, you must find out for
  yourself.

Sit a while dear son,
Here are biscuits to eat and here is milk to drink,
But as soon as you sleep and renew yourself in sweet
  clothes, I kiss you with a good-by kiss and open
  the gate for your egress hence.

Long enough have you dream'd contemptible dreams,
Now I wash the gum from your eyes,
You must habit yourself to the dazzle of the light and
  of every moment of your life.

Long have you timidly waded holding a plank by the
  shore,
Now I will you to be a bold swimmer,
To jump off in the midst of the sea, rise again, nod
  to me, shout, and laughingly dash with your hair.

47

I am the teacher of athletes,
He that by me spreads a wider breast than my own
    proves the width of my own,
He most honors my style who learns under it to destroy
    the teacher.

The boy I love, the same becomes a man not through
    derived power, but in his own right,
Wicked rather than virtuous out of conformity or fear,
Fond of his sweetheart, relishing well his steak,
Unrequited love or a slight cutting him worse than
    sharp steel cuts,
First-rate to ride, to fight, to hit the bull's eye, to sail
    a skiff, to sing a song or play on the banjo,
Preferring scars and the beard and faces pitted with
    small-pox over all latherers,
And those well-tann'd to those that keep out of the
    sun.

I teach straying from me, yet who can stray from me?
I follow you whoever you are from the present hour,
My words itch at your ears till you understand them.

I do not say these things for a dollar or to fill up the
    time while I wait for a boat,
(It is you talking just as much as myself, I act as the
    tongue of you,
Tied in your mouth, in mine it begins to be loosen'd.)

I swear I will never again mention love or death inside
    a house,
And I swear I will never translate myself at all, only
    to him or her who privately stays with me in the
    open air.

If you would understand me go to the heights or
    water-shore,
The nearest gnat is an explanation, and a drop or
    motion of waves a key,
The maul, the oar, the hand-saw, second my words.

No shutter'd room or school can commune with me,
But roughs and little children better than they.

The young mechanic is closest to me, he knows me
    well,
The woodman that takes his axe and jug with him
    shall take me with him all day,
The farm-boy ploughing in the field feels good at the
    sound of my voice,
In vessels that sail my words sail, I go with fishermen
    and seamen and love them.

The soldier camp'd or upon the march is mine,
On the night ere the pending battle many seek me,
    and I do not fail them,
On that solemn night (it may be their last) those
    that know me seek me.

My face rubs to the hunter's face when he lies down
    alone in his blanket,
The driver thinking of me does not mind the jolt of
    his wagon,
The young mother and old mother comprehend me,
The girl and the wife rest the needle a moment and
    forget where they are,
They and all would resume what I have told them.

48

I have said that the soul is not more than the body,
And I have said that the body is not more than the
    soul,
And nothing, not God, is greater to one than one's
    self is,

And whoever walks a furlong without sympathy walks
    to his own funeral drest in his shroud,
And I or you pocketless of a dime may purchase the
    pick of the earth,
And to glance with an eye or show a bean in its pod
    confounds the learning of all times,
And there is no trade or employment but the young
    man following it may become a hero,
And there is no object so soft but it makes a hub for
    the wheel'd universe,
And I say to any man or woman, Let your soul stand
    cool and composed before a million universes.

And I say to mankind, Be not curious about God,
For I who am curious about each am not curious
    about God,
(No array of terms can say how much I am at peace
    about God and about death.)

I hear and behold God in every object, yet under-
    stand God not in the least,
Nor do I understand who there can be more wonder-
    ful than myself.

Why should I wish to see God better than this day?
I see something of God each hour of the twenty-four,
    and each moment then,
In the faces of men and women I see God, and in my
    own face in the glass,
I find letters from God dropt in the street, and every
    one is sign'd by God's name,
And I leave them where they are, for I know that
    wheresoe'er I go,
Others will punctually come for ever and ever.

49

And as to you Death, and you bitter hug of mortality,
    it is idle to try to alarm me.

To his work without flinching the accoucheur comes,
I see the elder-hand pressing receiving supporting,
I recline by the sills of the exquisite flexible doors,
And mark the outlet, and mark the relief and escape.

And as to you Corpse I think you are good manure,
    but that does not offend me,
I smell the white roses sweet-scented and growing,
I reach to the leafy lips, I reach to the polish'd breasts
    of melons.

And as to you Life I reckon you are the leavings of
    many deaths,
(No doubt I have died myself ten thousand times
    before.)

I hear you whispering there O stars of heaven,
O suns—O grass of graves—O perpetual transfers and
    promotions,
If you do not say any thing how can I say any thing?

Of the turbid pool that lies in the autumn forest,
Of the moon that descends the steeps of the soughing
    twilight,
Toss, sparkles of day and dusk—toss on the black stems
    that decay in the muck,
Toss to the moaning gibberish of the dry limbs.

I ascend from the moon, I ascend from the night,
I perceive that the ghastly glimmer is noonday sun-
    beams reflected,
And debouch to the steady and central from the off-
    spring great or small.

50

There is that in me—I do not know what it is—but I
    know it is in me.

Wrench'd and sweaty—calm and cool then my body
    becomes,
I sleep—I sleep long.

I do not know it—it is without name—it is a word
unsaid,
It is not in any dictionary, utterance, symbol.

Something it swings on more than the earth I swing
on,
To it the creation is the friend whose embracing
awakes me.

Perhaps I might tell more. Outlines! I plead for my
brothers and sisters.

Do you see O my brothers and sisters?
It is not chaos or death—it is form, union, plan—it is
eternal life—it is Happiness.

51

The past and present wilt—I have fill'd them, emptied
them,
And proceed to fill my next fold of the future.

Listener up there! what have you to confide to me?
Look in my face while I snuff the sidle of evening,
(Talk honestly, no one else hears you, and I stay only
a minute longer.)

Do I contradict myself?
Very well then I contradict myself,
(I am large, I contain multitudes.)

I concentrate toward them that are nigh, I wait on
the door-slab.

Who has done his day's work? who will soonest be
through with his supper?
Who wishes to walk with me?

Will you speak before I am gone? will you prove
already too late?

52

The spotted hawk swoops by and accuses me, he
  complains of my gab and my loitering.

I too am not a bit tamed, I too am untranslatable,
I sound my barbaric yawp over the roofs of the world.

The last scud of day holds back for me,
It flings my likeness after the rest and true as any on
  the shadow'd wilds,
It coaxes me to the vapor and the dusk.

I depart as air, I shake my white locks at the runaway
  sun,
I effuse my flesh in eddies, and drift it in lacy jags.

I bequeath myself to the dirt to grow from the grass
  I love,
If you want me again look for me under your boot-
  soles.

You will hardly know who I am or what I mean,
But I shall be good health to you nevertheless,
And filter and fibre your blood.

Failing to fetch me at first keep encouraged,
Missing me one place search another,
I stop somewhere waiting for you.

OUT OF THE CRADLE ENDLESSLY ROCKING

Out of the cradle endlessly rocking,
Out of the mocking-bird's throat, the musical shuttle,
Out of the Ninth-month midnight,
Over the sterile sands and the fields beyond, where
  the child leaving his bed wander'd alone, bare-
  headed, barefoot,

Down from the shower'd halo,
Up from the mystic play of shadows twining and
    twisting as if they were alive,
Out from the patches of briers and blackberries,
From the memories of the bird that chanted to me,
From your memories sad brother, from the fitful ris-
    ings and fallings I heard,
From under that yellow half-moon late-risen and
    swollen as if with tears,
From those beginning notes of yearning and love
    there in the mist,
From the thousand responses of my heart never to
    cease,
From the myriad thence-arous'd words,
From the word stronger and more delicious than any,
From such as now they start the scene revisiting,
As a flock, twittering, rising, or overhead passing,
Borne hither, ere all eludes me, hurriedly,
A man, yet by these tears a little boy again,
Throwing myself on the sand, confronting the waves,
I, chanter of pains and joys, uniter of here and
    hereafter,
Taking all hints to use them, but swiftly leaping be-
    yond them.
A reminiscence sing.

Once Paumanok,
When the lilac-scent was in the air and Fifth-month
    grass was growing,
Up this seashore in some briers,
Two feather'd guests from Alabama, two together,
And their nest, and four light-green eggs spotted with
    brown,
And every day the he-bird to and fro near at hand,
And every day the she-bird crouch'd on her nest,
    silent, with bright eyes,
And every day I, a curious boy, never too close, never
    disturbing them,
Cautiously peering, absorbing, translating.

Shine! shine! shine!
Pour down your warmth, great sun!
While we bask, we two together.

Two together!
Winds blow south, or winds blow north,
Day come white, or night come black,
Home, or rivers and mountains from home,
Singing all time, minding no time,
While we two keep together.

Till of a sudden,
May-be kill'd, unknown to her mate,
One forenoon the she-bird crouch'd not on the nest,
Nor return'd that afternoon, nor the next
Nor ever appear'd again.

And thenceforward all summer in the sound of the
    sea,
And at night under the full of the moon in calmer
    weather,
Over the hoarse surging of the sea,
Or flitting from brier to brier by day,
I saw, I heard at intervals the remaining one, the
    he-bird,
The solitary guest from Alabama.

Blow! blow! blow!
Blow up sea-winds along Paumanok's shore;
I wait and I wait till you blow my mate to me.

Yes, when the stars glisten'd,
All night long on the prong of a moss-scallop'd stake,
Down almost amid the slapping waves,
Sat the lone singer wonderful causing tears.

He call'd on his mate,
He pour'd forth the meanings which I of all men
    know.

Yes, my brother I know,
The rest might not, but I have treasur'd every note,
For more than once dimly down to the beach gliding,
Silent, avoiding the moonbeams, blending myself with
    the shadows,
Recalling now the obscure shapes, the echoes, the
    sounds and sights after their sorts,
The white arms out in the breakers tirelessly tossing,
I, with bare feet, a child, the wind wafting my hair,
Listen'd long and long.

Listen'd to keep, to sing, now translating the notes,
Following you my brother.

Soothe! soothe! soothe!
Close on its wave soothes the wave behind,
And again another behind embracing and lapping,
    every one close,
But my love soothes not me, not me.

Low hangs the moon, it rose late,
It is lagging—O I think it is heavy with love, with love.

O madly the sea pushes upon the land,
With love, with love.

O night! do I not see my love fluttering out among
    the breakers?
What is that little black thing I see there in the white?

Loud! loud! loud!
Loud I call to you, my love!

High and clear I shoot my voice over the waves,
Surely you must know who is here, is here,
You must know who I am, my love.

Low-hanging moon!
What is that dusky spot in your brown yellow?
O it is the shape, the shape of my mate!
O moon do not keep her from me any longer.

Land! land! O land!
Whichever way I turn, O I think you could give me
my mate back again if you only would,
For I am almost sure I see her dimly whichever way
I look.

O rising stars!
Perhaps the one I want so much will rise, will rise
with some of you.

O throat! O trembling throat!
Sound clearer through the atmosphere!
Pierce the woods, the earth,
Somewhere listening to catch you must be the one I
want.

Shake out carols!
Solitary here, the night's carols!
Carols of lonesome love! death's carols!
Carols under that lagging, yellow, waning moon!
O under that moon where she droops almost down
into the sea!
O reckless despairing carols.

But soft! sink low!
Soft! let me just murmur,
And do you wait a moment you husky-nois'd sea,
For somewhere I believe I heard my mate responding
to me,
So faint, I must be still, be still to listen,
But not altogether still, for then she might not come
immediately to me.

Hither my love!
Here I am! here!
With this just-sustain'd note, I announce myself to
you,
This gentle call is for you my love, for you.

Do not be decoy'd elsewhere,
That is the whistle of the wind, it is not my voice,
That is the fluttering, the fluttering of the spray,
Those are the shadows of leaves.

O darkness! O in vain!
O I am very sick and sorrowful.

O brown halo in the sky near the moon, drooping
  upon the sea!
O troubled reflection in the sea!
O throat! O throbbing heart!
And I singing uselessly, uselessly all the night.

O past! O happy life! O songs of joy!
In the air, in the woods, over fields,
Loved! loved! loved! loved! loved!
But my mate no more, no more with me!
We two together no more.

The aria sinking,
All else continuing, the stars shining,
The winds blowing, the notes of the bird continuous
  echoing,
With angry moans the fierce old mother incessantly
  moaning,
On the sands of Paumanok's shore gray and rustling,
The yellow half-moon enlarged, sagging down, droop-
  ing, the face of the sea almost touching,
The boy ecstatic, with his bare feet the waves, with
  his hair the atmosphere dallying,
The love in the heart long pent, now loose, now at
  last tumultuously bursting,
The aria's meaning, the ears, the soul, swiftly de-
  positing,
The strange tears down the cheeks coursing,
The colloquy there, the trio, each uttering,
The undertone, the savage old mother incessantly
  crying,

To the boy's soul's questions sullenly timing, some
   drown'd secret hissing,
To the outsetting bard.

Demon or bird! (said the boy's soul,)
Is it indeed toward your mate you sing? or is it really
   to me?
For I, that was a child, my tongue's use sleeping,
   now I have heard you,
Now in a moment I know what I am for, I awake,
And already a thousand singers, a thousand songs,
   clearer, louder and more sorrowful than yours,
A thousand warbling echoes have started to life within
   me, never to die.

O you singer solitary, singing by yourself, projecting
   me,
O solitary me listening, never more shall I cease per-
   petuating you,
Never more shall I escape, never more the rever-
   berations,
Never more the cries of unsatisfied love be absent
   from me,
Never again leave me to be the peaceful child I was
   before what there in the night,
By the sea under the yellow and sagging moon,
The messenger there arous'd, the fire, the sweet hell
   within,
The unknown want, the destiny of me.

O give me the clew! (it lurks in the night here
   somewhere,)
O if I am to have so much, let me have more!
A word then, (for I will conquer it,)
The word final, superior to all,
Subtle, sent up—what is it?—I listen;
Are you whispering it, and have been all the time,
   you sea-waves?
Is that it from your liquid rims and wet sands?

Whereto answering, the sea,
Delaying not, hurrying not,
Whisper'd me through the night, and very plainly
before daybreak,
Lisp'd to me the low and delicious word death,
And again death, death, death, death,
Hissing melodious, neither like the bird nor like my
arous'd child's heart,
But edging near as privately for me rustling at my
feet,
Creeping thence steadily up to my ears and laving
me softly all over,
Death, death, death, death, death.

Which I do not forget,
But fuse the song of my dusky demon and brother,
That he sang to me in the moonlight on Paumanok's
gray beach,
With the thousand responsive songs at random,
My own songs awaked from that hour,
And with them the key, the word up from the waves,
The word of the sweetest song and all songs,
That strong and delicious word which, creeping to
my feet,
(Or like some old crone rocking the cradle, swathed
in sweet garments, bending aside,)
The sea whisper'd me.

COME UP FROM THE FIELDS FATHER

Come up from the fields father, here's a letter from
our Pete,
And come to the front door mother, here's a letter
from thy dear son.

Lo, 'tis autumn,
Lo, where the trees, deeper green, yellower and
redder,

Cool and sweeten Ohio's villages with leaves fluttering
    in the moderate wind,
Where apples ripe in the orchards hang and grapes
    on the trellis'd vines,
(Smell you the smell of the grapes on the vines?
Smell you the buckwheat where the bees were lately
    buzzing?)
Above all, lo, the sky so calm, so transparent after the
    rain, and with wondrous clouds,
Below too, all calm, all vital and beautiful, and the
    farm prospers well.

Down in the fields all prospers well,
But now from the fields come father, come at the
    daughter's call,
And come to the entry mother, to the front door come
    right away.

Fast as she can she hurries, something ominous, her
    steps trembling,
She does not tarry to smooth her hair nor adjust her
    cap.

Open the envelope quickly,
O this is not our son's writing, yet his name is sign'd,
O a strange hand writes for our dear son, O stricken
    mother's soul!
All swims before her eyes, flashes with black, she
    catches the main words only,
Sentences broken, *gunshot wound in the breast, cav-*
*   alry skirmish, taken to hospital,*
At present low, but will soon be better.

Ah now the single figure to me,
Amid all teeming and wealthy Ohio with all its cities
    and farms,
Sickly white in the face and dull in the head, very
    faint,
By the jamb of a door leans.

Grieve not so, dear mother, (the just-grown daughter
    speaks through her sobs,
The little sisters huddle around speechless and dis-
    may'd,)
*See, dearest mother, the letter says Pete will soon be
    better.*

Alas poor boy, he will never be better, (nor may-be
    needs to be better, that brave and simple soul,)
While they stand at home at the door he is dead
    already,
The only son is dead.

But the mother needs to be better,
She with thin form presently drest in black,
By day her meals untouch'd, then at night fitfully
    sleeping, often waking,
In the midnight waking, weeping, longing with one
    deep longing,
O that she might withdraw unnoticed, silent from life
    escape and withdraw,
To follow, to seek, to be with her dear dead son.

VIGIL STRANGE I KEPT ON THE FIELD ONE NIGHT

Vigil strange I kept on the field one night;
When you my son and my comrade dropt at my side
    that day,
One look I but gave which your dear eyes return'd
    with a look I shall never forget,
One touch of your hand to mine O boy, reach'd up as
    you lay on the ground,
Then onward I sped in the battle, the even-contested
    battle,
Till late in the night reliev'd to the place at last again
    I made my way,

Found you in death so cold dear comrade, found your
    body son of responding kisses, (never again on
    earth responding,)

Bared your face in the starlight, curious the scene,
    cool blew the moderate night-wind,

Long there and then in vigil I stood, dimly around me
    the battle-field spreading,

Vigil wondrous and vigil sweet there in the fragrant
    silent night,

But not a tear fell, not even a long-drawn sigh, long,
    long I gazed,

Then on the earth partially reclining sat by your side
    leaning my chin in my hands,

Passing sweet hours, immortal and mystic hours with
    you dearest comrade—not a tear, not a word,

Vigil of silence, love and death, vigil for you my son
    and my soldier,

As onward silently stars aloft, eastward new ones up-
    ward stole,

Vigil final for you brave boy, (I could not save you,
    swift was your death,

I faithfully loved you and cared for you living, I think
    we shall surely meet again,)

Till at latest lingering of the night, indeed just as the
    dawn appear'd,

My comrade I wrapt in his blanket, envelop'd well his
    form,

Folded the blanket well, tucking it carefully over head
    and carefully under feet,

And there and then and bathed by the rising sun, my
    son in his grave, in his rude-dug grave I de-
    posited,

Ending my vigil strange with that, vigil of night and
    battle-field dim,

Vigil for boy of responding kisses, (never again on
    earth responding,)

Vigil for comrade swiftly slain, vigil I never forget,
    how as day brighten'd,

I rose from the chill ground and folded my soldier
    well in his blanket,
And buried him where he fell.

AS TOILSOME I WANDER'D
VIRGINIA'S WOODS

As toilsome I wander'd Virginia's woods,
To the music of rustling leaves kick'd by my feet, (for
    'twas autumn,)
I mark'd at the foot of a tree the grave of a soldier;
Mortally wounded he and buried on the retreat,
    (easily all could I understand,)
The halt of a mid-day hour, when up! no time to lose
    —yet this sign left,
On a tablet scrawl'd and nail'd on the tree by the
    grave,
Bold, cautious, true, and my loving comrade.

Long, long I muse, then on my way go wandering,
Many a changeful season to follow, and many a scene
    of life,
Yet at times through changeful season and scene,
    abrupt, alone, or in the crowded street,
Comes before me the unknown soldier's grave, comes
    the inscription rude in Virginia's woods,
Bold, cautious, true, and my loving comrade.

HENRY TIMROD

1828–1867

Timrod, the most talented poet in the Confederacy, was a native of Charleston, South Carolina, then a regional literary center. When he died at thirty-nine, he had published only one brief volume, *Poems* (1860); after serving in the Confederate Army in 1861–1862 (he was discharged for ill health), he edited a newspaper. The war became the central subject of his later, more mature poetry, posthumously collected by Paul Hamilton Hayne in *The Poems of Henry Timrod* (1873). Timrod wrote with clarity, concreteness, and intensity; his best work is free of the rhetoric and sentimentality that were the faults of his Southern contemporaries Hayne and Sidney Lanier.

CHARLESTON

Calm as that second summer which precedes
    The first fall of snow,
In the broad sunlight of heroic deeds,
    The City bides the foe.

As yet, behind their ramparts stern and proud,
    Her bolted thunders sleep—
Dark Sumter, like a battlemented cloud,
    Looms o'er the solemn deep.

No Calpe frowns from lofty cliff or scar
    To guard the holy strand;
But Moultrie holds in leash her dogs of war
    Above the level sand.

And down the dunes a thousand guns lie couched,
  Unseen, beside the flood—
Like tigers in some Orient jungle crouched
  That wait and watch for blood.

Meanwhile, through streets still echoing with trade,
  Walk grave and thoughtful men,
Whose hand may one day wield the patriot's blade
  As lightly as the pen.

And maidens, with such eyes as would grow dim
  Over a bleeding hound,
Seem each one to have caught the strength of him
  Whose sword she sadly bound.

Thus girt without and garrisoned at home,
  Day patient following day,
Old Charleston looks from roof, and spire, and dome,
  Across her tranquil bay.

Ships, through a hundred foes, from Saxon lands
  And spicy Indian ports,
Bring Saxon steel and iron to her hands,
  And Summer to her courts.

But still, along yon dim Atlantic line,
  The only hostile smoke
Creeps like a harmless mist above the brine,
  From some frail, floating oak.

Shall the Spring dawn, and she still clad in smiles,
  And with an unscathed brow,
Rest in the strong arms of her palm-crowned isles,
  As fair and free as now?

We know not; in the temple of the Fates
  God has inscribed her doom;
And, all untroubled in her faith, she waits
  The triumph or the tomb.

ODE

SUNG ON THE OCCASION OF DECORAT-
ING THE GRAVES OF THE CONFEDERATE
DEAD, AT MAGNOLIA CEMETERY,
CHARLESTON, S.C., 1867

I

Sleep sweetly in your humble graves,
    Sleep, martyrs of a fallen cause;
Though yet no marble column craves
    The pilgrim here to pause.

II

In seeds of laurel in the earth
    The blossom of your fame is blown,
And somewhere, waiting for its birth,
    The shaft is in the stone!

III

Meanwhile, behalf the tardy years
    Which keep in trust your storied tombs,
Behold! your sisters bring their tears,
    And these memorial blooms.

IV

Small tributes! but your shades will smile
    More proudly on these wreaths to-day,
Than when some cannon-moulded pile
    Shall overlook this bay.

V

Stoop, angels, hither from the skies!
    There is no holier spot of ground
Than where defeated valor lies,
    By mourning beauty crowned!

HERMAN MELVILLE

1819–1891

Melville began to write poetry in earnest in 1859. He had returned two years earlier from a visit to Palestine; his poems, on impressions of the Old World, failed to interest publishers and did not appear until he included them in *Timoleon,* privately printed in the last year of his life. His first book of verse (after nine novels and a book of shorter tales) was *Battle-Pieces and Aspects of the War.* His preface explains, "The Pieces in this volume originated in an impulse imparted by the fall of Richmond. . . . Yielding instinctively, one after another, to feelings not inspired from any one source exclusively, and unmindful, without purposing to be, of consistency, I seem, in most of these verses, to have but placed a harp in a window, and noted the contrasted airs which wayward winds have played upon the strings." The image recurs in a later poem, "The Aeolian Harp," explicitly defining Melville's aesthetic. Indeed his inspiration was varied; like his readings in fiction, philosophy, and theology, in verse he read eclectically, marking whatever served his inner needs in the writings of such poets as Arnold, Chaucer, Churchill, Collins, Fergusson, Heine, Moore, Shakespeare, and Thomson. In the early 1860's he was reading Schiller, Madame de Staël, and Emerson; he wrote "admirable" next to Emerson's observation, "Language is made up of images, or tropes, which now, in their secondary use, have long ceased to remind us of their poetic origin. But the poet names the thing because he sees it, or comes one step nearer to it than any other." In addition to the three volumes of lyrics named below, Melville wrote a long narrative poem of a pilgrimage to the Holy Land, *Clarel* (1876). From 1863 to 1883 he lived in New York and worked as a Customs Inspector; after 1857 he wrote no fiction save the story "Billy Budd" (written 1891, published posthumously).

His verse was little noticed. The author of *Moby-Dick* seemed to have disappeared from the earth.

TEXTS: *Moby-Dick* (1851); *Battle-Pieces* (1866, reprinted in facsimile, 1960); *John Marr and Other Sailors* (1888); *Timoleon* (1891); for comment on Melville's verse see Newton Arvin, *Herman Melville* (1950); Richard Chase, *Herman Melville* (1949); and Robert Penn Warren, *Selected Essays* (1946).

FATHER MAPPLE'S HYMN

The ribs and terrors in the whale,
    Arched over me a dismal gloom,
While all God's sun-lit waves rolled by,
    And lift me deepening down to doom.

I saw the opening maw of hell,
    With endless pains and sorrows there;
Which none but they that feel can tell—
    Oh, I was plunging to despair.

In black distress, I called my God,
    When I could scarce believe him mine,
He bowed his ear to my complaints—
    No more the whale did me confine.

With speed he flew to my relief,
    As on a radiant dolphin borne;
Awful, yet bright, as lightning shone
    The face of my Deliverer God.

My song for ever shall record
    That terrible, that joyful hour;
I give the glory to my God,
    His all the mercy and the power.

THE PORTENT

(1859)

Hanging from the beam,
   Slowly swaying (such the law),
Gaunt the shadow on your green,
   Shenandoah!
The cut is on the crown
   (Lo, John Brown),
And the stabs shall heal no more.

Hidden in the cap
   Is the anguish none can draw;
So your future veils its face,
   Shenandoah!
But the streaming beard is shown
   (Weird John Brown),
The meteor of the war.

THE MARCH INTO VIRGINIA

ENDING IN THE FIRST MANASSAS.
(JULY, 1861.)

Did all the lets and bars appear
   To every just or larger end,
Whence should come the trust and cheer?
   Youth must its ignorant impulse lend—
Age finds place in the rear.
   All wars are boyish, and are fought by boys,
The champions and enthusiasts of the state:
   Turbid ardors and vain joys
     Not barrenly abate—
Stimulants to the power mature,
   Preparatives of fate.

Who here forecasteth the event?
What heart but spurns at precedent
And warnings of the wise,
Contemned foreclosures of surprise?
The banners play, the bugles call,
The air is blue and prodigal.
   No berrying party, pleasure-wooed,
No picnic party in the May,
Ever went less loth than they
   Into that leafy neighborhood.
In Bacchic glee they file toward Fate,
Moloch's uninitiate;
Expectancy, and glad surmise
Of battle's unknown mysteries.
All they feel is this; 'tis glory,
A rapture sharp, though transitory,
Yet lasting in belaureled story.
So they gayly go to fight,
Chatting left and laughing right.

But some who this blithe mood present,
   As on in lightsome files they fare,
Shall die experienced ere three days are spent—
   Perish, enlightened by the vollied glare;
Or shame survive, and, like to adamant,
   The throe of Second Manassas share.

A UTILITARIAN VIEW OF THE MONITOR'S FIGHT

Plain be the phrase, yet apt the verse,
   More ponderous than nimble;
For since grimed War here laid aside
His Orient pomp, 'twould ill befit
     Overmuch to ply
   The rhyme's barbaric cymbal.

Hail to victory without the gaud
   Of glory; zeal that needs no fans
Of banners; plain mechanic power
Plied cogently in War now placed—
     Where War belongs—
   Among the trades and artisans.

Yet this was battle, and intense—
   Beyond the strife of fleets heroic;
Deadlier, closer, calm 'mid storm;
No passion; all went on by crank,
     Pivot, and screw,
   And calculations of caloric.

Needless to dwell; the story's known.
   The ringing of those plates on plates
Still ringeth round the world—
The clangor of that blacksmiths' fray.
     The anvil-din
   Resounds this message from the Fates:

War shall yet be, and to the end;
   But war-paint shows the streaks of weather;
War yet shall be, but warriors
Are now but operatives; War's made
     Less grand than Peace,
   And a singe runs through lace and feather.

THE HOUSE-TOP

A NIGHT PIECE
(JULY, 1863.)

No sleep. The sultriness pervades the air
And binds the brain—a dense oppression, such
As tawny tigers feel in matted shades,
Vexing their blood and making apt for ravage.
Beneath the stars the roofy desert spreads
Vacant as Libya. All is hushed near by.

Yet fitfully from far breaks a mixed surf
Of muffled sound, the Atheist roar of riot.
Yonder, where parching Sirius set in drought,
Balefully glares red Arson—there—and there.
The Town is taken by its rats—ship-rats
And rats of the wharves. All civil charms
And priestly spells which late held hearts in awe—
Fear-bound, subjected to a better sway
Than sway of self; these like a dream dissolve,
And man rebounds whole æons back in nature.*
Hail to the low dull rumble, dull and dead,
And ponderous drag that jars the wall.
Wise Draco comes, deep in the midnight roll
Of black artillery; he comes, though late;
In code corroborating Calvin's creed
And cynic tyrannies of honest kings;
He comes, nor parlies; and the Town, redeemed,
Gives thanks devout; nor, being thankful, heeds
The grimy slur on the Republic's faith implied,
Which holds that Man is naturally good,
And—more—is Nature's Roman, never to be scourged.

THE AEOLIAN HARP

AT THE SURF INN

List the harp in window wailing
    Stirred by fitful gales from sea:
Shrieking up in mad crescendo—
    Dying down in plaintive key!

Listen: less a strain ideal
Than Ariel's rendering of the Real.
    What that Real is, let hint
    A picture stamped in memory's mint.

* "I dare not write the horrible and inconceivable atrocities committed," says Froissart, in alluding to the remarkable sedition in France during his time. The like may be hinted of some proceedings of the draft-rioters.—H. M.

Braced well up, with beams aslant,
Betwixt the continents sails the *Phocion,*
For Baltimore bound from Alicant.
Blue breezy skies white fleeces fleck
Over the chill blue white-capped ocean:
From yard-arm comes—"Wreck ho, a wreck!"

Dismasted and adrift,
Longtime a thing forsaken;
Overwashed by every wave
Like the slumbering kraken;
Heedless if the billow roar,
Oblivious of the lull,
Leagues and leagues from shoal or shore,
It swims—a levelled hull:
Bulwarks gone—a shaven wreck,
Nameless and a grass-green deck.
A lumberman: perchance, in hold
Prostrate pines with hemlocks rolled.

It has drifted, waterlogged,
Till by trailing weeds beclogged:
    Drifted, drifted, day by day,
    Pilotless on pathless way.
It has drifted till each plank
Is oozy as the oyster-bank:
    Drifted, drifted, night by night,
    Craft that never shows a light;
Nor ever, to prevent worse knell,
Tolls in fog the warning bell.

From collision never shrinking,
Drive what may through darksome smother;
Saturate, but never sinking,
Fatal only to the *other!*
    Deadlier than the sunken reef
Since still the snare it shifteth,
    Torpid in dumb ambuscade
Waylayingly it drifteth.

O, the sailors—O, the sails!
O, the lost crews never heard of!
Well the harp of Ariel wails
Thought that tongue can tell no word of!

THE MALDIVE SHARK

About the Shark, phlegmatical one,
Pale sot of the Maldive sea,
The sleek little pilot-fish, azure and slim,
How alert in attendance be.
From his saw-pit of mouth, from his charnel of maw
They have nothing of harm to dread,
But liquidly glide on his ghastly flank
Or before his Gorgonian head:
Or lurk in the port of serrated teeth
In white triple tiers of glittering gates,
And there find a haven when peril's abroad,
An asylum in jaws of the Fates!
They are friends; and friendly they guide him to prey,
Yet never partake of the treat—
Eyes and brains to the dotard lethargic and dull,
Pale ravener of horrible meat.

THE BERG

A DREAM

I saw a ship of martial build
(Her standards set, her brave apparel on)
Directed as by madness mere
Against a stolid iceberg steer,
Nor budge it, though the infatuate ship went down.
The impact made huge ice-cubes fall
Sullen, in tons that crashed the deck;
But that one avalanche was all—
No other movement save the foundering wreck.

Along the spurs of ridges pale,
Not any slenderest shaft and frail,
A prism over glass—green gorges lone,
Toppled; nor lace of traceries fine,
Nor pendant drops in grot or mine
Were jarred, when the stunned ship went down.
Nor sole the gulls in cloud that wheeled
Circling one snow-flanked peak afar,
But nearer fowl the floes that skimmed
And crystal beaches, felt no jar.
No thrill transmitted stirred the lock
Of jackstraw needle-ice at base;
Towers undermined by waves—the block
Atilt impending—kept their place.
Seals, dozing sleek on sliddery ledges
Slipt never, when by loftier edges
Through very inertia overthrown,
The impetuous ship in bafflement went down.
Hard Berg (methought), so cold, so vast,
With mortal damps self-overcast;
Exhaling still thy dankish breath—
Adrift dissolving, bound for death;
Though lumpish thou, a lumbering one—
A lumbering lubbard loitering slow,
Impingers rue thee and go down,
Sounding thy precipice below,
Nor stir the slimy slug that sprawls
Along thy dense stolidity of walls.

FROM PEBBLES

Healed of my hurt, I laud the inhuman Sea—
Yea, bless the Angels Four that there convene;
For healed I am ever by their pitiless breath
Distilled in wholesome dew named rosmarine.

MONODY

To have known him, to have loved him
    After loneness long;
And then to be estranged in life,
    And neither in the wrong;
And now for death to set his seal—
    Ease me, a little ease, my song!

By wintry hills his hermit-mound
    The sheeted snow-drifts drape,
And houseless there the snow-bird flits
    Beneath the fir-trees' crape:
Glazed now with ice the cloistral vine
    That hid the shyest grape.

THE RAVAGED VILLA

In shards the sylvan vases lie,
    Their links of dance undone,
And brambles wither by thy brim,
    Choked fountains of the sun!
The spider in the laurel spins,
    The weed exiles the flower;
And, flung to kiln, Apollo's bust
    Makes lime for Mammon's tower.

GOLD IN THE MOUNTAIN

Gold in the mountain
And gold in the glen,
And greed in the heart,
Heaven having no part,
And unsatisfied men.

GREEK ARCHITECTURE

Not magnitude, not lavishness,
But Form—the Site;
Not innovating wilfulness,
But reverence for the Archetype.

ART

In placid hours well-pleased we dream
Of many a brave unbodied scheme.
But form to lend, pulsed life create,
What unlike things must meet and mate:
A flame to melt—a wind to freeze;
Sad patience—joyous energies;
Humility—yet pride and scorn;
Instinct and study; love and hate;
Audacity—reverence. These must mate,
And fuse with Jacob's mystic heart,
To wrestle with the angel—Art.

EMILY DICKINSON

1830–1886

Except for brief trips to Washington, Philadelphia, and Boston, Emily Dickinson lived out her life in the home of her father, who was a prominent attorney and treasurer of Amherst College. For an account of the posthumous publication of her poems see p. 415.

TEXT: *Poems of Emily Dickinson,* edited by Mabel Loomis Todd and Thomas Wentworth Higginson (1890); *Poems by Emily Dickinson,* Second Series (1891), and Third Series (1896), edited by Todd and Higginson; *Further Poems of Emily Dickinson,* edited by Martha Dickinson Bianchi and Alfred Leete Hampson (1932). The chronology of the poems and the assignment of poem numbers follows *The Poems of Emily Dickinson,* 3 vols., edited by Thomas H. Johnson (1955); eight poems, substantively altered by their first editors, are reprinted from this edition in Emily Dickinson's rather erratic punctuation. For biographical and critical studies see George F. Whicher, *This Was a Poet* (1938); Richard Chase, *Emily Dickinson* (1951); Thomas H. Johnson, *Emily Dickinson* (1955); and essays by R. P. Blackmur in *The Expense of Greatness* (1940) and by Allen Tate in *Collected Essays* (1959).

[49]

I never lost as much but twice,
And that was in the sod;
Twice have I stood a beggar
Before the door of God!

Angels, twice descending,
Reimbursed my store.
Burglar, banker, father,
I am poor once more!

[126]

To fight aloud is very brave,
But gallanter, I know,
The charge within the bosom,
The cavalry of woe.

Who win, and nations do not see,
Who fall, and none observe,
Whose dying eyes no country
Regards with patriot love.

We trust, in plumed procession,
For such the angels go,
Rank after rank, with even feet
And uniforms of snow.

[165]

A wounded deer leaps highest,
I've heard the hunter tell;
'Tis but the ecstasy of death,
And then the brake is still.

The smitten rock that gushes,
The trampled steel that springs:
A cheek is always redder
Just where the hectic stings!

Mirth is the mail of anguish,
In which it cautious arm,
Lest anybody spy the blood
And "You're hurt" exclaim!

[201]

Two swimmers wrestled on the spar
Until the morning sun,
When one turned smiling to the land.
O God, the other one!

The stray ships passing spied a face
Upon the waters borne,
With eyes in death still begging raised,
And hands beseeching thrown.

[258]

There's a certain Slant of light,
Winter Afternoons—
That oppresses, like the Heft
Of Cathedral Tunes—

Heavenly Hurt, it gives us—
We can find no scar,
But internal difference,
Where the Meanings, are—

None may teach it—Any—
'Tis the Seal Despair—
An imperial affliction
Sent us of the Air—

When it comes, the Landscape listens—
Shadows—hold their breath—
When it goes, 'tis like the Distance
On the look of Death—

[280]

I felt a Funeral, in my Brain,
And Mourners to and fro
Kept treading—treading—till it seemed
That Sense was breaking through—

And when they all were seated,
A Service, like a Drum—
Kept beating—beating—till I thought
My Mind was going numb—

And then I heard them lift a Box
And creak across my Soul
With those same Boots of Lead, again,
Then Space—began to toll,

As all the Heavens were a Bell,
And Being, but an Ear,
And I, and Silence, some strange Race
Wrecked, solitary, here—

And then a Plank in Reason, broke,
And I dropped down, and down—
And hit a World, at every plunge,
And Finished knowing—then—

[303]

The soul selects her own society,
Then shuts the door;
On her divine majority
Obtrude no more.

Unmoved, she notes the chariot's pausing
At her low gate;
Unmoved, an emperor is kneeling
Upon her mat.

I've known her from an ample nation
Choose one;
Then close the valves of her attention
Like stone.

[341]

After great pain, a formal feeling comes—
The Nerves sit ceremonious, like Tombs—
The stiff Heart questions was it He, that bore,
And Yesterday, or Centuries before?

The Feet, mechanical, go round—
Of Ground, or Air, or Ought—
A Wooden way
Regardless grown,
A Quartz contentment, like a stone—

This is the Hour of Lead—
Remembered, if outlived,
As Freezing persons, recollect the Snow—
First—Chill—then Stupor—then the letting go—

[435]

Much madness is divinest sense
To a discerning eye;
Much sense the starkest madness.
'Tis the majority
In this, as all, prevails.
Assent, and you are sane;
Demur,—you're straightway dangerous,
And handled with a chain.

[436]

The wind tapped like a tired man,
And like a host, "Come in,"
I boldly answered; entered then
My residence within

A rapid, footless guest,
To offer whom a chair
Were as impossible as hand
A sofa to the air.

No bone had he to bind him,
His speech was like the push
Of numerous humming-birds at once
From a superior bush.

His countenance a billow,
His fingers, if he pass,
Let go a music, as of tunes
Blown tremulous in glass.

He visited, still flitting;
Then, like a timid man,
Again he tapped—'twas flurriedly—
And I became alone.

[465]

I heard a Fly buzz—when I died—
The Stillness in the Room
Was like the Stillness in the Air—
Between the Heaves of Storm—

The Eyes around—had wrung them dry—
And Breaths were gathering firm
For that last Onset—when the King
Be witnessed—in the Room—

I willed my Keepsakes—Signed away
What portion of me be
Assignable—and then it was
There interposed a Fly—

With Blue—uncertain stumbling Buzz—
Between the light—and me—
And then the Windows failed—and then
I could not see to see—

[520]

I started early, took my dog,
And visited the sea;
The mermaids in the basement
Came out to look at me,

And frigates in the upper floor
Extended hempen hands,
Presuming me to be a mouse
Aground, upon the sands.

But no man moved me till the tide
Went past my simple shoe,
And past my apron and my belt,
And past my bodice too,

And made as he would eat me up
As wholly as a dew
Upon a dandelion's sleeve—
And then I started too.

And he—he followed close behind;
I felt his silver heel
Upon my ankle,—then my shoes
Would overflow with pearl.

Until we met the solid town,
No man he seemed to know;
And bowing with a mighty look
At me, the sea withdrew.

[585]

I like to see it lap the miles,
And lick the valleys up,
And stop to feed itself at tanks;
And then, prodigious, step

Around a pile of mountains,
And, supercilious, peer
In shanties by the sides of roads;
And then a quarry pare

To fit its sides, and crawl between,
Complaining all the while
In horrid, hooting stanza;
Then chase itself down hill

And neigh like Boanerges;
Then, punctual as a star,
Stop—docile and omnipotent—
At its own stable door.

[632]

The brain is wider than the sky,
    For, put them side by side,
The one the other will include
    With ease, and you beside.

The brain is deeper than the sea,
  For, hold them, blue to blue,
The one the other will absorb
  As sponges, buckets do.

The brain is just the weight of God,
  For, lift them, pound for pound,
And they will differ, if they do,
  As syllable from sound.

[650]

Pain—has an Element of Blank—
It cannot recollect
When it begun—or if there were
A time when it was not—

It has no Future—but itself—
Its Infinite contain
Its Past—enlightened to perceive
New Periods—of Pain.

[657]

I dwell in Possibility
A fairer house than Prose,
More numerous of windows,
Superior of doors.

Of chambers, as the cedars—
Impregnable of eye;
And for an everlasting roof
The gables of the sky.

Of visitors—the fairest—
For occupation—this—
The spreading wide my narrow hands
To gather Paradise.

[686]

> They say that "time assuages"—
>   Time never did assuage;
> An actual suffering strengthens,
>   As sinews do, with age.
>
> Time is a test of trouble,
>   But not a remedy.
> If such it prove, it prove too
>   There was no malady.

[712]

> Because I could not stop for Death—
> He kindly stopped for me—
> The Carriage held but just Ourselves—
> And Immortality.
>
> We slowly drove—He knew no haste
> And I had put away
> My labor and my leisure too,
> For His Civility—
>
> We passed the School, where Children strove
> At Recess—in the Ring—
> We passed the Fields of Gazing Grain—
> We passed the Setting Sun—
>
> Or rather—He passed Us—
> The Dews grew quivering and chill—
> For only Gossamer, my Gown—
> My Tippet—only Tulle—

We paused before a House that seemed
A Swelling of the Ground—
The Roof was scarcely visible—
The Cornice—in the Ground—

Since then—'tis Centuries—and yet
Feels shorter than the Day
I first surmised the Horses Heads
Were toward Eternity—

[986]

A narrow fellow in the grass
Occasionally rides;
You may have met him,—did you not?
His notice sudden is.

The grass divides as with a comb,
A spotted shaft is seen;
And then it closes at your feet
And opens further on.

He likes a boggy acre,
A floor too cool for corn.
Yet when a child, and barefoot,
I more than once, at morn,

Have passed, I thought, a whip-lash
Unbraiding in the sun,—
When, stooping to secure it,
It wrinkled, and was gone.

Several of nature's people
I know, and they know me;
I feel for them a transport
Of cordiality;

But never meet this fellow,
Attended or alone,
Without a tighter breathing,
And zero at the bone.

[1068]

Further in Summer than the Birds
Pathetic from the Grass
A minor Nation celebrates
Its unobtrusive Mass.

No Ordinance be seen
So gradual the Grace
A pensive Custom it becomes
Enlarging Loneliness.

Antiquest felt at Noon
When August burning low
Arise this spectral Canticle
Repose to typify.

Remit as yet no Grace
No Furrow on the Glow
Yet a Druidic Difference
Enhances Nature now.

[1075]

The sky is low, the clouds are mean,
A travelling flake of snow
Across a barn or through a rut
Debates if it will go.

A narrow wind complains all day
How some one treated him;
Nature, like us, is sometimes caught
Without her diadem.

[1304]

Not with a Club, the Heart is broken
Nor with a Stone—
A Whip so small you could not see it
I've known

To lash the Magic Creature
Till it fell,
Yet that Whip's Name
Too noble then to tell.

Magnanimous as Bird
By Boy descried—
Singing unto the Stone
Of which it died—

Shame need not crouch
In such an Earth as Ours—
Shame—stand erect—
The Universe is yours.

[1393]

Lay this laurel on the one
Too intrinsic for renown.
Laurel! veil your deathless tree—
Him you chasten, that is he!

[1459]

Belshazzar had a letter,—
He never had but one;
Belshazzar's correspondent
Concluded and begun

In that immortal copy
The conscience of us all
Can read without its glasses
On revelation's wall.

[1670]

In winter, in my room,
I came upon a worm,
Pink, lank, and warm.
But as he was a worm
And worms presume,
Not quite with him at home—
Secured him with a string
To something neighboring,
And went along.

A trifle afterward
A thing occurred,
I'd not believe it if I heard—
But state with creeping blood;
A snake, with mottles rare,
Surveyed my chamber floor,
In feature as the worm before,
But ringed with power.
The very string
With which I tied him, too,
When he was mean and new,
That string was there.

I shrank—'How fair you are!'
Propitiation's claw—
'Afraid,' he hissed,
'Of me?'
'No cordiality?'
He fathomed me.

Then, to a rhythm slim
Secreted in his form,
As patterns swim,
Projected him.

That time I flew,
Both eyes his way,
Lest he pursue—
Nor ever ceased to run,
Till, in a distant town,
Towns on from mine—
I set me down;
This was a dream.

[1732]

My life closed twice before its close;
    It yet remains to see
If immortality unveil
    A third event to me,

So huge, so hopeless to conceive,
    As these that twice befell.
Parting is all we know of heaven,
    And all we need of hell.

[1740]

Sweet is the swamp with its secrets,
    Until we meet a snake;
'T is then we sigh for houses,
    And our departure take
At that enthralling gallop
    That only childhood knows.
A snake is summer's treason,
    And guile is where it goes.

[1755]

> To make a prairie it takes a clover and one bee,
> One clover, and a bee,
> And revery.
> The revery alone will do,
> If bees are few.

[1760]

> Elysium is as far as to
> The very nearest room,
> If in that room a friend await
> Felicity or doom.
>
> What fortitude the soul contains,
> That it can so endure
> The accent of a coming foot,
> The opening of a door!

STEPHEN CRANE

1871–1900

"I understand that a man is born into this world with his own pair of eyes, and that he is not at all responsible for his vision—he is merely responsible for his quality of personal honesty. To keep close to this personal honesty is my supreme ambition." Holding such views, Crane went further than any writer of his time in repudiating the genteel diction and evasive idealism in the verse of Victorian America. Although his novel *The Red Badge of Courage* made him famous, he considered *The Black Riders and Other Lines* "a more ambitious effort." Crane published *War is Kind* in 1899; about two dozen further poems have been posthumously printed. His antiheroic statement, ironic paradox, and a style determinedly contrary to established models made his "lines" seem willfully eccentric. Later critics found his work similar to that of Laforgue, Corbière, and other symbolists. But Crane wrote in ignorance of French poetics. He made similar repudiations, and held assumptions similar to theirs of the autonomy of the literary work and the relation of form and meaning. These conceptions more probably reached him through his desultory reading in standard American authors —Hawthorne, perhaps Whitman, certainly Emerson. He was introduced to Emily Dickinson's work in 1893 by William Dean Howells, who read her poems aloud when Crane first called on him. (See Howells' review of *Poems of Emily Dickinson*, p. 426; her poem No. 201 was doubtless a starting-point for Crane's "A man adrift on a slim spar.") Crane, born within three years of Robinson and Frost, came nearer than either to anticipating the dominant twentieth-century poetic movement. But at twenty-nine, in the first year of the new century, he was dead.

TEXTS: *The Black Riders* (1895); *War is Kind* (1899); *Collected Poems*, edited by Wilson Follett (1930); *The Poetry of Stephen Crane* by Daniel G. Hoffman (1957).

FROM THE BLACK RIDERS

I

Black riders came from the sea.
There was clash and clang of spear and shield,
And clash and clash of hoof and heel,
Wild shouts and the wave of hair
In the rush upon the wind:
Thus the ride of Sin.

III

In the desert
I saw a creature, naked, bestial,
Who, squatting upon the ground,
Held his heart in his hands,
And ate of it.
I said, "Is it good, friend?"
"It is bitter—bitter," he answered;
"But I like it
Because it is bitter,
And because it is my heart."

VI

God fashioned the ship of the world carefully.
With the infinite skill of an All-Master
Made He the hull and the sails,
Held He the rudder
Ready for adjustment.
Erect stood He, scanning His work proudly.
Then—at fateful time—a wrong called,
And God turned, heeding.
Lo, the ship, at this opportunity, slipped slyly,
Making cunning noiseless travel down the ways.
So that, for ever rudderless, it went upon the seas
Going ridiculous voyages,
Making quaint progress,
Turning as with serious purpose
Before stupid winds.
And there were many in the sky
Who laughed at this thing.

XXVII

A youth in apparel that glittered
Went to walk in a grim forest.
There he met an assassin
Attired in garb of old days;
He, scowling through the thickets,
And dagger poised quivering,
Rushed upon the youth.
"Sir," said this latter,
"I am enchanted, believe me,
To die, thus,
In this medieval fashion,
According to the best legends.
Ah, what joy!"
Then took he the wound, smiling,
And died, content.

LIV

"It was wrong to do this," said the angel.
"You should live like a flower,
Holding malice like a puppy,
Waging war like a lambkin."

"Not so," quoth the man
Who had no fear of spirits:
"It is only wrong for angels
Who can live like the flowers,
Holding malice like the puppies,
Waging war like the lambkins."

LVI

A man feared that he might find an assassin;
Another that he might find a victim.
One was more wise than the other.

FROM WAR IS KIND

I

Do not weep, maiden, for war is kind.
Because your lover threw wild hands toward the sky
And the affrighted steed ran on alone,
Do not weep,
War is kind.

Hoarse, booming drums of the regiment,
Little souls who thirst for fight,
These men were born to drill and die.
The unexplained glory flies above them,
Great is the battle god, great, and his kingdom—
A field where a thousand corpses lie.

Do not weep, babe, for war is kind.
Because your father tumbled in the yellow trenches,
Raged at his breast, gulped and died,
Do not weep,
War is kind.

Swift blazing flag of the regiment,
Eagle with crest of red and gold,
These men were born to drill and die.
Point for them the virtue of slaughter,
Make plain to them the excellence of killing
And a field where a thousand corpses lie.

Mother whose heart hung humble as a button
On the bright splendid shroud of your son,
Do not weep.
War is kind.

VIII

Fast rode the knight
With spurs, hot and reeking.
Ever waving an eager sword,
"To save my lady!"
Fast rode the knight,
And leaped from saddle to war.
Men of steel flickered and gleamed
Like riot of silver lights,
And the gold of the knight's good banner
Still waved on a castle wall.

❋   ❋   ❋   ❋   ❋

A horse,
Blowing, staggering, bloody thing,
Forgotten at foot of castle wall.
A horse
Dead at foot of castle wall.

XII

A newspaper is a collection of half-injustices
Which, bawled by boys from mile to mile,
Spreads its curious opinion
To a million merciful and sneering men,
While families cuddle the joys of the fireside
When spurred by tale of dire lone agony.
A newspaper is a court
Where every one is kindly and unfairly tried
By a squalor of honest men.
A newspaper is a market
Where wisdom sells its freedom
And melons are crowned by the crowd.
A newspaper is a game
Where his error scores the player victory
While another's skill wins death.

A newspaper is a symbol;
It is feckless life's chronicle,
A collection of loud tales
Concentrating eternal stupidities,
That in remote ages lived unhaltered,
Roaming through a fenceless world.

XIII

The wayfarer,
Perceiving the pathway to truth,
Was struck with astonishment.
It was thickly grown with weeds.
"Ha," he said,
"I see that none has passed here
In a long time."
Later he saw that each weed
Was a singular knife.
"Well," he mumbled at last,
"Doubtless there are other roads."

XXI

A man said to the universe:
"Sir, I exist!"
"However," replied the universe,
"The fact has not created in me
A sense of obligation."

A MAN ADRIFT ON A SLIM SPAR

A man adrift on a slim spar
A horizon smaller than the rim of a bottle
Tented waves rearing lashy dark points
The near whine of froth in circles.

God is cold.

The incessant raise and swing of the sea
And growl after growl of crest
The sinkings, green, seething, endless
The upheaval half-completed.

God is cold.

The seas are in the hollow of The Hand;
Oceans may be turned to a spray
Raining down through the stars
Because of a gesture of pity toward a babe,
Oceans may become grey ashes,
Die with a long moan and a roar
Amid the tumult of the fishes
And the cries of the ships,
Because The Hand beckons the mice.

A horizon smaller than a dommed assassin's cap,
Inky, surging tumults
A reeling, drunken sky and no sky
A pale hand sliding from a polished spar.

God is cold.

The puff of a coat imprisoning air:
A face kissing the water-death
A weary slow sway of a lost hand
And the sea, the moving sea.

God is cold.

FROM BOTTLES AND BOTTLES AND BOTTLES

Bottles and bottles and bottles
In a merry den
And the wan smiles of women
Untruthing license and joy.
Countless lights
Making oblique and confusing multiplication
In mirrors
And the light returns again to the faces.

*   *   *   *

A cellar, and a pale death-child,
A woman
Ministering commonly, degradedly,
Without manners,
A murmur and a silence
Or silence and a murmur
And then a finished silence
The moon beats practically upon the cheap bed.

THE PATENT OF A LORD

The patent of a lord
And the bangle of a bandit
Make argument
Which God solves
Only after lighting more candles.

GEORGE SANTAYANA

1863–1952

Santayana was born in Spain but came early to the United States. After graduation from Harvard he taught philosophy there for many years. Among his major writings are *The Sense of Beauty* (1896), *The Life of Reason* (1905), *Three Philosophical Poets* (1910), *Realms of Being* (1927–1930), and a novel, *The Last Puritan* (1935). Most of his poetry was written between 1885 and 1900. Of his poems he has written, "If their prosody is worn and traditional, like a liturgy, it is because they represent the initiation of a mind into a world older and larger than itself . . . Here is the uncertain hand of an apprentice, but of an apprentice in a great school . . . As to the subject of these poems, it is simply my philosophy in the making." Santayana's verse has been criticized for its Platonism, for the conventionality of its language, and for the detachment of its images from experience; yet these are the faults of the period, and in several of the Petrarchan sonnets and Sapphic odes there is a union of concrete observation, felicity of language, and intellectual rigor which claims for them a lasting place. Santayana's aesthetic ideas are expressed in an essay reprinted in this volume (see p. 432).

TEXTS: *Sonnets and Other Verses* (1894), enlarged edition (1896); *The Hermit of Carmel* (1901); see also Santayana's preface to *Poems* (1923). For discussion of Santayana as a poet see G. W. Howgate, *George Santayana* (1938); and Philip Blair Rice's essay "The Philosopher as Poet and Critic" in *The Philosophy of George Santayana*, edited by P. A. Schilpp (1940).

FROM SONNETS, 1883–1893

III

O world, thou choosest not the better part!
It is not wisdom to be only wise,
And on the inward vision of the eyes,
But it is wisdom to believe the heart.
Columbus found a world, and had no chart,
Save one that faith deciphered in the skies;
To trust the soul's invincible surmise
Was all his science and his only art.
Our knowledge is a torch of smoky pine
That lights the pathway but one step ahead
Across a void of mystery and dread.
Bid, then, the tender light of faith to shine
By which alone the mortal heart is led
Unto the thinking of the thought divine.

V

Dreamt I to-day the dream of yesternight,
Sleep ever feigning one evolving theme,—
Of my two lives which should I call the dream?
Which action vanity? which vision sight?
Some greater waking must pronounce aright,
If aught abideth of the things that seem,
And with both currents swell the flooded stream
Into an ocean infinite of light.
Even such a dream I dream, and know full well
My waking passeth like a midnight spell,
But know not if my dreaming breaketh through
Into the deeps of heaven and of hell.
I know but this of all I would I knew:
Truth is a dream, unless my dream is true.

ODES

II

My heart rebels against my generation,
That talks of freedom and is slave to riches,
And, toiling 'neath each day's ignoble burden,
    Boasts of the morrow.

No space for noonday rest or midnight watches,
No purest joy of breathing under heaven!
Wretched themselves, they heap, to make them
    happy,
    Many possessions.

But thou, O silent Mother, wise, immortal,
To whom our toil is laughter,—take, divine one,
This vanity away, and to thy lover
    Give what is needful:—

A staunch heart, nobly calm, averse to evil,
The windy sky for breath, the sea, the mountain,
A well-born, gentle friend, his spirit's brother,
    Ever beside him.

What would you gain, ye seekers, with your striving,
Or what vast Babel raise you on your shoulders?
You multiply distresses, and your children
    Surely will curse you.

O leave them rather friendlier gods, and fairer
Orchards and temples, and a freer bosom!
What better comfort have we, or what other
    Profit in living,

Than to feel, sobered by the truth of Nature,
Awhile upon her bounty and her beauty,
And hand her torch of gladness to the ages
     Following after?

She hath not made us, like her other children,
Merely for peopling of her spacious kingdoms,
Beasts of the wild, or insects of the summer,
     Breeding and dying,

But also that we might, half knowing, worship
The deathless beauty of her guiding vision,
And learn to love, in all things mortal, only
     What is eternal.

V

Of thee the Northman by his beachèd galley
Dreamt, as he watched the never-setting Ursa
And longed for summer and thy light, O sacred
     Mediterranean.

Unseen he loved thee; for the heart within him
Knew earth had gardens where he might be blessed,
Putting away long dreams and aimless, barbarous
     Hunger for battle.

The foretaste of thy languors thawed his bosom;
A great need drove him to thy caverned islands
From the gray, endless reaches of the outer
     Desert of ocean.

He saw thy pillars, saw thy sudden mountains
Wrinkled and stark, and in their crooked gorges,
'Neath peeping pine and cypress, guessed the torrent
     Smothered in flowers.

Thine incense to the sun, thy gathered vapours,
He saw suspended on the flanks of Taurus,
Or veiling the snowed bosom of the virgin
  Sister of Atlas.

He saw the luminous top of wide Olympus,
Fit for the happy gods; he saw the pilgrim
River, with rains of Ethiopia flooding
  Populous Egypt.

And having seen, he loved thee. His racked spirit,
By thy breath tempered and the light that clothes
  thee,
Forgot the monstrous gods, and made of Nature
  Mistress and mother.

The more should I, O fatal sea, before thee
Of alien words make echoes to thy music;
For I was born where first the rills of Tagus
  Turn to the westward,

And wandering long, alas! have need of drinking
Deep of the patience of thy perfect sadness,
O thou that constant through the change of ages,
  Beautiful ever,

Never wast wholly young and void of sorrows,
Nor ever canst be old, while yet the morning
Kindles thy ripples, or the golden evening
  Dyes thee in purple.

Thee, willing to be tamed but still untamable,
The Roman called his own until he perished,
As now the busy English hover o'er thee,
  Stalwart and noble;

But all is naught to thee, while no harsh winter
Congeals thy fountains, and the blown Sahara
Chokes not with dreadful sand thy deep and placid
  Rock-guarded havens.

Thou carest not what men may tread thy margin;
Nor I, while from some heather-scented headland
I may behold thy beauty, the eternal
    Solace of mortals.

CAPE COD

The low sandy beach and the thin scrub pine,
The wide reach of bay and the long sky line,—
    O, I am far from home!

The salt, salt smell of the thick sea air,
And the smooth round stones that the ebbtides
    wear,—
    When will the good ship come?

The wretched stumps all charred and burned,
And the deep soft rut where the cartwheel turned,—
    Why is the world so old?

The lapping wave, and the broad gray sky
Where the cawing crows and the slow gulls fly,—
    Where are the dead untold?

The thin slant willows by the flooded bog,
The huge stranded hulks and the floating log,—
    Sorrow with life began!

And among the dark pines, and along the flat shore,
O the wind, and the wind, for evermore!
    What will become of man?

FROM SONNETS, 1895

XXV

As in the midst of battle there is room
For thoughts of love, and in foul sin for mirth;
As gossips whisper of a trinket's worth
Spied by the death-bed's flickering candle-gloom;
As in the crevices of Cæsar's tomb
The sweet herbs flourish on a little earth:
So in this great disaster of our birth
We can be happy, and forget our doom.
For morning, with a ray of tenderest joy
Gilding the iron heaven, hides the truth,
And evening gently woos us to employ
Our grief in idle catches. Such is youth;
Till from that summer's trance we wake, to find
Despair before us, vanity behind.

EDWIN ARLINGTON
ROBINSON

1869–1935

A descendant of Anne Bradstreet's sister, Robinson was born at Head Tide, Maine, and grew up in Gardiner, the "Tilbury Town" of his poems. Poverty and family illness kept Robinson from going to college until he had to spend a year in Boston for treatment of an injury and enrolled as a special student at Harvard. His early enthusiasms were for Emerson's essays, Kipling's ballads, and Crabbe's directness; he was influenced by Browning's treatment of character and probably by the versification of W. M. Praed. His first book, *The Torrent and the Night Before* (1896), was published at his own expense; a friend paid for *Children of the Night* (1897). When *Captain Craig* appeared in 1902 Robinson, as yet unheralded and unread, was working in the New York subway. Then President Theodore Roosevelt became his advocate, persuaded Scribner's to re-issue *Children of the Night*, reviewed the book in *The Outlook* (1905), and secured the poet a job —like Melville's before him—in the New York Customhouse, where Robinson worked for five years. After *The Town Down the River* (1910) Robinson tried to write plays; then he turned to psychological novels in verse. In 1921 his *Collected Poems* appeared and won a Pulitzer Prize, but not until *Tristram* (1927), the third of his Arthurian poems, did his work reach a popular audience and bring him financial independence. For some years a group of twelve guarantors had given $1200 a year to Robinson through a bank; now their help was no longer needed. At his death in 1935 he had published twenty-seven books. In a preface to *King Jasper*, Robinson's last book, his friend Robert Frost wrote that "Robinson stayed content with the old-fashioned way to be new."

TEXT: *Collected Poems* (1937); see also Herman Hagedorn, *Edwin Arlington Robinson: A Biography* (1938); Yvor Winters, *Edwin Arlington Robinson* (1948).

SONNET

Oh for a poet—for a beacon bright
To rift this changless glimmer of dead gray;
To spirit back the Muses, long astray,
And flush Parnassus with a newer light;
To put these little sonnet-men to flight
Who fashion, in a shrewd, mechanic way,
Songs without souls, that flicker for a day,
To vanish in irrevocable night.

What does it mean, this barren age of ours?
Here are the men, the women, and the flowers,
The seasons, and the sunset, as before.
What does it mean? Shall not one bard arise
To wrench one banner from the western skies,
And mark it with his name forevermore?

CREDO

I cannot find my way: there is no star
In all the shrouded heavens anywhere;
And there is not a whisper in the air
Of any living voice but one so far
That I can hear it only as a bar
Of lost, imperial music, played when fair
And angel fingers wove, and unaware,
Dead leaves to garlands where no roses are.

No, there is not a glimmer, nor a call,
For one that welcomes, welcomes when he fears,
The black and awful chaos of the night;
For through it all,—above, beyond it all,—
I know the far-sent message of the years,
I feel the coming glory of the Light!

LUKE HAVERGAL

Go to the western gate, Luke Havergal,—
There where the vines cling crimson on the wall,—
And in the twilight wait for what will come.
The wind will moan, the leaves will whisper some—
Whisper of her, and strike you as they fall;
But go, and if you trust her she will call.
Go to the western gate, Luke Havergal—
Luke Havergal.

No, there is not a dawn in eastern skies
To rift the fiery night that's in your eyes;
But there, where western glooms are gathering,
The dark will end the dark, if anything:
God slays Himself with every leaf that flies,
And hell is more than half of paradise.
No, there is not a dawn in eastern skies—
In eastern skies.

Out of a grave I come to tell you this,—
Out of a grave I come to quench the kiss
That flames upon your forehead with a glow
That blinds you to the way that you must go.
Yes, there is yet one way to where she is,—
Bitter, but one that faith can never miss.
Out of a grave I come to tell you this—
To tell you this.

There is the western gate, Luke Havergal,
There are the crimson leaves upon the wall.
Go,—for the winds are tearing them away,—
Nor think to riddle the dead words they say,
Nor any more to feel them as they fall;
But go! and if you trust her she will call.
There is the western gate, Luke Havergal—
Luke Havergal.

JOHN EVERELDOWN

"Where are you going to-night, to-night,—
    Where are you going, John Evereldown?
There's never the sign of a star in sight,
    Nor a lamp that's nearer than Tilbury Town.
Why do you stare as a dead man might?
Where are you pointing away from the light?
And where are you going to-night, to-night,—
    Where are you going, John Evereldown?"

"Right through the forest, where none can see,
    There's where I'm going, to Tilbury Town.
The men are asleep,—or awake, may be,—
    But the women are calling John Evereldown.
Ever and ever they call for me,
And while they call can a man be free?
So right through the forest, where none can see,
    There's where I'm going, to Tilbury Town."

"But why are you going so late, so late,—
    Why are you going, John Evereldown?
Though the road be smooth and the path be straight,
    There are two long leagues to Tilbury Town.
Come in by the fire, old man, and wait!
Why do you chatter out there by the gate?
And why are you going so late, so late,—
    Why are you going, John Evereldown?"

"I follow the women wherever they call,—
    That's why I'm going to Tilbury Town.
God knows if I pray to be done with it all,
    But God is no friend to John Evereldown.
So the clouds may come and the rain may fall,
The shadows may creep and the dead men crawl,—
But I follow the women wherever they call,
    And that's why I'm going to Tilbury Town."

WALT WHITMAN

The master-songs are ended, and the man
That sang them is a name. And so is God
A name; and so is love, and life, and death,
And everything. But we, who are too blind
To read what we have written, or what faith
Has written for us, do not understand:
We only blink, and wonder.

Last night it was the song that was the man,
But now it is the man that is the song.
We do not hear him very much to-day:
His piercing and eternal cadence rings
Too pure for us—too powerfully pure,
Too lovingly triumphant, and too large;
But there are some that hear him, and they know
That he shall sing to-morrow for all men,
And that all time shall listen.

The master-songs are ended? Rather say
No songs are ended that are ever sung,
And that no names are dead names. When we write
Men's letters on proud marble or on sand,
We write them there forever.

RICHARD CORY

Whenever Richard Cory went down town,
We people on the pavement looked at him:
He was a gentleman from sole to crown,
Clean favored, and imperially slim.

And he was always quietly arrayed,
And he was always human when he talked;
But still he fluttered pulses when he said,
"Good-morning," and he glittered when he walked.

And he was rich,—yes, richer than a king,—
And admirably schooled in every grace:
In fine, we thought that he was everything
To make us wish that we were in his place.

So on we worked, and waited for the light,
And went without the meat, and cursed the bread;
And Richard Cory, one calm summer night,
Went home and put a bullet through his head.

CLIFF KLINGENHAGEN

Cliff Klingenhagen had me in to dine
With him one day; and after soup and meat,
And all the other things there were to eat,
Cliff took two glasses and filled one with wine
And one with wormwood. Then, without a sign
For me to choose at all, he took the draught
Of bitterness himself, and lightly quaffed
It off, and said the other one was mine.

And when I asked him what the deuce he meant
By doing that, he only looked at me
And grinned, and said it was a way of his.
And though I know the fellow, I have spent
Long time a-wondering when I shall be
As happy as Cliff Klingenhagen is.

REUBEN BRIGHT

Because he was a butcher and thereby
Did earn an honest living (and did right),
I would not have you think that Reuben Bright
Was any more a brute than you or I;
For when they told him that his wife must die,
He stared at them, and shook with grief and fright,
And cried like a great baby half that night,
And made the women cry to see him cry.

And after she was dead, and he had paid
The singers and the sexton and the rest,
He packed a lot of things that she had made
Most mournfully away in an old chest
Of hers, and put some chopped-up cedar boughs
In with them, and tore down the slaughter-house.

HOW ANNANDALE WENT OUT

'They called it Annandale—and I was there
To flourish, to find words, and to attend:
Liar, physician, hypocrite, and friend,
I watched him; and the sight was not so fair
As one or two that I have seen elsewhere:
An apparatus not for me to mend—
A wreck, with hell between him and the end,
Remained of Annandale; and I was there.

'I knew the ruin as I knew the man;
So put the two together, if you can.
Remembering the worst you know of me.
Now view yourself as I was, on the spot—
With a slight kind of engine. Do you see?
Like this . . . You wouldn't hang me? I thought not.'

MINIVER CHEEVY

Miniver Cheevy, child of scorn,
    Grew lean while he assailed the seasons;
He wept that he was ever born,
    And he had reasons.

Miniver loved the days of old
    When swords were bright and steeds were prancing;
The vision of a warrior bold
    Would set him dancing.

Miniver sighed for what was not,
    And dreamed, and rested from his labors;
He dreamed of Thebes and Camelot,
    And Priam's neighbors.

Miniver mourned the ripe renown
    That made so many a name so fragrant;
He mourned Romance, now on the town,
    And Art, a vagrant.

Miniver loved the Medici,
    Albeit he had never seen one;
He would have sinned incessantly
    Could he have been one.

Miniver cursed the commonplace
    And eyed a khaki suit with loathing;
He missed the mediaeval grace
    Of iron clothing.

Miniver scorned the gold he sought,
    But sore annoyed was he without it;
Miniver thought, and thought, and thought,
    And thought about it.

Miniver Cheevy, born too late,
    Scratched his head and kept on thinking;
Miniver coughed, and called it fate,
    And kept on drinking.

FOR A DEAD LADY

No more with overflowing light
Shall fill the eyes that now are faded,
Nor shall another's fringe with night
Their woman-hidden world as they did.
No more shall quiver down the days
The flowing wonder of her ways,
Whereof no language may requite
The shifting and the many-shaded.

The grace, divine, definitive,
Clings only as a faint forestalling;
The laugh that love could not forgive
Is hushed, and answers to no calling;
The forehead and the little ears
Have gone where Saturn keeps the years;
The breast where roses could not live
Has done with rising and with falling.

The beauty, shattered by the laws
That have creation in their keeping,
No longer trembles at applause,
Or over children that are sleeping;
And we who delve in beauty's lore
Know all that we have known before
Of what inexorable cause
Makes Time so vicious in his reaping.

ROBERT FROST

Born 1874

Although Frost is famous as the author of *North of Boston* and *New Hampshire,* he was born in San Francisco and was named for Confederate General Robert E. Lee. It is true that his father was an anti-New England New Englander, whose will (he died when Frost was eleven) specified that his remains be sent home to New England. Thus Robert Frost grew up in New Hampshire after all; his coming back East so late in childhood may have made him especially aware of the distinctive speech, character, and landscape of the region. He grew up without apparent direction, dropping out of Dartmouth after a year. He married in 1895 and attended Harvard for two more years but again left without taking a degree. He tried for a decade to run a poultry farm, teaching school intermittently. He was writing poems based on speech and directness instead of the then-prevalent diffuseness and melody; his prosaic surface did not appeal to magazines, but like his "Oven Bird," Frost knew "in singing not to sing." In 1912 Frost went to England with his family, and at once found a publisher. The appearance of *A Boy's Will* and *North of Boston* (1913, 1914) coincided with a shift in taste and the emergence of the poetry of the expatriates Pound and Eliot. Returning to America the following year, Frost found himself famous. He has won the Pulitzer Prize four times and has received honorary degrees from over forty American institutions and from Oxford and Cambridge. The ten books of his verse published between 1913 and 1947 were collected in *The Complete Poems of Robert Frost* (1949). Frost was appointed Consultant in Poetry to the Library of Congress by President Eisenhower; President Kennedy invited him to take part in the inauguration ceremony in 1961.

TEXT: *Complete Poems* (1949). See also: Randall Jarrell, *Poetry and the Age* (1953); Lawrance Thompson, *Robert Frost* (1959); John F. Lynen, *The Pastoral Art of Robert Frost* (1960).

AFTER APPLE-PICKING

My long two-pointed ladder's sticking through a tree
Toward heaven still,
And there's a barrel that I didn't fill
Beside it, and there may be two or three
Apples I didn't pick upon some bough.
But I am done with apple-picking now.
Essence of winter sleep is on the night,
The scent of apples: I am drowsing off.
I cannot rub the strangeness from my sight
I got from looking through a pane of glass
I skimmed this morning from the drinking trough
And held against the world of hoary grass.
It melted, and I let it fall and break.
But I was well
Upon my way to sleep before it fell,
And I could tell
What form my dreaming was about to take.
Magnified apples appear and disappear.
Stem end and blossom end,
And every fleck of russet showing clear.
My instep arch not only keeps the ache,
It keeps the pressure of a ladder-round.
I feel the ladder sway as the boughs bend.
And I keep hearing from the cellar bin
The rumbling sound
Of load on load of apples coming in.
For I have had too much
Of apple-picking: I am overtired
Of the great harvest I myself desired.

There were ten thousand thousand fruit to touch,
Cherish in hand, lift down, and not let fall.
For all
That struck the earth,
No matter if not bruised or spiked with stubble,
Went surely to the cider-apple heap
As of no worth.
One can see what will trouble
This sleep of mine, whatever sleep it is.
Were he not gone,
The woodchuck could say whether it's like his
Long sleep, as I describe its coming on,
Or just some human sleep.

THE OVEN BIRD

There is a singer everyone has heard,
Loud, a mid-summer and a mid-wood bird,
Who makes the solid tree trunks sound again.
He says that leaves are old and that for flowers
Mid-summer is to spring as one to ten.
He says the early petal-fall is past
When pear and cherry bloom went down in showers
On sunny days a moment overcast;
And comes that other fall we name the fall.
He says the highway dust is over all.
The bird would cease and be as other birds
But that he knows in singing not to sing.
The question that he frames in all but words
Is what to make of a diminished thing.

'OUT, OUT—'

The buzz-saw snarled and rattled in the yard
And made dust and dropped stove-length sticks of
    wood,
Sweet-scented stuff when the breeze drew across it.
And from there those that lifted eyes could count
Five mountain ranges one behind the other
Under the sunset far into Vermont.
And the saw snarled and rattled, snarled and rattled,
As it ran light, or had to bear a load.
And nothing happened: day was all but done.
Call it a day, I wish they might have said
To please the boy by giving him the half hour
That a boy counts so much when saved from work.
His sister stood beside them in her apron
To tell them 'Supper.' At the word, the saw,
As if to prove saws knew what supper meant,
Leaped out at the boy's hand, or seemed to leap—
He must have given the hand. However it was,
Neither refused the meeting. But the hand!
The boy's first outcry was a rueful laugh,
As he swung toward them holding up the hand
Half in appeal, but half as if to keep
The life from spilling. Then the boy saw all—
Since he was old enough to know, big boy
Doing a man's work, though a child at heart—
He saw all spoiled. 'Don't let him cut my hand off—
The doctor, when he comes. Don't let him, sister!'
So. But the hand was gone already.
The doctor put him in the dark of ether.
He lay and puffed his lips out with his breath.
And then—the watcher at his pulse took fright.
No one believed. They listened at his heart.
Little—less—nothing!—and that ended it.
No more to build on there. And they, since they
Were not the one dead, turned to their affairs.

THE WITCH OF COÖS

I stayed the night for shelter at a farm
Behind the mountain, with a mother and son,
Two old-time believers. They did all the talking.

MOTHER. Folks think a witch who has familiar spirits
She could call up to pass a winter evening,
But won't, should be burned at the stake or some-
    thing.
Summoning spirits isn't 'Button, button,
Who's got the button,' I would have them know.

SON. Mother can make a common table rear
And kick with two legs like an army mule.

MOTHER. And when I've done it, what good have I
    done?
Rather than tip a table for you, let me
Tell you what Ralle the Sioux Control once told me.
He said the dead had souls, but when I asked him
How that could be—I thought the dead were souls,
He broke my trance. Don't that make you suspicious
That there's something the dead are keeping back?
Yes, there's something the dead are keeping back.

SON. You wouldn't want to tell him what we have
Up attic, mother?

MOTHER. Bones—a skeleton.

SON. But the headboard of mother's bed is pushed
Against the attic door: the door is nailed.
It's harmless. Mother hears it in the night
Halting perplexed behind the barrier
Of door and headboard. Where it wants to get
Is back into the cellar where it came from.

MOTHER. We'll never let them, will we, son! We'll
never!

SON. It left the cellar forty years ago
And carried itself like a pile of dishes
Up one flight from the cellar to the kitchen,
Another from the kitchen to the bedroom,
Another from the bedroom to the attic,
Right past both father and mother, and neither
stopped it.
Father had gone upstairs; mother was downstairs.
I was a baby: I don't know where I was.

MOTHER. The only fault my husband found with me—
I went to sleep before I went to bed,
Especially in winter when the bed
Might just as well be ice and the clothes snow.
The night the bones came up the cellar-stairs
Toffile had gone to bed alone and left me,
But left an open door to cool the room off
So as to sort of turn me out of it.
I was just coming to myself enough
To wonder where the cold was coming from,
When I heard Toffile upstairs in the bedroom
And thought I heard him downstairs in the cellar.
The board we had laid down to walk dry-shod on
When there was water in the cellar in spring
Struck the hard cellar bottom. And then someone
Began the stairs, two footsteps for each step,
The way a man with one leg and a crutch,
Or a little child, comes up. It wasn't Toffile:
It wasn't anyone who could be there.
The bulkhead double-doors were double-locked
And swollen tight and buried under snow.
The cellar windows were banked up with sawdust
And swollen tight and buried under snow.
It was the bones. I knew them—and good reason.
My first impulse was to get to the knob
And hold the door. But the bones didn't try
The door; they halted helpless on the landing,

Waiting for things to happen in their favor.
The faintest restless rustling ran all through them.
I never could have done the thing I did
If the wish hadn't been too strong in me
To see how they were mounted for this walk.
I had a vision of them put together
Not like a man, but like a chandelier.
So suddenly I flung the door wide on him.
A moment he stood balancing with emotion,
And all but lost himself. (A tongue of fire
Flashed out and licked along his upper teeth.
Smoke rolled inside the sockets of his eyes.)
Then he came at me with one hand outstretched,
The way he did in life once; but this time
I struck the hand off brittle on the floor,
And fell back from him on the floor myself.
The finger-pieces slid in all directions.
(Where did I see one of those pieces lately?
Hand me my button-box—it must be there.)
I sat up on the floor and shouted, 'Toffile,
It's coming up to you.' It had its choice
Of the door to the cellar or the hall.
It took the hall door for the novelty,
And set off briskly for so slow a thing,
Still going every which way in the joints, though,
So that it looked like lightning or a scribble,
From the slap I had just now given its hand.
I listened till it almost climbed the stairs
From the hall to the only finished bedroom,
Before I got up to do anything;
Then ran and shouted, 'Shut the bedroom door,
Toffile, for my sake!' 'Company?' he said,
'Don't make me get up; I'm too warm in bed.'
So lying forward weakly on the handrail
I pushed myself upstairs, and in the light
(The kitchen had been dark) I had to own
I could see nothing. 'Toffile, I don't see it.
It's with us in the room though. It's the bones.'
'What bones?' 'The cellar bones—out of the grave.'

That made him throw his bare legs out of bed
And sit up by me and take hold of me.
I wanted to put out the light and see
If I could see it, or else mow the room,
With our arms at the level of our knees,
And bring the chalk-pile down. 'I'll tell you what—
It's looking for another door to try.
The uncommonly deep snow has made him think
Of his old song, *The Wild Colonial Boy,*
He always used to sing along the tote-road.
He's after an open door to get out-doors.
Let's trap him with an open door up attic.'
Toffile agreed to that, and sure enough,
Almost the moment he was given an opening,
The steps began to climb the attic stairs.
I heard them. Toffile didn't seem to hear them.
'Quick!' I slammed to the door and held the knob.
'Toffile, get nails.' I made him nail the door shut
And push the headboard of the bed against it.
Then we asked was there anything
Up attic that we'd ever want again.
The attic was less to us than the cellar.
If the bones liked the attic, let them have it.
Let them stay in the attic. When they sometimes
Come down the stairs at night and stand perplexed
Behind the door and headboard of the bed,
Brushing their chalky skull with chalky fingers,
With sounds like the dry rattling of a shutter,
That's what I sit up in the dark to say—
To no one any more since Toffile died.
Let them stay in the attic since they went there.
I promised Toffile to be cruel to them
For helping them be cruel once to him.

SON. We think they had a grave down in the cellar.

MOTHER. We know they had a grave down in the
cellar.

SON. We never could find out whose bones they were.

MOTHER. Yes, we could too, son. Tell the truth for
      once
They were a man's his father killed for me.
I mean a man he killed instead of me.
The least I could do was to help dig their grave.
We were about it one night in the cellar.
Son knows the story: but 'twas not for him
To tell the truth, suppose the time had come.
Son looks surprised to see me end a lie
We'd kept all these years between ourselves
So as to have it ready for outsiders.
But tonight I don't care enough to lie—
I don't remember why I ever cared.
Toffile, if he were here, I don't believe
Could tell you why he ever cared himself. . . .

She hadn't found the finger-bone she wanted
Among the buttons poured out in her lap.
I verified the name next morning: Toffile.
The rural letter box said Toffile Lajway.

ACQUAINTED WITH THE NIGHT

I have been one acquainted with the night.
I have walked out in rain—and back in rain.
I have outwalked the furthest city light.

I have looked down the saddest city lane.
I have passed the watchman on his beat
And dropped my eyes, unwilling to explain.

I have stood still and stopped the sound of feet
When far away an interrupted cry
Came over houses from another street,

But not to call me back or say good-bye;
And further still at an unearthly height,
One luminary clock against the sky

Proclaimed the time was neither wrong nor right.
I have been one acquainted with the night.

DESIGN

I found a dimpled spider, fat and white,
On a white heal-all, holding up a moth
Like a white piece of rigid satin cloth—
Assorted characters of death and blight
Mixed ready to begin the morning right,
Like the ingredients of a witches' broth—
A snow-drop spider, a flower like froth,
And dead wings carrying a paper kite.

What had that flower to do with being white,
The wayside blue and innocent heal-all?
What brought the kindred spider to that height,
Then steered the white moth thither in the night?
What but design of darkness to appall?—
If design govern in a thing so small.

DIRECTIVE

Back out of all this now too much for us,
Back in a time made simple by the loss
Of detail, burned, dissolved, and broken off
Like graveyard marble sculpture in the weather,
There is a house that is no more a house
Upon a farm that is no more a farm
And in a town that is no more a town.
The road there, if you'll let a guide direct you
Who only has at heart your getting lost,
May seem as if it should have been a quarry—
Great monolithic knees the former town
Long since gave up pretence of keeping covered.
And there's a story in a book about it:
Beside the wear of iron wagon wheels
The ledges show lines ruled southeast northwest,

The chisel work of an enormous Glacier
That braced his feet against the Arctic Pole.
You must not mind a certain coolness from him
Still said to haunt this side of Panther Mountain.
Nor need you mind the serial ordeal
Of being watched from forty cellar holes
As if by eye pairs out of forty firkins.
As for the woods' excitement over you
That sends light rustle rushes to their leaves,
Charge that to upstart inexperience.
Where were they all not twenty years ago?
They think too much of having shaded out
A few old pecker-fretted apple trees.
Make yourself up a cheering song of how
Someone's road home from work this once was,
Who may be just ahead of you on foot
Or creaking with a buggy load of grain.
The height of the adventure is the height
Of country where two village cultures faded
Into each other. Both of them are lost.
And if you're lost enough to find yourself
By now, pull in your ladder road behind you
And put a sign up CLOSED to all but me.
Then make yourself at home. The only field
Now left's no bigger than a harness gall.
First there's the children's house of make believe,
Some shattered dishes underneath a pine,
The playthings in the playhouse of the children.
Weep for what little things could make them glad.
Then for the house that is no more a house,
But only a belilaced cellar hole,
Now slowly closing like a dent in dough.
This was no playhouse but a house in earnest.
Your destination and your destiny's
A brook that was the water of the house,
Cold as a spring as yet so near its source,
Too lofty and original to rage.
(We know the valley streams that when aroused
Will leave their tatters hung on barb and thorn.)

I have kept hidden in the instep arch
Of an old cedar at the waterside
A broken drinking goblet like the Grail
Under a spell so the wrong ones can't find it,
So can't get saved, as Saint Mark says they mustn't.
(I stole the goblet from the children's playhouse.)
Here are your waters and your watering place.
Drink and be whole again beyond confusion.

PART II

CRITICAL THEORY

Selected Documents

JOHN COTTON

1584–1652

John Cotton, teacher of the Boston church, emigrated to Massachusetts after being forced to resign his pulpit in Lincolnshire in 1633. He was a theological and intellectual leader among the Puritans on both sides of the Atlantic. Cotton Mather's account of the Massachusetts Puritans' translation of the psalms, in his *Magnalia Christi Americani*, led many to suppose that his grandfather Richard Mather was primarily responsible for the "Preface" to the *Bay Psalm Book*, or, more properly, *The Whole Booke of Psalmes Faithfully Translated into English Metre*; it has recently been shown, however, that John Cotton drafted the preface and, in conjunction with several other ministers, translated the psalms. Their book was the first work in English to be printed in the New World. The preface seeks the sanction of Biblical precedent to justify singing in the holy service and to defend the use of meter and music in worship against the charge of sinful indulgence of sensuous pleasure.

TEXT: *The Whole Booke of Psalmes* (1640), reprinted in facsimile as *The Bay Psalm Book* (1956). See also Zoltan Haraszti, *The Enigma of the Bay Psalm Book* (1956).

PREFACE TO THE BAY PSALM BOOK

The singing of Psalms, though it breathe forth nothing but holy harmony and melody, yet such is the subtilty of the enemy and the enmity of our nature against the Lord and His ways, that our hearts can find matter of discord in this harmony, and crotchets of division in this holy melody. For there have been three questions especially stirring concerning singing. First, what psalms are to be sung in churches? whether David's and other scripture psalms or the psalms invented by the gifts of godly men in every age of the church. Secondly, if scripture psalms, whether in their own words, or in such meter as English poetry is wont to run in? Thirdly, by whom are they to be sung? whether by the whole church together with their voices? or by one man singing alone and the rest joining in silence, and in the close of saying amen.

Touching the first, certainly the singing of David's psalms was an acceptable worship of God, not only in his own, but in succeeding times, as in Solomon's time 2 *Chron.* 5. 13; in Jehosaphat's time 2 *Chron.* 20. 21; in Ezra's time *Ezra* 3. 10, 11; and the text is evident in Hezekiah's time they are commanded to sing praise in the words of David and Asaph, 2 *Chron.* 29, 30; which one place may serve to resolve two of the questions (the first and the last) at once, for this commandment was it ceremonial or moral? Some things in it indeed were ceremonial, as their musical instruments &c., but what ceremony was there in singing praise with the words of David and Asaph? What if David was a type of Christ, was Asaph also? Was everything of David typical? are his words (which are of moral, universal, and perpetual authority in all nations and ages) are they typical? what type can be imagined in making use of his songs to praise the Lord? . . .

If the singing David's psalms be a moral duty & therefore perpetual, then we under the New Testament are bound to sing them as well as they under the Old. And if we are expressly commanded to sing Psalms, Hymns, and spiritual songs, then either we must sing David's psalms, or else may affirm they are not spiritual songs, which being penned by an extraordinary gift of the Spirit, for the sake especially of God's spiritual Israel, not to be read and preached only (as other parts of holy writ) but to be sung also; they are therefore most spiritual, and still to be sung of all the Israel of God. . . .

Obj. 1. If it be said that the Saints in the primitive Church did compile spiritual songs of their own inditing, and sing them before the Church. 1 *Cor.* 14, 15, 16.

Ans. We answer first, that those Saints compiled these

spiritual songs by the extraordinary gifts of the spirit (common in those days) whereby they were enabled to praise the Lord in strange tongues, wherein learned *Paraeus* proves those psalms were uttered, in his Comment on that place (verse 14) which extraordinary gifts, if they were still in the Churches, we should allow them the like liberty now. Secondly, suppose those psalms were sung by an ordinary gift (which we suppose cannot be evicted) doth it therefore follow that they did not, and that we ought not to, sing David's psalms? Must the ordinary gifts of a private man quench the spirit still speaking to us by the extraordinary gifts of his servant David? There is not the least foot-step of example, or precept, or colour reason for such a bold practice.

Obj. 2. Ministers are allowed to pray conceived prayers, and why not to sing conceived psalms? Must we not sing in the spirit as well as pray in the spirit?

Ans. First because every good minister hath not a gift of spiritual poetry to compose extemporary psalms as he hath of prayer. Secondly, suppose he had, yet seeing psalms are to be sung by a joint consent and harmony of all the Church in heart and voice (as we shall prove) this cannot be done except he that composeth a psalm, bringeth into the Church set forms of psalms of his own invention; for which we find no warrant or precedent in any ordinary officers of the Church throughout the scriptures. Thirdly, because the book of psalms is so complete a System of psalms, which the Holy-Ghost himself in infinite wisdom hath made to suit all the conditions, necessities, temptations, affections, &c. of men in all ages (as most of all our interpreters on the psalms have fully and particularly cleared), therefore by this the Lord seemeth to stop all men's mouths and minds ordinarily to compile or sing any other psalms (under colour that the occasions and conditions of the Church are new) &c. for the public use of the Church, seeing, let our condition be what it will, the Lord Himself hath supplied us with far better. . . .

As for the scruple that some take at the translation of the book of psalms into meter, because David's psalms were sung in his own words without meter, we answer:

First, there are many verses together in several psalms of
David which run in rhythms . . . which shews at least
the lawfulness of singing psalms in English rhythms.

Secondly, the psalms are penned in such verses as are
suitable to the poetry of the Hebrew language, and not
in the common style of such other books of the Old Testament as are not poetical. Now no protestant doubteth but
that all the books of the scripture should by God's ordinance be extant in the mother tongue of each nation, that
they may be understood of all; hence the psalms are to
be translated into our English tongue. And if in our English tongue we are to sing them, then as all our English
songs (according to the course of our English poetry) do
run in meter, so ought David's psalms to be translated into
meter that so we may sing the Lord's songs as in our
English tongue so in such verses as are familiar to an
English ear—which are commonly metrical. And as it can
be no just offence to any good conscience to sing David's
Hebrew songs in English words, so neither to sing his
poetical verses in English poetical meter. Men might as
well stumble at singing the Hebrew psalms in our English
tunes and not in Hebrew tunes, as at singing them in English meter, which are our verses, and not in such verses as
are generally used by David according to the poetry of
the Hebrew language. But the truth is, as the Lord hath
hid from us the Hebrew tunes, lest we should think ourselves bound to imitate them, so also the course and frame
(for the most part) of their Hebrew poetry, that we might
not think ourselves bound to imitate that, but that every
nation without scruple might follow as the graver sort of
tunes of their own country songs, so the graver sort of
verses of their own country poetry.

Neither let any think that for the meter's sake we have
taken liberty or poetical license to depart from the true
and proper sence of David's words in the Hebrew verses;
no, but it hath been one part of our religious care and
faithful endeavour to keep close to the original text. . . .
We have therefore done our endeavour to make a plain
and familiar translation of the psalms and words of David
into English meter, and have not so much as presumed

to paraphrase to give the sense of his meaning in other words. . . . We have with our English Bibles (to which next to the Original we have had respect) used the Idioms of our own tongue instead of Hebraisms, lest they might seem English barbarisms. . . .

If therefore the verses are not always so smooth and elegant as some may desire or expect, let them consider that God's Altar needs not our polishings (Exod. 20) for we have respected rather a plain translation than to smooth our verses with the sweetness of any paraphrase, and so have attended Conscience rather than Elegance, fidelity rather than poetry, in translating the Hebrew words into English language, and David's poetry into English meter; that so we may sing in Sion the Lord's songs of praise according to his own will, until he take us from hence, and wipe away our tears, & bid us enter into our master's joy to sing eternal Halleluiahs.

COTTON MATHER

1663–1728

Cotton Mather was the grandson of John Cotton and of Richard Mather, and the son of Increase Mather, President of Harvard College. The inheritor of their religious authority and intellectual eminence became a leading voice of orthodoxy. Mather was an indefatigable writer who published over 450 separate works, including *Magnalia Christi Americani; or, The Ecclesiastical History of New England* (1702); biographies of John Eliot and Sir William Phips; accounts of witchcraft; a treatise on inoculation for smallpox; poetry; a translation of the Psalms in blank verse; numerous theological works; and *Manuductio ad Ministerium* (1726), the manual for the instruction of ministers from which the following passage is excerpted. In those writings intended for the commonality Mather followed the precepts of the Puritan plain style, but in his *Magnalia* and elsewhere his prose is studded with allusions and stylistic complexities. In *Manuductio*, written two years before his death, he shows how far both he and Puritan New England had departed from the devotion of the first generation to the austerities of utilitarian plainness. Now, writes Mather, although rhyme has been attacked "as if it were a sort of Morris dancing with bells, yet I cannot wish you a soul that shall be wholly unpoetical," and he advises his ministerial candidate to try his hand at verse but forewarns him against harlot Muses. Mather's discourse on style portends the shift of sensibility toward the eighteenth-century conception of polite letters.

TEXT: *Manuductio ad Ministerium* (1726, reprinted in facsimile, 1938), chapter 8.

ON POETRY AND STYLE

I proceed now to say, That if (under the guidance of a *Vida*) you try your young wings now and then to see what flights you can make, at least for an *Epigram*, it may a little sharpen your *Sense*, and polish your *Style*, for more important performances. For this purpose you are now even overstocked with patterns, and—*Poemata passim.* You may, like Nazianzen, all your days make a little recreation of poetry in the midst of your more painful studies. Nevertheless, I cannot but advise you, *Withhold thy throat from thirst.* Be not so set upon poetry as to be always poring on the passionate and measured pages. Let not what should be sauce rather than food for you engross all your application. Beware of a boundless and sickly appetite for the reading of poems, which now the rickety Nation swarms withal: and let not the Circaean cup intoxicate you. But especially preserve the chastity of your soul from the dangers you may incur by a conversation with Muses that are no better than Harlots: among which are others besides Ovid's Epistles, which for their tendency to excite and foment impure flames, and cast coals into your bosom, deserve rather to be thrown into the fire, than to be laid before the eye which a covenant should be made withal. Indeed, not merely for the impurities which they convey, but also on some other accounts, the Powers of Darkness have a Library among us, whereof the poets have been the most numerous as well as the most venomous authors. Most of the modern plays as well as the romances and novels and fictions, which are a sort of poems, do belong to the catalogue of this cursed Library. The plays, I say, in which there are so many passages that have a tendency to overthrow all piety that one whose name is Bedford has extracted near Seven Thousand Instances of them from the plays chiefly of but five years preceding; and says awfully upon them, *They are National Sins, and therefore call for National Plagues; And if GOD should enter into Judgment all the Blood in the Nation would not be able to atone for them.* How much do I wish that such pestilences, and indeed all those worse than Egyptian Toads, [the spawns of a Butler, & a Brown, and a Ward, and a company whose name is legion!] might never crawl into your chamber! *The unclean spirits that come like frogs out of the mouth of the dragon, and of the beast,* which go forth unto the young people of the earth, and expose them to be dealt with as enemies of GOD, in the *Battle of the Great Day of the Almighty.* As for those wretched scribbles of madmen, my son, *Touch them not, Taste them not, Handle them not.* Thou wilt perish in the using of them. They are *The dragons whose contagious breath peoples the dark retreats of Death.* To much better purpose will an excellent but envied Blackmore feast you than those vile rhapsodies (of that *Vinum Daemonum*) which you will find always leave a taint upon your mind, and among other ill effects will sensibly indispose you to converse with the Holy Oracles of GOD your SAVIOUR.

But there is what I may rather call a parenthesis than a digression, which this may be not altogether an improper place for the introducing of.

There has been a deal of ado about a STYLE, so much, that I must offer you my sentiments upon it. There is a *Way of Writing,* wherein the author endeavours that the reader may have *something to the purpose* in every paragraph. There is not only a vigour sensible in every sentence, but the paragraph is embellished with *profitable references,* even to something beyond what is *directly spoken.* Formal and painful quotations are not studied, yet all that could be learnt from them is insinuated. The writer pretends not unto reading, yet he could not have writ as he does if he had not read very much in his time; and his composures are not only a cloth of gold, but also stuck with as many jewels as the gown of a Russian ambassador. This way of writing has been decried by many, and is at this day more than ever so, for the same reason, that in the old story, the grapes were decried, *That they were not ripe.* A lazy, ignorant, conceited set of authors would persuade the whole tribe to lay aside that way of writing for the same reason that one would have persuaded his brethren to part with the encumbrance of their bushy tails. But, however fashion and humour may prevail, they must not think that the club at their coffee-house is *All the World,* but there will always be those who will in this cafe be governed by *Indisputable Reason,* and who will think that the real excellency of a book will never lie in saying of little; that the less one has for his money in a book, 'tis really the more valuable for it; and that the less one is instructed in a book, and the more of superfluous margin and superficial harangue, and the less of substantial matter one has in it, the more 'tis to be accounted of. And if a more massy way of writing be never so much disgusted at this day, a better gust will come on, as will some other thing, *quae iam cecidere.* In the mean time, nothing appears to me more impertinent and ridiculous than the modern way (I cannot say *Rule,* for they have *None!*) of criticising. The blades that set up for critics, I know not who constituted or commissioned 'em!—they appear to me for the most part as contemptible as they are a supercilious generation. For indeed no two of them have the same style; and they are as intolerably cross-grained and severe in their censures upon one another, as they are upon the rest of mankind. But while each of them, conceitedly enough, sets up for the *Standards of Perfection,* we are entirely at a loss which fire to follow. Nor can you easily find any one thing wherein they agree for their style, except perhaps a perpetual care to give us jejune and empty pages, without such *touches of erudition* (to speak in the style of an ingenious traveller) as may make the discourse less tedious and more enriching to the mind of him that peruses them. There is much talk of a *Florid Style* obtaining among the pens that are most in vogue, but how often would it puzzle one even with the best glasses to find the flowers! And if they were to be chastized for it, it would be with much what as much of Justice as Jerome was for being a Ciceronian. After all, every man will have his own style, which will distinguish him as much as his gait; and if you can attain to that which I have newly described, but always writing so as to give an early conveyance unto your ideas, I would not have you by any scourging be driven out of your gait, but if you must confess a fault in it, make a confession like that of the lad unto his father while he was beating him for his versifying.

However, since every man will have his own style, I would pray that we may learn to treat one another with mutual civilities and considerations, and handsomely indulge one another in this, as gentlemen do in other matters.

I wonder what ails people, that they can't let Cicero write in the style of Cicero, and Seneca write in the (much other!) style of Seneca; and own that both may please in their several ways. —But I will freely tell you what has made me consider the humourists that set up for critics upon style as the most unregardable set of mortals in the world is this: Far more illustrious critics than any of those to whom I am now bidding defiance, and no less men than your Erasmus and your Grotius, have taxed the Greek style of the New Testament with I know not what solecisms and barbarisms. And how many learned folks have obsequiously run away with the Notion! Whereas 'tis an ignorant and an insolent whimsey which they have been guilty of. It may be (and particularly by an ingenious Blackwall, it has been) demonstrated that the gentlemen are mistaken in every one of their pretended instances; all the unquestionable classics may be brought in to convince them of their mistakes. Those glorious oracles are as pure Greek as ever was written in the world; and so correct, so noble, so sublime is their style, that never any thing under the cope of Heaven but the Old Testament has equall'd it.

JOSEPH DENNIE

1768–1812

Until the acclaim of Washington Irving, Joseph Dennie was the most widely-read essayist and critic of his time. After graduation from Harvard in 1790 Dennie practiced law briefly; his literary career began in association with the Vermont playwright and novelist Royall Tyler, with whom he wrote light essays in the tradition of Addison and Goldsmith. Dennie was successively editor of *The Tablet* (1795), *Farmer's Weekly Museum* (1796), and, after his removal from New Hampshire to Philadelphia, *The Port Folio*. This journal, which he founded in 1801, survived him until 1827 and was America's foremost literary periodical before the establishment in 1815 of *The North American Review*. Dennie became a friend of Thomas Moore when the latter visited America; *The Port Folio* contains the first printings of poems by Moore and such other English writers as Thomas Campbell, Leigh Hunt, and "Monk" Lewis. Dennie was active in Federalist politics; his literary taste was modeled on the traditions of the English eighteenth century, and he abhorred democratic innovations. The review of Freneau, like many of his other contributions, was signed "Oliver Oldschool, Esq."

TEXT: *The Port Folio*, n.s. IV (1807), 251–53, 257–59, 313–15, 349–52 (17 and 24 Oct., 14 and 28 Nov.).

FRENEAU'S POEMS

There is nothing with which the inhabitants of the United States have been so much reproached, as the little encouragement given by them to the Belles Lettres. No traveller, or Journalist, can mention us without making this charge; and even they who kindly endeavour to apologize for our defects, for the most part find our excuse in a poverty of genius, or negation of intellect with which nature has cursed our unhappy land; and for which, they think, as her operations were beyond our control, we should rather be excused than condemned.

If foreigners, however, would take the trouble to view the scenes which we present to their observation, they could not avoid seeing, at a glance, why the works of fancy or imagination are less attended to than the crudest political theories, or the dryest details of mercantile calculation.

In this country, though, perhaps, a moderate competency is more general than in any other part of the world, large fortunes are rare, and the youth released from college, immediately applies himself to some business or profession, to which he finds it necessary to devote an assiduous attention in order to obtain a proper rank in society; and thus a period of life is passed in close application to business, in which, otherwise, a taste for polite literature would have been either formed or fixed; and the lustre of that eye is extinguished, which else, perhaps, had rolled "in a fine frenzy" of poetick inspiration. Youthful leisure, which *alat formetque poetam*,[1] is almost unknown to us. How many of the English poets have felt—I might, indeed, ask, how few have not felt the *res augusta domi?* And when the poverty of their bards is so common as even to be proverbial, in a nation, the birthright of whose numerous nobility and gentry it should be to foster the Muses; shall

[1] "Nourishes and moulds poets."

we be reproached if, as fortune here is within the reach of every man of talents, he forsake the barren steeps of Parnassus for the rich lowlands of domestick comfort and independence? In popular governments, eloquence has justly been called the road to wealth and power, and our foes themselves will not deny that in the United States it is a well beaten one, and that some of our oratours might safely challenge a comparison with the most exalted names which Europe could oppose to them. The literature encouraged by us is solid and useful, and although it may not have the fragrance of the flower-garden, it assuredly has the fruitfulness of the harvest field.

Among the few in this country who have wandered from "the main road of business" to stray in the paths of poesy, is PHILIP FRENEAU, who, as I have been informed, was born in New-Jersey, educated at Princeton College, and, with a singular versatility of character, has been alternately a commander of a ship, and an editor of a newspaper. A volume of this gentleman's poems, "printed at the press of the authour," is now before me, and as I think it much deserving of attention, I shall devote some pages to an examination of it.

The poet, as well as the oratour, is to be encouraged in his race *clamore plausuque;* our authour, however, if we may judge from the following lines, appears to have anticipated very little of either: [See "To an Author," p. 16].

Freneau's habits of life led to an acquaintance with Nature, and he did not pass by her with a regardless eye. The measures of his poetry, like the subjects of his Muse, are various and desultory. The following lines, on an Indian burying-ground, are extremely beautiful: the two last stanzas are in the sweetest style of Collins: [See "The Indian Burying Ground," p. 15].

Many a volume has been written on the comparative advantages of the civilized and savage life; and the expansion of intellect and personal comforts of the one have been opposed by the few wants, and proud feeling of independence of the other.

"What happier natures shrink from with affright,
   The hard inhabitant contends is right."

It is a difficult subject to give an opinion on, for to do so impartially, it would be necessary that we should add the mental improvement of the one to the hardihood of body of the other. Sitting in our study, surrounded by books, and fenced from the least inclemency of air, we shudder at the thoughts of the difficulties to which the life of the savage is exposed; while he, whose body is hardened almost beyond the sensation of pain, would view with sovereign contempt a man employing his life in turning over page after page, or scrawling black marks on paper. Notwithstanding all that has been said in favour of the civilized state, it is very certain that the Indians who have been educated at our seminaries of learning, have sighed for their former mode of life, and on returning to their tribes, immediately assumed their old habits. The following little poem very beautifully describes what may be supposed to have been the feelings of an Indian lad, who, separated from his companions, had been some time immured in a New-England College.

THE INDIAN STUDENT

From Susquehanna's western springs,
   Where savage tribes pursue their game,
His blanket tied with yellow strings,
   A native of the forest came.

Not long before, a wandering priest
   Exprest his wish, with visage sad;
"Ah why," he cried, "in Satan's waste,
   "Ah why detain so fine a lad?

"In *Yankee land* there stands a town,
   "*Where learning may be purchased low:*
"Exchange his blanket for a gown,
   "And let the lad to college go."

From long debate the council rose,
    And viewing Shallum's tricks with joy,
To *Harvard Hall,* o'er wastes of snows,
    They sent the copper-coloured boy.

One generous chief a bow supplied,
    This gave a sheaf, and that a skin;
The feathers, in vermillion dy'd,
    Himself did from a turkey win.

Thus dress'd so gay, he took his way
    O'er barren hills, alone, alone!
His guide a star, he wander'd far,
    His pillow ev'ry night a stone.

At last he came, with foot so lame,
    Where learned men talk heathen Greek,
And Hebrew lore is gabbled o'er,
    To please the Muses, twice a week.

Awhile he writ, awhile he read,
    Awhile he conn'd their grammar rules—
An Indian savage so well bred,
    Great credit promis'd to the schools.

Some thought he would in *law* excel,
    Some said in *physick* he would shine;
And one, who knew him passing well,
    Beheld, in him, a sound divine.

But those of more discerning eye,
    Even then could other prospects show,
And saw him lay his *Virgil* by
    To wander with his dearer *bow.*

The tedious hours of study spent,
    The heavy-moulded lecture done,
He to the woods a hunting went,
    Through lonely wastes he'd walk, he'd run.

No mystick wonders fir'd his mind;
  He sought to gain no learn'd degree,
But only sense enough to find
  The squirrel in the hollow tree.

The shady bank, the purling stream,
  The woody wild his heart possess'd;
The dewy lawn his morning dream
  In Fancy's gayest colours dress'd.

"And why (he cry'd) did I forsake
  "My native woods for gloomy walls!
"The silver brook, the limpid lake,
  "For musty books and college halls!

"A little could my wants supply:
  "Can wealth and honour give me more?
"Or will the sylvan god deny
  "The humble treat he gave before?

"Let seraphs gain the bright abode,
  "And Heaven's sublimest mansions see;
"I only bow to NATURE's GOD,
  "The land of shades will do for me.

"These dreadful secrets of the sky
  "Alarm my soul with chilling fear—
"Do planets in their orbits fly?
  "And is the earth, indeed, a sphere?

"Let planets still their *course* pursue,
  "And comets to the CENTRE run;
"In him my faithful friend I view,
  "The image of my God—the SUN.

"Where Nature's ancient forests grow,
  "And mingled laurel never fades,
"My heart is fix'd;—and I must go
  "To die among my native shades."

He spoke, and to the western springs,
   (His gown discharg'd, his money spent,
His blanket tied with yellow strings)
   The native of the forest went.

Freneau very seldom attuned his lyre to love, and in his works we find none of those "fabled tortures, quaint and tame," so common in the writings of the amatory poets. The following stanzas conclude an address, in a seaman's phrase, to a "scornful lady;" and although the threat of Time punishing the fair one for her cruelty is very common, yet the introduction of this personage in the last line is certainly very uncommon:

Ah, Celia, what a strange mistake,
   To ruin thus for ruin's sake;
Thus to delude us, in distress,
   And quit the prize you should possess.

Years may advance with silent pace,
   And rob that form of ev'ry grace;
And all your conquests be repaid
   By—Teague O'Murphy, and his spade.

In many passages he evinces a capacity for the pathetick; but in general passes rapidly to other sensations. The following lines are not unlike some written by Cowper on seeing a favourite grove of trees cut down:

Inspir'd at the sound, while the *name* she repeats,
Wild fancy conveys me to Hudson's retreats—
At sweet recollection of juvenile dreams,
In the groves and the forests that skirted his streams!
How often with rapture those streams were survey'd,
When, sick of city, I flew to the shade!
How often the bard and the peasant shall mourn
Ere those groves shall revive, and those shades shall
    return!

And again, with a happy allusion to one of the emblems of Time:

> But days such as these were too happy to last;
> The *sand of felicity settled too fast!*

The lines to his dog are an affectionate recollection of that faithful animal, and all who read them will remember the days of their boyhood.

> How oft in the year shall I visit your grave,
> Amid the lone forest that shadows the wave!
> How often lament, when the day's at its close,
> That a mile from my cot is your place of repose!
>
> Ah here (I will say) in this path he has run;
> And there stands a tree where a squirrel he won;
> And here, in this spot where the willow trees grow,
> He dragg'd out a rabbit that lurk'd in the snow.

Speaking of the battle of Eutaw springs, his language is both pathetick and forcible, and the epitaph on those who were slain in the action, is, at once, beautifully simple and comprehensive:

> Ah! had our friends that led the fray
> Surviv'd the ruins of that day,
> We should not mix our joy with pain,
> Nor, sympathizing, now complain.
>
> Strange! that of those who nobly dare
> Death always claims so large a share!
> That those of virtues most refin'd,
> Are soonest to the grave consign'd!
>
> But fame is theirs—and future days
> On pillar'd brass shall tell their praise;
> Shall tell—when cold neglect is dead—
> *"These"* for their country fought and bled."

Freneau has given several translations and imitations from the Latin and French. The conclusion of the sixteenth ode of the second book of Horace,

> On me a poor and small domain,
> With something of a poet's vein,
> Kind fate bestow'd—*and share of pride*
> *To spurn a scoundrel from my side,*

is extremely indignant, and expresses the very sensations of the Prince of lyrick poets:

> ——Mihi parva rura, et
> Spiritum Graiæ tenuem camenæ
> Parca non mendax dedit, et malignum
> Spernere vulgus.

The Address to a Jug of Rum is very much in the manner of Swift, who with all his power of condensing his expression, could not afford us a better example of the *multum in parvo* than the following:

> Here only by a cork control'd,
> And slender walls of earthen mould,
> In all the pomp of death repose
> The seeds of many a bloody nose;
> The chattering tongue, the horrid oath,
> The fist for fighting nothing loth,
> The passion which no words can tame,
> That bursts, like sulphur, into flame;
> The nose carbuncled, glowing red,
> The bloated eye, the broken head;
> The tree that bears the deadly fruit
> Of murder, maiming, and dispute;
> Assault that Innocence assails,
> The images of gloomy jails,
> The giddy thought, on mischief bent,
> The midnight hour in riot spent:
> All these within this jug appear,
> And Jack, the hangman, in the rear!

Falconer, Captain Thompson, and Freneau have shown that the Muses may be induced to accommodate themselves to the boisterous habits of a sailor's life, and sing as melodiously on board a ship, as on Parnassus. Æschylus was, at the same time, a poet and a sailor. Homer, Virgil, Appolonius Rhodius, and others, with the maritime adventures of their respective heroes, describe the vessels on board of which they were embarked: these, however, with little rigging, and of simple structure required no great art to introduce, with a description of all their parts, into poetry, in comparison with the complex machinery of modern navigation. When, a soldier was at once, by a mandate of his officer, transformed into a sailor, and a general, upon stepping on board a galley, became an admiral: now, years are necessary to acquire a requisite knowledge of the science of directing a ship, as well as of the language spoken on board it, which is perfectly unintelligible to a landsman; and which some of our best writers have in vain endeavoured to use. Shakespeare's "Lay her a-hold!" and Dryden's "Veer starboard sea and land," would be understood neither at sea nor on shore. Falconer first wrote a nautical poem in nautical language, and his work may justly be termed classical in a new department of poetry.

Sannazarius, stepping out of the beaten path of pastoral, wrote his Piscatory Idylls; but this required little invention, and although they talked of mullets, tunnies, oysters, &c. the language and sentiments of his fishermen, and the language and sentiments of the shepherds of the pastoral bards, who have all servilely imitated each other in committing so great an outrage on nature, as to cause rivers to weep and rocks to groan whenever some country wench was supposed to be in an ill humour.

The following lines describe the building, sailing, and capture of the Aurora with great beauty. [Here follow 172 lines of "The British Prison Ship."]

Too many criticks judge of the excellence of a poet by the length of his pieces. Freneau, measured by this scale, would not rank high; for he never detains his reader long on one subject. He, in too many places, shows a disrespect for the pulpit, which deserves to be highly censured; but although we touch, with much reverence, in whatever is connected with that guardian of our happiness both here and hereafter, we cannot avoid smiling at the odd association in the stanzas on the crew of a certain vessel several of whom happened to be of the same name with celebrated clergymen.

> In life's unsettled, odd career
> What changes every day appear
>   To please, or plague the eye;
> A goodly brotherhood of priests
> Are here transformed to swearing beasts
>   That heaven and hell defy.
>
> Here Bonner, bruised with many a knock,
> Has chang'd his surplice for a frock;
>   Old Erskine swabs the decks:
> And Watts, that once such pleasure took
> In writing hymns, here turn'd a cook,
>   No more shall sinners vex.
>
> Here Burnet, Tillotson, and Blair,
> With Jemmy Hervey, curse and swear;
>   Here Cudworth mixes grog;
> Pearson the crew to dinner hails,
> A graceless Serlock trims the sails,
>   And Bunyan heaves the log.

Our authour has, in a very desultory manner, rambled from subject to subject, but satire appears to be his favourite one. Here, however, we cannot, in general, praise him. He is far from being elegant in the choice of his language, which is, for the most part, downright railing; and this we do not think sufficiently justified by the examples of the ancient satyrists, the vulgarity of whose expressions affords no favourable ideas of their own manners. His subjects also, which are local, have lost much of their interest; and we are unwilling to recall the recollection of feuds long past. In the phrase of the aborigines, the tomahawk is buried, and we wish not to dig it up. It is the more to

be regretted, that Freneau wasted so much of his time in
this manner, as he has convinced us that he is capable of
better things. As a proof of that kind of satire, which can

"Tickle, while it gently probes the wound."

we select the following lines from The Life of Hugh Gaine,
which we are disposed to mention with much encomium.
[EDITOR'S NOTE: Here follows 155 lines of anti-Tory
satire.]

Having thus rambled through Freneau's Poems, with a
spirit of no illiberal criticism, it may not be amiss to mention our regret at the authour, in several places giving us
cause to censure him for principles, which in this country,
are rarely in union with genius. Providence, while she permits the pest of Jacobinism to range at large among us,
has kindly shown her in her foulest colours; she displays
no elegance of form, no fascination of manners, no persuasion of eloquence, but rude and deformed, is equally
disgusting to the spirit of philosophy and to the eye of
taste.

We have mentioned some causes of the little encouragement given to our *bards;* but we confidently look forward
to a time not distant, when we may say, in the words of
Cicero: *Rudem enin esse omnino in nostris poetis, aut
inertissimæ signitiæ est, aut fastidii delicatissimi. Mihi
quidem nulli satis eruditi videntur, quibus nostra ignota
sunt.*[2]

[Dennie concludes by listing 75 of Freneau's poems
which he considers worthy of reprinting.]

[2] "To be totally ignorant of our own poets is typical either of
the most inert sloth or of the most exquisite overfastidiousness.
No one seems to me sufficiently learned to whom our own
writings are unknown."

WILLIAM CULLEN BRYANT

1794–1878

"On Poetry in Its Relation to Our Age and Country" is the third of four lectures Bryant gave to the Athenaeum Society during his first year in New York, 1825. The other three were titled "On the Nature of Poetry," "On the Value and Uses of Poetry," and "On Originality and Imitation." Bryant consistently defined poetry as "that which takes the strongest hold of the feelings" and "not only addresses the passions and the imagination; it appeals to the understanding also. . . . Nor is it merely didactic; but this does not prevent it from teaching truths which the mind instinctively acknowledges. The elements of moral truth are few and simple, but their combinations with human actions are innumerable and diversified as the combinations of the language." Since poetry is a suggestive, not a mimetic art, it engages the imagination and the reader participates by following "the path which the poet only points out." The lectures were first printed in 1884.

TEXT: *Prose Writings of William Cullen Bryant,* edited by Parke Godwin, 2 vols. (1884).

ON POETRY IN ITS RELATION TO OUR AGE AND COUNTRY

Our citizens are held to possess, in a remarkable degree, the heedful, calculating, prosaic spirit of the age, while our country is decried as peculiarly barren of the materials of poetry. The scenery of our land these reasoners admit to be beautiful, but they urge that it is the beauty of a face without expression; that it wants the associations of tradition which are the soul and interest of scenery; that it wants the national superstitions which linger yet in every district in Europe, and the legends of distant and dark ages and of wild and unsettled times of which the old world reminds you at every step. Nor can our country, they say, ever be more fruitful of these materials than at present. For this is not an age to give birth to new superstitions, but to explode and root out old, however harmless and agreeable they may be, while half the world is already wondering how little the other half will finally believe. Is it likely, then, that a multitude of interesting traditions will spring up in our land to ally themselves with every mountain, every hill, every forest, every river, and every tributary brook. There may be some passages of our early history which associate themselves with particular places, but the argument is that the number of these will never be greatly augmented. The genius of our nation is quiet and commercial. Our people are too much in love with peace and gain, the state of society is too settled, and the laws too well enforced and respected, to allow of wild and strange adventures. There is no romance either in our character, our history, or our condition of society; and, therefore, it is neither likely to encourage poetry, nor capable of supplying it with those materials—materials drawn from domestic traditions and manners—which render it popular.

If these views of the tendency of the present age, and the state of things in our own country, are to be received as true, it must be acknowledged that they are not only exceedingly discouraging to those who make national literature a matter of pride, but, what is worse, that they go far toward causing that very inferiority on which they so strongly insist. Not that there is any danger that the demand for contemporary poetry will entirely cease. Verses have always been, and always will be written, and will always find readers; but it is of some consequence that they should be good verses, that they should exert the healthful and beneficial influences which I consider as belonging to the highest productions of the art; not feebly and imperfectly, but fully and effectually. . . .

What, then, were the circumstances which fostered the art of poetry in ancient times? They have been defined to be the mystery impressed on all the operations of nature as yet not investigated and traced to their laws—the beautiful systems of ancient mythology, and, after their extinction, the superstitions that linger like ghosts in the twilight of a later age. Let us examine separately each of these alleged advantages. That there is something in whatever is unknown and inscrutable which strongly excites the imagination and awes the heart, particularly when connected with things of unusual vastness and grandeur, is not to be denied. But I deny that much of this mystery is apparent to an ignorant age, and I maintain that no small degree of inquiry and illumination is necessary to enable the mind to perceive it. He who takes all things to be as they appear, who supposes the earth to be a great plain, the sun a moving ball of fire, the heavens a vault of sapphire, and the stars a multitude of little flames lighted up in its arches—what does he think of mysteries, or care for them? But enlighten him a little further. Teach him that the earth is an immense sphere; that the wide land whose bounds he knows so imperfectly is an isle in the great oceans that flows all over it; talk to him of that boundlessness of the skies, and the army of worlds that move through them—and, by means of the knowledge that you have communicated, you have opened to him a vast field of the unknown and the wonderful. Thus it ever was and ever will be with the human mind; everything which it knows introduces to its observation a greater multitude of things which it does not know; the clearing up of one mystery conducts it to another. . . . It is a pledge of the immortal destinies of the human intellect that it is forever drawn by a strong attraction to . . . penetrate the obscurities beyond. The old world, then, is welcome to its mysteries; we need not envy it on that account: for, in addition to our superior knowledge and as a consequence of it, we have even more of them than it, and they are loftier, deeper, and more spiritual.

But the mythologies of antiquity!—in particular, the beautiful mythologies of Greece and Rome, of which so much enters into the charming remains of ancient poetry! Beautiful those mythologies unquestionably were, and exceedingly varied and delightfully adapted to many of the purposes of poetry; yet it may be doubted whether, on the whole, the art gained more by them than it lost. For remark that, so far as mystery is a quality of poetry, it has been taken away almost entirely by the myth. It has a god for every operation of nature. . . . It left nothing in obscurity; everything was seen. Its very beauty consisted in minute disclosures. Thus the imagination was delighted, but neither the imagination nor the feelings were stirred up from utmost depths. That system gave us the story of a superior and celestial race of beings who were, like ourselves, susceptible of suffering; but it elevated them so far above the creatures of earth in power, in knowledge, and in security from the calamities of our condition, that they could be the subjects of little sympathy. Therefore it is that the mythological poetry of the ancients is as cold as it is beautiful, as unaffecting as it is faultless. And the genius of this mythological poetry, carried into the literature of a later age, where it was cultivated with a less sincere and earnest spirit, has been the destruction of all nature and simplicity. Men forsook the sure guidance of their own feelings and impressions, and fell into gross offences against taste. They wished to describe the passion of love, and they talked of Venus and her boy Cupid and his bow; they would speak of the freshness and glory of morning, and they fell to prattling of Phoebus and his steeds. No wonder that poetry has been thought a trifling art when thus practiced. For my part I cannot but think that human beings, placed among the things of this earth, with their affections and sympathies, their joys and sorrows, and the accidents of fortune to which they are liable, are infinitely a better subject for poetry than any imaginary race of creatures whatsoever. Let the fountain tell me of the flocks that have drank at it; of the village girl that has gathered spring flowers on its margin; the traveller that has slaked his thirst there in the hot noon, and blessed its waters; . . . let it speak of youth and health and purity and gladness, and I care not for the naiad that pours it out. If it must have a religious association, let it murmur of the invisible goodness that fills and feeds its reservoirs in the darkness of the earth. . . .

With respect to later superstitions, traces of which linger yet in so many districts of the civilized world—such as the belief in witchcraft, astrology, the agency of foul spirits in the affairs of men, in ghosts, fairies, water-sprites, and goblins of the wood and the mine—I would observe that the ages which gave birth to this fantastic brood are not those which have produced the noblest specimens of poetry. . . . Poetry, it is true, sometimes produces a powerful effect by appealing to that innate love of the supernatural which lies at the bottom of every man's heart and mind, and which all are willing to indulge, some freely and some by stealth, but it does this for the most part by means of those superstitions which exist rather in tradition than in serious belief. It finds them more flexible and accommodating; it is able to mould them to its purposes, and at liberty to reject all that is offensive. Accordingly, we find that even the poets of superstitious ages have been fond of going back to the wonders and prodigies of elder days. . . . The best witch ballad, with the exception, perhaps, of "Tam o'Shanter," that I know of is Hogg's "Witch of Fyfe," yet both these were written long after the belief in witches had been laughed out of countenance.

It is especially the privilege of an age which has no engrossing superstitions of its own, to make use in its poetry of those of past ages; to levy contributions from the credulity of all time, and thus to diversify indefinitely the situations in which its human agents are placed. If these materials are managed with sufficient skill to win the temporary assent of the reader to the probability of the supernatural circumstances related, the purpose of the poet is answered. This is precisely the condition of the present age; it has the advantage over all ages that have preceded it in the abundance of those collected materials, and its poets have not been slow to avail themselves of their aid.

In regard to the circumstances which are thought in the present age to repress and limit the exercise of the poetical faculty, the principal if not the only one is supposed to be the prevalence of studies and pursuits unfavorable to the

cultivation of imagination and to enthusiasm of feeling.
. . . Yet I cannot see that . . . because the chemist
prosecutes his science successfully, therefore the poet
should lose his inspiration. Take the example of Great
Britain. In no country are the sciences studied with greater
success, yet in no country is poetry pursued with more
ardor. . . . Does the poetry of that island at the present
day—the poetry of Wordsworth, Scott, Coleridge, Byron,
Southey, Shelley, and others—smack of the chilling tendencies of the physical sciences? Or, rather, is it not bold,
varied, impassioned, irregular, and impatient of precise
laws, beyond that of any former age? Indeed, has it not
the freshness, the vigor, and perhaps also the disorder, of
a new literature?

The amount of knowledge necessary to be possessed by
all who would keep pace with the age, as much greater as
it is than formerly, is not, I apprehend, in danger of
smothering poetical talent. Knowledge is the material with
which Genius builds her fabrics. The greater its abundance, the more power is required to dispose it into order
and beauty, but the more vast and magnificent will be the
structure. All great poets have been men of great knowledge. Some have gathered it from books, as Spenser and
Milton; others from keen observation of men and things,
as Homer and Shakespeare. On the other hand, the poetry
of Ossian, whether genuine or not, is an instance of no
inconsiderable poetical talent struggling with the disad-
vantage of a want of knowledge. It is this want which
renders it so singularly monotonous. The poverty of the
poet's ideas confined his mind to a narrow circle, and his
poems are a series of changes run upon a few thoughts
and a few images. Single passages are beautiful and affecting, but each poem, as a whole, is tiresome and un-
interesting.

I come, in the last place, to the question of our own
expectations in literature, and the probability of our producing in the new world anything to rival the immortal
poems of the old. . . . Where the fountains of knowledge
are by the roadside, and where the volumes from which
poetic enthusiasms are caught and fed are in everybody's

hands, it would be singularly strange if, amid the multitude of pursuits which occupy our citizens, nobody should think of taking verse as a path to fame. Yet, if it shall be chosen and pursued with the characteristic ardor of our countrymen, what can prevent its being brought to the same degree of perfection here as in other countries? . . . With respect to the paucity of national traditions, it will be time to complain of it when all those of which we are possessed are exhausted. Besides, as I have already shown, it is the privilege of poets, when they suppose themselves in need of materials, to seek them in other countries. The best English poets have done this. The events of Spenser's celebrated poem take place within the shadowy limits of fairy-land. Shakespeare laid the scene of many of his finest tragedies in foreign countries. Milton went out of the world for the subject of his two epics. Byron has taken the incidents of all his poems from outside of England. Southey's best work is a poem of Spain—of chivalry, and of the Roman Church. For the story of one of his narrative poems, Moore went to Persia; for that of another, to the antediluvian world. Wordsworth and Crabbe, each in a different way, and each with great power, abjuring all heroic traditions and recollections, and all aid from the supernatural and the marvellous, have drawn their subjects from modern manners and the simple occurrences of common life. Are they read, for that reason, with any the less avidity by the multitudes who resort to their pages for pastime, for edification, for solace, for noble joy, and for the ecstasies of pure delight?

It has been urged by some, as an obstacle to the growth of elegant literature among us, that our language is a transplanted one, framed for a country and for institutions different from ours, and, therefore, not likely to be wielded by us with such force, effect, and grace, as it would have been if it had grown up with our nation, and received its forms and its accessions from the exigencies of our experience. It seems to me that this is one of the most insubstantial of all the brood of phantoms which have been conjured up to alarm us. Let those who press this opinion descend to particulars. Let them point out the peculiar de-

fects of our language in its application to our natural and
political situation. Let them show in what respects it refuses to accommodate itself easily and gracefully to all
the wants of expression that are felt among us. Till they
do this, let us be satisfied that the copious and flexible
dialect we speak is as equally proper to be used at the
equator as at the poles, and at any intermediate latitude;
and alike in monarchies or republics. It has grown up, as
every forcible and beautiful language has done, among a
simple and unlettered people; it has accommodated itself,
in the first place, to the things of nature, and, as civilization advanced, to the things of art; and thus it has become
a language full of picturesque forms of expression, yet
fitted for the purposes of science. If a new language were
to arise among us in our present condition of society, I
fear that it would derive too many of its words from the
roots used to signify canals, railroads, and steam-boats—
things which, however well thought of at present, may
perhaps a century hence be superseded by still more ingenious inventions. To try this notion about a transplanted
dialect, imagine one of the greatest living poets of England
emigrated to this country. Can anyone be simple enough
to suppose that his poetry would be the worse for it?

I infer, then, that all the materials of poetry exist in our
own country, with all the ordinary encouragements and
opportunities for making a successful use of them. The
elements of beauty and grandeur, intellectual greatness and
moral truth, the stormy and the gentle passions, the casu-
alties and the changes of life, and the light shed upon
man's nature by the story of past times and the knowledge
of foreign manners, have not made their sole abode in the
old world beyond the waters. If under these circumstances
our poetry should finally fail of rivalling that of Europe,
it will be because Genius sits idle in the midst of its
treasures.

EDGAR ALLAN POE

1809–1849

"Letter to B——," published as the preface of Poe's *Poems* (1831) when he was twenty-two years old, is his earliest literary platform. Poe here defines his own position in the context of Wordsworth's and Coleridge's. Although his attack on Wordsworth is rather intemperate and labored, Poe's denial that the aim of poetry can be instruction becomes a major element in his later critical theory. His tribute to Coleridge is especially significant and suggests the derivation of his concluding definition of poetry as having for its object not truth but an indefinite pleasure. These doctrines are elaborated in "The Poetic Principle." The identity of "B——" is uncertain; it is possibly the publisher of the 1831 volume, Elam Bliss.

In "The Philosophy of Composition," first published in *Graham's Magazine* (April, 1846), Poe professes to have written "The Raven" to conform to his preconceived plan of what a poem should be. His theories demanded that it deal with Beauty, be melancholy in tone, be of a length appropriate to "elevate the soul" of the reader at a single sitting, and reinforce its effect with a sonorous refrain. T. S. Eliot has observed "that if Poe plotted out his poem with such calculation, he might have taken a little more pains over it; the result hardly does credit to the method," but shows that Poe's method emphasized incantatory sound at the expense of rational sense. As Eliot makes clear, the essay should be taken as part of Poe's own *art poétique*. Poe's emphasis upon the self-consciousness of the poet's manipulation of language toward the ends of "pure poetry" has had great influence on Baudelaire, Mallarmé, and, through them, on post-Symbolist poetry and poetic theory.

"The Poetic Principle," Poe's final statement of his doctrines, was prepared as a lecture and delivered often during the last few years of Poe's life. It was posthumously published in the *New York Home Journal* and in *Sartain's Union Magazine* in 1850.

TEXTS: *The Complete Works of Edgar Allan Poe*, edited by James A. Harrison, 17 vols. (1902). See T. S. Eliot, "From Poe to Valery," *Hudson Review*, III (1949), 327–42; comment on Poe in Yvor Winters, *Maule's Curse* (1938).

LETTER TO B——

It has been said that a good critique on a poem may be written by one who is no poet himself. This, according to *your* idea and *mine* of poetry, I feel to be false—the less poetical the critic, the less just the critique, and the converse. On this account, and because there are but few B——'s in the world, I would be as much ashamed of the world's good opinion as proud of your own. Another than yourself might here observe, Shakespeare is in possession of the world's good opinion, and yet Shakespeare is the greatest of poets. It appears then that the world judge correctly, why should you be ashamed of their favorable judgment? The difficulty lies in the interpretation of the word "judgment" or "opinion." The opinion is the world's, truly, but it may be called theirs as a man would call a book his, having bought it; he did not write the book, but it is his; they did not originate the opinion, but it is theirs. A fool, for example, thinks Shakespeare a great poet—yet the fool has never read Shakespeare. But the fool's neighbor, who is a step higher on the Andes of the mind, whose head (that is to say, his more exalted thought) is too far above the fool to be seen or understood, but whose feet (by which I mean his every-day actions) are sufficiently near to be discerned, and by means of which that superiority is ascertained, which *but* for them would never have been discovered—this neighbor asserts that Shakespeare is a great poet—the fool believes him, and it is henceforward his *opinion*. This neighbor's opinion has, in like manner, been adopted from one above *him*, and so, ascendingly, to a few gifted individuals who kneel around the summit, beholding, face to face, the master spirit who stands upon the pinnacle.

You are aware of the great barrier in the path of an American writer. He is read, if at all, in preference to the combined and established wit of the world. I say established; for it is with literature as with law or empire—an established name is an estate in tenure, or a throne in possession. Besides, one might suppose that books, like their authors, improve by travel—their having crossed the sea is, with us, so great a distinction. Our antiquaries abandon time for distance; our very fops glance from the binding to the bottom of the title-page, where the mystic characters which spell London, Paris, or Genoa, are precisely so many letters of recommendation.

I mentioned just now a vulgar error as regards criticism. I think the notion that no poet can form a correct estimate of his own writings is another. I remarked before, that in proportion to the poetical talent, would be the justice of a critique upon poetry. Therefore, a bad poet would, I grant, make a false critique, and his self-love would infallibly bias his little judgment in his favor; but a poet, who is indeed a poet, could not, I think, fail of making a just critique. Whatever should be deducted on the score of self-love, might be replaced on account of his intimate acquaintance with the subject; in short, we have more instances of false criticism than of just, where one's own writings are the test, simply because we have more bad poets than good. There are of course many objections to what I say: Milton is a great example of the contrary; but his opinion with respect to the Paradise Regained, is by no means fairly ascertained. By what trivial circumstances men are often led to assert what they do not really believe! Perhaps an inadvertent word has descended to posterity. But, in fact, the Paradise Regained is little, if at all, inferior to the Paradise Lost, and is only supposed so to be, because men do not like epics, whatever they may say to the contrary, and reading those of Milton in their natural order, are too much wearied with the first to derive any pleasure from the second.

I dare say Milton preferred Comus to either—if so—justly.

As I am speaking of poetry, it will not be amiss to touch lightly upon the most singular heresy in its modern history —the heresy of what is called very foolishly, the Lake School. Some years ago I might have been induced, by an occasion like the present, to attempt a formal refutation of their doctrine; at present it would be a work of super-erogation. The wise must bow to the wisdom of such men as Coleridge and Southey, but being wise, have laughed at poetical theories so prosaically exemplified.

Aristotle, with singular assurance, has declared poetry the most philosophical of all writings—but it required a Wordsworth to pronounce it the most metaphysical. He seems to think that the end of poetry is, or should be, in-struction—yet it is a truism that the end of our existence is happiness; if so, the end of every separate part of our existence—every thing connected with our existence should be still happiness. Therefore the end of instruction should be happiness; and happiness is another name for pleasure; —therefore the end of instruction should be pleasure: yet we see the above mentioned opinion implies precisely the reverse.

To proceed: *ceteris paribus,* he who pleases, is of more importance to his fellow men than he who instructs, since utility is happiness, and pleasure is the end already ob-tained which instruction is merely the means of obtaining.

I see no reason, then, why our metaphysical poets should plume themselves so much on the utility of their works, unless indeed they refer to instruction with eternity in view; in which case, sincere respect for their piety would not allow me to express my contempt for their judgment; contempt which it would be difficult to conceal, since their writings are professedly to be understood by the few, and it is the many who stand in need of salvation. In such case I should no doubt be tempted to think of the devil in Melmoth, who labors indefatigably through three octavo volumes, to accomplish the destruction of one or two souls, while any common devil would have demolished one or two thousand.

Against the subtleties which would make poetry a study —not a passion—it becomes the metaphysician to reason— but the poet to protest. Yet Wordsworth and Coleridge are men in years; the one imbued in contemplation from his childhood, the other a giant in intellect and learning. The diffidence, then, with which I venture to dispute their authority, would be overwhelming, did I not feel, from the bottom of my heart, that learning has little to do with the imagination—intellect with the passions—or age with poetry.

> "Trifles, like straws, upon the surface flow,
> He who would search for pearls must dive below,"

are lines which have done much mischief. As regards the greater truths, men oftener err by seeking them at the bottom than at the top; the depth lies in the huge abysses where wisdom is sought—not in the palpable places where she is found. The ancients were not always right in hiding the goddess in a well: witness the light which Bacon has thrown upon philosophy; witness the principles of our divine faith—that moral mechanism by which the simplicity of a child may overbalance the wisdom of a man.

We see an instance of Coleridge's liability to err, in his Biographia Literaria—professedly his literary life and opinions, but, in fact, a treatise *de omni scibili et quibusdam aliis.* He goes wrong by reason of his very profundity, and of his error we have a natural type in the contemplation of a star. He who regards it directly and intensely sees, it is true, the star, but it is the star without a ray—while he who surveys it less inquisitively is conscious of all for which the star is useful to us below—its brilliancy and its beauty.

As to Wordsworth, I have no faith in him. That he had, in youth, the feelings of a poet I believe—for there are glimpses of extreme delicacy in his writings—(and delicacy is the poet's own kingdom—his *El Dorado*)—but they have the appearance of a better day recollected; and glimpses, at best, are little evidence of present poetic fire—we know that a few straggling flowers spring up daily in the crevices of the glacier.

He was to blame for wearing away his youth in contemplation with the end of poetizing in his manhood. With the increase of his judgment the light which should make it apparent has faded away. His judgment consequently is too correct. This may not be understood,—but the old Goths of Germany would have understood it, who used it to debate matters of importance to their State twice, once when drunk, and once when sober—sober that they might not be deficient in formality—drunk lest they should be destitute of vigor.

The long wordy discussions by which he tries to reason us into admiration of his poetry, speak very little in his favor: they are full of such assertions as this—(I have opened one of his volumes at random) "Of genius the only proof is the act of doing well what is worthy to be done, and what was never done before"—indeed! then it follows that in doing what is *un*worthy to be done, or what *has* been done before, no genius can be evinced; yet the picking of pockets is an unworthy act, pockets have been picked time immemorial, and Barrington, the pick-pocket, in point of genius, would have thought hard of a comparison with William Wordsworth, the poet.

Again—in estimating the merit of certain poems, whether they be Ossian's or M'Pherson's, can surely be of little consequence, yet, in order to prove their worthlessness, Mr. W. has expended many pages in the controversy. *Tantaene animis?* Can great minds descend to such absurdity? But worse still: that he may bear down every argument in favor of these poems, he triumphantly drags forward a passage, in his abomination of which he expects the reader to sympathize. It is the beginning of the epic poem *"Temora."* "The blue waves of Ullin roll in light; the green hills are covered with day; trees shake their dusky heads in the breeze." And this—this gorgeous, yet simple imagery, where all is alive and panting with immortality—this, William Wordsworth, the author of "Peter Bell," has *selected* for his contempt. We shall see what better he, in his own person, has to offer. Imprimis:

"And now she's at the pony's head,
And now she's at the pony's tail,
On that side now, and now on this,
And almost stifled her with bliss—
A few sad tears does Betty shed,
She pats the pony where or when
She knows not: happy Betty Foy!
O, Johnny! never mind the Doctor!"

Secondly:

"The dew was falling fast, the—stars began to blink,
I heard a voice; it said—drink, pretty creature, drink;
And, looking o'er the hedge, be—fore me I espied
A snow-white mountain lamb, with a—maiden at its
   side.
No other sheep were near, the lamb was all alone,
And by a slender cord was—tether'd to a stone."

Now, we have no doubt this is all true; we *will* believe
it, indeed, we will, Mr. W. Is it sympathy for the sheep
you wish to excite? I love a sheep from the bottom of my
heart.

But there *are* occasions, dear B——, there are occasions
when even Wordsworth is reasonable. Even Stamboul, it
is said, shall have an end, and the most unlucky blunders
must come to a conclusion. Here is an extract from his
preface—

"Those who have been accustomed to the phraseology
of modern writers, if they persist in reading this book to a
conclusion (*impossible!*) will, no doubt, have to struggle
with feelings of awkwardness; (ha! ha! ha!) and will be
induced to inquire by what species of courtesy these attempts have been permitted to assume that title." Ha! ha!
ha! ha! ha!

Yet let not Mr. W. despair; he has given immortality to
a wagon, and the bee Sophocles has transmitted to eternity
a sore toe, and dignified a tragedy with a chorus of
turkeys.

Of Coleridge I cannot speak but with reverence. His
towering intellect! his gigantic power! He is one more evi-

dence of the fact "que la plupart des sectes ont raison dans une bonne partie de ce qu'elles avancent, mais non pas en ce qu'elles nient." He has imprisoned his own conceptions by the barrier he has erected against those of others. It is lamentable to think that such a mind should be buried in metaphysics, and, like the Nyctanthes, waste its perfume upon the night alone. In reading his poetry, I tremble, like one who stands upon a volcano, conscious, from the very darkness bursting from the crater, of the fire and the light that are weltering below.

What is Poetry?—Poetry! that proteus-like idea, with as many appellations as the nine-titled Corcyra! Give me, I demanded of a scholar some time ago, give me a definition of poetry. "Tres-volontiers," and he proceeded to his library, brought me a Dr. Johnson, and overwhelmed me with a definition. Shade of the immortal Shakespeare! I imagine to myself the scowl of your spiritual eye upon the profanity of that scurrilous Ursa Major. Think of poetry, dear B——, think of poetry, and then think of—Dr. Samuel Johnson! Think of all that is airy and fairy-like, and then of all that is hideous and unwieldy; think of his huge bulk, the Elephant! and then—and then think of the Tempest— the Midsummer Night's Dream—Prospero—Oberon—and Titania!

A poem, in my opinion, is opposed to a work of science by having, for its *immediate* object, pleasure, not truth; to romance, by having for its object an *indefinite* instead of a *definite* pleasure, being a poem only so far as this object is attained; romance presenting perceptible images with definite, poetry with *in*definite sensations, to which end music is an *essential*, since the comprehension of sweet sound is our most indefinite conception. Music, when combined with a pleasurable idea, is poetry; music without the idea is simply music; the idea without the music is prose from its very definitiveness.

What was meant by the invective against him who had no music in his soul?

To sum up this long rigmarole, I have, dear B——, what you no doubt perceive, for the metaphysical poets, *as* poets, the most sovereign contempt. That they have followers proves nothing—

> The Indian prince has to his palace
> More followers than a thief to the gallows.

THE PHILOSOPHY OF COMPOSITION

Charles Dickens, in a note now lying before me, alluding to an examination I once made of the mechanism of "Barnaby Rudge," says—"By the way, are you aware that Godwin wrote his 'Caleb Williams' backwards? He first involved his hero in a web of difficulties, forming the second volume, and then, for the first, cast about him for some mode of accounting for what had been done."

I cannot think this the *precise* mode of procedure on the part of Godwin—and indeed what he himself acknowledges, is not altogether in accordance with Mr. Dickens' idea—but the author of "Caleb Williams" was too good an artist not to perceive the advantage derivable from at least a somewhat similar process. Nothing is more clear than that every plot, worth the name, must be elaborated to its *dénouement* before anything be attempted with the pen. It is only with the *dénouement* constantly in view that we can give a plot its indispensable air of consequence, or causation, by making the incidents, and especially the tone at all points, tend to the development of the intention.

There is a radical error, I think, in the usual mode of constructing a story. Either history affords a thesis—or one is suggested by an incident of the day—or, at best, the author sets himself to work in the combination of striking events to form merely the basis of his narrative—designing, generally, to fill in with description, dialogue, or autorial comment, whatever crevices of fact, or action, may, from page to page, render themselves apparent.

I prefer commencing with the consideration of an *effect*. Keeping originality *always* in view—for he is false to himself who ventures to dispense with so obvious and so easily attainable a source of interest—I say to myself, in the first place, "Of the innumerable effects, or impressions, of which the heart, the intellect, or (more generally) the soul is susceptible, what one shall I, on the present occasion, select?" Having chosen a novel, first, and secondly a vivid effect, I consider whether it can be best wrought by incident or tone—whether by ordinary incidents and peculiar tone, or the converse, or by peculiarity both of incident and tone—afterward looking about me (or rather within) for such combinations of event, or tone, as shall best aid me in the construction of the effect.

I have often thought how interesting a magazine paper might be written by any author who would—that is to say who could—detail, step by step, the processes by which any one of his compositions attained its ultimate point of completion. Why such a paper has never been given to the world, I am much at a loss to say—but, perhaps, the autorial vanity has had more to do with the omission than any one other cause. Most writers—poets in especial—prefer having it understood that they compose by a species of fine frenzy—an ecstatic intuition—and would positively shudder at letting the public take a peep behind the scenes, at the elaborate and vacillating crudities of thought—at the true purposes seized only at the last moment—at the innumerable glimpses of idea that arrived not at the maturity of full view—at the fully matured fancies discarded in despair as unmanageable—at the cautious selections and rejections—at the painful erasures and interpolations—in a word, at the wheels and pinions—the tackle for scene-shifting—the step-ladders and demon-traps—the cock's feathers, the red paint and the black patches, which, in ninety-nine cases out of the hundred, constitute the properties of the literary *histrio*.

I am aware, on the other hand, that the case is by no means common, in which an author is at all in condition to retrace the steps by which his conclusions have been attained. In general, suggestions, having arisen pell-mell, are pursued and forgotten in a similar manner.

For my own part, I have neither sympathy with the repugnance alluded to, nor, at any time the least difficulty in recalling to mind the progressive steps of any of my compositions; and, since the interest of an analysis, or reconstruction, such as I have considered a *desideratum*, is quite independent of any real or fancied interest in the thing analyzed, it will not be regarded as a breach of decorum on my part to show the *modus operandi* by which some one of my own works was put together. I select "The Raven," as most generally known. It is my design to render it manifest that no one point in its composition is referable either to accident or intuition—that the work proceeded, step by step, to its completion with the precision and rigid consequence of a mathematical problem.

Let us dismiss, as irrelevant to the poem, *per se*, the circumstance—or say the necessity—which, in the first place, gave rise to the intention of composing *a* poem that should suit at once the popular and the critical taste.

We commence, then, with this intention.

The initial consideration was that of extent. If any literary work is too long to be read at one sitting, we must be content to dispense with the immensely important effect derivable from unity of impression—for, if two sittings be required, the affairs of the world interfere, and every thing like totality is at once destroyed. But since, *ceteris paribus*, no poet can afford to dispense with *any thing* that may advance his design, it but remains to be seen whether there is, in extent, any advantage to counterbalance the loss of unity which attends it. Here I say no, at once. What we term a long poem is, in fact, merely a succession of brief ones—that is to say, of brief poetical effects. It is needless to demonstrate that a poem is such, only inasmuch as it intensely excites, by elevating, the soul; and all intense excitements are, through a psychal necessity, brief. For this reason, at least one half of the "Paradise Lost" is essentially prose—a succession of poetical excitements interspersed, *inevitably*, with corresponding depressions—the whole being deprived, through the extremeness of its length, of the vastly important artistic element, totality, or unity, of effect.

It appears evident, then, that there is a distinct limit, as regards length, to all works of literary art—the limit of a single sitting—and that, although in certain classes of prose composition, such as "Robinson Crusoe," (demanding no unity,) this limit may be advantageously overpassed, it can never properly be overpassed in a poem. Within this limit, the extent of a poem may be made to bear mathematical relation to its merit—in other words, to the excitement or elevation—again in other words, to the degree of the true poetical effect which it is capable of inducing; for it is clear that the brevity must be in direct ratio of the intensity of the intended effect:—this, with one proviso —that a certain degree of duration is absolutely requisite for the production of any effect at all.

Holding in view these considerations, as well as that degree of excitement which I deemed not above the popular, while not below the critical, taste, I reached at once what I conceived the proper *length* for my intended poem—a length of about one hundred lines. It is, in fact, a hundred and eight.

My next thought concerned the choice of an impression, or effect, to be conveyed: and here I may as well observe that, throughout the construction, I kept steadily in view the design of rendering the work *universally* appreciable. I should be carried too far out of my immediate topic were I to demonstrate a point upon which I have repeatedly insisted, and which, with the poetical, stands not in the slightest need of demonstration—the point, I mean, that Beauty is the sole legitimate province of the poem. A few words, however, in elucidation of my real meaning, which some of my friends have evinced a disposition to misrepresent. That pleasure which is at once the most intense, the most elevating, and the most pure, is, I believe, found in the contemplation of the beautiful. When, indeed, men speak of Beauty, they mean, precisely, not a quality, as is supposed, but an effect—they refer, in short, just to that intense and pure elevation of *soul—not* of intellect, or of heart— upon which I have commented, and which is experienced in consequence of contemplating "the beautiful." Now I designate Beauty as the province of the poem, merely because it is an obvious rule of Art that effects should be made to spring from direct causes—that objects should be attained through means best adapted for their attainment —no one as yet having been weak enough to deny that the peculiar elevation alluded to is *most readily* attained in the poem. Now the object, Truth, or the satisfaction of the intellect, and the object Passion, or the excitement of the heart, are, although attainable, to a certain extent, in poetry, far more readily attainable in prose. Truth, in fact, demands a precision, and Passion a *homeliness* (the truly passionate will comprehend me) which are absolutely antagonistic to that Beauty which, I maintain, is the excitement, or pleasurable elevation, of the soul. It by no means follows from any thing here said, that passion, or even truth, may not be introduced, and even profitably introduced, into a poem—for they may serve in elucidation, or aid the general effect, as do discords in music, by contrast—but the true artist will always contrive, first, to tone them into proper subservience to the predominant aim, and, secondly, to enveil them, as far as possible, in that Beauty which is the atmosphere and the essence of the poem.

Regarding, then, Beauty as my province, my next question referred to the *tone* of its highest manifestation—and all experience has shown that this tone is one of *sadness*. Beauty of whatever kind, in its supreme development, invariably excites the sensitive soul to tears. Melancholy is thus the most legitimate of all the poetical tones.

The length, the province, and the tone, being thus determined, I betook myself to ordinary induction, with the view of obtaining some artistic piquancy which might serve me as a key-note in the construction of the poem— some pivot upon which the whole structure might turn. In carefully thinking over all the usual artistic effects—or more properly *points,* in the theatrical sense—I did not fail to perceive immediately that no one had been so universally employed as that of the *refrain.* The universality of its employment sufficed to assure me of its intrinsic value, and spared me the necessity of submitting it to analysis. I considered it, however, with regard to its susceptibility of improvement, and soon saw it to be in a primitive condition. As commonly used, the *refrain,* or burden, not only is limited to lyric verse, but depends for its impression upon the force of monotone—both in sound and thought. The pleasure is deduced solely from the sense of identity—of repetition. I resolved to diversify, and so heighten, the effect, by adhering, in general, to the monotone of sound, while I continually varied that of thought: that is to say, I determined to produce continuously novel effects, by the variation *of the application* of the *refrain*—the *refrain* itself remaining, for the most part, unvaried.

These points being settled, I next bethought me of the *nature* of my *refrain*. Since its application was to be repeatedly varied, it was clear that the *refrain* itself must be brief, for there would have been an insurmountable difficulty in frequent variations of application in any sentence of length. In proportion to the brevity of the sentence, would, of course, be the facility of the variation. This led me at once to a single word as the best *refrain*.

The question now arose as to the *character* of the word. Having made up my mind to a *refrain*, the division of the poem into stanzas was, of course, a corollary: the *refrain* forming the close of each stanza. That such a close, to have force, must be sonorous and susceptible of protracted emphasis, admitted no doubt: and these considerations inevitably led me to the long *o* as the most sonorous vowel, in connection with *r* as the most producible consonant.

The sound of the *refrain* being thus determined, it became necessary to select a word embodying this sound, and at the same time in the fullest possible keeping with that melancholy which I had predetermined as the tone of the poem. In such a search it would have been absolutely impossible to overlook the word "Nevermore." In fact, it was the very first which presented itself.

The next *desideratum* was a pretext for the continuous use of the one word "nevermore." In observing the difficulty which I at once found in inventing a sufficiently plausible reason for its continuous repetition, I did not fail to perceive that this difficulty arose solely from the preassumption that the word was to be so continuously or monotonously spoken by *a human* being—I did not fail to perceive, in short, that the difficulty lay in the reconciliation of this monotony with the exercise of reason on the part of the creature repeating the word. Here, then, immediately arose the idea of a *non*-reasoning creature capable of speech; and, very naturally, a parrot, in the first instance, suggested itself, but was superseded forthwith by a Raven, as equally capable of speech, and infinitely more in keeping with the intended *tone*.

I had now gone so far as the conception of a Raven—the bird of ill omen—monotonously repeating the one word, "Nevermore," at the conclusion of each stanza, in a poem of melancholy tone, and in length about one hundred lines. Now, never losing sight of the object *supremeness*, or perfection, at all points, I asked myself—"Of all melancholy topics, what, according to the *universal* understanding of mankind, is the *most* melancholy?" Death was the obvious reply. "And when," I said, "is this most melancholy of topics most poetical?" From what I have already explained at some length, the answer, here also, is obvious—"When it most closely allies itself to *Beauty*: the death, then, of a beautiful woman is, unquestionably, the most poetical topic in the world—and equally is it beyond doubt that the lips best suited for such topic are those of a bereaved lover."

I had now to combine the two ideas, of a lover lamenting his deceased mistress and a Raven continuously repeating the word "Nevermore."—I had to combine these, bearing in mind my design of varying, at every turn, the *application* of the word repeated; but the only intelligible mode of such combination is that of imagining the Raven employing the word in answer to the queries of the lover. And here it was that I saw at once the opportunity afforded for the effect on which I had been depending—that is to say, the effect of the *variation of application.* I saw that I could make the first query propounded by the lover—the first query to which the Raven should reply "Nevermore"—that I could make this first query a commonplace one—the second less so—the third still less, and so on—until at length the lover, startled from his original *nonchalance* by the melancholy character of the word itself—by its frequent repetition—and by a consideration of the ominous reputation of the fowl that uttered it—is at length excited to superstition, and wildly propounds queries of a far different character—queries whose solution he has passionately at heart—propounds them half in superstition and half in that species of despair which delights in self-torture—propounds them not altogether because he believes in the prophetic or demoniac character of the bird (which, reason assures him, is merely repeating a lesson learned by rote) but because he experiences a phrenzied pleasure in so modeling his questions as to receive from the *expected* "Nevermore" the most delicious because the most intolerable of sorrow. Perceiving the opportunity thus afforded me—or, more strictly, thus forced upon me in the progress of the construction—I first established in mind the climax, or concluding query—that query to which "Nevermore" should be in the last place an answer—that in reply to which this word "Nevermore" should involve the utmost conceivable amount of sorrow and despair.

Here then the poem may be said to have its beginning—at the end, where all works of art should begin—for it was here, at this point of my preconsideration, that I first put pen to paper in the composition of the stanza:

"Prophet," said I, "thing of evil! prophet still if bird or devil!
By that heaven that bends above us—by that God we both adore,
Tell this soul with sorrow laden, if within the distant Aidenn,
It shall clasp a sainted maiden whom the angels name Lenore—
Clasp a rare and radiant maiden whom the angels name Lenore."
Quoth the Raven "Nevermore."

I composed this stanza, at this point, first that, by establishing the climax, I might the better vary and graduate, as regards seriousness and importance, the preceding queries of the lover—and, secondly, that I might definitely settle the rhythm, the metre, and the length and general arrangement of the stanza—as well as graduate the stanzas which were to precede, so that none of them might surpass this in rhythmical effect. Had I been able, in the subsequent composition, to construct more vigorous stanzas, I should, without scruple, have purposely enfeebled them, so as not to interfere with the climacteric effect.

And here I may as well say a few words of the versification. My first object (as usual) was originality. The extent to which this has been neglected, in versification, is one of the most unaccountable things in the world. Admitting that there is little possibility of variety in mere *rhythm*, it is still clear that the possible varieties of metre and stanza are absolutely infinite—and yet, *for centuries, no man, in verse, has ever done, or ever seemed to think of doing, an original thing.* The fact is, that originality (unless in minds of very unusual force) is by no means a matter, as some suppose, of impulse or intuition. In general, to be found, it must be elaborately sought, and although a positive merit of the highest class, demands in its attainment less of invention than negation.

Of course, I pretend to no originality in either the rhythm or metre of the "Raven." The former is trochaic—the latter is octameter acatalectic, alternating with heptameter catalectic repeated in the *refrain* of the fifth verse, and terminating with tetrameter catalectic. Less pedantically—the feet employed throughout (trochees) consist of a long syllable followed by a short: the first line of the stanza consists of eight of these feet—the second of seven and a half (in effect two-thirds)—the third of eight—the fourth of seven and a half—the fifth the same—the sixth three and a half. Now, each of these lines, taken individually, has been employed before, and what originality the "Raven" has, is in their *combination into stanza;* nothing even remotely approaching this combination has ever been attempted. The effect of this originality of combination is aided by other unusual, and some altogether novel effects, arising from an extension of the application of the principles of rhyme and alliteration.

The next point to be considered was the mode of bringing together the lover and the Raven—and the first branch of this consideration was the *locale*. For this the most natural suggestion might seem to be a forest, or the fields—but it has always appeared to me that a close *circumscription of space* is absolutely necessary to the effect of insulated incident:—it has the force of a frame to a picture. It has an indisputable moral power in keeping concentrated the attention, and, of course, must not be confounded with mere unity of place.

I determined, then, to place the lover in his chamber—in a chamber rendered sacred to him by memories of her who had frequented it. The room is represented as richly furnished—this in mere pursuance of the ideas I have already explained on the subject of Beauty, as the sole true poetical thesis.

The *locale* being thus determined, I had now to introduce the bird—and the thought of introducing him through the window, was inevitable. The idea of making the lover suppose, in the first instance, that the flapping of the wings of the bird against the shutter, is a "tapping" at the door, originated in a wish to increase, by prolonging, the reader's curiosity, and in a desire to admit the incidental effect arising from the lover's throwing open the door, finding all dark, and thence adopting the half-fancy that it was the spirit of his mistress that knocked.

I made the night tempestuous, first, to account for the Raven's seeking admission, and secondly, for the effect of contrast with the (physical) serenity within the chamber.

I made the bird alight on the bust of Pallas, also for the effect of contrast between the marble and the plumage—it being understood that the bust was absolutely *suggested* by the bird—the bust of *Pallas* being chosen, first, as most in keeping with the scholarship of the lover, and, secondly, for the sonorousness of the word, Pallas, itself.

About the middle of the poem, also, I have availed myself of the force of contrast, with a view of deepening the ultimate impression. For example, an air of the fantastic—approaching as nearly to the ludicrous as was admissible—is given to the Raven's entrance. He comes in "with many a flirt and flutter."

Not the *least obeisance made he*—not a moment
    stopped or stayed he,
But with mien of lord or lady, perched above my
    chamber door.

In the two stanzas which follow, the design is more
obviously carried out:—

Then this ebony bird beguiling my sad fancy into
    smiling
By the *grave and stern decorum of the countenance
    it wore*,
"Though thy *crest be shorn and shaven* thou," I said,
    "art sure no craven,
Ghastly grim and ancient Raven wandering from the
    nightly shore—
Tell me what thy lordly name is on the Night's
    Plutonian shore?"
      Quoth the Raven "Nevermore."

Much I marvelled *this ungainly fowl* to hear discourse
    so plainly
Though its answer little meaning—little relevancy bore;
For we cannot help agreeing that no living human
    being
*Ever yet was blessed with seeing bird above his
    chamber door*—
*Bird or beast upon the sculptured bust above his
    chamber door*,
      With such name as "Nevermore."

The effect of the *dénouement* being thus provided for,
I immediately drop the fantastic for a tone of the most
profound seriousness:—this tone commencing in the stanza
directly following the one last quoted, with the line,

But the Raven, sitting lonely on that placid bust,
    spoke only, etc.

From this epoch the lover no longer jests—no longer
sees any thing even of the fantastic in the Raven's de-

meanor. He speaks of him as a "grim, ungainly, ghastly, gaunt, and ominous bird of yore," and feels the "fiery eyes" burning into his "bosom's core." This revolution of thought, or fancy, on the lover's part, is intended to induce a similar one on the part of the reader—to bring the mind into a proper frame for the *dénouement*—which is now brought about as rapidly and as *directly* as possible.

With the *dénouement* proper—with the Raven's reply, "Nevermore," to the lover's final demand if he shall meet his mistress in another world—the poem, in its obvious phase, that of a simple narrative, may be said to have its completion. So far, every thing is within the limits of the accountable—of the real. A raven, having learned by rote the single word "Nevermore," and having escaped from the custody of its owner, is driven at midnight, through the violence of a storm, to seek admission at a window from which a light still gleams—the chamber-window of a student, occupied half in poring over a volume, half in dreaming of a beloved mistress deceased. The casement being thrown open at the fluttering of the bird's wings, the bird itself perches on the most convenient seat out of the immediate reach of the student, who, amused by the incident and the oddity of the visitor's demeanor, demands of it, in jest and without looking for a reply, its name. The raven addressed, answers with its customary word, "Nevermore"—a word which finds immediate echo in the melancholy heart of the student, who, giving utterance aloud to certain thoughts suggested by the occasion, is again startled by the fowl's repetition of "Nevermore." The student now guesses the state of the case, but is impelled, as I have before explained, by the human thirst for self-torture, and in part by superstition, to propound such queries to the bird as will bring him, the lover, the most of the luxury of sorrow, through the anticipated answer "Nevermore." With the indulgence, to the extreme, of this self-torture, the narration, in what I have termed its first or obvious phase, has a natural termination, and so far there has been no overstepping of the limits of the real.

But in subjects so handled, however skilfully, or with however vivid an array of incident, there is always a certain hardness or nakedness, which repels the artistical eye. Two things are invariably required—first, some amount of complexity, or more properly, adaptation; and, secondly, some amount of suggestiveness—some under-current, however indefinite, of meaning. It is this latter, in especial, which imparts to a work of art so much of that *richness* (to borrow from colloquy a forcible term) which we are too fond of confounding with *the ideal*. It is the *excess* of the suggested meaning—it is the rendering this the upper instead of the under current of the theme—which turns into prose (and that of the very flattest kind) the so called poetry of the so called transcendentalists.

Holding these opinions, I added the two concluding stanzas of the poem—their suggestiveness being thus made to pervade all the narrative which has preceded them. The under-current of meaning is rendered first apparent in the lines—

> "Take thy beak from out *my heart,* and take thy form
>   from off my door!"
>   Quoth the Raven "Nevermore!"

It will be observed that the words, "from out my heart," involve the first metaphorical expression in the poem. They, with the answer, "Nevermore," dispose the mind to seek a moral in all that has been previously narrated. The reader begins now to regard the Raven as emblematical—but it is not until the very last line of the very last stanza, that the intention of making him emblematical of *Mournful and Never-Ending Remembrance* is permitted distinctly to be seen:

> And the Raven, never flitting, still is sitting, still is
>   sitting,
> On the pallid bust of Pallas, just above my chamber
>   door;
> And his eyes have all the seeming of a demon's that
>   is dreaming,
> And the lamplight o'er him streaming throws his
>   shadow on the floor;

And my soul *from out that shadow* that lies floating
    on the floor
        Shall be lifted—nevermore.

THE POETIC PRINCIPLE

In speaking of the Poetic Principle, I have no design
to be either thorough or profound. While discussing, very
much at random, the essentiality of what we call Poetry,
my principal purpose will be to cite for consideration, some
few of those minor English or American poems which best
suit my own taste, or which, upon my own fancy, have
left the most definite impression. By "minor poems" I mean,
of course, poems of little length. And here, in the beginning, permit me to say a few words in regard to a somewhat peculiar principle, which, whether rightfully or
wrongfully, has always had its influence in my own critical
estimate of the poem. I hold that a long poem does not
exist. I maintain that the phrase, "a long poem," is simply
a flat contradiction in terms.

I need scarcely observe that a poem deserves its title
only inasmuch as it excites, by elevating the soul. The value
of the poem is in the ratio of this elevating excitement.
But all excitements are, through a psychal necessity,
transient. That degree of excitement which would entitle
a poem to be so called at all, cannot be sustained throughout a composition of any great length. After the lapse of
half an hour, at the very utmost, it flags—fails—a revulsion
ensues—and then the poem is, in effect, and in fact, no
longer such.

There are, no doubt, many who have found difficulty
in reconciling the critical dictum that the "Paradise Lost"
is to be devoutly admired throughout, with the absolute
impossibility of maintaining for it, during perusal, the
amount of enthusiasm which that critical dictum would
demand. This great work, in fact, is to be regarded as
poetical, only when, losing sight of that vital requisite in
all works of Art, Unity, we view it merely as a series of
minor poems. If, to preserve its Unity—its totality of effect

or impression—we read it (as would be necessary) at a single sitting, the result is but a constant alternation of excitement and depression. After a passage of what we feel to be true poetry, there follows, inevitably, a passage of platitude which no critical pre-judgment can force us to admire; but if, upon completing the work, we read it again; omitting the first book—that is to say, commencing with the second—we shall be surprised at now finding that admirable which we before condemned—that damnable which we had previously so much admired. It follows from all this that the ultimate, aggregate, or absolute effect of even the best epic under the sun, is a nullity:—and this is precisely the fact.

In regard to the Iliad, we have, if not positive proof, at least very good reason, for believing it intended as a series of lyrics; but, granting the epic intention, I can say only that the work is based in an imperfect sense of art. The modern epic is, of the supposititious ancient model, but an inconsiderate and blindfold imitation. But the day of these artistic anomalies is over. If, at any time, any very long poem *were* popular in reality, which I doubt, it is at least clear that no very long poem will ever be popular again.

That the extent of a poetical work is, *ceteris paribus,* the measure of its merit, seems undoubtedly, when we thus state it, a proposition sufficiently absurd—yet we are indebted for it to the Quarterly Reviews. Surely there can be nothing in mere *size,* abstractly considered—there can be nothing in mere *bulk,* so far as a volume is concerned, which has so continuously elicited admiration from these saturnine pamphlets! A mountain, to be sure, by the mere sentiment of physical magnitude which it conveys, *does* impress us with a sense of the sublime—but no man is impressed after *this* fashion by the material grandeur of even "The Columbiad." Even the Quarterlies have not instructed us to be so impressed by it. *As yet,* they have not *insisted* on our estimating Lamartine by the cubic foot, or Pollok by the pound—but what else are we to *infer* from their continual prating about "sustained effort"? If, by "sustained effort," any little gentleman has accomplished an epic, let us frankly commend him for the effort—if this indeed be a thing commendable—but let us forbear praising the epic on the effort's account. It is to be hoped that common sense, in the time to come, will prefer deciding upon a work of art, rather by the impression it makes, by the effect it produces, than by the time it took to impress the effect or by the amount of "sustained effort" which had been found necessary in effecting the impression. The fact is, that perseverance is one thing, and genius quite another —nor can all the Quarterlies in Christendom confound them. By-and-by, this proposition, with many which I have been just urging, will be received as self-evident. In the meantime, by being generally condemned as falsities, they will not be essentially damaged as truths.

On the other hand, it is clear that a poem may be improperly brief. Undue brevity degenerates into mere epigrammatism. A *very* short poem, while now and then producing a brilliant or vivid, never produces a profound or enduring effect. There must be the steady pressing down of the stamp upon the wax. De Béranger has wrought innumerable things, pungent and spirit-stirring; but, in general, they have been too imponderous to stamp themselves deeply into the public attention; and thus, as so many feathers of fancy, have been blown aloft only to be whistled down the wind.

A remarkable instance of the effect of undue brevity in depressing a poem—in keeping it out of the popular view— is afforded by the following exquisite little Serenade:

> I arise from dreams of thee
>   In the first sweet sleep of night,
> When the winds are breathing low,
>   And the stars are shining bright;
> I arise from dreams of thee,
>   And a spirit in my feet
> Hath led me—who knows how?—
>   To thy chamber-window, sweet!
>
> The wandering airs, they faint
>   On the dark, the silent stream—
> The champak odours fail
>   Like sweet thoughts in a dream;

The nightingale's complaint,
  It dies upon her heart,
As I must die on thine,
  O, beloved as thou art!

O, lift me from the grass!
  I die, I faint, I fail!
Let thy love in kisses rain
  On my lips and eyelids pale.
My cheek is cold and white, alas!
  My heart beats loud and fast:
Oh! press it close to thine again,
  Where it will break at last!

Very few, perhaps, are familiar with these lines—yet no less a poet than Shelley is their author. Their warm, yet delicate and ethereal imagination will be appreciated by all—but by none so thoroughly as by him who has himself arisen from sweet dreams of one beloved to bathe in the aromatic air of a southern midsummer night.

One of the finest poems by Willis—the very best, in my opinion, which he has ever written—has, no doubt, through this same defect of undue brevity, been kept back from its proper position, not less in the critical than in the popular view.

The shadows lay along Broadway,
  'Twas near the twilight-tide—
And slowly there a lady fair
  Was walking in her pride.
Alone walk'd she; but, viewlessly,
  Walk'd spirits at her side.

Peace charm'd the street beneath her feet,
  And Honour charm'd the air;
And all astir looked kind on her,
  And call'd her good and fair—
For all God ever gave to her
  She kept with chary care.

She kept with care her beauties rare
　　From lovers warm and true—
For her heart was cold to all but gold,
　　And the rich came not to woo—
But honour'd well are charms to sell,
　　If priests the selling do.

Now walking there was one more fair—
　　A slight girl, lily-pale;
And she had unseen company
　　To make the spirit quail—
'Twixt Want and Scorn she walk'd forlorn,
　　And nothing could avail.

No mercy now can clear her brow
　　For this world's peace to pray;
For, as love's wild prayer dissolved in air,
　　Her woman's heart gave way!—
But the sin forgiven by Christ in Heaven
　　By man is cursed alway!

In this composition we find it difficult to recognise the
Willis who has written so many mere "verses of society."
The lines are not only richly ideal, but full of energy;
while they breathe an earnestness—an evident sincerity of
sentiment—for which we look in vain throughout all the
other works of this author.

While the epic mania—while the idea that, to merit in
poetry, prolixity is indispensable—has, for some years past,
been gradually dying out of the public mind, by mere dint
of its own absurdity—we find it succeeded by a heresy too
palpably false to be long tolerated, but one which, in the
brief period it has already endured, may be said to have
accomplished more in the corruption of our Poetical Literature than all its other enemies combined. I allude to the
heresy of *The Didactic*. It has been assumed, tacitly and
avowedly, directly and indirectly, that the ultimate object
of all Poetry is Truth. Every poem, it is said, should inculcate a moral; and by this moral is the poetical merit of
the work to be adjudged. We Americans especially have

patronised this happy idea; and we Bostonians, very especially, have developed it in full. We have taken it into our heads that to write a poem simply for the poem's sake, and to acknowledge such to have been our design, would be to confess ourselves radically wanting in the true Poetic dignity and force:—but the simple fact is, that, would we but permit ourselves to look into our own souls, we should immediately there discover that under the sun there neither exists nor *can* exist any work more thoroughly dignified—more supremely noble than this very poem—this poem *per se*—this poem which is a poem and nothing more—this poem written solely for the poem's sake.

With as deep a reverence for the True as ever inspired the bosom of man, I would, nevertheless, limit, in some measure, its modes of inculcation. I would limit to enforce them. I would not enfeeble them by dissipation. The demands of Truth are severe. She has no sympathy with the myrtles. All *that* which is so indispensable in Song, is precisely all *that* with which *she* has nothing whatever to do. It is but making her a flaunting paradox, to wreathe her in gems and flowers. In enforcing a truth, we need severity rather than efflorescence of language. We must be simple, precise, terse. We must be cool, calm, unimpassioned. In a word, we must be in that mood which, as nearly as possible, is the exact converse of the poetical. *He* must be blind, indeed, who does not perceive the radical and chasmal differences between the truthful and the poetical modes of inculcation. He must be theory-mad beyond redemption who, in spite of these differences, shall still persist in attempting to reconcile the obstinate oils and waters of Poetry and Truth.

Dividing the world of mind into its three most immediately obvious distinctions, we have the Pure Intellect, Taste, and the Moral Sense. I place Taste in the middle, because it is just this position which, in the mind, it occupies. It holds intimate relations with either extreme; but from the Moral Sense is separated by so faint a difference that Aristotle has not hesitated to place some of its operations among the virtues themselves. Nevertheless, we find the *offices* of the trio marked with a sufficient distinction.

Just as the Intellect concerns itself with Truth, so Taste informs us of the Beautiful while the Moral Sense is regardful of Duty. Of this latter, while Conscience teaches the obligation, and Reason the expediency, Taste contents herself with displaying the charms:—waging war upon Vice solely on the ground of her deformity—her disproportion—her animosity to the fitting, to the appropriate, to the harmonious—in a word, to Beauty.

An immortal instinct, deep within the spirit of man, is thus, plainly, a sense of the Beautiful. This it is which administers to his delight in the manifold forms, and sounds, and odours, and sentiments amid which he exists. And just as the lily is repeated in the lake, or the eyes of Amaryllis in the mirror, so is the mere oral or written repetition of these forms, and sounds, and colours, and odours, and sentiments, a duplicate source of delight. But this mere repetition is not poetry. He who shall simply sing, with however glowing enthusiasm, or with however vivid a truth of description, of the sights, and sounds, and odours, and colours, and sentiments, which greet *him* in common with all mankind—he, I say, has yet failed to prove his divine title. There is still a something in the distance which he has been unable to attain. We have still a thirst unquenchable, to allay which he has not shown us the crystal springs. This thirst belongs to the immortality of Man. It is at once a consequence and an indication of his perennial existence. It is the desire of the moth for the star. It is no mere appreciation of the Beauty before us—but a wild effort to reach the Beauty above. Inspired by an ecstatic prescience of the glories beyond the grave, we struggle, by multiform combinations among the things and thoughts of Time, to attain a portion of that Loveliness whose very elements, perhaps, appertain to eternity alone. And thus when by Poetry—or when by Music, the most entrancing of the Poetic moods—we find ourselves melted into tears —we weep them—not as the Abbate Gravina supposes— through excess of pleasure, but through a certain, petulant, impatient sorrow at our inability to grasp *now*, wholly, here on earth, at once and for ever, those divine and rapturous joys, of which *through* the poem, or *through* the music, we attain to but brief and indeterminate glimpses.

The struggle to apprehend the supernal Loveliness—this struggle, on the part of souls fittingly constituted—has given to the world all *that* which it (the world) has ever been enabled at once to understand and *to feel* as poetic.

The Poetic Sentiment, of course, may develop itself in various modes—in Painting, in Sculpture, in Architecture, in the Dance—very especially in Music—and very peculiarly, and with a wide field, in the composition of the Landscape Garden. Our present theme, however, has regard only to its manifestation in words. And here let me speak briefly on the topic of rhythm. Contenting myself with the certainty that Music, in its various modes of metre, rhythm, and rhyme, is of so vast a moment in Poetry as never to be wisely rejected—is so vitally important an adjunct, that he is simply silly who declines its assistance, I will not now pause to maintain its absolute essentiality. It is in Music, perhaps, that the soul most nearly attains the great end for which, when inspired by the Poetic Sentiment, it struggles —the creation of supernal Beauty. It *may* be, indeed, that here this sublime end is, now and again, attained *in fact*. We are often made to feel, with a shivering delight, that from an earthly harp are stricken notes which *cannot* have been unfamiliar to the angels. And thus there can be little doubt that in the union of Poetry with Music in its popular sense, we shall find the widest field for the Poetic development. The old Bards and Minnesingers had advantages which we do not possess—and Thomas Moore, singing his own songs, was, in the most legitimate manner, perfecting them as poems.

To recapitulate, then:—I would define, in brief, the Poetry of words as *The Rhythmical Creation of Beauty*. Its sole arbiter is Taste. With the Intellect or with the Conscience, it has only collateral relations. Unless incidentally, it has no concern whatever either with Duty or with Truth.

A few words, however, in explanation. *That* pleasure which is at once the most pure, the most elevating, and the most intense, is derived, I maintain, from the contemplation of the Beautiful. In the contemplation of Beauty we alone find it possible to attain that pleasurable elevation, or excitement, *of the soul,* which we recognise as the Poetic Sentiment, and which is so easily distinguished from Truth, which is the satisfaction of the Reason, or from Passion, which is the excitement of the heart. I make Beauty, therefore—using the word as inclusive of the sublime—I make Beauty the province of the poem, simply because it is an obvious rule of Art that effects should be made to spring as directly as possible from their causes:—no one as yet having been weak enough to deny that the peculiar elevation in question is at least *most readily* attainable in the poem. It by no means follows, however, that the incitements of Passion, or the precepts of Duty, or even the lessons of Truth, may not be introduced into a poem, and with advantage; for they may subserve, incidentally, in various ways, the general purposes of the work:—but the true artist will always contrive to tone them down in proper subjection to that *Beauty* which is the atmosphere and the real essence of the poem.

I cannot better introduce the few poems which I shall present for your consideration, than by the citation of the Proem to Mr. Longfellow's "Waif":

The day is done, and the darkness
    Falls from the wings of Night,
As a feather is wafted downward
    From an Eagle in his flight.

I see the lights of the village
    Gleam through the rain and the mist,
And a feeling of sadness comes o'er me,
    That my soul cannot resist;

A feeling of sadness and longing,
    That is not akin to pain,
And resembles sorrow only
    As the mist resembles the rain.

Come, read to me some poem,
　Some simple and heartfelt lay,
That shall soothe this restless feeling,
　And banish the thoughts of day.

Not from the grand old masters,
　Not from the bards sublime,
Whose distant footsteps echo
　Through the corridors of Time.

For, like strains of martial music,
　Their mighty thoughts suggest
Life's endless toil and endeavour;
　And to-night I long for rest.

Read from some humbler poet,
　Whose songs gushed from his heart,
As showers from the clouds of summer,
　Or tears from the eyelids start;

Who through long days of labour,
　And nights devoid of ease,
Still heard in his soul the music
　Of wonderful melodies.

Such songs have power to quiet
　The restless pulse of care,
And come like the benediction
　That follows after prayer.

Then read from the treasured volume
　The poem of thy choice
And lend to the rhyme of the poet
　The beauty of thy voice.

And the night shall be filled with music,
　And the cares that infest the day,
Shall fold their tents, like the Arabs,
　And as silently steal away.

With no great range of imagination, these lines have been justly admired for their delicacy of expression. Some of the images are very effective. Nothing can be better than—

>————The bards sublime,
> Whose distant footsteps echo
> Down the corridors of Time.

The idea of the last quatrain is also very effective. The poem, on the whole, however, is chiefly to be admired for the graceful *insouciance* of its metre, so well in accordance with the character of the sentiments, and especially for the *ease* of the general manner. This "ease," or naturalness, in a literary style, it has long been the fashion to regard as ease in appearance alone—as a point of really difficult attainment. But not so:—a natural manner is difficult only to him who should never meddle with it—to the unnatural. It is but the result of writing with the understanding, or with the instinct, that *the tone*, in composition, should always be that which the mass of mankind would adopt—and must perpetually vary, of course, with the occasion. The author who, after the fashion of "The North American Review," should be, upon *all* occasions, merely "quiet," must necessarily upon *many* occasions, be simply silly, or stupid; and has no more right to be considered "easy," or "natural," than a Cockney exquisite, or than the sleeping Beauty in the wax-works.

Among the minor poems of Bryant, none has so much impressed me as the one which he entitles "June." I quote only a portion of it:

> There, through the long, long summer hours,
>   The golden light should lie,
> And thick young herbs and groups of flowers
>   Stand in their beauty by.
> The oriole should build and tell
> His love-tale, close beside my cell;
>   The idle butterfly
> Should rest him there, and there be heard
> The housewife-bee and humming-bird.

And what if cheerful shouts, at noon,
　　Come, from the village sent,
Or songs of maids, beneath the moon,
　　With fairy laughter blent?
And what, if in the evening light,
Betrothed lovers walk in sight
　　Of my low monument?
I would the lovely scene around
Might know no sadder sight nor sound.

I know, I know I should not see
　　The season's glorious show,
Nor would its brightness shine for me,
　　Nor its wild music flow;
But if, around my place of sleep,
The friends I love should come to weep,
　　They might not haste to go.
Soft airs, and song, and light, and bloom
Should keep them lingering by my tomb.

These to their softened hearts should bear
　　The thought of what has been,
And speak of one who cannot share
　　The gladness of the scene;
Whose part, in all the pomp that fills
The circuit of the summer hills,
　　Is—that his grave is green;
And deeply would their hearts rejoice
To hear again his living voice.

The rhythmical flow, here, is even voluptuous—nothing
could be more melodious. The poem has always affected
me in a remarkable manner. The intense melancholy which
seems to well up, perforce, to the surface of all the poet's
cheerful sayings about his grave, we find thrilling us to
the soul—while there is the truest poetic elevation in the
thrill. The impression left is one of a pleasurable sadness.
And if, in the remaining compositions which I shall introduce to you, there be more or less of a similar tone always
apparent, let me remind you that (how or why we know

not) this certain taint of sadness is inseparably connected with all the higher manifestations of true Beauty. . . . [Here Poe quotes, without significant comment, poems then popular by Edward Coate Pinckney, Thomas Moore, Thomas Hood, and Byron.]

From Alfred Tennyson—although in perfect sincerity I regard him as the noblest poet that ever lived—I have left myself time to cite only a very brief specimen. I call him, and *think* him the noblest of poets—*not* because the impressions he produces are, at *all* times, the most profound —*not* because the poetical excitement which he induces is, at *all* times, the most intense—but because it *is*, at all times, the most ethereal—in other words, the most elevating and the most pure. No poet is so little of the earth, earthy. What I am about to read is from his last long poem, "The Princess":

> Tears, idle tears, I know not what they mean,
> Tears from the depth of some divine despair
> Rise in the heart, and gather to the eyes,
> In looking on the happy Autumn-fields,
> And thinking of the days that are no more.
>
> Fresh as the first beam glittering on a sail,
> That brings our friends up from the underworld,
> Sad as the last which reddens over one
> That sinks with all we love below the verge;
> So sad, so fresh, the days that are no more.
>
> Ah, sad and strange as in dark summer dawns
> The earliest pipe of half-awaken'd birds
> To dying ears, when unto dying eyes
> The casement slowly grows a glimmering square;
> So sad, so strange, the days that are no more.
>
> Dear as remember'd kisses after death,
> And sweet as those by hopeless fancy feign'd
> On lips that are for others; deep as love,
> Deep as first love, and wild with all regret;
> O Death in Life, the days that are no more.

Thus, although in a very cursory and imperfect manner, I have endeavoured to convey to you my conception of the Poetic Principle. It has been my purpose to suggest that, while this Principle itself is, strictly and simply, the Human Aspiration for Supernal Beauty, the manifestation of the Principle is always found in *an elevating excitement of the Soul*—quite independent of that passion which is the intoxication of the heart—or of that Truth which is the satisfaction of the Reason. For, in regard to Passion, alas! its tendency is to degrade, rather than to elevate the Soul. Love, on the contrary—Love—the true, the divine Eros—the Uranian, as distinguished from the Dionæan Venus—is unquestionably the purest and truest of all poetical themes. And in regard to Truth—if, to be sure, through the attainment of a truth, we are led to perceive a harmony where none was apparent before, we experience, at once, the true poetical effect—but this effect is referable to the harmony alone, and not in the least degree to the truth which merely served to render the harmony manifest.

We shall reach, however, more immediately a distinct conception of what the true Poetry is, by mere reference to a few of the simple elements which induce in the Poet himself the true poetical effect. He recognises the ambrosia which nourishes his soul, in the bright orbs that shine in Heaven—in the volutes of the flower—in the clustering of low shrubberies—in the waving of the grain-fields—in the slanting of tall, Eastern trees—in the blue distance of mountains—in the grouping of clouds—in the twinkling of half-hidden brooks—in the gleaming of silver rivers—in the repose of sequestered lakes—in the star-mirroring depths of lonely wells. He perceives it in the songs of birds —in the harp of Æolus—in the sighing of the night-wind —in the repining voice of the forest—in the surf that complains to the shore—in the fresh breath of the woods—in the scent of the violet—in the voluptuous perfume of the hyacinth—in the suggestive odour that comes to him, at eventide, from far-distant, undiscovered islands, over dim oceans, illimitable and unexplored. He owns it in all noble thoughts—in all unworldly motives—in all holy impulses

—in all chivalrous, generous, and self-sacrificing deeds. He feels it in the beauty of woman—in the grace of her step —in the lustre of her eye—in the melody of her voice—in her soft laughter—in her sigh—in the harmony of the rustling of her robes. He deeply feels it in her winning endearments—in her burning enthusiasms—in her gentle charities —in her meek and devotional endurances—but above all— ah, far above all—he kneels to it—he worships it in the faith, in the purity, in the strength, in the altogether divine majesty—of her *love.*

Let me conclude—by the recitation of yet another brief poem—one very different in character from any that I have before quoted. It is by Motherwell, and is called "The Song of the Cavalier." With our modern and altogether rational ideas of the absurdity and impiety of warfare, we are not precisely in that frame of mind best adapted to sympathise with the sentiments, and thus to appreciate the real excellence of the poem. To do this fully, we must identify ourselves, in fancy, with the soul of the old cavalier.

> Then mounte! then mounte, brave gallants, all,
>   And don your helmes amaine:
> Deathe's couriers, Fame and Honour, call
>   Us to the field againe.
> No shrewish teares shall fill our eye
>   When the sword-hilt's in our hand,—
> Heart-whole we'll part, and no whit sighe
>   For the fayrest of the land;
> Let piping swaine, and craven wight,
>   Thus weepe and puling crye,
> Our business is like men to fight,
>   And hero-like to die!

HENRY TIMROD

1828–1867

Timrod prepared "A Theory of Poetry" as a lecture to the Methodist Female College at Columbia, South Carolina, in 1863. It was published posthumously in the *Atlantic Monthly* (1905). Though concerned with the aesthetic problems for which Poe had offered solutions, Timrod approached them with a broader range of sensibility than Poe's. Timrod's Wordsworthian reverence for nature and his conviction that the greatest poetry must be ethical in content made him find Poe's poetic principles untenable. His sensitive reading of *Paradise Lost* convinced him not only that the long poem is possible, but that the variety of its texture is a positive asset. In this, as in his judgment that Poe's critical theory was in part an attempt to make universal laws of personal limitations, Timrod anticipates more recent views of Poe, such as T. S. Eliot's. Although Sidney Lanier was reputed the major Southern poet-critic of the latter nineteenth century, Timrod's importance has been affirmed by his modern successors John Crowe Ransom and Allen Tate.

TEXT: *The Essays of Henry Timrod*, edited by Edd Winfield Parks (1942), reprinted by permission of the University of Georgia Press.

A THEORY OF POETRY

I desire to arrive, if possible, at a comprehensive and satisfactory theory of poetry, but more especially to examine, and to enter my protest against certain narrow creeds which seem to me to be growing into fashion, to expose the falsity of that taste which is formed by particular schools, and which lead necessarily to a narrow and limited culture, and to assist, as far as it lies in my power, in the establishment of a generous and catholic criticism. . . .

There have been few poetical eras without their peculiar theories of poetry. But no age was ever so rich in poetical creeds as the first half of the present century. . . . I shall pass most of these theories to consider only two—one of which I shall discuss at some length. The first is that definition of poetry which represents it simply as the expression in verse of thought, sentiment, or passion; and which measures the difference between the poet and the versifier only by the difference between the depth, power, and vivacity of their several productions. This definition was ably advocated not long ago in a well-known Southern periodical, by one of the most acute of Southern writers.[1] It would not be difficult to prove its total inadequacy, but I do not think it necessary to do so, except so far as the proof of that inadequacy may be involved in the establishment of a theory altogether opposed to it. I am the less inclined to give it a minute examination, because though the idea is an old one, and in strict accordance with the common usage of the word poetry, it has never become popular, nor is it likely to become so, as it fails to satisfy even those who displeased they do not know why, and dimly conscious of the true faith, are yet unable to discover in their undefined emotions a logical refutation of the heresy. The genuine lovers of poetry feel that its essential characteristics underlie the various forms which it assumes, however dim and shadowy those characteristics may seem to them, and notwithstanding that they elude the search like the jar of gold which is fabled to be buried at the foot of the rainbow.

The second theory which I desire to examine critically was propounded a number of years ago.

Poe begins his disquisition with the dogma that a long poem is simply a flat contradiction in "terms." . . .

But I deny boldly and without reservation the truth of

[1] William John Grayson, "What is Poetry?" *Russell's Magazine*, I, 327–37 (July, 1857), reprinted in *The Essays of Henry Timrod*, ed. E. W. Parks.

that assertion on which the whole argument hinges, that to preserve in effect the unity of a great poem, it should be read through at a single sitting. And to substantiate my denial, I shall not fear to examine the effect of that very poem to which Poe has appealed.

I suppose then the Reader who takes up Paradise Lost to begin its perusal in a spirit not unbecoming that divine production, and with the reverence of one who enters upon holy ground. He must have "docile thoughts, and purgèd ears." A poem the aim of which is "to justify the ways of God to man" is not to be entered upon at any season, and never when our only wish is to beguile a vacant moment. The time and even the place should be in harmony with the lofty theme. Charles Lamb in a spirit of proper appreciation says "that Milton almost needs a solemn service of music to be played" before we approach him. . . . I affirm that he who takes up Paradise Lost in this spirit will lay it down at the completion of the first [book], or if (as is not unlikely) he should have been beguiled further, at the completion of the second book, not simply with an impression of satisfied[,] still less of satiated gratification, but in a state of mind in which awe and delight are blended together in a deep though sober rapture. I say too that upon his resuming the book at some future time, if he come to it with the same reverential precautions, and not as one who must finish a book to-night because he began it yesterday, there will occur no such utter disconnection between his perusal of the first, and his perusal of the second part of the poem as will produce an effect at all similar to that which is produced by the perusal of two distinct poems. I say that no hiatus of platitude, whether real or the result merely of jaded attention, is sufficient so to separate two parts of an artistically constructed poem like Paradise Lost, as to disturb the general harmony of its effect. And the thoughtful reader instead of sitting down to the study of the third book as to a new poem, brings with him all the impressions of his former reading to heighten the colour and deepen the effect of that which is before him. The continuation of the poem seems all the more beautiful because he is familiar with the beginning, and necessarily so from the roundness and completeness of a structure the parts of which add alike to the strength and grace of the whole and of each other. . . . Every portion of Paradise Lost is bound together by the closest relations, and helps to give force to all; and as the light about us is not produced solely by the direct rays of the Sun, but is composed of millions of atmospherical and other reflections, so the ultimate and aggregate effect of this truly great creation is made up of the innumerable lights and cross-lights which each book sheds upon the other[s]. So as day by day the reader, such a reader, at least, as I have described, moves onward through the varied beauties and sublimities of the poem, its grand purport and harmonious proportions become more and more clearly apparent;—it is "vastness which grows, but grows to harmonize, All musical in its immensities—". . . .

I shall not notice the sarcasms which Poe directs against those who measure the merit of a book by its length, as I have said nothing from which it could be inferred that I regard size as a criterion of excellence. It is one thing to say that a poem of twelve books may be good, and another thing to say that a poem is good because it contains twelve books. I am not going to deny, however, that a poem may be extended to so great a length as to preclude the possibility of its operating upon our feelings with unity of effect, as witness the Fairy Queen. Yet, it should be observed in justice to Spenser that *that* production is in fact, what Poe maintains the epic of Milton to be, a succession of poems having no real connection with each other. Perhaps the same may be said of the Iliad of Homer. I do not refer to the Columbiad[2] because if that ponderous production could be crushed into a space no bigger than that occupied by an epigram, not a drop of genuine poetry could be forced from it. If I should be asked to fix the limit beyond which a poem should not be extended, I can only answer that that must be left to the taste and judgment of the Poet based upon a careful and appreciative study of the few great masters. The ordeal of criticism

[2] By Joel Barlow (1807).

will settle afterwards how far unity has been preserved or violated. In general it may be remarked that the plot of a poem should be so compact, as not to involve scenes and subjects of too great diversity. As a consequence of this principle, I have always regarded the Divine Comedy of Dante in its progress through Hell, Purgatory and Heaven as three distinct poems.

I do not wish it to be supposed that I look upon Paradise Lost as in all respects a perfect poem. It has many of the faults inseparable from all human productions. Indeed I so far agree with Poe that I concede that by no possibility can a poem as long as Paradise Lost be all poetry (Coleridge, the profoundest poetical critic of any age, says [it] ought not to be all poetry[3]) from beginning to end. However noble the theme, there will be parts and aspects which do not admit of the presence of genuine poetry. Herein, however, I differ from Poe, inasmuch as I maintain that these parts may be so raised above the ordinary level of prose by skillful verse as to preserve the general harmony of the poem, and not materially to injure its unity as a work of art. And in the distinction between poetry and a poem, between the spirit and its body which Poe recognizes when he comes to develope his theory, but which he blinks, or ignores altogether in his remarks upon Paradise Lost, I shall look for the justification of my position.

I hold that the confusion of these terms, of the subjective essence with the objective form[,] is the source of most of the errors and contradictions of opinion prevalent upon this subject. The two should be carefully distinguished, and should never, in any critical discussion, be allowed to mean the same thing. What then is Poetry? . . . The poets who attempt to solve the question look rather into themselves than into the poems which they have written. One, very characteristically, when his own poems are considered, defines it as "emotions recollected in tranquillity," and another as "the recollection of the best and happiest moments of the best and happiest minds." These definitions—if definitions they can be called—are unsatisfactory

[3] *Biographia Literaria,* chapter XIV.

enough, but they indicate correctly the direction in which the distinctive principle of poetry is to be sought.

I think that Poe in his eloquent description of the poetic sentiment as the sense of the beautiful, and in its loftiest action as a struggle to apprehend a supernal loveliness, a wild effort to reach a beauty above that which is about us, has certainly fixed with some definiteness one phase of its merely subjective manifestation. It is indeed to the inspiration which lies in the ethereal, the remote, and the unknown, that the world owes some of its sweetest poems; and the poetry of words has never so strange a fascination as when it seems to suggest more than it utters, to call up by implication rather than by expression those thoughts which refuse to be embodied in language, and to hint at something ineffable and mysterious of which the mind can attain but partial glimpses. But in making this feeling, and this feeling only, constitute the poetic sentiment, Poe only verifies the remark of one of the most luminous critics of this century, that it is as little to men of peculiar and original genius as to the multitude, that we must look for broad and comprehensive critical theories. Such men have usually one faculty developed at the expense of others; and the very clearness of their perception of one kind of excellence, impairs their perception of other and different kinds of excellence. Their theories being drawn from their own particular tastes and talents, just suffice to cover themselves and those who resemble them. The theory of Poe leads directly to the conclusion (and this he boldly avows) that Tennyson is the noblest Poet that ever lived; since no other poet that ever lived has possessed so much of that ethereality and dim suggestiveness which Poe regards, if not as the sole, at least as the highest characteristic of a poem. I am constrained to add too that while the theory leads to the conclusion that Tennyson is the noblest of poets, it leads as surely to the conclusion that Poe is next to the noblest. At the same time I must do Poe the justice to acquit him of the petty vanity of wishing to lead his readers to such a conclusion—his theory I regard as a natural and logical result evolved from his own beautiful and very peculiar genius. Like the fabled Narcissus, he fell in love unconsciously with his own shadow in the water. I yield to few, and only to that extravagant few who would put him over the head of Milton himself, in my admiration of Poe; and to *none* in a love which is almost a worship of Tennyson with whose poems I have been familiar from my boyhood, and whom I yet continue to study with ceaseless profit and pleasure. But I can by no means consent to regard him as the first of Poets, and I am sure that Tennyson himself would repudiate the compliment, and the theory which seems to justify it. The very merit which that theory mainly insists upon, is not characteristic of more than one third part of the poems of Tennyson, who as a poet possesses (what Poe had *not*) other qualities besides his intense spiritualism, of a more human and earthly tendency which could not fail to bring him into affinity with other tastes, and constrain him to demand a broader creed.

In order to perceive the real narrowness of Poe's theory, it is but necessary to examine the list of those elements which he says induces in the poet the true poetical effect, and mark how carefully he selects only such appearances as are simply beautiful or simply mysterious, and how sedulously he excludes all that is sublime and terrible in the phenomena of nature. "The Poet," he says, "recognizes the ambrosia which nourishes his soul in the bright orbs of heaven,—in the volutes of the flower,—in the clustering of low shrubberies—in the slanting of tall Eastern trees—in the blue distance of mountains—in the grouping of clouds —in the gleaming of silver rivers—in the repose of sequestered lakes. He perceives [it] in the songs of birds—in the harp of Æolus—in the sighing of the night-wind—in the perfume of the violet—and in the suggestive odours that come to him at eventide over dim oceans from far distant and undiscovered lands." I have not enumerated all the influences to which he refers, but every one of them, will be found upon examination to bear the same general character of quiet and gentle beauty. Let me ask, in my turn, if there be no excitement of the poetical faculty in the clouded night as well as in the bright one,—in the rack of clouds by which the stars are driven in, as well as in the purple islands and crimson archipelagoes of sunset,—in the terror-stricken rain fleeing before the tempest, as well as in the gentle and refreshing showers of April—in the craggy dangers, as well as in the blue distance of mountains—in the rush of the tornado which opens a road through deep, untravelled and illimitable forests, as well as in the faint and fragrant sigh of the zephyr—in the lightening which shatters some great Admiral doomed never again to be heard of—in the ear-splitting crash of the thunder, the stricken pine, and the blasted heath—in the tiger haunted jungles of India—in the vast Sahara over which the sirocco sweeps like the breath of hell—in the barren and lonely cape strown with wrecks, and the precipitous promontory which refuses to preserve even a single plank of the ships that have been crushed against it—in the fearful tale suggested by the discovery of a human skeleton upon a desert and uninhabited island—in the march of the Pestilence—in the bloody battle of freedom—and in the strange noises and wild risks of an Arctic night when the Great Pack has broken up, and an Arctic storm is grinding and hurling the floes in thunder against each other.

In the same manner when the eloquent Poet comes to seek the mental stimulants of poetry, he finds them "in all unworldly motives—in all holy impulses—in all chivalrous and self-sacrificing deeds"; but he does not, like the profounder Wordsworth, see them in the tranquil comforts of home,—in the dignity of honest labour—in the charities of the beggar—and in those every-day virtues over which the human soul of Wordsworth's Muse broods in pleased contemplation. He sees no appeal to the faculty in "the common things that round us lie",—[4] in the fairy tales of Science—in the magic of machinery—in the pen that writes and the types that immortalize his argument—in truth as truth merely—and in the lessons of which Nature is so bountiful that they may be gathered from the very dust that we tread beneath our feet.

I think that when we recall the many and varied sources of Poetry, we must perforce confess that it is wholly impossible to reduce them all to the simple element of beauty.

[4] Wordsworth, "A Poet's Epitaph," l. 49.

Two other elements at least must be added: and these are *power* when it is developed in some noble shape, and *truth* —whether abstract or not—when it affects the common heart of mankind. For the suggestion of these two additional principles, I suppose I ought to say that I am indebted to Hunt; but I cannot help adding that I had fixed upon the same trinity of elements long before I became acquainted with his delightful book on Imagination and Fancy.

It is then in the feelings awakened by certain moods of the mind when we stand in the presence of Truth, Power, and Beauty, that I recognize what we all agree to call Poetry. To analyze the nature of these feelings, inextricably tangled as they are with the different faculties of the mind, and especially with that great faculty which is the prime minister of Poetry,—Imagination—is not absolutely necessary to the present purpose. Let us be satisfied with having ascertained the elements which excite in us the sentiment of Poetry, and, with having thus in a measure fixed its boundaries; and proceed at once to consider it as it appears when embodied in language. . . .

I look upon every poem as strictly a work of art, and on the Poet, in the act of putting poetry into verse, simply as an artist. If the Poet have his hour of inspiration (though I am so sick of the cant of which this word has been the fruitful source, that I dislike to use it) it is not during the work of composition. A distinction must be made between the moment when the great thought strikes for the first time along the brain, and flushes the cheek with the sudden revelation of beauty, or grandeur,—and the hour of patient and elaborate execution. The soul of the Poet, though constrained to utter itself at some time or other, does not burst into song as readily as a maiden of sixteen bursts into musical laughter. Many poets have written of grief, but no poet with the first agony at his heart, ever sat down to strain that grief through iambics. Many poets have given expression to the first raptures of successful love, but no poet, in the delirium of the joy, has ever babbled it in anapests. Could this have been possible, the poet would be the most wonderful of improvisers, and perhaps a poem would be no better than what improvisations always are.

It would be easy to prove the truth of these remarks by the confessions of the Poets themselves. Poe has described to the world the manner in which he slowly built up the poem of the Raven. A greater poet than Poe speaks of himself as "not used to make A present joy the matter of his song," and of his poems, which the "Muse accepts, *deliberately* pleased,"[5] as "*thoughtfully* fitted to the Orphean lyre." The labour through which Tennyson has attained that perfection of style which is characteristic of his poems, must have been almost infinite. And Matthew Arnold—a poet not widely known in this country, but one who in the estimation of the English critical Public—sits not very far below Tennyson—separates as I have separated the hour of insight, from the hour of labour.

> "We cannot kindle when we will
>   The fire that in the heart resides;
> The spirit bloweth and is still;
>   In mystery our soul abides;
> *But tasks in hours of insight willed*
> *May be through hours of gloom fulfilled.*"

Does this fact lessen the merit of the Poet, or the charm of his poem? . . .

It must not be forgotten that my present aim is to show how it is possible that a poem, without being all poetry from beginning to end, may be complete as a work of art. Now there are two classes of poets differing essentially in their several characters. The one class desires only to utter musically its own peculiar feelings, thoughts, sentiments, or passion, without regard to their truth, or falsehood, their morality or their want of morality, but in simple reference to their poetical effect. The other class with more poetry at its command than the first, regards Poetry simply as the minister—the highest minister indeed but still only the minister—of Truth, and refuses to address itself to the

[5] Wordsworth, *The Prelude*, I, 47; *The Excursion*, II, 105–6.

sense of the Beautiful alone. The former class is content only to create Beauty, and writes such poems as the Raven of Poe, or the Corsair of Byron. The latter class aims to create Beauty also, but it desires at the same time to mould this Beauty into the shape of a temple dedicated to Truth. It is to this class we owe the authorship of such poems as the Paradise Lost of Milton, the lines on Tintern Abbey, and the Excursion of Wordsworth, and the In Memoriam of Tennyson. The former class can afford to write brief and faultless poems because its end is a narrow one; the latter class is forced to demand an ampler field, because it is influenced by a vaster purpose.

Take a poet of the last mentioned class at the commencement of his work. Imbued with a love of truth, conscious of the noble character of his mission as a poet, convinced that a poem should, to use the words of Bacon, help and confer to magnanimity, morality as well as delectation, he chooses a subject the beauty of which may be so developed as to subserve an ulterior and loftier end. The end of Milton's poem is the glory of God and a justification of his ways toward man. The end of the poems of Wordsworth is to evolve the spiritual meanings that lie behind the phenomena of Nature, and to show that the materials of Poetry may be gathered from the common and familiar things of existence. The end of the poems of Tennyson who, in his large Nature touches Poe upon the one side, and Wordsworth on the other, is at times, as purely the creation of beauty as Poe could desire it to be. But it is not less often to inculcate the profoundest lessons of a human philosophy, and to do this he sounds in one poem the remotest metaphysical depths, he embodies the whole history of a sorrow in another, and in a third he converts into magnificent verse, the doubts, fears and perplexities through which the soul attains at last a ground on which to rest its hopes of immortality.

The poet who has such ends as these in view is not likely to measure the length of his poem by the rules of Poe's theory. If his subject be in the main poetical, he is careless if its complete development, involve the treatment of here and there a prosaic topic, and necessitate the composition of a few thousand instead of one hundred and fourteen lines. But at the same time in the development of this subject, he will not forget that he is an artist; and that he is bound to produce, as far as possible, an harmonious work of art. He will take care that all his topics have reference to the general purpose of his poem; and when they are unpoetical, he may not seldom use them as the musician uses his discords, or as the painter his shadows, to strengthen by contrast the effect of that which is genuinely poetical. He will endeavour also, by every artifice of verse and language, to raise these necessarily unpoetical portions, as near as may be, to the height of the loftier portions of his creation. Thus Milton has contrived, by a melodious arrangement, to impart a wonderful charm to a mere list of geographical names. And thus Tennyson by clearness and sometimes picturesqueness of expression, and by the unequalled perfection of his rhythm, has succeeded in giving a poetical air to thoughts which in any other hands would have been the baldest and most prosaic abstractions.

It seems to me that I have now made plain what I mean when I say that a poem may be complete without being, in the highest and most legitimate sense, poetical in all its parts. If a poem have one purpose, and the materials of which it is composed be so selected and arranged as to help enforce it, we have no right to regard it as a series of minor poems because there may occur an occasional flaw in the structure. And he who persists in reading such a poem as so many short ones, besides losing the pleasure of contemplating the symmetrical development of work [of] art, will fail to grasp the central purpose of the Poet.

It seems to me that I may strengthen still farther my theory that truth as much as beauty is a source of poetry, by a reference to the works of a Poet who always refuses to separate them. When Poe speaks of the impossibility of "reconciling the obstinate oils and waters of Poetry and Truth," he is, unconsciously to himself, confounding Truth with Science and Matter of fact. It is of course impossible to see poetry in the details of business, in the arguments and commonplaces of politicians, or in the fact that the three angles of any triangle are equal to two right angles. But there *is* poetry in the truths of the mind and heart, in the truths that affect us in our daily relations as men, and even in the grand, general truths of Science, when they become familiar to us, and help us to understand and appreciate the beauty of the Universe. This is what Coleridge meant in part when he represents Poetry as "the blossom and the fragrance of all human knowledge, human thoughts, human passions, emotions, language," and what Wordsworth meant when he not less eloquently describes it "as the breath and finer spirit of all knowledge; the impassioned expression which is in the countenance of all Science."6 . . .

Wordsworth could never have been brought to agree with Poe that a true poem is written for the poem's sake alone. The theory which Poe very naturally evolved from his own genius, Wordsworth quite as naturally would have thought incompatible with the high office of a poet as thinker, seer, teacher, and bard. On the other hand, the broader vision of Tennyson has enabled him to detect the truth which lies upon the side of Poe, and the truth which lies upon the side of Wordsworth. The proof that a poet may aim at beauty alone without respect to an ulterior purpose, he sees in every daisy and buttercup of an English meadow.

"O, to what uses shall we put
 The wild-weed flower that simply blows?
And is there any moral shut
 Within the bosom of the rose?"

But not the less does he recognize the right of the poet to make his art the vehicle of great moral and philosophical lessons, not less does he recognize his right to grapple with the darkest problems of man's destiny, to discuss the fears and perplexities of the spirit, and the faith which triumphs over them, and even to drop now and then, a silken line into the dim sea of metaphysics.

6 Quoted from Coleridge, *Biographia Literaria*, chapter XV; and Wordsworth, "Observations prefixed to 'Lyrical Ballads.'"

I have been induced to undertake a refutation of Poe's theory while attempting to establish another which (such is the difficulty of the subject) may not improbably turn out to be equally objectionable, not because I believe it to be the one most prevalently adopted, but because I regard it as the one most artfully put, and at the same time most likely to excite interest in a Southern audience. I have not time to examine any other of those theories which seem to me to present false views of poetry. There is an admirably written essay prefixed to the second edition of the poems of Matthew Arnold in which that poet endeavours to show that all the poets of the present century have been working on mistaken principles, and that the ancients were the only true masters of the poetical art. A theory (to the full as true as Poe's) might also be drawn from the works of the Brownings which would lead to the exclusion of Poe from the roll of great poets, as surely as the theory of Poe would lead to the exclusion of the Brownings. I do not regret, however, the necessity of passing over the many plausible half-truths which go to make up the creed of this or that poet, as the principal object I have proposed to myself in this essay, is to call attention to the narrowness of them all. A very little examination will generally prove that they have grown out of the idiosyncrasies of the poets themselves, and so necessarily seldom attain a greater breadth than suffices to shelter the theorist and the models from which he has drawn his arguments and his inspiration. Yet every one of these creeds has its disciples; and the consequence is, the growth of particular schools in the study of which the taste becomes limited, and the poetic vision, except in one direction, is deprived of all its clearness. I am not protesting against an evil existing only in my imagination. I have known more than one young lover of poetry who read nothing but Browning, and there are hundreds who have drowned all the poets of the past and present in the deep music of Tennyson. But is it not possible with the whole wealth of English literature at our command to attain views broad enough to enable us to do justice to genius of every class and character[?] That certainly can be no true poetical creed which leads directly to the neglect of those masterpieces which though wrought hundreds or thousands of years ago, still preserve the freshness of their perennial youth. It is not from gratitude simply—though we owe them much—to the many poets whose "thoughts have made rich the blood of the world" that I desire to press their claims upon attention. In the possession of a fame as immortal as Truth and Nature, they can afford to look with indifference upon a temporary suspension of admiration. The injury falls only on such as slight them, and the penalty they pay, is a contracted and contracting insight, the shutting on them forever of many glorious vistas into the universe of mind and matter, and the loss of thousands of images of grace and beauty and grandeur. Oh! rest assured that there are no stereotyped forms of poetry. It is a vital power, and may assume any guise, and take any shape—at one time towering like an Alp in the darkness, and at another sunning itself in the bell of a tulip, or the cup of a lily. Until you shall have learned to recognize it in all its various developments, you will have no right to echo back the benison of Wordsworth,

"Blessings be on them and eternal praise,
The poets who on earth have made us heirs
Of *Truth* and *pure delight* in heavenly lays!"

ALEXIS DE TOCQUEVILLE

1805–1859

Born in Paris to a family of Norman petty nobility, Tocqueville at twenty-one became a magistrate in the court at Versailles. After the fall of the Bourbons in the revolution of July, 1830, Tocqueville found himself out of sympathy with the new government. With a fellow-magistrate, Gustave de Beaumont, he proposed a tour of the United States to inspect penal institutions, and in 1831 the two set out on a nine-month visit, traversing seven thousand miles between Boston, Sault Ste. Marie, Green Bay, and New Orleans. Tocqueville's chief interest in visiting America was to observe the workings of democracy in a nation which had no fixed aristocratic class. The first part of *La Democratie en Amérique,* dealing with political institutions, appeared in 1835; the second volume, from which the following chapter is taken, five years later. *Democracy in America* was quickly translated into English and was immediately recognized—by J. S. Mill, Lord Bryce, and Edward Everett, among others—as a seminal work of political theory. Tocqueville's analysis of the effects of democratic institutions upon religion, philosophy, language, and literature, although based on careful observation and cogent argument, is more accurate as a description of possibilities than of existing conditions.

TEXT: *Democracy in America,* translated by Henry Reeve (1840). See also George Wilson Pierson, *Tocqueville and Beaumont in America* (1938); introduction by Phillips Bradley to *Democracy in America* (1945).

FROM DEMOCRACY IN AMERICA

OF SOME OF THE SOURCES OF POETRY AMONG DEMOCRATIC NATIONS

Various different significations have been given to the word Poetry. It would weary my readers if I were to lead them into a discussion as to which of these definitions ought to be selected: I prefer telling them at once that which I have chosen. In my opinion, Poetry is the search and the delineation of the Ideal.

The Poet is he who, by suppressing a part of what exists, by adding some imaginary touches to the picture, and by combining certain real circumstances, but which do not in fact concurrently happen, completes and extends the work of nature. Thus the object of poetry is not to represent what is true, but to adorn it, and to present to the mind some loftier imagery. Verse, regarded as the ideal beauty of language, may be eminently poetical; but verse does not, of itself, constitute poetry.

I now proceed to inquire whether, among the actions, the sentiments, and the opinions of democratic nations, there are any which lead to a conception of ideal beauty, and which may for this reason be considered as natural sources of poetry.

It must, in the first place, be acknowledged that the taste for ideal beauty, and the pleasure derived from the expression of it, are never so intense or so diffused among a democratic as among an aristocratic people. In aristocratic nations it sometimes happens that the body goes on to act as it were spontaneously, while the higher faculties are bound and burdened by repose. Among these nations the people will very often display poetic tastes, and sometimes allow their fancy to range beyond and above what surrounds them.

But in democracies the love of physical gratification, the notion of bettering one's condition, the excitement of competition, the charm of anticipated success, are so many spurs to urge men onward in the active professions they have embraced, without allowing them to deviate for an instant from the track. The main stress of the faculties is to this point. The imagination is not extinct; but its chief function is to devise what may be useful, and to represent what is real.

The principle of equality not only diverts men from the description of ideal beauty—it also diminishes the number of objects to be described.

Aristocracy, by maintaining society in a fixed position, is favourable to the solidity and duration of positive religions, as well as to the stability of political institutions. It not only keeps the human mind within a certain sphere of belief, but it predisposes the mind to adopt one faith rather than another. An aristocratic people will always be prone to place intermediate powers between God and man. In this respect it may be said that the aristocratic element is favourable to poetry. When the universe is peopled with supernatural creatures, not palpable to the senses but discovered by the mind, the imagination ranges freely, and poets, finding a thousand subjects to delineate, also find a countless audience to take an interest in their productions.

In democratic ages it sometimes happens, on the contrary, that men are as much afloat in matters of belief as they are in their laws. Scepticism then draws the imagination of poets back to earth, and confines them to the real and visible world. Even when the principle of equality does not disturb religious belief, it tends to simplify it, and to divert attention from secondary agents, to fix it principally on the Supreme Power.

Aristocracy naturally leads the human mind to the contemplation of the past, and fixes it there. Democracy, on the contrary, gives men a sort of instinctive distaste for what is ancient. In this respect aristocracy is far more favourable to poetry; for things commonly grow larger and more obscure as they are more remote; and for this twofold reason they are better suited to the delineation of the ideal.

After having deprived poetry of the past, the principle

of equality robs it in part of the present. Among aristocratic nations there are a certain number of privileged personages, whose situation is, as it were, without and above the condition of man; to these, power, wealth, fame, wit, refinement, and distinction in all things appear peculiarly to belong. The crowd never sees them very closely, or does not watch them in minute details; and little is needed to make the description of such men poetical. On the other hand, among the same people, you will meet with classes so ignorant, low, and enslaved, that they are no less fit objects for poetry from the excess of their rudeness and wretchedness, than the former are from their greatness and refinement. Besides, as the different classes of which an aristocratic community is composed are widely separated, and imperfectly acquainted with each other, the imagination may always represent them with some addition to, or some subtraction from, what they really are.

In democratic communities, where men are all insignificant and very much alike, each man instantly sees all his fellows when he surveys himself.

The poets of democratic ages can never, therefore, take any man in particular as the subject of a piece; for an object of slender importance, which is distinctly seen on all sides, will never lend itself to an ideal composition.

Thus the principle of equality, in proportion as it has established itself in the world, has dried up most of the old springs of poetry. Let us now attempt to show what new ones it may disclose.

When scepticism has depopulated heaven, and the progress of equality has reduced each individual to smaller and better known proportions, the poets, not yet aware of what they could substitute for the great themes which were departing together with the aristocracy, turned their eyes to inanimate nature. As they lost sight of gods and heroes, they set themselves to describe streams and mountains. Thence originated, in the last century, that kind of poetry which has been called, by way of distinction, the descriptive. Some have thought that this sort of delineation, embellished with all the physical and inanimate objects which cover the earth, was the kind of poetry peculiar to democratic ages; but I believe this to be an error, and that it only belongs to a period of transition.

I am persuaded that in the end democracy diverts the imagination from all that is external to man, and fixes it on man alone. Democratic nations may amuse themselves for a while with considering the productions of nature; but they are only excited in reality by a survey of themselves. Here, and here alone, the true sources of poetry among such nations are to be found; and it may be believed that the poets who shall neglect to draw their inspiration hence, will lose all sway over the minds which they would enchant, and will be left in the end with none but unimpassioned spectators of their transports.

I have shown how the ideas of progression and of the indefinite perfectibility of the human race belong to democratic ages. Democratic nations care but little for what has been, but they are haunted by visions of what will be: in this direction their unbounded imagination grows and dilates beyond all measure. Here then is the widest range open to the genius of poets, which allows them to remove their performances to a sufficient distance from the eye. Democracy shuts the past against the poet, but opens the future before him.

As all the citizens who compose a democratic community are nearly equal and alike, the poet cannot dwell upon any one of them; but the nation itself invites the exercise of his powers. The general similitude of individuals, which renders any one of them taken separately an improper subject of poetry, allows poets to include them all in the same imagery, and to take a general survey of the people itself. Democratic nations have a clearer perception than any others of their own aspect; and an aspect so imposing is admirably fitted to the delineation of the ideal.

I readily admit that the Americans have no poets; I cannot allow that they have no poetic ideas. In Europe people talk a great deal of the wilds of America, but the Americans themselves never think about them: they are insensible to the wonders of inanimate nature, and they may be said not to perceive the mighty forests which surround them till they fall beneath the hatchet. Their eyes are fixed upon another sight: the American people views its own march across these wilds—drying swamps, turning the course of rivers, peopling solitudes, and subduing nature. This magnificent image of themselves does not meet the gaze of the Americans at intervals only; it may be said to haunt every one of them in his least as well as in his most important actions, and to be always flitting before his mind.

Nothing conceivable is so petty, so insipid, so crowded with paltry interests, in one word so anti-poetic, as the life of a man in the United States. But among the thoughts which it suggests, there is always one which is full of poetry, and that is the hidden nerve which gives vigour to the frame.

In aristocratic ages each people, as well as each individual, is prone to stand separate and aloof from all others. In democratic ages, the extreme fluctuations of men and the impatience of their desires keep them perpetually on the move; so that the inhabitants of different countries intermingle, see, listen to, and borrow from each other's stores. It is not only then the members of the same community who grow more alike; communities are themselves assimilated to one another, and the whole assemblage presents to the eye of the spectator one vast democracy, each citizen of which is a people. This displays the aspect of mankind for the first time in the broadest light. All that belongs to the existence of the human race taken as a whole, to its vicissitudes and to its future, becomes an abundant mine for poetry.

The poets who lived in aristocratic ages have been eminently successful in their delineations of certain incidents in the life of a people or a man; but none of them ever ventured to include within his performances the destinies of mankind—a task which poets writing in democratic ages may attempt.

At the same time at which every man, raising his eyes above his country, begins at length to discern mankind at large, the Divinity is more and more manifest to the human mind in full and entire majesty. If in democratic ages faith in positive religions be often shaken, and the belief in intermediate agents, by whatever name they are called, be overcast; on the other hand men are disposed to conceive a far broader idea of Providence itself, and its interference in human affairs assumes a new and more imposing appearance to their eyes. Looking at the human race as one great whole, they easily conceive that its destinies are regulated by the same design; and in the actions of every individual they are led to acknowledge a trace of that universal and eternal plan on which God rules our race. This consideration may be taken as another prolific source of poetry which is opened in democratic ages.

Democratic poets will always appear trivial and frigid if they seek to invest gods, demons, or angels with corporeal forms, and if they attempt to draw them down from heaven to dispute the supremacy of earth. But if they strive to connect the great events they commemorate with the general providential designs which govern the universe, and, without showing the finger of the Supreme Governor, reveal the thoughts of the Supreme Mind, their works will be admired and understood, for the imagination of their contemporaries takes this direction of its own accord.

It may be foreseen in like manner that poets living in democratic ages will prefer the delineation of passions and ideas to that of persons and achievements. The language, the dress, and the daily actions of men in democracies are repugnant to ideal conceptions. These things are not poetical in themselves; and if it were otherwise, they would cease to be so, because they are too familiar to all those to whom the poet would speak of them. This forces the poet constantly to search below the external surface which is palpable to the senses, in order to read the inner soul: and nothing lends itself more to the delineation of the Ideal than the scrutiny of the hidden depths of the immaterial nature of man. I need not ramble over earth and sky to discover a wondrous object woven of contrasts, of greatness and littleness infinite, of intense gloom and of amazing brightness—capable at once of exciting pity, admiration, terror, contempt. I find that object in myself. Man springs out of nothing, crosses Time, and disappears for ever in the bosom of God: he is seen but for a moment, staggering on the verge of two abysses, and there he is lost.

If man were wholly ignorant of himself, he would have no poetry in him; for it is impossible to describe what the mind does not conceive. If man clearly discerned his own nature, his imagination would remain idle, and would have nothing to add to the picture. But the nature of man is sufficiently disclosed for him to apprehend something of himself; and sufficiently obscure for all the rest to be plunged in thick darkness, in which he gropes for ever—and for ever in vain—to lay hold on some completer notion of his being.

Among a democratic people poetry will not be fed with legendary lays or the memories of old traditions. The poet will not attempt to people the universe with supernatural beings in whom his readers and his own fancy have ceased to believe; nor will he present virtues and vices under the mask of frigid personification, which are better received under their own features. All these resources fail him; but Man remains, and the poet needs no more. The destinies of mankind—man himself, taken aloof from his age and his country, and standing in the presence of Nature and of God, with his passions, his doubts, his rare prosperities and inconceivable wretchedness—will become the chief, if not the sole theme of poetry among these nations.

Experience may confirm this assertion, if we consider the productions of the greatest poets who have appeared since the world has been turned to democracy. The authors of our age who have so admirably delineated the features of [Faust], Childe Harold, Réné, and Jocelyn, did not seek to record the actions of an individual, but to enlarge and to throw light on some of the obscurer recesses of the human heart.

Such are the poems of democracy. The principle of equality does not then destroy all the subjects of poetry: it renders them less numerous, but more vast.

RALPH WALDO EMERSON

1803–1882

To present Emerson as the author of a poetic theory necessarily truncates the cyclical movement of his thought. His conception of language, here excerpted from his first book, *Nature*, is intrinsically bound with his ideas of morality and his theory of knowledge. The entire essay is prefaced by the questions, "Why should we not enjoy an original relation to the universe? Why should we not have a poetry and philosophy of insight and not of tradition, and a religion by revelation to us?" Emerson's radical synthesis is deeply influenced by Coleridge and by Emanuel Swedenborg, whom he regarded as a supreme "translator of nature into thought."

Emerson, a son of the minister of the First Church, Boston, grew up among elders whose Unitarianism accommodated their Puritan heritage to the intellectual impact of the Enlightenment by stressing social responsibility and the rational bases of religious belief. Emerson was graduated from Harvard in 1821 and, after teaching school to help his brothers through college, he entered Harvard Divinity School in 1825 and in 1829 was ordained as junior minister in the Second Church of Boston, the church of Increase and Cotton Mather. Increasingly Emerson felt that the church he served was formalistic and historical. He did not wish to "grope among the dry bones of the past"; unable to acknowledge the sacrament of communion—to him man is at every moment in communion with the Divine—he resigned his ministry. Henceforth he preached from secular pulpits, calling to his generation to recapture the spiritual immediacy by which the religious life is experienced. In his view the poet is the seer who realizes the spiritual unity of things with the soul, of man with the universe. His conception of artistic form is based upon his conviction that the universe is a metaphor of the human mind; art is organic, style is functional, ornament extraneous, and the materials of poetry are those of life itself. "America is a poem in our eyes," he says in a passage that Whitman heeded; and again, he invokes "that *dream-power* . . . transcending all limit and privacy . . . by virtue of which a man is the conductor of the whole river of electricity . . . Comes he to that power, his genius is no longer exhaustible." Emerson in his own poems rarely tapped that subconscious power, but he showed the way to its conduits for Whitman. After a life of outward serenity, lived in Concord except for occasional trips abroad and lecture tours across the country, Emerson died in 1882.

TEXT: *Complete Works,* edited by Edward Waldo Emerson, 12 vols. (1903–1904). See also: Charles Feidelson, *Symbolism in American Literature* (1953); F. O. Matthiessen, *American Renaissance* (1941); Perry Miller, "From Jonathan Edwards to Emerson," *New England Quarterly,* XIII (1940); Stephen Whicher, *Freedom and Fate: An Inner Life of Ralph Waldo Emerson* (1953).

FROM NATURE

LANGUAGE

Language is a third use which Nature subserves to man. Nature is the vehicle of thought, and in a simple, double, and threefold degree.

1. Words are signs of natural facts.

2. Particular natural facts are symbols of particular spiritual facts.

3. Nature is the symbol of spirit.

1. Words are signs of natural facts. The use of natural history is to give us aid in supernatural history; the use of the outer creation, to give us language for the beings and changes of the inward creation. Every word which is used to express a moral or intellectual fact, if traced to its root, is found to be borrowed from some material appearance. *Right* means *straight; wrong* means *twisted. Spirit* primarily means *wind; transgression,* the crossing of a *line; super-*

cilious, the *raising of the eyebrow.* We say the *heart* to express emotion, the *head* to denote thought; and *thought* and *emotion* are words borrowed from sensible things, and now appropriated to spiritual nature. Most of the process by which this transformation is made, is hidden from us in the remote time when language was framed; but the same tendency may be daily observed in children. Children and savages use only nouns or names of things, which they convert into verbs, and apply to analogous mental acts.

2. But this origin of all words that convey a spiritual import,—so conspicuous a fact in the history of language,—is our least debt to nature. It is not words only that are emblematic; it is things which are emblematic. Every natural fact is a symbol of some spiritual fact. Every appearance in nature corresponds to some state of the mind, and that state of the mind can only be described by presenting that natural appearance as its picture. An enraged man is a lion, a cunning man is a fox, a firm man is a rock, a learned man is a torch. A lamb is innocence; a snake is subtle spite; flowers express to us the delicate affections. Light and darkness are our familiar expression for knowledge and ignorance; and heat for love. Visible distance behind and before us, is respectively our image of memory and hope.

Who looks upon a river in a meditative hour and is not reminded of the flux of all things? Throw a stone into the stream, and the circles that propagate themselves are the beautiful type of all influence. Man is conscious of a universal soul within or behind his individual life, wherein, as in a firmament, the natures of Justice, Truth, Love, Freedom, arise and shine. This universal soul he calls Reason: it is not mine, or thine, or his, but we are its; we are its property and men. And the blue sky in which the private earth is buried, the sky with its eternal calm, and full of everlasting orbs, is the type of Reason. That which intellectually considered we call Reason, considered in relation to nature, we call Spirit. Spirit is the Creator. Spirit hath life in itself. And man in all ages and countries embodies it in his language as the FATHER.

It is easily seen that there is nothing lucky or capricious in these analogies, but that they are constant, and pervade nature. These are not the dreams of a few poets, here and there, but man is an analogist, and studies relations in all objects. He is placed in the centre of beings, and a ray of relation passes from every other being to him. And neither can man be understood without these objects, nor these objects without man. All the facts in natural history taken by themselves, have no value, but are barren, like a single sex. But marry it to human history, and it is full of life. Whole floras, all Linnæus' and Buffon's volumes, are dry catalogues of facts; but the most trivial of these facts, the habit of a plant, the organs, or work, or noise of an insect, applied to the illustration of a fact in intellectual philosophy, or in any way associated to human nature, affects us in the most lively and agreeable manner. The seed of a plant,—to what affecting analogies in the nature of man is that little fruit made use of, in all discourse, up to the voice of Paul, who calls the human corpse a seed,—"It is sown a natural body; it is raised a spiritual body." The motion of the earth round its axis and round the sun, makes the day and the year. These are certain amounts of brute light and heat. But is there no intent of an analogy between man's life and the seasons? And do the seasons gain no grandeur or pathos from that analogy? The instincts of the ant are very unimportant considered as the ant's; but the moment a ray of relation is seen to extend from it to man, and the little drudge is seen to be a monitor, a little body with a mighty heart, then all its habits, even that said to be recently observed, that it never sleeps, become sublime.

Because of this radical correspondence between visible things and human thoughts, savages, who have only what is necessary, converse in figures. As we go back in history, language becomes more picturesque, until its infancy, when it is all poetry; or all spiritual facts are represented by natural symbols. The same symbols are found to make the original elements of all languages. It has moreover been observed, that the idioms of all languages approach each other in passages of the greatest eloquence and power. And as this is the first language, so is it the last. This immediate dependence of language upon nature, this conversion of an outward phenomenon into a type of somewhat in human life, never loses its power to affect us. It is this which gives that piquancy to the conversation of a strong-natured farmer or backwoodsman, which all men relish.

A man's power to connect his thought with its proper symbol, and so to utter it, depends on the simplicity of his character, that is, upon his love of truth and his desire to communicate it without loss. The corruption of man is followed by the corruption of language. When simplicity of character and the sovereignty of ideas is broken up by the prevalence of secondary desires,—the desire of riches, of pleasure, of power, and of praise,—and duplicity and falsehood take place of simplicity and truth, the power over nature as an interpreter of the will is in a degree lost; new imagery ceases to be created, and old words are perverted to stand for things which are not; a paper currency is employed, when there is no bullion in the vaults. In due time the fraud is manifest, and words lose all power to stimulate the understanding or the affections. Hundreds of writers may be found in every long-civilized nation who for a short time believe and make others believe that they see and utter truths, who do not of themselves clothe one thought in its natural garment, but who feed unconsciously on the language created by the primary writers of the country, those, namely, who hold primarily on nature.

But wise men pierce this rotten diction and fasten words again to visible things; so that picturesque language is at once a commanding certificate that he who employs it is a man in alliance with truth and God. The moment our discourse rises above the ground line of familiar facts and is inflamed with passion or exalted by thought, it clothes itself in images. A man conversing in earnest, if he watch his intellectual processes, will find that a material image more or less luminous arises in his mind, contemporaneous with every thought, which furnishes the vestment of the thought. Hence, good writing and brilliant discourse are perpetual allegories. This imagery is spontaneous. It is the blending of experience with the present action of the mind.

It is proper creation. It is the working of the Original Cause through the instruments he has already made.

These facts may suggest the advantage which the country-life possesses, for a powerful mind, over the artificial and curtailed life of cities. We know more from nature than we can at will communicate. Its light flows into the mind evermore, and we forget its presence. The poet, the orator, bred in the woods, whose senses have been nourished by their fair and appeasing changes, year after year, without design and without heed,—shall not lose their lesson altogether, in the roar of cities or the broil of politics. Long hereafter, amidst agitation and terror in national councils,— in the hour of revolution,—these solemn images shall reappear in their morning lustre, as fit symbols and words of the thoughts which the passing events shall awaken. At the call of a noble sentiment, again the woods wave, the pines murmur, the river rolls and shines, and the cattle low upon the mountains, as he saw and heard them in his infancy. And with these forms, the spells of persuasion, the keys of power are put into his hands.

3. We are thus assisted by natural objects in the expression of particular meanings. But how great a language to convey such pepper-corn informations! Did it need such noble races of creatures, this profusion of forms, this host of orbs in heaven, to furnish man with the dictionary and grammar of his municipal speech? Whilst we use this grand cipher to expedite the affairs of our pot and kettle, we feel that we have not yet put it to its use, neither are able. We are like travellers using the cinders of a volcano to roast their eggs. Whilst we see that it always stands ready to clothe what we would say, we cannot avoid the question whether the characters are not significant of themselves. Have mountains, and waves, and skies, no significance but what we consciously give them when we employ them as emblems of our thoughts? The world is emblematic. Parts of speech are metaphors, because the whole of nature is a metaphor of the human mind. The laws of moral nature answer to those of matter as face to face in a glass. "The visible world and the relation of its parts, is the dial plate of the invisible." The axioms of physics

translate the laws of ethics. Thus, "the whole is greater than its part;" "reaction is equal to action;" "the smallest weight may be made to lift the greatest, the difference of weight being compensated by time;" and many the like propositions, which have an ethical as well as physical sense. These propositions have a much more extensive and universal sense when applied to human life, than when confined to technical use.

In like manner, the memorable words of history and the proverbs of nations consist usually of a natural fact, selected as a picture or parable of a moral truth. Thus; A rolling stone gathers no moss; A bird in the hand is worth two in the bush; A cripple in the right way will beat a racer in the wrong; Make hay while the sun shines; 'Tis hard to carry a full cup even; Vinegar is the son of wine; The last ounce broke the camel's back; Long-lived trees make roots first;—and the like. In their primary sense these are trivial facts, but we repeat them for the value of their analogical import. What is true of proverbs, is true of all fables, parables, and allegories.

This relation between the mind and matter is not fancied by some poet, but stands in the will of God, and so is free to be known by all men. It appears to men, or it does not appear. When in fortunate hours we ponder this miracle, the wise man doubts if at all other times he is not blind and deaf;

> "Can such things be,
> And overcome us like a summer's cloud,
> Without our special wonder?"

for the universe becomes transparent, and the light of higher laws than its own shines through it. It is the standing problem which has exercised the wonder and the study of every fine genius since the world began; from the era of the Egyptians and the Brahmins to that of Pythagoras, of Plato, of Bacon, of Leibnitz, of Swedenborg. There sits the Sphinx at the roadside, and from age to age, as each prophet comes by, he tries his fortune at reading her riddle. There seems to be a necessity in spirit to manifest itself in material forms; and day and night, river and storm, beast and bird, acid and alkali, preëxist in necessary Ideas in the mind of God, and are what they are by virtue of preceding affections in the world of spirit. A Fact is the end or last issue of spirit. The visible creation is the terminus or the circumference of the invisible world. "Material objects," said a French philosopher, "are necessarily kinds of *scoriæ* of the substantial thoughts of the Creator, which must always preserve an exact relation to their first origin; in other words, visible nature must have a spiritual and moral side."

This doctrine is abstruse, and though the images of "garment," "scoriæ," "mirror," etc., may stimulate the fancy, we must summon the aid of subtler and more vital expositors to make it plain. "Every scripture is to be interpreted by the same spirit which gave it forth,"—is the fundamental law of criticism. A life in harmony with Nature, the love of truth and of virtue, will purge the eyes to understand her text. By degrees we may come to know the primitive sense of the permanent objects of nature, so that the world shall be to us an open book, and every form significant of its hidden life and final cause.

A new interest surprises us, whilst, under the view now suggested, we contemplate the fearful extent and multitude of objects; since "every object rightly seen, unlocks a new faculty of the soul." That which was unconscious truth, becomes, when interpreted and defined in an object, a part of the domain of knowledge,—a new weapon in the magazine of power.

THE POET

A moody child and wildly wise
Pursued the game with joyful eyes,
Which chose, like meteors, their way,
And rived the dark with private ray:
They overleapt the horizon's edge,
Searched with Apollo's privilege;

Through man, and woman, and sea, and star
Saw the dance of nature forward far;
Through worlds, and races, and terms, and times
Saw musical order, and pairing rhymes.

Olympian bards who sung
Divine ideas below,
Which always find us young,
And always keep us so.

Those who are esteemed umpires of taste are often persons who have acquired some knowledge of admired pictures or sculptures, and have an inclination for whatever is elegant; but if you inquire whether they are beautiful souls, and whether their own acts are like fair pictures, you learn that they are selfish and sensual. Their cultivation is local, as if you should rub a log of dry wood in one spot to produce fire, all the rest remaining cold. Their knowledge of the fine arts is some study of rules and particulars, or some limited judgment of color or form, which is exercised for amusement or for show. It is a proof of the shallowness of the doctrine of beauty as it lies in the minds of our amateurs, that men seem to have lost the perception of the instant dependence of form upon soul. There is no doctrine of forms in our philosophy. We were put into our bodies, as fire is put into a pan to be carried about; but there is no accurate adjustment between the spirit and the organ, much less is the latter the germination of the former. So in regard to other forms, the intellectual men do not believe in any essential dependence of the material world on thought and volition. Theologians think it a pretty air-castle to talk of the spiritual meaning of a ship or a cloud, of a city or a contract, but they prefer to come again to the solid ground of historical evidence; and even the poets are contented with a civil and conformed manner of living, and to write poems from the fancy, at a safe distance from their own experience. But the highest minds of the world have never ceased to explore the double meaning, or shall I say the quadruple or the centuple or much more manifold meaning, of every sensuous fact; Orpheus,

Empedocles, Heraclitus, Plato, Plutarch, Dante, Swedenborg, and the masters of sculpture, picture and poetry. For we are not pans and barrows, nor even porters of the fire and torchbearers, but children of the fire, made of it, and only the same divinity transmuted and at two or three removes, when we know least about it. And this hidden truth, that the fountains whence all this river of Time and its creatures floweth are intrinsically ideal and beautiful, draws us to the consideration of the nature and functions of the Poet, or the man of Beauty; to the means and materials he uses, and to the general aspect of the art in the present time.

The breadth of the problem is great, for the poet is representative. He stands among partial men for the complete man, and apprises us not of his wealth, but of the common wealth. The young man reveres men of genius, because, to speak truly, they are more himself than he is. They receive of the soul as he also receives, but they more. Nature enhances her beauty, to the eye of loving men, from their belief that the poet is beholding her shows at the same time. He is isolated among his contemporaries by truth and by his art, but with this consolation in his pursuits, that they will draw all men sooner or later. For all men live by truth and stand in need of expression. In love, in art, in avarice, in politics, in labor, in games, we study to utter our painful secret. The man is only half himself, the other half is his expression.

Notwithstanding this necessity to be published, adequate expression is rare. I know not how it is that we need an interpreter, but the great majority of men seem to be minors, who have not yet come into possession of their own, or mutes, who cannot report the conversation they have had with nature. There is no man who does not anticipate a supersensual utility in the sun and stars, earth and water. These stand and wait to render him a peculiar service. But there is some obstruction or some excess of phlegm in our constitution, which does not suffer them to yield the due effect. Too feeble fall the impressions of nature on us to make us artists. Every touch should thrill. Every man should be so much an artist that he could report in conversation what had befallen him. Yet, in our experience, the rays or appulses have sufficient force to arrive at the senses, but not enough to reach the quick and compel the reproduction of themselves in speech. The poet is the person in whom these powers are in balance, the man without impediment, who sees and handles that which others dream of, traverses the whole scale of experience, and is representative of man, in virtue of being the largest power to receive and to impart.

For the Universe has three children, born at one time, which reappear under different names in every system of thought, whether they be called cause, operation and effect; or, more poetically, Jove, Pluto, Neptune; or, theologically, the Father, the Spirit and the Son; but which we will call here the Knower, the Doer and the Sayer. These stand respectively for the love of truth, for the love of good, and for the love of beauty. These three are equal. Each is that which he is, essentially, so that he cannot be surmounted or analyzed, and each of these three has the power of the others latent in him and his own, patent.

The poet is the sayer, the namer, and represents beauty. He is a sovereign, and stands on the centre. For the world is not painted or adorned, but is from the beginning beautiful; and God has not made some beautiful things, but Beauty is the creator of the universe. Therefore the poet is not any permissive potentate, but is emperor in his own right. Criticism is infested with a cant of materialism, which assumes that manual skill and activity is the first merit of all men, and disparages such as say and do not, overlooking the fact that some men, namely poets, are natural sayers, sent into the world to the end of expression, and confounds them with those whose province is action but who quit it to imitate the sayers. But Homer's words are as costly and admirable to Homer as Agamemnon's victories are to Agamemnon. The poet does not wait for the hero or the sage, but, as they act and think primarily, so he writes primarily what will and must be spoken, reckoning the others, though primaries also, yet, in respect to him, secondaries and servants; as sitters or models in the studio of a painter, or as assistants who bring building-materials to an architect.

For poetry was all written before time was, and whenever we are so finely organized that we can penetrate into that region where the air is music, we hear those primal warblings and attempt to write them down, but we lose ever and anon a word or a verse and substitute something of our own, and thus miswrite the poem. The men of more delicate ear write down these cadences more faithfully, and these transcripts, though imperfect, become the songs of the nations. For nature is as truly beautiful as it is good, or it is reasonable, and must as much appear as it must be done, or be known. Words and deeds are quite indifferent modes of the divine energy. Words are also actions, and actions are a kind of words.

The sign and credentials of the poet are that he announces that which no man foretold. He is the true and only doctor; he knows and tells; he is the only teller of news, for he was present and privy to the appearance which he describes. He is a beholder of ideas and an utterer of the necessary and causal. For we do not speak now of men of poetical talents, or of industry and skill in metre, but of the true poet. I took part in a conversation the other day concerning a recent writer of lyrics, a man of subtle mind, whose head appeared to be a music-box of delicate tunes and rhythms, and whose skill and command of language we could not sufficiently praise. But when the question arose whether he was not only a lyrist but a poet, we were obliged to confess that he is plainly a contemporary, not an eternal man. He does not stand out of our low limitations, like a Chimborazo under the line, running up from a torrid base through all the climates of the globe, with belts of the herbage of every latitude on its high and mottled sides; but this genius is the landscape-garden of a modern house, adorned with fountains and statues, with well-bred men and women standing and sitting in the walks and terraces. We hear, through all the varied music, the ground-tone of conventional life. Our poets are men of talents who sing, and not the children of music. The argument is secondary, the finish of the verses is primary.

For it is not metres, but a metre-making argument that makes a poem,—a thought so passionate and alive that like the spirit of a plant or an animal it has an architecture of its own, and adorns nature with a new thing. The thought and the form are equal in the order of time, but in the order of genesis the thought is prior to the form. The poet has a new thought; he has a whole new experience to unfold; he will tell us how it was with him, and all men will be the richer in his fortune. For the experience of each new age requires a new confession, and the world seems always waiting for its poet. I remember when I was young how much I was moved one morning by tidings that genius had appeared in a youth who sat near me at table. He had left his work and gone rambling none knew whither, and had written hundreds of lines, but could not tell whether that which was in him was therein told; he could tell nothing but that all was changed,—man, beast, heaven, earth and sea. How gladly we listened! how credulous! Society seemed to be compromised. We sat in the aurora of a sunrise which was to put out all the stars. Boston seemed to be at twice the distance it had the night before, or was much farther than that. Rome,—what was Rome? Plutarch and Shakespeare were in the yellow leaf, and Homer no more should be heard of. It is much to know that poetry has been written this very day, under this very roof, by your side. What! that wonderful spirit has not expired! These stony moments are still sparkling and animated! I had fancied that the oracles were all silent, and nature had spent her fires; and behold! all night, from every pore, these fine auroras have been streaming. Every one has some interest in the advent of the poet, and no one knows how much it may concern him. We know that the secret of the world is profound, but who or what shall be our interpreter, we know not. A mountain ramble, a new style of face, a new person, may put the key into our hands. Of course the value of genius to us is in the veracity of its report. Talent may frolic and juggle; genius realizes and adds. Mankind in good earnest have availed so far in understanding themselves and their work, that the foremost watchman on the peak announces his news. It is the truest word ever spoken, and the phrase will be the fittest, most musical, and the unerring voice of the world for that time.

All that we call sacred history attests that the birth of a poet is the principal event in chronology. Man, never so often deceived, still watches for the arrival of a brother who can hold him steady to a truth until he has made it his own. With what joy I begin to read a poem which I confide in as an inspiration! And now my chains are to be broken; I shall mount above these clouds and opaque airs in which I live,—opaque, though they seem transparent, —and from the heaven of truth I shall see and comprehend my relations. That will reconcile me to life and renovate nature, to see trifles animated by a tendency, and to know what I am doing. Life will no more be a noise; now I shall see men and women, and know the signs by which they may be discerned from fools and satans. This day shall be better than my birthday: then I became an animal; now I am invited into the science of the real. Such is the hope, but the fruition is postponed. Oftener it falls that this winged man, who will carry me into the heaven, whirls me into mists, then leaps and frisks about with me as it were from cloud to cloud, still affirming that he is bound heavenward; and I, being myself a novice, am slow in perceiving that he does not know the way into the heavens, and is merely bent that I should admire his skill to rise like a fowl or a flying fish, a little way from the ground or the water; but the all-piercing, all-feeding and ocular air of heaven that man shall never inhabit. I tumble down again soon into my old nooks, and lead the life of exaggerations as before, and have lost my faith in the possibility of any guide who can lead me thither where I would be.

But, leaving these victims of vanity, let us, with new hope, observe how nature, by worthier impulses, has insured the poet's fidelity to his office of announcement and affirming, namely by the beauty of things, which becomes a new and higher beauty when expressed. Nature offers all her creatures to him as a picture-language. Being used as a type, a second wonderful value appears in the object, far better than its old value; as the carpenter's stretched cord, if you hold your ear close enough, is musical in the breeze. "Things more excellent than every image," says Jamblichus, "are expressed through images." Things admit of being used as symbols because nature is a symbol, in the whole, and in every part. Every line we can draw in the sand has expression; and there is no body without its spirit or genius. All form is an effect of character; all condition, of the quality of the life; all harmony, of health; and for this reason a perception of beauty should be sympathetic, or proper only to the good. The beautiful rests on the foundations of the necessary. The soul makes the body, as the wise Spenser teaches:—

"So every spirit, as it is more pure,
And hath in it the more of heavenly light,
So it the fairer body doth procure
To habit in, and it more fairly dight,
With cheerful grace and amiable sight.
For, of the soul, the body form doth take,
For soul is form, and doth the body make."

Here we find ourselves suddenly not in a critical speculation but in a holy place, and should go very warily and reverently. We stand before the secret of the world, there where Being passes into Appearance and Unity into Variety.

The Universe is the externization of the soul. Wherever the life is, that bursts into appearance around it. Our science is sensual, and therefore superficial. The earth and the heavenly bodies, physics and chemistry, we sensually treat, as if they were self-existent; but these are the retinue of that Being we have. "The mighty heaven," said Proclus, "exhibits, in its transfigurations, clear images of the splendor of intellectual perceptions; being moved in conjunction with the unapparent periods of intellectual natures." Therefore science always goes abreast with the just elevation of the man, keeping step with religion and metaphysics; or the state of science is an index of our self-knowledge. Since every thing in nature answers to a moral power, if any phenomenon remains brute and dark it is because the corresponding faculty in the observer is not yet active.

No wonder then, if these waters be so deep, that we hover over them with a religious regard. The beauty of the fable proves the importance of the sense; to the poet, and to all others; or, if you please, every man is so far a poet as to be susceptible of these enchantments of nature; for all men have the thoughts whereof the universe is the celebration. I find that the fascination resides in the symbol. Who loves nature? Who does not? Is it only poets, and men of leisure and cultivation, who live with her? No; but also hunters, farmers, grooms and butchers, though they express their affection in their choice of life and not in their choice of words. The writer wonders what the coachman or the hunter values in riding, in horses and dogs. It is not superficial qualities. When you talk with him he holds these at as slight a rate as you. His worship is sympathetic; he has no definitions, but he is commanded in nature by the living power which he feels to be there present. No imitation or playing of these things would content him; he loves the earnest of the north wind, of rain, of stone and wood and iron. A beauty not explicable is dearer than a beauty which we can see to the end of. It is nature the symbol, nature certifying the supernatural, body overflowed by life which he worships with coarse but sincere rites.

The inwardness and mystery of this attachment drive men of every class to the use of emblems. The schools of poets and philosophers are not more intoxicated with their symbols than the populace with theirs. In our political parties, compute the power of badges and emblems. See the great ball which they roll from Baltimore to Bunker Hill! In the political processions, Lowell goes in a loom, and Lynn in a shoe, and Salem in a ship. Witness the cider-barrel, the log-cabin, the hickory stick, the palmetto, and all the cognizances of party. See the power of national emblems. Some stars, lilies, leopards, a crescent, a lion, an eagle, or other figure which came into credit God knows how, on an old rag of bunting, blowing in the wind on a fort at the ends of the earth, shall make the blood tingle under the rudest or the most conventional exterior. The people fancy they hate poetry, and they are all poet and mystics!

Beyond this universality of the symbolic language, we are apprised of the divineness of this superior use of things, whereby the world is a temple whose walls are covered with emblems, pictures and commandments of the Deity, —in this, that there is no fact in nature which does not carry the whole sense of nature; and the distinctions which we make in events and in affairs, of low and high, honest and base, disappear when nature is used as a symbol. Thought makes everything fit for use. The vocabulary of an omniscient man would embrace words and images excluded from polite conversation. What would be base, or even obscene, to the obscene, becomes illustrious, spoken in a new connection of thought. The piety of the Hebrew prophets purges their grossness. The circumcision is an example of the power of poetry to raise the low and offensive. Small and mean things serve as well as great symbols. The meaner the type by which a law is expressed, the more pungent it is, and the more lasting in the memories of men; just as we choose the smallest box or case in which any needful utensil can be carried. Bare lists of words are found suggestive to an imaginative and excited mind; as it is related of Lord Chatham that he was accustomed to read in Bailey's Dictionary when he was preparing to speak in Parliament. The poorest experience is rich enough for all the purposes of expressing thought. Why covet a knowledge of new facts? Day and night, house and garden, a few books, a few actions, serve us as well as would all trades and all spectacles. We are far from having exhausted the significance of the few symbols we use. We can come to use them yet with a terrible simplicity. It does not need that a poem should be long. Every word was once a poem. Every new relation is a new word. Also we use defects and deformities to a sacred purpose, so expressing our sense that the evils of the world are such only to the evil eye. In the old mythology, mythologists observe, defects are ascribed to divine natures, as lameness to Vulcan, blindness to Cupid, and the like,—to signify exuberances.

For as it is dislocation and detachment from the life of God that makes things ugly, the poet, who re-attaches things to nature and the Whole,—re-attaching even artificial things and violation of nature, to nature, by a deeper insight,—disposes very easily of the most disagreeable facts. Readers of poetry see the factory-village and the railway, and fancy that the poetry of the landscape is broken up by these; for these works of art are not yet consecrated in their reading; but the poet sees them fall within the great Order not less than the beehive or the spider's geometrical web. Nature adopts them very fast into her vital circles, and the gliding train of cars she loves like her own. Besides, in a centred mind, it signifies nothing how many mechanical inventions you exhibit. Though you add millions, and never so surprising, the fact of mechanics has not gained a grain's weight. The spiritual fact remains unalterable, by many or by few particulars; as no mountain is of any appreciable height to break the curve of the sphere. A shrewd country-boy goes to the city for the first time, and the complacent citizen is not satisfied with his little wonder. It is not that he does not see all the fine houses and know that he never saw such before, but he disposes of them as easily as the poet finds place for the railway. The chief value of the new fact is to enhance the great and constant fact of Life, which can dwarf any and every circumstance, and to which the belt of wampum and the commerce of America are alike.

The world being thus put under the mind for verb and noun, the poet is he who can articulate it. For though life is great, and fascinates and absorbs; and though all men are intelligent of the symbols through which it is named; yet they cannot originally use them. We are symbols and inhabit symbols; workmen, work, and tools, words and things, birth and death, all are emblems; but we sympathize with the symbols, and being infatuated with the economical uses of things, we do not know that they are thoughts. The poet, by an ulterior intellectual perception, gives them a power which makes their old use forgotten, and puts eyes and a tongue into every dumb and inanimate object. He perceives the independence of the thought on the symbol, the stability of the thought, the accidency and fugacity of the symbol. As the eyes of Lyncæus were said to see through the earth, so the poet turns the world to glass, and shows us all things in their right series and procession. For through that better perception he stands one step nearer to things, and sees the flowing or metamorphosis; perceives that thought is multiform; that within the form of every creature is a force impelling it to ascend into a higher form; and following with his eyes the life, uses the forms which express that life, and so his speech flows with the flowing of nature. All the facts of the animal economy, sex, nutriment, gestation, birth, growth, are symbols of the passage of the world into the soul of man, to suffer there a change and reappear a new and higher fact. He uses forms according to the life, and not according to the form. This is true science. The poet alone knows astronomy, chemistry, vegetation and animation, for he does not stop at these facts, but employs them as signs. He knows why the plain or meadow of space was strown with these flowers we call suns and moons and stars; why the great deep is adorned with animals, with men, and gods; for in every word he speaks he rides on them as the horses of thought.

By virtue of this science the poet is the Namer or Language-maker, naming things sometimes after their appearance, sometimes after their essence, and giving to every one its own name and not another's, thereby rejoicing the intellect, which delights in detachment or boundary. The poets made all the words, and therefore language is the archives of history, and, if we must say it, a sort of tomb of the muses. For though the origin of most of our words is forgotten, each word was at first a stroke of genius, and obtained currency because for the moment it symbolized the world to the first speaker and to the hearer. The etymologist finds the deadest word to have been once a brilliant picture. Language is fossil poetry. As the limestone of the continent consists of infinite masses of the shells of animalcules, so language is made up of images or tropes, which now, in their secondary use, have long ceased to remind us of their poetic origin. But the poet names the thing because he sees it, or comes one step nearer to it than any other. This expression or naming is not art, but a second nature, grown out of the first, as a leaf out of a tree. What we call nature is a certain self-regulated motion or change; and nature does all things by her own hands, and does not leave another to baptize her but baptizes herself; and this through the metamorphosis again. I remember that a certain poet described it to me thus:—

Genius is the activity which repairs the decays of things, whether wholly or partly of a material and finite kind. Nature, through all her kingdoms, insures herself. Nobody cares for planting the poor fungus; so she shakes down from the gills of one agaric countless spores, any one of which, being preserved, transmits new billions of spores to-morrow or next day. The new agaric of this hour has a chance which the old one had not. This atom of seed is thrown into a new place, not subject to the accidents which destroyed its parent two rods off. She makes a man; and having brought him to ripe age, she will no longer run the risk of losing this wonder at a blow, but she detaches from him a new self, that the kind may be safe from accidents to which the individual is exposed. So when the soul of the poet has come to ripeness of thought, she detaches and sends away from it its poems or songs,—a fearless, sleepless, deathless progeny, which is not exposed to the accidents of the weary kingdom of time; a fearless, vivacious offspring, clad with wings (such was the virtue of the soul out of which they came) which carry them fast and far, and infix them irrecoverably into the hearts of men. These wings are the beauty of the poet's soul. The songs, thus flying immortal from their mortal parent, are pursued by clamorous flights of censures, which swarm in far greater numbers and threaten to devour them; but these last are not winged. At the end of a very short leap they fall plump down and rot, having received from the souls out of which they came no beautiful wings. But the melodies of the poet ascend and leap and pierce into the deeps of infinite time.

So far the bard taught me, using his freer speech. But nature has a higher end, in the production of new individuals, than security, namely *ascension,* or the passage of the soul into higher forms. I knew in my younger days the sculptor who made the statue of the youth which stands in the public garden. He was, as I remember, unable to tell directly what made him happy or unhappy, but by wonderful indirections he could tell. He rose one day, according to his habit, before the dawn, and saw the morning break, grand as the eternity out of which it came, and for many days after, he strove to express this tranquillity, and lo! his chisel had fashioned out of marble the form of a beautiful youth, Phosphorus, whose aspect is such that it is said all persons who look on it become silent. The poet also resigns himself to his mood, and that thought which agitated him is expressed, but *alter idem,* in a manner totally new. The expression is organic, or the new type which things themselves take when liberated. As, in the sun, objects paint their images on the retina of the eye, so they, sharing the aspiration of the whole universe, tend to paint a far more delicate copy of their essence in his mind. Like the metamorphosis of things into higher organic forms is their change into melodies. Over everything stands its dæmon or soul, and, as the form of the thing is reflected by the eye, so the soul of the thing is reflected by a melody. The sea, the mountain-ridge, Niagara, and every flower-bed, pre-exist, or super-exist, in pre-cantations, which sail like odors in the air, and when any man goes by with an ear sufficiently fine, he overhears them and endeavors to write down the notes without diluting or depraving them. And herein is the legitimation of criticism, in the mind's faith that the poems are a corrupt version of some text in nature with which they ought to be made to tally. A rhyme in one of our sonnets should not be less pleasing than the iterated nodes of a seashell, or the resembling difference of a group of flowers. The pairing of the birds is an idyl, not tedious as our idyls are; a tempest is a rough ode, without falsehood or rant; a summer, with its harvest sown, reaped and stored, is an epic song, subordinating how many admirably executed parts. Why should not the symmetry and truth that modulate these, glide into our spirits, and we participate the invention of nature?

This insight, which expresses itself by what is called Imagination, is a very high sort of seeing, which does not come by study, but by the intellect being where and what it sees; by sharing the path or circuit of things through forms, and so making them translucid to others. The path of things is silent. Will they suffer a speaker to go with them? A spy they will not suffer; a lover, a poet, is the transcendency of their own nature,—him they will suffer. The condition of true naming, on the poet's part, is his resigning himself to the divine *aura* which breathes through forms, and accompanying that.

It is a secret which every intellectual man quickly learns, that beyond the energy of his possessed and conscious intellect he is capable of a new energy (as of an intellect doubled on itself), by abandonment to the nature of things; that beside his privacy of power as an individual man, there is a great public power on which he can draw, by unlocking, at all risks, his human doors, and suffering the ethereal tides to roll and circulate through him; then he is caught up into the life of the Universe, his speech is thunder, his thought is law, and his words are universally intelligible as the plants and animals. The poet knows that he speaks adequately then only when he speaks somewhat wildly, or "with the flower of the mind;" not with the intellect used as an organ, but with the intellect released from all service and suffered to take its direction from its celestial life; or as the ancients were wont to express themselves, not with intellect alone but with the intellect inebriated by nectar. As the traveller who has lost his way throws his reins on his horse's neck and trusts to the instinct of the animal to find his road, so must we do with the divine animal who carries us through this world. For if in any manner we can stimulate this instinct, new passages are opened for us into nature; the mind flows into and through things hardest and highest, and the metamorphosis is possible.

This is the reason why bards love wine, mead, narcotics, coffee, tea, opium, the fumes of sandalwood and tobacco, or whatever other procurers of animal exhilaration. All men avail themselves of such means as they can, to add this extraordinary power to their normal powers; and to this end they prize conversation, music, pictures, sculpture, dancing, theatres, travelling, war, mobs, fires, gaming, politics, or love, or science, or animal intoxication,—which are several coarser or finer *quasi*-mechanical substitutes for the true nectar, which is the ravishment of the intellect by coming nearer to the fact. These are auxiliaries to the centrifugal tendency of a man, to his passage out into free space, and they help him to escape the custody of that body in which he is pent up, and of that jail-yard of individual relations in which he is enclosed. Hence a great number of such as were professionally expressers of Beauty, as painters, poets, musicians and actors, have been more than others wont to lead a life of pleasure and indulgence; all but the few who received the true nectar; and, as it was a spurious mode of attaining freedom, as it was an emancipation not into the heavens but into the freedom of baser places, they were punished for that advantage they won, by a dissipation and deterioration. But never can any advantage be taken of nature by a trick. The spirit of the world, the great calm presence of the Creator, comes not forth to the sorceries of opium or of wine. The sublime vision comes to the pure and simple soul in a clean and chaste body. That is not an inspiration, which we owe to narcotics, but some counterfeit excitement and fury. Milton says that the lyric poet may drink wine and live generously, but the epic poet, he who shall sing of the gods and their descent unto men, must drink water out of a wooden bowl. For poetry is not "Devil's wine," but God's wine. It is with this as it is with toys. We fill the hands and nurseries of our children with all manner of dolls, drums and horses; withdrawing their eyes from the plain face and sufficing objects of nature, the sun and moon, the animals, the water and stones, which should be their toys. So the poet's habit of living should be set on a key so low that the common influences should delight him. His cheerfulness should be the gift of the sunlight; the air should suffice for his inspiration, and he should be tipsy with water. That spirit which suffices quiet hearts, which seems to come forth to such from every dry knoll of sere grass, from every pine stump and half-imbedded stone on which the dull March sun shines, comes forth to the poor and hungry, and such as are of simple taste. If thou fill thy brain with Boston and New York, with fashion and covetousness, and wilt stimulate thy jaded senses with wine and French coffee, thou shalt find no radiance of wisdom in the lonely waste of the pine woods.

If the imagination intoxicates the poet, it is not inactive in other men. The metamorphosis excites in the beholder an emotion of joy. The use of symbols has a certain power of emancipation and exhilaration for all men. We seem to be touched by a wand which makes us dance and run about happily, like children. We are like persons who come out of a cave or cellar into the open air. This is the effect on us of tropes, fables, oracles and all poetic forms. Poets are thus liberating gods. Men have really got a new sense, and found within their world another world, or nest of worlds; for, the metamorphosis once seen, we divine that it does not stop. I will not now consider how much this makes the charm of algebra and the mathematics, which also have their tropes, but it is felt in every definition; as when Aristotle defines *space* to be an immovable vessel in which things are contained;—or when Plato defines a *line* to be a flowing point; or *figure* to be a bound of solid; and many the like. What a joyful sense of freedom we have when Vitruvius announces the old opinion of artists that no architect can build any house well who does not know something of anatomy. When Socrates, in Charmides, tells us that the soul is cured of its maladies by certain incantations, and that these incantations are beautiful reasons, from which temperance is generated in souls; when Plato calls the world an animal, and Timæus affirms that the plants also are animals; or affirms a man to be a heavenly tree, growing with his root, which is his head, upward; and, as George Chapman, following him, writes,

"So in our tree of man, whose nervie root
   Springs in his top;"—

when Orpheus speaks of hoariness as "that white flower which marks extreme old age;" when Proclus calls the universe the statue of the intellect; when Chaucer, in his praise of "Gentilesse," compares good blood in mean condition to fire, which, though carried to the darkest house betwixt this and the mount of Caucasus, will yet hold its natural office and burn as bright as if twenty thousand men did it behold; when John saw, in the Apocalypse, the ruin of the world through evil, and the stars fall from heaven as the fig tree casteth her untimely fruit; when Æsop reports the whole catalogue of common daily relations through the masquerade of birds and beasts;—we take the cheerful hint of the immortality of our essence and its versatile habit and escapes, as when the gypsies say of themselves "it is in vain to hang them, they cannot die."

The poets are thus liberating gods. The ancient British bards had for the title of their order, "Those who are free throughout the world." They are free, and they make free. An imaginative book renders us much more service at first, by stimulating us through its tropes, than afterward when we arrive at the precise sense of the author. I think nothing is of any value in books excepting the transcendental and extraordinary. If a man is inflamed and carried away by his thought, to that degree that he forgets the authors and the public and heeds only this one dream which holds him like an insanity, let me read his paper, and you may have all the arguments and histories and criticism. All the value which attaches to Pythagoras, Paracelsus, Cornelius Agrippa, Cardan, Kepler, Swedenborg, Schelling, Oken, or any other who introduces questionable facts into his cosmogony, as angels, devils, magic, astrology, palmistry, mesmerism, and so on, is the certificate we have of departure from routine, and that here is a new witness. That also is the best success in conversation, the magic of liberty, which puts the world like a ball in our hands. How cheap even the liberty then seems; how mean to study, when an emotion communicates to the intellect the power to sap and upheave nature; how great the perspective! nations, times, systems, enter and disappear like threads in tapestry of large figure and many colors; dream delivers us to dream, and while the drunkenness lasts we will sell our bed, our philosophy, our religion, in our opulence.

There is good reason why we should prize this liberation. The fate of the poor shepherd, who, blinded and lost in the snow-storm, perishes in a drift within a few feet of his cottage door, is an emblem of the state of man. On the brink of the waters of life and truth, we are miserably dying. The inaccessibleness of every thought but that we are in, is wonderful. What if you come near to it; you are as remote when you are nearest as when you are farthest. Every thought is also a prison; every heaven is also a prison. Therefore we love the poet, the inventor, who in any form, whether in an ode or in an action or in looks and behavior, has yielded us a new thought. He unlocks our chains and admits us to a new scene.

This emancipation is dear to all men, and the power to impart it, as it must come from greater depth and scope of thought, is a measure of intellect. Therefore all books of the imagination endure, all which ascend to that truth that the writer sees nature beneath him, and uses it as his exponent. Every verse or sentence possessing this virtue will take care of its own immortality. The religions of the world are the ejaculations of a few imaginative men.

But the quality of the imagination is to flow, and not to freeze. The poet did not stop at the color or the form, but read their meaning; neither may he rest in this meaning, but he makes the same objects exponents of his new thought. Here is the difference betwixt the poet and the mystic, that the last nails a symbol to one sense, which was a true sense for a moment, but soon becomes old and false. For all symbols are fluxional; all language is vehicular and transitive, and is good, as ferries and horses are, for conveyance, not as farms and houses are, for homestead. Mysticism consists in the mistake of an accidental and individual symbol for an universal one. The morning-redness happens to be the favorite meteor to the eyes of Jacob Behmen, and comes to stand to him for truth and faith; and, he believes, should stand for the same realities to every reader. But the first reader prefers as naturally the symbol of a mother and child, or a gardener and his bulb, or a jeweller polishing a gem. Either of these, or of a myriad more, are equally good to the person to whom they are significant. Only they must be held lightly, and be very willingly translated into the equivalent terms which others use. And the mystic must be steadily told,—All that you say is just as true without the tedious use of that symbol as with it. Let us have a little algebra, instead of this trite rhetoric,—universal signs, instead of these village symbols, —and we shall both be gainers. The history of hierarchies seems to show that all religious error consisted in making the symbol too stark and solid, and was at last nothing but an excess of the organ of language.

Swedenborg, of all men in the recent ages, stands emi-nently for the translator of nature into thought. I do not know the man in history to whom things stood so uni-formly for words. Before him the metamorphosis continu-ally plays. Everything on which his eye rests, obeys the impulses of moral nature. The figs become grapes whilst he eats them. When some of his angels affirmed a truth, the laurel twig which they held blossomed in their hands. The noise which at a distance appeared like gnashing and thumping, on coming nearer was found to be the voice of disputants. The men in one of his visions, seen in heavenly light, appeared like dragons, and seemed in darkness; but to each other they appeared as men, and when the light from heaven shone into their cabin, they complained of the darkness, and were compelled to shut the window that they might see.

There was this perception in him which makes the poet or seer an object of awe and terror, namely that the same man or society of men may wear one aspect to themselves and their companions, and a different aspect to higher in-telligences. Certain priests, whom he describes as convers-ing very learnedly together, appeared to the children who were at some distance, like dead horses; and many the like misappearances. And instantly the mind inquires whether these fishes under the bridge, yonder oxen in the pasture, those dogs in the yard, are immutably fishes, oxen and dogs, or only so appear to me, and perchance to themselves appear upright men; and whether I appear as a man to all eyes. The Brahmins and Pythagoras propounded the same question, and if any poet has witnessed the transformation he doubtless found it in harmony with various experiences. We have all seen changes as considerable in wheat and caterpillars. He is the poet and shall draw us with love and terror, who sees through the flowing vest the firm nature, and can declare it.

I look in vain for the poet whom I describe. We do not with sufficient plainness or sufficient profoundness address ourselves to life, nor dare we chaunt our own times and social circumstance. If we filled the day with bravery, we should not shrink from celebrating it. Time and nature yield us many gifts, but not yet the timely man, the new religion, the reconciler, whom all things await. Dante's praise is that he dared to write his autobiography in colossal cipher, or into universality. We have yet had no genius in America, with tyrannous eye, which knew the value of our incomparable materials, and saw, in the barbarism and materialism of the times, another carnival of the same gods whose picture he so much admires in Homer; then in the Middle Age; then in Calvinism. Banks and tariffs, the newspaper and caucus, Methodism and Unitarianism, are flat and dull to dull people, but rest on the same foundations of wonder as the town of Troy and the temple of Delphi, and are as swiftly passing away. Our log-rolling, our stumps and their politics, our fisheries, our Negroes and Indians, our boats and our repudiations, the wrath of rogues and the pusillanimity of honest men, the northern trade, the southern planting, the western clearing, Oregon and Texas, are yet unsung. Yet America is a poem in our eyes; its ample geography dazzles the imagination, and it will not wait long for metres. If I have not found that excellent combination of gifts in my countrymen which I seek, neither could I aid myself to fix the idea of the poet by reading now and then in Chalmers's collection of five centuries of English poets. These are wits more than poets, though there have been poets among them. But when we adhere to the ideal of the poet, we have our difficulties even with Milton and Homer. Milton is too literary, and Homer too literal and historical.

But I am not wise enough for a national criticism, and must use the old largeness a little longer, to discharge my errand from the muse to the poet concerning his art.

Art is the path of the creator to his work. The paths or methods are ideal and eternal, though few men ever see them; not the artist himself for years, or for a lifetime, unless he come into the conditions. The painter, the sculptor, the composer, the epic rhapsodist, the orator, all partake one desire, namely to express themselves symmetrically and abundantly, not dwarfishly and fragmentarily. They found or put themselves in certain conditions, as, the painter and sculptor before some impressive human figures; the orator into the assembly of the people; and the others in such scenes as each has found exciting to his intellect; and each presently feels the new desire. He hears a voice, he sees a beckoning. Then he is apprised, with wonder, what herds of dæmons hem him in. He can no more rest; he says, with the old painter, "By God it is in me and must go forth of me." He pursues a beauty, half seen, which flies before him. The poet pours out verses in every solitude. Most of the things he says are conventional, no doubt; but by and by he says something which is original and beautiful. That charms him. He would say nothing else but such things. In our way of talking we say "That is yours, this is mine;" but the poet knows well that it is not his; that it is as strange and beautiful to him as to you; he would fain hear the like eloquence at length. Once having tasted this immortal ichor, he cannot have enough of it, and as an admirable creative power exists in these intellections, it is of the last importance that these things get spoken. What a little of all we know is said! What drops of all the sea of our science are baled up! and by what accident it is that these are exposed, when so many secrets sleep in nature! Hence the necessity of speech and song; hence these throbs and heart-beatings in the orator, at the door of the assembly, to the end namely that thought may be ejaculated as Logos, or Word.

Doubt not, O poet, but persist. Say "It is in me, and shall out." Stand there, balked and dumb, stuttering and stammering, hissed and hooted, stand and strive, until at last rage draw out of thee that *dream*-power which every night shows thee is thine own; a power transcending all limit and privacy, and by virtue of which a man is the conductor of the whole river of electricity. Nothing walks, or creeps, or grows, or exists, which must not in turn arise and walk before him as exponent of his meaning. Comes he to that power, his genius is no longer exhaustible. All the creatures by pairs and by tribes pour into his mind as into a Noah's ark, to come forth again to people a new world. This is like the stock of air for our respiration or for the combustion of our fireplace; not a measure of gallons, but the entire atmosphere if wanted. And therefore the rich poets, as Homer, Chaucer, Shakespeare, and Raphael, have obviously no limits to their works except the limits of their lifetime, and resemble a mirror carried through the street, ready to render an image of every created thing.

O poet! a new nobility is conferred in groves and pastures, and not in castles or by the sword-blade any longer. The conditions are hard, but equal. Thou shalt leave the world, and know the muse only. Thou shalt not know any longer the times, customs, graces, politics, or opinions of men, but shalt take all from the muse. For the time of towns is tolled from the world by funereal chimes, but in nature the universal hours are counted by succeeding tribes of animals and plants, and by growth of joy on joy. God wills also that thou abdicate a manifold and duplex life, and that thou be content that others speak for thee. Others shall be thy gentlemen and shall represent all courtesy and worldly life for thee; others shall do the great and resounding actions also. Thou shalt lie close hid with nature, and canst not be afforded to the Capitol or the Exchange. The world is full of renunciations and apprenticeships, and this is thine; thou must pass for a fool and a churl for a long season. This is the screen and sheath in which Pan has protected his well-beloved flower, and thou shalt be known only to thine own, and they shall console thee with tenderest love. And thou shalt not be able to rehearse the names of thy friends in thy verse, for an old shame before the holy ideal. And this is the reward; that the ideal shall be real to thee, and the impressions of the actual world shall fall like summer rain, copious, but not troublesome to thy invulnerable essence. Thou shalt have the whole land for thy park and manor, the sea for thy bath and navigation, without tax and without envy; the woods and the rivers thou shalt own, and thou shalt possess that wherein others are only tenants and boarders. Thou true land-lord! sea-lord! air-lord! Wherever snow falls or water flows or birds fly, wherever day and night meet in twilight, wherever the blue heaven is hung by clouds or sown with stars, wherever are forms with transparent boundaries, wherever are outlets into celestial space, wherever is danger, and awe, and love,—there is Beauty, plenteous as rain, shed for thee, and though thou shouldst walk the world over, thou shalt not be able to find a condition inopportune or ignoble.

WALT WHITMAN

1819–1892

The first edition of *Leaves of Grass* was prefaced by Whitman's manifesto. Much indebted to Emerson as it is in thought and style, the "Preface" is yet wholly Whitman's own. In epigrammatic sentences it announces the bases of the poems in the 1855 volume and of poems yet to come: "The United States themselves are essentially the greatest poem." "The expression of the American poet is to be transcendant and new. It is to be indirect, and not direct or descriptive or epic." "The greatest poem forms the consistence of what is to be from what has been and is." "Each precise object or condition or combination or process exhibits a beauty." To his readers the poet will "indicate the path between reality and their souls." Hopeful, magnanimous, and triumphant, this preface is a central document in Whitman's achievement.

Thirty-three years later he wrote "A Backward Glance O'er Travel'd Roads," the preface to the ninth and last edition of *Leaves of Grass*. The original thirteen poems are still present (though rewritten), plus hundreds of pages of later work, all subsumable under the same title, the same poetic personality, the same intention. Now, as Whitman writes "in the early candlelight of old age," he takes a less iconoclastic view of the heritage he had thrown aside in his youth. "The New World receives with joy the poems of the antique, with European feudalism's rich find of epics, plays, and ballads." Now he "could not have written *Leaves of Grass*" had he not reverenced Homer, Aeschylus, Sophocles, Dante, Shakespeare. He acknowledges room for Poe ("The Poetic area . . . has so many mansions!"), and paradoxically accepts Poe's arguments against the long poem. He is still certain "that really great poetry is always . . . the result of a national spirit," that "the strongest and sweetest songs yet remain to be sung." But he now sees perils as well as promises in democracy: "leveling tendencies" which endanger "that primal and interior something in man . . . giving the last majesty to him." Yet still he seeks to prepare the way "for grander individualities than ever."

Whitman composed his prose journal *Specimen Days* between 1862 and 1882. It contains reminiscences of his boyhood, a remarkable account of his Civil War experiences, and detailed observations of nature. The excerpts reprinted here give Whitman's impressions, late in his life, of Poe, Emerson, Bryant, Whittier, and Longfellow.

TEXT: *Leaves of Grass* (1855); *Complete Prose Works* (1892).

PREFACE, 1855, TO FIRST ISSUE OF

"LEAVES OF GRASS."

Brooklyn, N.Y.

America does not repel the past or what it has produced under its forms or amid other politics or the idea of castes or the old religions . . . . accepts the lesson with calmness . . . is not so impatient as has been supposed that the slough still sticks to opinions and manners and literature while the life which served its requirements has passed into the new life of the new forms . . . perceives that the corpse is slowly borne from the eating and sleeping rooms of the house . . . perceives that it waits a little while in the door . . . that it was fittest for its days . . . that its action has descended to the stalwart and well-shaped heir who approaches . . . and that he shall be fittest for his days.

The Americans of all nations at any time upon the earth have probably the fullest poetical nature. The United States themselves are essentially the greatest poem. In the history of the earth hitherto the largest and most stirring appear tame and orderly to their ampler largeness and stir. Here at last is something in the doings of man that corresponds with the broadcast doings of the day and night. Here is not merely a nation but a teeming nation of nations. Here is action untied from strings necessarily blind to particulars and details magnificently moving in vast masses. Here is the hospitality which forever indicates heroes . . . . Here are the roughs and beards and space and ruggedness and nonchalance that the soul loves. Here the performance disdaining the trivial unapproached in the tremendous audacity of its crowds and groupings and the push of its perspective spreads with crampless and flowing breadth and showers its prolific and splendid extravagance. One sees it must indeed own the riches of the summer and winter, and need never be bankrupt while corn grows from the ground or the orchards drop apples or the bays contain fish or men beget children upon women.

Other states indicate themselves in their deputies . . . . but the genius of the United States is not best or most in its executives or legislatures, nor in its ambassadors or authors or colleges or churches or parlors, nor even in its newspapers or inventors . . . but always most in the common people. Their manners speech dress friendships—the freshness and candor of their physiognomy—the picturesque looseness of their carriage . . . their deathless attachment to freedom—their aversion to anything indecorous or soft or mean—the practical acknowledgment of the citizens of one state by the citizens of all other states—the fierceness of their roused resentment—their curiosity and welcome of novelty—their self-esteem and wonderful sympathy—their susceptibility to a slight—the air they have of persons who never knew how it felt to stand in the presence of superiors —the fluency of their speech—their delight in music, the sure symptom of manly tenderness and native elegance of soul . . . their good temper and openhandedness—the terrible significance of their elections—the President's taking off his hat to them not they to him—these too are unrhymed poetry. It awaits the gigantic and generous treatment worthy of it.

The largeness of nature or the nation were monstrous without a corresponding largeness and generosity of the spirit of the citizen. Not nature nor swarming states nor

streets and steamships nor prosperous business nor farms
nor capital nor learning may suffice for the ideal of man
. . . nor suffice the poet. No reminiscences may suffice
either. A live nation can always cut a deep mark and can
have the best authority the cheapest . . . namely from its
own soul. This is the sum of the profitable uses of individuals or states and of present action and grandeur and
of the subjects of poets.—As if it were necessary to trot
back generation after generation to the eastern records! As
if the beauty and sacredness of the demonstrable must fall
behind that of the mythical! As if men do not make their
mark out of any times! As if the opening of the western
continent by discovery and what has transpired since in
North and South America were less than the small theatre
of the antique or the aimless sleepwalking of the middle
ages! The pride of the United States leaves the wealth and
finesse of the cities and all returns of commerce and agriculture and all the magnitude of geography or shows of
exterior victory to enjoy the breed of fullsized men or one
fullsized man unconquerable and simple.

The American poets are to enclose old and new for
America is the race of races. Of them a bard is to be com-
mensurate with a people. To him the other continents arrive as contributions . . . he gives them reception for their
sake and his own sake. His spirit responds to his country's
spirit . . . . he incarnates its geography and natural life
and rivers and lakes. Mississippi with annual freshets and
changing chutes, Missouri and Columbia and Ohio and
Saint Lawrence with the falls and beautiful masculine Hudson, do not embouchure where they spend themselves more
than they embouchure into him. The blue breadth over
the inland sea of Virginia and Maryland and the sea of
Massachusetts and Maine and over Manhattan bay and
over Champlain and Erie and over Ontario and Huron and
Michigan and Superior, and over the Texan and Mexican
and Floridian and Cuban seas and over the seas off California and Oregon, is not tallied by the blue breadth of
the waters below more than the breadth of above and below is tallied by him. When the long Atlantic coast
stretches longer and the Pacific coast stretches longer he

easily stretches with them north or south. He spans between them also from east to west and reflects what is between them. On him rise solid growths that offset the growths of pine and cedar and hemlock and liveoak and locust and chestnut and cypress and hickory and limetree and cottonwood and tuliptree and cactus and wildvine and tamarind and persimmon . . . . and tangles as tangled as any canebrake or swamp . . . . and forests coated with transparent ice and icicles hanging from the boughs and crackling in the wind . . . . and sides and peaks of mountains . . . . and pasturage sweet and free as savannah or upland or prairie . . . . with flights and songs and screams that answer those of the wild-pigeon and highhold and orchard-oriole and coot and surf-duck and redshouldered-hawk and fish-hawk and white-ibis and indian-hen and cat-owl and water-pheasant and qua-bird and pied-sheldrake and blackbird and mockingbird and buzzard and condor and night-heron and eagle. To him the hereditary countenance descends both mother's and father's. To him enter the essences of the real things and past and present events—of the enormous diversity of temperature and agriculture and mines—the tribes of red aborigines—the weatherbeaten vessels entering new ports or making landings on rocky coasts—the first settlements north or south—the rapid stature and muscle—the haughty defiance of '76, and the war and peace and formation of the constitution . . . . the union always surrounded by blatherers and always calm and impregnable—the perpetual coming of immigrants—the wharfhem'd cities and superior marine—the unsurveyed interior—the loghouses and clearings and wild animals and hunters and trappers . . . . the free commerce —the fisheries and whaling and gold-digging—the endless gestation of new states—the convening of Congress every December, the members duly coming up from all climates and the uttermost parts . . . . the noble character of the young mechanics and of all free American workmen and workwomen . . . . the general ardor and friendliness and enterprise—the perfect equality of the female with the male . . . . the large amativeness—the fluid movement of the population—the factories and mercantile life and laborsaving machinery—the Yankee swap—the New-York firemen and the target excursion—the southern plantation life—the character of the northeast and of the northwest and southwest—slavery and the tremulous spreading of hands to protect it, and the stern opposition to it which shall never cease till it ceases or the speaking of tongues and the moving of lips cease. For such the expression of the American poet is to be transcendant and new. It is to be indirect and not direct or descriptive or epic. Its quality goes through these to much more. Let the age and wars of other nations be chanted and their eras and characters be illustrated and that finish the verse. Not so the great Psalm of the republic. Here the theme is creative and has vista. Here comes one among the wellbeloved stonecutters and plans with decision and science and sees the solid and beautiful forms of the future where there are now no solid forms.

Of all nations the United States with veins full of poetical stuff most need poets and will doubtless have the greatest and use them the greatest. Their Presidents shall not be their common referee so much as their poets shall. Of all mankind the great poet is the equable man. Not in him but off from him things are grotesque or eccentric or fail of their sanity. Nothing out of its place is good and nothing in its place is bad. He bestows on every object or quality its fit proportions neither more nor less. He is the arbiter of the diverse and he is the key. He is the equalizer of his age and land . . . . he supplies what wants supplying and checks what wants checking. If peace is the routine out of him speaks the spirit of peace, large, rich, thrifty, building vast and populous cities, encouraging agriculture and the arts and commerce—lighting the study of man, the soul, immortality—federal, state or municipal government, marriage, health, free-trade, intertravel by land and sea . . . . nothing too close, nothing too far off . . . the stars not too far off. In war he is the most deadly force of the war. Who recruits him recruits horse and foot . . . he fetches parks of artillery the best that engineer ever knew. If the time becomes slothful and heavy he knows how to arouse it . . . he can make every word he speaks draw blood. Whatever stagnates in the flat of custom or obedience or legislation he never stagnates. Obedience does not master him, he masters it. High up out of reach he stands turning a concentrated light . . . he turns the pivot with his finger . . . he baffles the swiftest runners as he stands and easily overtakes and envelops them. The time straying toward infidelity and confections and persiflage he withholds by his steady faith . . . he spreads out his dishes . . . he offers the sweet firmfibred meat that grows men and women. His brain is the ultimate brain. He is no arguer . . . he is judgment. He judges not as the judge judges but as the sun falling around a helpless thing. As he sees the farthest he has the most faith. His thoughts are the hymns of the praise of things. In the talk on the soul and eternity and God off of his equal plane he is silent. He sees eternity less like a play with a prologue and denouement . . . . he sees eternity in men and women . . . he does not see men and women as dreams or dots. Faith is the antiseptic of the soul . . . it pervades the common people and preserves them . . . they never give up believing and expecting and trusting. There is that indescribable freshness and unconsciousness about an illiterate person that humbles and mocks the power of the noblest expressive genius. The poet sees for a certainty how one not a great artist may be just as sacred and perfect as the greatest artist. . . . . . The power to destroy or remould is freely used by him but never the power of attack. What is past is past. If he does not expose superior models and prove himself by every step he takes he is not what is wanted. The presence of the greatest poet conquers . . . not parleying or struggling or any prepared attempts. Now he has passed that way see after him! there is not left any vestige of despair or misanthropy or cunning or exclusiveness or the ignominy of a nativity or color or delusion of hell or the necessity of hell . . . . . and no man thenceforward shall be degraded for ignorance or weakness or sin.

The greatest poet hardly knows pettiness or triviality. If he breathes into any thing that was before thought small it dilates with the grandeur and life of the universe. He is a seer . . . . he is individual . . . he is complete in himself . . . . the others are as good as he, only he sees it and they do not. He is not one of the chorus . . . . he does not stop for any regulation . . . he is the president of regulation. What the eyesight does to the rest he does to the rest. Who knows the curious mystery of the eyesight? The other senses corroborate themselves, but this is removed from any proof but its own and foreruns the identities of the spiritual world. A single glance of it mocks all the investigations of man and all the instruments and books of the earth and all reasoning. What is marvellous? what is unlikely? what is impossible or baseless or vague? after you have once just opened the space of a peachpit and given audience to far and near and to the sunset and had all things enter with electric swiftness softly and duly without confusion or jostling or jam.

The land and sea, the animals fishes and birds, the sky of heaven and the orbs, the forests mountains and rivers, are not small themes . . . but folks expect of the poet to indicate more than the beauty and dignity which always attach to dumb real objects . . . . they expect him to indicate the path between reality and their souls. Men and women perceive the beauty well enough . . probably as well as he. The passionate tenacity of hunters, woodmen, early risers, cultivators of gardens and orchards and fields, the love of healthy women for the manly form, seafaring persons, drivers of horses, the passion for light and the open air, all is an old varied sign of the unfailing perception of beauty and of a residence of the poetic in outdoor people. They can never be assisted by poets to perceive . . . some may but they never can. The poetic quality is not marshalled in rhyme or uniformity or abstract addresses to things nor in melancholy complaints or good precepts, but is the life of these and much else and is in the soul. The profit of rhyme is that it drops seeds of a sweeter and more luxuriant rhyme, and of uniformity that it conveys itself into its own roots in the ground out of sight. The rhyme and uniformity of perfect poems show the free growth of metrical laws and bud from them as unerringly and loosely as lilacs or roses on a bush, and take shapes as compact as the shapes of chestnuts and oranges and melons and pears, and shed the perfume impalpable to form. The fluency and ornaments of the finest poems or music or orations or recitations are not independent but dependent. All beauty comes from beautiful blood and a beautiful brain. If the greatnesses are in conjunction in a man or woman it is enough . . . . the fact will prevail through the universe . . . . but the gaggery and gilt of a million years will not prevail. Who troubles himself about his ornaments or fluency is lost. This is what you shall do: Love the earth and sun and the animals, despise riches, give alms to every one that asks, stand up for the stupid and crazy, devote your income and labor to others, hate tyrants, argue not concerning God, have patience and indulgence toward the people, take off your hat to nothing known or unknown or to any man or number of men, go freely with powerful uneducated persons and with the young and with the mothers of families, read these leaves in the open air every season of every year of your life, reexamine all you have been told at school or church or in any book, dismiss whatever insults your own soul, and your very flesh shall be a great poem and have the richest fluency not only in its words but in the silent lines of its lips and face and between the lashes of your eyes and in every motion and joint of your body. . . . . The poet shall not spend his time in unneeded work. He shall know that the ground is always ready ploughed and manured . . . . others may not know it but he shall. He shall go directly to the creation. His trust shall master the trust of everything he touches . . . . and shall master all attachment.

The known universe has one complete lover and that is the greatest poet. He consumes an eternal passion and is indifferent which chance happens and which possible contingency of fortune or misfortune and persuades daily and hourly his delicious pay. What balks or breaks others is fuel for his burning progress to contact and amorous joy. Other proportions of the reception of pleasure dwindle to nothing to his proportions. All expected from heaven or from the highest he is rapport with in the sight of the daybreak or a scene of the winter woods or the presence of children playing or with his arm round the neck of a man or woman. His love above all love has leisure and expanse . . . . he leaves room ahead of himself. He is no irresolute or suspicious lover . . . he is sure . . . he scorns intervals. His experience and the showers and thrills are not for nothing. Nothing can jar him . . . . suffering and darkness cannot—death and fear cannot. To him complaint and jealousy and envy are corpses buried and rotten in the earth . . . . he saw them buried. The sea is not surer of the shore or the shore of the sea than he is of the fruition of his love and of all perfection and beauty.

The fruition of beauty is no chance of hit or miss . . . it is inevitable as life . . . . it is exact and plumb as gravitation. From the eyesight proceeds another eyesight and from the hearing proceeds another hearing and from the voice proceeds another voice eternally curious of the harmony of things with man. To these respond perfections not only in the committees that were supposed to stand for the rest but in the rest themselves just the same. These understand the law of perfection in masses and floods . . . that its finish is to each for itself and onward from itself . . . that it is profuse and impartial . . . that there is not a minute of the light or dark nor an acre of the earth or sea without it—nor any direction of the sky nor any trade or employment nor, any turn of events. This is the reason that about the proper expression of beauty there is precision and balance . . . one part does not need to be thrust above another. The best singer is not the one who has the most lithe and powerful organ . . . the pleasure of poems is not in them that take the handsomest measure and similes and sound.

Without effort and without exposing in the least how it is done the greatest poet brings the spirit of any or all events and passions and scenes and persons some more and some less to bear on your individual character as you hear or read. To do this well is to compete with the laws that pursue and follow time. What is the purpose must surely be there and the clue of it must be there . . . . and the faintest indication is the indication of the best and then becomes the clearest indication. Past and present and future are not disjoined but joined. The greatest poet forms the consistence of what is to be from what has been and is. He drags the dead out of their coffins and stands them again on their feet . . . . he says to the past, Rise and walk before me that I may realize you. He learns the lesson . . . . he places himself where the future becomes present. The greatest poet does not only dazzle his rays over character and scenes and passions . . . he finally ascends and finishes all . . . he exhibits the pinnacles that no man can tell what they are for or what is beyond . . . . he glows a moment on the extremest verge. He is most wonderful in his last half-hidden smile or frown . . . by that flash of the moment of parting the one that sees it shall be encouraged or terrified afterward for many years. The greatest poet does not moralize or make applications of morals . . . he knows the soul. The soul has that measureless pride which consists in never acknowledging any lessons but its own. But it has sympathy as measureless as its pride and the one balances the other and neither can stretch too far while it stretches in company with the other. The inmost secrets of art sleep with the twain. The greatest poet has lain close betwixt both and they are vital in his style and thoughts.

The art of art, the glory of expression and the sunshine of the light of letters is simplicity. Nothing is better than simplicity . . . . nothing can make up for excess or for the lack of definiteness. To carry on the heave of impulse and pierce intellectual depths and give all subjects their articulations are powers neither common nor very uncommon. But to speak in literature with the perfect rectitude and insouciance of the movements of animals and the unimpeachableness of the sentiment of trees in the woods and grass by the roadside is the flawless triumph of art. If you have looked on him who has achieved it you have looked on one of the masters of the artists of all nations and times. You shall not contemplate the flight of the graygull over the bay or the mettlesome action of the blood horse or the tall leaning of sunflowers on their stalk or the appearance of the sun journeying through heaven or the appearance of the moon afterward with any more satisfaction than you shall contemplate him. The greatest poet has less a marked style and is more the channel of thoughts and things without increase or diminution, and is the free channel of himself. He swears to his art, I will not be meddlesome, I will not have in my writing any elegance or effect or originality to hang in the way between me and the rest like curtains. I will have nothing hang in the way, not the richest curtains. What I tell I tell for precisely what it is. Let who may exalt or startle or fascinate or sooth I will have purposes as health or heat or snow has and be as regardless of observation. What I experience or portray shall go from my composition without a shred of my composition. You shall stand by my side and look in the mirror with me.

The old red blood and stainless gentility of great poets will be proved by their unconstraint. A heroic person walks at his ease through and out of that custom or precedent or authority that suits him not. Of the traits of the brotherhood of writers savans musicians inventors and artists nothing is finer than silent defiance advancing from new free forms. In the need of poems philosophy politics mechanism science behaviour, the craft of art, an appropriate native grand-opera, shipcraft, or any craft, he is greatest forever and forever who contributes the greatest original practical example. The cleanest expression is that which finds no sphere worthy of itself and makes one.

The messages of great poets to each man and woman are, Come to us on equal terms, Only then can you understand us, We are no better than you, What we enclose you enclose, What we enjoy you may enjoy. Did you suppose there could be only one Supreme? We affirm there can be unnumbered Supremes, and that one does not countervail another any more than one eyesight countervails another . . and that men can be good or grand only of the consciousness of their supremacy within them. What do you think is the grandeur of storms and dismemberments and the deadliest battles and wrecks and the wildest fury of the elements and the power of the sea and the motion of nature and of the throes of human desires and dignity and hate and love? It is that something in the soul which says, Rage on, Whirl on, I tread master here and everywhere, Master of the spasms of the sky and of the shatter of the sea, Master of nature and passion and death, And of all terror and all pain.

The American bards shall be marked for generosity and affection and for encouraging competitors . . They shall be kosmos . . without monopoly or secresy . . glad to pass any thing to any one . . hungry for equals night and day. They shall not be careful of riches and privilege . . . . they shall be riches and privilege . . . . they shall perceive who the most affluent man is. The most affluent man is he that confronts all the shows he sees by equivalents out of the stronger wealth of himself. The American bard shall delineate no class of persons nor one or two out of the strata of interests nor love most nor truth most nor the soul most nor the body most . . . . and not be for the eastern states more than the western or the northern states more than the southern.

Exact science and its practical movements are no checks on the greatest poet but always his encouragement and support. The outset and remembrance are there . . there the arms that lifted him first and brace him best . . . . there he returns after all his goings and comings. The sailor and traveler . . the anatomist chemist astronomer geologist phrenologist spiritualist mathematician historian and lexicographer are not poets, but they are the lawgivers of poets and their construction underlies the structure of every perfect poem. No matter what rises or is uttered they sent the seed of the conception of it . . . of them and by them stand the visible proofs of souls . . . . . always of their fatherstuff must be begotten the sinewy races of bards. If there shall be love and content between the father and the son and if the greatness of the son is the exuding of the greatness of the father there shall be love between the poet and the man of demonstrable science. In the beauty of poems are the tuft and final applause of science.

Great is the faith of the flush of knowledge and of the investigation of the depths of qualities and things. Cleaving and circling here swells the soul of the poet yet is president of itself always. The depths are fathomless and therefore

calm. The innocence and nakedness are resumed . . . they
are neither modest nor immodest. The whole theory of
the special and supernatural and all that was twined with
it or educed out of it departs as a dream. What has ever
happened . . . . what happens and whatever may or shall
happen, the vital laws enclose all . . . . they are sufficient
for any case and for all cases . . . none to be hurried or
retarded . . . . any miracle of affairs or persons inadmis-
sible in the vast clear scheme where every motion and
every spear of grass and the frames and spirits of men and
women and all that concerns them are unspeakably perfect miracles all referring to all and each distinct and in
its place. It is also not consistent with the reality of the
soul to admit that there is anything in the known universe
more divine than men and women.

Men and women and the earth and all upon it are simply
to be taken as they are, and the investigation of their past
and present and future shall be unintermitted and shall
be done with perfect candor. Upon this basis philosophy
speculates ever looking toward the poet, ever regarding the
eternal tendencies of all toward happiness never inconsistent with what is clear to the senses and to the soul.
For the eternal tendencies of all toward happiness make
the only point of sane philosophy. Whatever compre-
hends less than that . . . whatever is less than the laws
of light and of astronomical motion . . . or less than the
laws that follow the thief the liar the glutton and the
drunkard through this life and doubtless afterward
. . . . . . or less than vast stretches of time or the slow
formation of density or the patient upheaving of strata—
is of no account. Whatever would put God in a poem or
system of philosophy as contending against some being or
influence is also of no account. Sanity and ensemble char-
acterise the great master . . . spoilt in one principle all
is spoilt. The great master has nothing to do with miracles.
He sees health for himself in being one of the mass . . . .
he sees the hiatus in singular eminence. To the perfect
shape comes common ground. To be under the general
law is great for that is to correspond with it. The master
knows that he is unspeakably great and that all are un-

speakably great . . . . that nothing for instance is greater than to conceive children and bring them up well . . . that to be is just as great as to perceive or tell.

In the make of the great masters the idea of political liberty is indispensable. Liberty takes the adherence of heroes wherever men and women exist . . . . but never takes any adherence or welcome from the rest more than from poets. They are the voice and exposition of liberty. They out of ages are worthy the grand idea . . . . to them it is confided and they must sustain it. Nothing has precedence of it and nothing can warp or degrade it. The attitude of great poets is to cheer up slaves and horrify despots. The turn of their necks, the sound of their feet, the motions of their wrists, are full of hazard to the one and hope to the other. Come nigh them awhile and though they neither speak or advise you shall learn the faithful American lesson. Liberty is poorly served by men whose good intent is quelled from one failure or two failures or any number of failures, or from the casual indifference or ingratitude of the people, or from the sharp show of the tushes of power, or the bringing to bear soldiers and cannon or any penal statutes. Liberty relies upon itself, invites no one, promises nothing, sits in calmness and light, is positive and composed, and knows no discouragement. The battle rages with many a loud alarm and frequent advance and retreat . . . . the enemy triumphs . . . . the prison, the handcuffs, the iron necklace and anklet, the scaffold, garrote and leadballs do their work . . . . the cause is asleep . . . . the strong throats are choked with their own blood . . . . the young men drop their eyelashes toward the ground when they pass each other . . . . and is liberty gone out of that place? No never. When liberty goes it is not the first to go nor the second or third to go . . it waits for all the rest to go . . it is the last. . . When the memories of the old martyrs are faded utterly away . . . . when the large names of patriots are laughed at in the public halls from the lips of the orators . . . . when the boys are no more christened after the same but christened after tyrants and traitors instead . . . . when the laws of the free are grudgingly permitted and laws for informers and bloodmoney are sweet to the taste of the people . . . . when I and you walk abroad upon the earth stung with compassion at the sight of numberless brothers answering our equal friendship and calling no man master —and when we are elated with noble joy at the sight of slaves . . . . when the soul retires in the cool communion of the night and surveys its experience and has much extasy over the word and deed that put back a helpless innocent person into the gripe of the gripers or into any cruel inferiority . . . . when those in all parts of these states who could easier realize the true American character but do not yet—when the swarms of cringers, suckers, doughfaces, lice of politics, planners of sly involutions for their own preferment to city officers or state legislatures or the judiciary or congress or the presidency, obtain a response of love and natural deference from the people whether they get the offices or no . . . . when it is better to be a bound booby and rogue in office at a high salary than the poorest free mechanic or farmer with his hat unmoved from his head and firm eyes and a candid and generous heart . . . . and when servility by town or state or the federal government or any oppression on a large scale or small scale can be tried on without its own punishment following duly after in exact proportion against the smallest chance of escape . . . . or rather when all life and all the souls of men and women are discharged from any part of the earth—then only shall the instinct of liberty be discharged from that part of the earth.

As the attributes of the poets of the kosmos concentre in the real body and soul and in the pleasure of things they possess the superiority of genuineness over all fiction and romance. As they emit themselves facts are showered over with light . . . . the daylight is lit with more volatile light . . . . also the deep between the setting and rising sun goes deeper many fold. Each precise object or condition or combination or process exhibits a beauty . . . . the multiplication table its—old age its—the carpenter's trade its—the grand-opera its . . . . the hugehulled cleanshaped New-York clipper at sea under steam or full sail gleams with unmatched beauty . . . . the American circles and large harmonies of government gleam with theirs . . . . and the commonest definite intentions and actions with theirs. The poets of the kosmos advance through all interpositions and coverings and turmoils and stratagems to first principles. They are of use . . . . they dissolve poverty from its need and riches from its conceit. You large proprietor they say shall not realize or perceive more than any one else. The owner of the library is not he who holds a legal title to it having bought and paid for it. Any one and every one is owner of the library who can read the same through all the varieties of tongues and subjects and styles, and in whom they enter with ease and take residence and force toward paternity and maternity, and make supple and powerful and rich and large. . . . . These American states strong and healthy and accomplished shall receive no pleasure from violations of natural models and must not permit them. In paintings or mouldings or carvings in mineral or wood, or in the illustrations of books or newspapers, or in any comic or tragic prints, or in the patterns of woven stuffs or any thing to beautify rooms or furniture or costumes, or to put upon cornices or monuments or on the prows or sterns of ships, or to put anywhere before the human eye indoors or out, that which distorts honest shapes or which creates unearthly beings or places or contingencies is a nuisance and revolt. Of the human form especially it is so great it must never be made ridiculous. Of ornaments to a work nothing outre can be allowed . . but those ornaments can be allowed that conform to the perfect facts of the open air and that flow out of the nature of the work and come irrepressibly from it and are necessary to the completion of the work. Most works are most beautiful without ornament. . . Exaggerations will be revenged in human physiology. Clean and vigorous children are jetted and conceived only in those communities where the models of natural forms are public every day. . . . . Great genius and the people of these states must never be demeaned to romances. As soon as histories are properly told there is no more need of romances.

The great poets are also to be known by the absence

in them of tricks and by the justification of perfect personal candor. Then folks echo a new cheap joy and a divine voice leaping from their brains: How beautiful is candor! All faults may be forgiven of him who has perfect candor. Henceforth let no man of us lie, for we have seen that openness wins the inner and outer world and that there is no single exception, and that never since our earth gathered itself in a mass have deceit or subterfuge or prevarication attracted its smallest particle or the faintest tinge of a shade—and that through the enveloping wealth and rank of a state or the whole republic of states a sneak or sly person shall be discovered and despised . . . . and that the soul has never been once fooled and never can be fooled . . . . and thrift without the loving nod of the soul is only a fœtid puff . . . . and there never grew up in any of the continents of the globe nor upon any planet or satellite or star, nor upon the asteroids, nor in any part of ethereal space, nor in the midst of density, nor under the fluid wet of the sea, nor in that condition which precedes the birth of babes, nor at any time during the changes of life, nor in that condition that follows what we term death, nor in any stretch of abeyance or action afterward of vitality, nor in any process of formation or reformation anywhere, a being whose instinct hated the truth.

Extreme caution or prudence, the soundest organic health, large hope and comparison and fondness for women and children, large alimentiveness and destructiveness and causality, with a perfect sense of the oneness of nature and the propriety of the same spirit applied to human affairs . . these are called up of the float of the brain of the world to be parts of the greatest poet from his birth out of his mother's womb and from her birth out of her mother's. Caution seldom goes far enough. It has been thought that the prudent citizen was the citizen who applied himself to solid gains and did well for himself and his family and completed a lawful life without debt or crime. The greatest poet sees and admits these economies as he sees the economies of food and sleep, but has higher notions of prudence than to think he gives much when he gives a few slight attentions at the latch of the gate. The premises of the prudence of life are not the hospitality of it or the ripeness and harvest of it. Beyond the independence of a little sum laid aside for burial-money, and of a few clapboards around and shingles overhead on a lot of American soil owned, and the easy dollars that supply the year's plain clothing and meals, the melancholy prudence of the abandonment of such a great being as a man is to the toss and pallor of years of moneymaking with all their scorching days and icy nights and all their stifling deceits and underhanded dodgings, or infinitesimals of parlors, or shameless stuffing while others starve . . and all the loss of the bloom and odor of the earth and of the flowers and atmosphere and of the sea and of the true taste of the women and men you pass or have to do with in youth or middle age, and the issuing sickness and desperate revolt at the close of a life without elevation or naivete, and the ghastly chatter of a death without serenity or majesty, is the great fraud upon modern civilization and forethought, blotching the surface and system which civilization undeniably drafts, and moistening with tears the immense features it spreads and spreads with such velocity before the reached kisses of the soul. . . Still the right explanation remains to be made about prudence. The prudence of the mere wealth and respectability of the most esteemed life appears too faint for the eye to observe at all when little and large alike drop quietly aside at the thought of the prudence suitable for immortality. What is wisdom that fills the thinness of a year or seventy or eighty years to wisdom spaced out by ages and coming back at a certain time with strong reinforcements and rich presents and the clear faces of wedding-guests as far as you can look in every direction running gaily toward you? Only the soul is of itself . . . . all else has reference to what ensues. All that a person does or thinks is of consequence. Not a move can a man or woman make that affects him or her in a day or a month or any part of the direct lifetime or the hour of death but the same affects him or her onward afterward through the indirect lifetime. The indirect is always as great and real as the direct. The spirit receives from the body just as much as it gives to the

body. Not one name of word or deed . . not of venereal
sores or discolorations . . not the privacy of the onanist
. . not of the putrid veins of gluttons or rumdrinkers . . .
not peculation or cunning or betrayal or murder . . no
serpentine poison of those that seduce women . . not the
foolish yielding of women . . not prostitution . . not of
any depravity of young men . . not of the attainment of
gain by discreditable means . . not any nastiness of appetite . . not any harshness of officers to men or judges
to prisoners or fathers to sons or sons to fathers or of hus-
bands to wives or bosses to their boys . . not of greedy
looks or malignant wishes . . . nor any of the wiles prac-
tised by people upon themselves . . . ever is or ever can
be stamped on the programme but it is duly realized and
returned, and that returned in further performances . . .
and they returned again. Nor can the push of charity or
personal force ever be any thing else than the profoundest
reason, whether it bring arguments to hand or no. No
specification is necessary . . to add or subtract or divide
is in vain. Little or big, learned or unlearned, white or
black, legal or illegal, sick or well, from the first inspiration down the windpipe to the last expiration out of it,
all that a male or female does that is vigorous and benevolent and clean is so much sure profit to him or her in the
unshakable order of the universe and through the whole
scope of it forever. If the savage or felon is wise it is well
. . . . if the greatest poet or savan is wise it is simply the
same . . if the President or chief justice is wise it is the
same . . . if the young mechanic or farmer is wise it is no
more or less . . if the prostitute is wise it is no more nor
less. The interest will come round . . all will come round.
All the best actions of war and peace . . . all help given
to relatives and strangers and the poor and old and sorrowful and young children and widows and the sick, and to
all shunned persons . . all furtherance of fugitives and of
the escape of slaves . . all the self-denial that stood steady
and aloof on wrecks and saw others take the seats of the
boats . . . all offering of substance or life for the good old
cause, or for a friend's sake or opinion's sake . . . all pains
of enthusiasts scoffed at by their neighbors . . all the vast

sweet love and precious suffering of mothers . . . all honest men baffled in strifes recorded or unrecorded . . . . all the grandeur and good of the few ancient nations whose fragments of annals we inherit . . and all the good of the hundreds of far mightier and more ancient nations unknown to us by name or date or location . . . . all that was ever manfully begun, whether it succeeded or no . . . . all that has at any time been well suggested out of the divine heart of man or by the divinity of his mouth or by the shaping of his great hands . . and all that is well thought or done this day on any part of the surface of the globe . . or on any of the wandering stars or fixed stars by those there as we are here . . or that is henceforth to be well thought or done by you whoever you are, or by any one—these singly and wholly inured at their time and inure now and will inure always to the identities from which they sprung or shall spring. . . Did you guess any of them lived only its moment? The world does not so exist . . no parts palpable or impalpable so exist . . . no result exists now without being from its long antecedent result, and that from its antecedent, and so backward without the farthest mentionable spot coming a bit nearer the beginning than any other spot. . . . . Whatever satisfies the soul is truth. The prudence of the greatest poet answers at last the craving and glut of the soul, is not contemptuous of less ways of prudence if they conform to its ways, puts off nothing, permits no let-up for its own case or any case, has no particular sabbath or judgmentday, divides not the living from the dead or the righteous from the unrighteous, is satisfied with the present, matches every thought or act by its correlative, knows no possible forgiveness or deputed atonement . . knows that the young man who composedly periled his life and lost it has done exceeding well for himself, while the man who has not periled his life and retains it to old age in riches and ease has perhaps achieved nothing for himself worth mentioning . . and that only that person has no great prudence to learn who has learnt to prefer real longlived things, and favors body and soul the same, and perceives the indirect assuredly following the direct, and what evil or good

he does leaping onward and waiting to meet him again
—and who in his spirit in any emergency whatever neither
hurries or avoids death.

The direct trial of him who would be the greatest poet
is today. If he does not flood himself with the immediate
age as with vast oceanic tides . . . . . and if he does not
attract his own land body and soul to himself and hang on
its neck with incomparable love and plunge his semitic
muscle into its merits and demerits . . . and if he be not
himself the age transfigured . . . . and if to him is not
opened the eternity which gives similitude to all periods
and locations and processes and animate and inanimate
forms, and which is the bond of time, and rises up from
its inconceivable vagueness and infiniteness in the swimming shape of today, and is held by the ductile anchors
of life, and makes the present spot the passage from what
was to what shall be, and commits itself to the representa-
tion of this wave of an hour and this one of the sixty
beautiful children of the wave—let him merge in the general run and wait his development. . . . Still the final
test of poems or any character or work remains. The
prescient poet projects himself centuries ahead and judges
performer or performance after the changes of time. Does
it live through them? Does it still hold on untired? Will
the same style and the direction of genius to similar points
be satisfactory now? Has no new discovery in science or
arrival at superior planes of thought and judgment and
behavior fixed him or his so that either can be looked down
upon? Have the marches of tens and hundreds and thousands of years made willing detours to the right hand and
the left hand for his sake? Is he beloved long and long
after he is buried? Does the young man think often of
him? and the young woman think often of him? and do
the middleaged and the old think of him?

A great poem is for ages and ages in common and for
all degrees and complexions and all departments and sects
and for a woman as much as a man and a man as much
as a woman. A great poem is no finish to a man or woman
but rather a beginning. Has any once fancied he could
sit at last under some due authority and rest satisfied with

explanations and realize and be content and full? To no such terminus does the greatest poet bring . . . he brings neither cessation or sheltered fatness and ease. The touch of him tells in action. Whom he takes he takes with firm sure grasp into live regions previously unattained . . . . thenceforward is no rest . . . . they see the space and ineffable sheen that turn the old spots and lights into dead vacuums. The companion of him beholds the birth and progress of stars and learns one of the meanings. Now there shall be a man cohered out of tumult and chaos . . . . the elder encourages the younger and shows him how . . . they two shall launch off fearlessly together till the new world fits an orbit for itself and looks unabashed on the lesser orbits of the stars and sweeps through the ceaseless rings and shall never be quiet again.

There will soon be no more priests. Their work is done. They may wait a while . . perhaps a generation or two . . dropping off by degrees. A superior breed shall take their place . . . . the gangs of kosmos and prophets en masse shall take their place. A new order shall arise and they shall be the priests of man, and every man shall be his own priest. The churches built under their umbrage shall be the churches of men and women. Through the divinity of themselves shall the kosmos and the new breed of poets be interpreters of men and women and of all events and things. They shall find their inspiration in real objects today, symptoms of the past and future . . . . They shall not deign to defend immortality or God or the perfection of things or liberty or the exquisite beauty and reality of the soul. They shall arise in America and be responded to from the remainder of the earth.

The English language befriends the grand American expression . . . . it is brawny enough and limber and full enough. On the tough stock of a race who through all change of circumstance was never without the idea of political liberty, which is the animus of all liberty, it has attracted the terms of daintier and gayer and subtler and more elegant tongues. It is the powerful language of resistance . . . it is the dialect of common sense. It is the speech of the proud and melancholy races and of all who aspire. It is the chosen tongue to express growth faith self-esteem freedom justice equality friendliness amplitude prudence decision and courage. It is the medium that shall well nigh express the inexpressible.

No great literature nor any like style of behaviour or oratory or social intercourse or household arrangements or public institutions or the treatment by bosses of employed people, nor executive detail or detail of the army or navy, nor spirit of legislation or courts or police or tuition or architecture or songs or amusements or the costumes of young men, can long elude the jealous and passionate instinct of American standards. Whether or no the sign appears from the mouths of the people, it throbs a live interrogation in every freeman's and freewoman's heart after that which passes by or this built to remain. Is it uniform with my country? Are its disposals without ignominious distinctions? Is it for the evergrowing communes of brothers and lovers, large, well-united, proud beyond the old models, generous beyond all models? Is it something grown fresh out of the fields or drawn from the sea for use to me today here? I know that what answers for me an American must answer for any individual or nation that serves for a part of my materials. Does this answer? or is it without reference to universal needs? or sprung of the needs of the less developed society of special ranks? or old needs of pleasure overlaid by modern science and forms? Does this acknowledge liberty with audible and absolute acknowledgement, and set slavery at nought for life and death? Will it help breed one goodshaped and wellhung man, and a woman to be his perfect and independent mate? Does it improve manners? Is it for the nursing of the young of the republic? Does it solve readily with the sweet milk of the nipples of the breasts of the mother of many children? Has it too the old ever-fresh forbearance and impartiality? Does it look with the same love on the last born and on those hardening toward stature, and on the errant, and on those who disdain all strength of assault outside of their own?

The poems distilled from other poems will probably pass away. The coward will surely pass away. The expectation of the vital and great can only be satisfied by the demeanor of the vital and great. The swarms of the polished deprecating and reflectors and the polite float off and leave no remembrance. America prepares with composure and goodwill for the visitors that have sent word. It is not intellect that is to be their warrant and welcome. The talented, the artist, the ingenious, the editor, the statesman, the erudite . . they are not unappreciated . . they fall in their place and do their work. The soul of the nation also does its work. No disguise can pass on it . . no disguise can conceal from it. It rejects none, it permits all. Only toward as good as itself and toward the like of itself will it advance half-way. An individual is as superb as a nation when he has the qualities which make a superb nation. The soul of the largest and wealthiest and proudest nation may well go half-way to meet that of its poets. The signs are effectual. There is no fear of mistake. If the one is true the other is true. The proof of a poet is that his country absorbs him as affectionately as he has absorbed it.

FROM SPECIMEN DAYS

EDGAR POE'S SIGNIFICANCE

Jan. 1, '80.—In diagnosing this disease called humanity —to assume for the nonce what seems a chief mood of the personality and writings of my subject—I have thought that poets, somewhere or other on the list, present the most mark'd indications. Comprehending artists in a mass, musicians, painters, actors, and so on, and considering each and all of them as radiations or flanges of that furious whirling wheel, poetry, the centre and axis of the whole, where else indeed may we so well investigate the causes, growths, tally-marks of the time—the age's matter and malady?

By common consent there is nothing better for man or woman than a perfect and noble life, morally without flaw, happily balanced in activity, physically sound and pure, giving its due proportion, and no more, to the sympathetic, the human emotional element—a life, in all these, unhasting, unresting, untiring to the end. And yet there is another shape of personality dearer far to the artist-sense, (which likes the play of strongest lights and shades,) where the perfect character, the good, the heroic, although never attain'd, is never lost sight of, but through failures, sorrows, temporary downfalls, is return'd to again and again, and while often violated, is passionately adhered to as long as mind, muscles, voice, obey the power we call volition. This sort of personality we see more or less in Burns, Byron, Schiller, and George Sand. But we do not see it in Edgar Poe. (All this is the result of reading at intervals the last three days a new volume of his poems —I took it on my rambles down by the pond, and by degrees read it all through there.) While to the character first outlined the service Poe renders is certainly that entire contrast and contradiction which is next best to fully exemplifying it.

Almost without the first sign of moral principle, or of the concrete or its heroisms, or the simpler affections of the heart, Poe's verses illustrate an intense faculty for technical and abstract beauty, with the rhyming art to excess, an incorrigible propensity toward nocturnal themes, a demoniac undertone behind every page—and, by final judgment, probably belong among the electric lights of imaginative literature, brilliant and dazzling, but with no heat. There is an indescribable magnetism about the poet's life and reminiscences, as well as the poems. To one who could work out their subtle retracing and retrospect, the latter would make a close tally no doubt between the author's birth and antecedents, his childhood and youth, his physique, his so-call'd education, his studies and associates, the literary and social Baltimore, Richmond, Philadelphia and New York, of those times—not only the places and circumstances in themselves, but often, very often, in a strange spurning of, and reaction from them all.

The following from a report in the Washington "Star" of November 16, 1875, may afford those who care for it something further of my point of view toward this interesting figure and influence of our era. There occurr'd about that date in Baltimore a public reburial of Poe's remains, and dedication of a monument over the grave:

"Being in Washington on a visit at the time, 'the old gray' went over to Baltimore, and though ill from paralysis, consented to hobble up and silently take a seat on the platform, but refused to make any speech, saying, 'I have felt a strong impulse to come over and be here to-day myself in memory of Poe, which I have obey'd, but not the slightest impulse to make a speech, which, my dear friends, must also be obeyed.' In an informal circle, however, in conversation after the ceremonies, Whitman said: 'For a long while, and until lately, I had a distaste for Poe's writings. I wanted, and still want for poetry, the clear sun shining, and fresh air blowing—the strength and power of health, not of delirium, even amid the stormiest passions—with always the background of the eternal moralities. Non-complying with these requirements, Poe's genius has yet conquer'd a special recognition for itself, and I too have come to fully admit it, and appreciate it and him.

"'In a dream I once had, I saw a vessel on the sea, at midnight, in a storm. It was no great full-rigg'd ship, nor majestic steamer, steering firmly through the gale, but seem'd one of those superb little schooner yachts I had often seen lying anchor'd, rocking so jauntily, in the waters around New York, or up Long Island sound—now flying uncontroll'd with torn sails and broken spars through the wild sleet and winds and waves of the night. On the deck was a slender, slight, beautiful figure, a dim man, apparently enjoying all the terror, the murk, and the dislocation of which he was the centre and the victim. That figure of my lurid dream might stand for Edgar Poe, his spirit, his fortunes, and his poems—themselves all lurid dreams.'"

Much more may be said, but I most desired to exploit the idea put at the beginning. By its popular poets the calibres of an age, the weak spots of its embankments, its sub-currents, (often more significant than the biggest surface ones,) are unerringly indicated. The lush and the weird that have taken such extraordinary possession of Nineteenth century verse-lovers—what mean they? The inevitable tendency of poetic culture to morbidity, abnormal beauty—the sickliness of all technical thought or refinement in itself—the abnegation of the perennial and democratic concretes at first hand, the body, the earth and sea, sex and the like—and the substitution of something for them at second or third hand—what bearings have they on current pathological study?

MY TRIBUTE TO FOUR POETS

April 16 [*1881*].—A short but pleasant visit to Longfellow. I am not one of the calling kind, but as the author of "Evangeline" kindly took the trouble to come and see me three years ago in Camden, where I was ill, I felt not only the impulse of my own pleasure on that occasion, but a duty. He was the only particular eminence I called on in Boston, and I shall not soon forget his lit-up face and glowing warmth and courtesy, in the modes of what is called the old school.

And now just here I feel the impulse to interpolate something about the mighty four who stamp this first American century with its birth-marks of poetic literature. In a late magazine one of my reviewers, who ought to know better, speaks of my "attitude of contempt and scorn and intolerance" toward the leading poets—of my "deriding" them, and preaching their "uselessness." If anybody cares to know what I think—and have long thought and avow'd—about them, I am entirely willing to propound. I can't imagine any better luck befalling these States for a poetical beginning and initiation than has come from Emerson, Longfellow, Bryant and Whittier. Emerson, to me, stands unmistakably at the head, but for the others I am at a loss where to give any precedence. Each illustrious, each rounded, each distinctive. Emerson for his sweet, vital-tasting melody, rhym'd philosophy, and poems as amber-clear as the honey of the wild bee he loves to sing. Longfellow for rich color, graceful forms and incidents —all that makes life beautiful and love refined—competing with the singers of Europe on their own ground, and, with one exception, better and finer work than that of any of them. Bryant pulsing the first interior verse-throbs of a mighty world—bard of the river and the wood, ever conveying a taste of open air, with scents as from hayfields,

grapes, birch-borders—always lurkingly fond of threnodies
—beginning and ending his long career with chants of
death, with here and there through all, poems, or passages
of poems, touching the highest universal truths, enthusiasms, duties—morals as grim and eternal, if not as stormy
and fateful, as anything in Eschylus. While in Whittier,
with his special themes—(his outcropping love of heroism
and war, for all his Quakerdom, his verses at times like
the measur'd step of Cromwell's old veterans)—in Whittier
lives the zeal, the moral energy, that founded New England—the splendid rectitude and ardor of Luther, Milton,
George Fox—I must not, dare not, say the wilfulness and
narrowness—though doubtless the world needs now, and
always will need, almost above all, just such narrowness
and wilfulness.

DEATH OF LONGFELLOW

Camden, April 3, '82.—I have just return'd from an
old forest haunt, where I love to go occasionally away
from parlors, pavements, and the newspapers and magazines—and where, of a clear forenoon, deep in the shade
of pines and cedars and a tangle of old laurel-trees and
vines, the news of Longfellow's death first reach'd me. For
want of anything better, let me lightly twine a sprig of
the sweet ground-ivy trailing so plentifully through the
dead leaves at my feet, with reflections of that half hour
alone, there in the silence, and lay it as my contribution
on the dead bard's grave.

Longfellow in his voluminous works seems to me not
only to be eminent in the style and forms of poetical expression that mark the present age, (an idiosyncrasy, almost a sickness, of verbal melody,) but to bring what is
always dearest as poetry to the general human heart and
taste, and probably must be so in the nature of things.
He is certainly the sort of bard and counteractant most
needed for our materialistic, self-assertive, money-worship-
ping, Anglo-Saxon races, and especially for the present
age in America—an age tyrannically regulated with refer-

ence to the manufacturer, the merchant, the financier, the politician and the day workman—for whom and among whom he comes as the poet of melody, courtesy, deference —poet of the mellow twilight of the past in Italy, Germany, Spain, and in Northern Europe—poet of all sympathetic gentleness—and universal poet of women and young people. I should have to think long if I were ask'd to name the man who has done more, and in more valuable directions, for America.

I doubt if there ever was before such a fine intuitive judge and selecter of poems. His translations of many German and Scandinavian pieces are said to be better than the vernaculars. He does not urge or lash. His influence is like good drink or air. He is not tepid either, but always vital, with flavor, motion, grace. He strikes a splendid average, and does not sing exceptional passions, or humanity's jagged escapades. He is not revolutionary, brings nothing offensive or new, does not deal hard blows. On the contrary, his songs soothe and heal, or if they excite, it is a healthy and agreeable excitement. His very anger is gentle, is at second hand, (as in the "Quadroon Girl" and the "Witnesses.")

There is no undue element of pensiveness in Longfellow's strains. Even in the early translation, the Manrique, the movement is as of strong and steady wind or tide, holding up and buoying. Death is not avoided through his many themes, but there is something almost winning in his original verses and renderings on that dread subject— as, closing "the Happiest Land" dispute,

> And then the landlord's daughter
> Up to heaven rais'd her hand,
> And said, "Ye may no more contend,
> There lies the happiest land."

To the ungracious complaint-charge of his want of racy nativity and special originality, I shall only say that America and the world may well be reverently thankful—can never be thankful enough—for any such singing-bird vouchsafed out of the centuries, without asking that the notes be different from those of other songsters; adding what I have heard Longfellow himself say, that ere the New World can be worthily original, and announce herself and her own heroes, she must be well saturated with the originality of others, and respectfully consider the heroes that lived before Agamemnon.

A BACKWARD GLANCE O'ER
TRAVEL'D ROADS

Perhaps the best of songs heard, or of any and all true love, or life's fairest episodes, or sailors', soldiers' trying scenes on land or sea, is the *résumé* of them, or any of them, long afterwards, looking at the actualities away back past, with all their practical excitations gone. How the soul loves to float amid such reminiscences!

So here I sit gossiping in the early candle-light of old age—I and my book—casting backward glances over our travel'd road. After completing, as it were, the journey— (a varied jaunt of years, with many halts and gaps of intervals—or some lengthen'd ship-voyage, wherein more than once the last hour had apparently arrived, and we seem'd certainly going down—yet reaching port in a sufficient way through all discomfitures at last)—After completing my poems, I am curious to review them in the light of their own (at the time unconscious, or mostly unconscious) intentions, with certain unfoldings of the thirty years they seek to embody. These lines, therefore, will probably blend the weft of first purposes and speculations, with the warp of that experience afterwards, always bringing strange developments.

Result of seven or eight stages and struggles extending through nearly thirty years, (as I nigh my three-score-and-ten I live largely on memory,) I look upon "Leaves of Grass," now finish'd to the end of its opportunities and powers, as my definitive *carte visite* to the coming generations of the New World,* if I may assume to say so. That I have not gain'd the acceptance of my own time, but have fallen back on fond dreams of the future—anticipations— ("still lives the song, though Regnar dies")—That from a worldly and business point of view "Leaves of Grass" has been worse than a failure—that public criticism on the book and myself as author of it yet shows mark'd anger and contempt more than anything else—("I find a solid line of enemies to you everywhere,"—letter from W. S. K., Boston, May 28, 1884)—And that solely for publishing it I have been the object of two or three pretty serious special official buffetings—is all probably no more than I ought to have expected. I had my choice when I commenc'd. I bid neither for soft eulogies, big money returns, nor the approbation of existing schools and conventions. As fulfill'd, or partially fulfill'd, the best comfort of the whole business (after a small band of the dearest friends and upholders ever vouchsafed to man or cause—doubtless all the more faithful and uncompromising—this little phalanx!—for being so few) is that, unstopp'd and unwarp'd by any influence outside the soul within me, I have had my say entirely my own way, and put it unerringly on record—the value thereof to be decided by time.

In calculating that decision, William O'Connor and Dr. Bucke are far more peremptory than I am. Behind all else that can be said, I consider "Leaves of Grass" and its theory experimental—as, in the deepest sense, I consider our American republic itself to be, with its theory. (I think I have at least enough philosophy not to be too absolutely certain of any thing, or any results.) In the second place, the volume is a *sortie*—whether to prove triumphant, and conquer its field of aim and escape and construction, nothing less than a hundred years from now can fully answer. I consider the point that I have positively gain'd a hearing, to far more than make up for any and all other lacks and withholdings. Essentially, *that* was from the first, and has remain'd throughout, the main object. Now it seems to be

* When Champollion, on his death-bed, handed to the printer the revised proof of his "Egyptian Grammar," he said gayly, "Be careful of this—it is my *carte de visite* to posterity."

achiev'd, I am certainly contented to waive any otherwise momentous drawbacks, as of little account. Candidly and dispassionately reviewing all my intentions, I feel that they were creditable—and I accept the result, whatever it may be.

After continued personal ambition and effort, as a young fellow, to enter with the rest into competition for the usual rewards, business, political, literary, &c.—to take part in the great *mélée*, both for victory's prize itself and to do some good—After years of those aims and pursuits, I found myself remaining possess'd, at the age of thirty-one to thirty-three, with a special desire and conviction. Or rather, to be quite exact, a desire that had been flitting through my previous life, or hovering on the flanks, mostly indefinite hitherto, had steadily advanced to the front, defined itself, and finally dominated everything else. This was a feeling or ambition to articulate and faithfully express in literary or poetic form, and uncompromisingly, my own physical, emotional, moral, intellectual, and æsthetic Personality, in the midst of, and tallying, the momentous spirit and facts of its immediate days, and of current America—and to exploit that Personality, identified with place and date, in a far more candid and comprehensive sense than any hitherto poem or book.

Perhaps this is in brief, or suggests, all I have sought to do. Given the Nineteenth Century, with the United States, and what they furnish as area and points of view, "Leaves of Grass" is, or seeks to be, simply a faithful and doubtless self-will'd record. In the midst of all, it gives one man's— the author's—identity, ardors, observations, faiths, and thoughts, color'd hardly at all with any decided coloring from other faiths or other identities. Plenty of songs had been sung—beautiful, matchless songs—adjusted to other lands than these—another spirit and stage of evolution; but I would sing, and leave out or put in, quite solely with reference to America and to-day. Modern science and democracy seem'd to be throwing out their challenge to poetry to put them in its statements in contradistinction to the songs and myths of the past. As I see it now (perhaps too late,) I have unwittingly taken up that challenge and made an attempt at such statements—which I certainly would not assume to do now, knowing more clearly what it means.

For grounds for "Leaves of Grass," as a poem, I abandon'd the conventional themes, which do not appear in it: none of the stock ornamentation, or choice plots of love or war, or high, exceptional personages of Old-World song; nothing, as I may say, for beauty's sake—no legend, or myth, or romance, nor euphemism, nor rhyme. But the broadest average of humanity and its identities in the now ripening Nineteenth Century, and especially in each of their countless examples and practical occupations in the United States to-day.

One main contrast of the ideas behind every page of my verses, compared with establish'd poems, is their different relative attitude towards God, towards the objective universe, and still more (by reflection, confession, assumption, &c.) the quite changed attitude of the ego, the one chanting or talking, towards himself and towards his fellow-humanity. It is certainly time for America, above all, to begin this readjustment in the scope and basic point of view of verse; for everything else has changed. As I write, I see in an article on Wordsworth, in one of the current English magazines, the lines, "A few weeks ago an eminent French critic said that, owing to the special tendency to science and to its all-devouring force, poetry would cease to be read in fifty years." But I anticipate the very contrary. Only a firmer, vastly broader, new era begins to exist—nay, is already form'd—to which the poetic genius must emigrate. Whatever may have been the case in years gone by, the true use for the imaginative faculty of modern times is to give ultimate vivification to facts, to science, and to common lives, endowing them with the glows and glories and final illustriousness which belong to every real thing, and to real things only. Without that ultimate vivification—which the poet or other artist alone can give— reality would seem incomplete, and science, democracy, and life itself, finally in vain.

Few appreciate the moral revolutions, our age, which have been profounder far than the material or inventive or war-produced ones. The Nineteenth Century, now well towards its close (and ripening into fruit the seeds of the two preceding centuries*)—the uprisings of national masses and shiftings of boundary-lines—the historical and other prominent facts of the United States—the war of attempted Secession—the stormy rush and haste of nebulous forces—never can future years witness more excitement and din of action—never completer change of army front along the whole line, the whole civilized world. For all these new and evolutionary facts, meanings, purposes, new poetic messages, new forms and expressions, are inevitable.

My Book and I—what a period we have presumed to span! those thirty years from 1850 to '80—and America in them! Proud, proud indeed may we be, if we have cull'd enough of that period in its own spirit to worthily waft a few live breaths of it to the future!

Let me not dare, here or anywhere, for my own purposes, or any purposes, to attempt the definition of Poetry, nor answer the question what it is. Like Religion, Love, Nature, while those terms are indispensable, and we all give a sufficiently accurate meaning to them, in my opinion no definition that has ever been made sufficiently encloses the name Poetry; nor can any rule or convention ever so absolutely obtain but some great exception may arise and disregard and overturn it.

Also it must be carefully remember'd that first-class literature does not shine by any luminosity of its own; nor do its poems. They grow of circumstances, and are evolutionary. The actual living light is always curiously from elsewhere—follows unaccountable sources, and is lunar and relative at the best. There are, I know, certain controlling themes that seem endlessly appropriated to the poets—as war, in the past—in the Bible, religious rapture and adoration—always love, beauty, some fine plot, or pensive or

---

* The ferment and germination even of the United States today, dating back to, and in my opinion mainly founded on, the Elizabethan age in English history, the age of Francis Bacon and Shakspere. Indeed, when we pursue it, what growth or advent is there that does not date back, back, until lost—perhaps its most tantalizing clues lost—in the receded horizons of the past?

other emotion. But, strange as it may sound at first, I will say there is something striking far deeper and towering far higher than those themes for the best elements of modern song.

Just as all the old imaginative works rest, after their kind, on long trains of presuppositions, often entirely unmention'd by themselves, yet supplying the most important bases of them, and without which they could have had no reason for being, so "Leaves of Grass," before a line was written, presupposed something different from any other, and, as it stands, as the result of such presupposition. I should say, indeed, it were useless to attempt reading the book without first carefully tallying that preparatory background and quality in the mind. Think of the United States to-day—the facts of these thirty-eight or forty empires solder'd in one—sixty or seventy millions of equals, with their lives, their passions, their future—these incalculable, modern, American, seething multitudes around us, of which we are inseparable parts! Think, in comparison, of the petty environage and limited area of the poets of past or present Europe, no matter how great their genius. Think of the absence and ignorance, in all cases hitherto, of the multitudinousness, vitality, and the unprecedented stimulants of to-day and here. It almost seems as if a poetry with cosmic and dynamic features of magnitude and limitlessness suitable to the human soul, were never possible before. It is certain that a poetry of absolute faith and equality for the use of the democratic masses never was.

In estimating first-class song, a sufficient Nationality, or, on the other hand, what may be call'd the negative and lack of it, (as in Goethe's case, it sometimes seems to me,) is often, if not always, the first element. One needs only a little penetration to see, at more or less removes, the material facts of their country and radius, with the coloring of the moods of humanity at the time, and its gloomy or hopeful prospects, behind all poets and each poet, and forming their birth-marks. I know very well that my "Leaves" could not possibly have emerged or been fashion'd or completed, from any other era than the latter half of the Nineteenth Century, nor any other land than democratic

America, and from the absolute triumph of the National Union arms.

And whether my friends claim it for me or not, I know well enough, too, that in respect to pictorial talent, dramatic situations, and especially in verbal melody and all the conventional technique of poetry, not only the divine works that to-day stand ahead in the world's reading, but dozens more, transcend (some of them immeasurably transcend) all I have done, or could do. But it seem'd to me, as the objects in Nature, the themes of æstheticism, and all special exploitations of the mind and soul, involve not only their own inherent quality, but the quality, just as inherent and important, of *their point of view,** the time had come to reflect all themes and things, old and new, in the lights thrown on them by the advent of America and democracy—to chant those themes through the utterance of one, not only the grateful and reverent legatee of the past, but the born child of the New World—to illustrate all through the genesis and ensemble of to-day; and that such illustration and ensemble are the chief demands of America's prospective imaginative literature. Not to carry out, in the approved style, some choice plot of fortune or misfortune, or fancy, or fine thoughts, or incidents, or courtesies —all of which has been done overwhelmingly and well, probably never to be excell'd—but that while in such æsthetic presentation of objects, passions, plots, thoughts, &c., our lands and days do not want, and probably will never have, anything better than they already possess from the bequests of the past, it still remains to be said that there is even towards all those a subjective and contemporary point of view appropriate to ourselves alone, and to our new genius and environments, different from anything hitherto; and that such conception of current or gone-by life and art is for us the only means of their assimilation consistent with the Western world.

Indeed, and anyhow, to put it specifically, has not the time arrived when, (if it must be plainly said, for democratic America's sake, if for no other) there must impera-

* According to Immanuel Kant, the last essential reality, giving shape and significance to all the rest.

tively come a readjustment of the whole theory and nature
of Poetry? The question is important, and I may turn the
argument over and repeat it: Does not the best thought of
our day and Republic conceive of a birth and spirit of song
superior to anything past or present? To the effectual and
moral consolidation of our lands (already, as materially
establish'd, the greatest factors in known history, and far,
far greater through what they prelude and necessitate, and
are to be in future)—to conform with and build on the
concrete realities and theories of the universe furnish'd by
science, and henceforth the only irrefragable basis for anything, verse included—to root both influences in the emotional and imaginative action of the modern time, and
dominate all that precedes or opposes them—is not either a
radical advance and step forward, or a new verteber of the
best song indispensable?

The New World receives with joy the poems of the antique, with European feudalism's rich fund of epics, plays,
ballads—seeks not in the least to deaden or displace those
voices from our ear and area—holds them indeed as indispensable studies, influences, records, comparisons. But
though the dawn-dazzle of the sun of literature is in those
poems for us of to-day—though perhaps the best parts of
current character in nations, social groups, or any man's or
woman's individuality, Old World or New, are from them
—and though if I were ask'd to name the most precious
bequest to current American civilization from all the
hitherto ages, I am not sure but I would name those old
and less old songs ferried hither from east and west—some
serious words and debits remain; some acrid considerations
demand a hearing. Of the great poems receiv'd from
abroad and from the ages, and to-day enveloping and
penetrating America, is there one that is consistent with
these United States, or essentially applicable to them as
they are and are to be? Is there one whose underlying
basis is not a denial and insult to democracy? What a comment it forms, anyhow, on this ear of literary fulfilment,
with the splendid day-rise of science and resuscitation of
history, that our chief religious and poetical works are not
our own, nor adapted to our light, but have been furnish'd

by far-back ages out of their arriere and darkness, or, at most, twilight dimness! What is there in those works that so imperiously and scornfully dominates all our advanced civilization, and culture?

Even Shakspere, who so suffuses current letters and art (which indeed have in most degrees grown out of him,) belongs essentially to the buried past. Only he holds the proud distinction for certain important phases of that past, of being the loftiest of the singers life has yet given voice to. All, however, relate to and rest upon conditions, standards, politics, sociologies, ranges of belief, that have been quite eliminated from the Eastern hemisphere, and never existed at all in the Western. As authoritative types of song they belong in America just about as much as the persons and institutes they depict. True, it may be said, the emotional, moral, and æsthetic natures of humanity have not radically changed—that in these the old poems apply to our times and all times, irrespective of date; and that they are of incalculable value as pictures of the past. I willingly make those admissions, and to their fullest extent; then advance the points herewith as of serious, even paramount importance.

I have indeed put on record elsewhere my reverence and eulogy for those never-to-be-excell'd poetic bequests, and their indescribable preciousness as heirlooms for America. Another and separate point must now be candidly stated. If I had not stood before those poems with uncover'd head, fully aware of their colossal grandeur and beauty of form and spirit, I could not have written "Leaves of Grass." My verdict and conclusions as illustrated in its pages are arrived at through the temper and inculcation of the old works as much as through anything else—perhaps more than through anything else. As America fully and fairly construed is the legitimate result and evolutionary outcome of the past, so I would dare to claim for my verse. Without stopping to qualify the averment, the Old World has had the poems of myths, fictions, feudalism, conquest, caste, dynastic wars, and splendid exceptional characters and affairs, which have been great; but the New World needs the poems of realities and science and of the demo-

cratic average and basic equality, which shall be greater.
In the centre of all, and object of all, stands the Human
Being, towards whose heroic and spiritual evolution poems
and everything directly or indirectly tend, Old World or
New.

Continuing the subject, my friends have more than once
suggested—or may be the garrulity of advancing age is
possessing me—some further embryonic facts of "Leaves of
Grass," and especially how I enter'd upon them. Dr. Bucke
has, in his volume, already fully and fairly described the
preparation of my poetic field, with the particular and
general plowing, planting, seeding, and occupation of the
ground, till everything was fertilized, rooted, and ready to
start its own way for good or bad. Not till after all this,
did I attempt any serious acquaintance with poetic literature. Along in my sixteenth year I had become possessor of
a stout, well-cramm'd one thousand page octavo volume
(I have it yet,) containing Walter Scott's poetry entire—
an inexhaustible mine and treasury of poetic forage (especially the endless forests and jungles of notes)—has been so
to me for fifty years, and remains so to this day.*

Later, at intervals, summers and falls, I used to go off,
sometimes for a week at a stretch, down in the country, or
to Long Island's seashores—there, in the presence of outdoor influences, I went over thoroughly the Old and New
Testaments, and absorb'd (probably to better advantage
for me than in any library or indoor room—it makes such
difference *where* you read,) Shakspere, Ossian, the best
translated versions I could get of Homer, Eschylus, Sopho-

---

* Sir Walter Scott's COMPLETE POEMS; especially including
BORDER MINSTRELSY; then Sir Tristrem; Lay of the Last Min-
strel; Ballads from the German; Marmion; Lady of the Lake;
Vision of Don Roderick; Lord of the Isles; Rokeby; Bridal of
Triermain; Field of Waterloo; Harold the Dauntless; all the
Dramas; various Introductions, endless interesting Notes, and
Essays on Poetry, Romance, &c.

Lockhart's 1833 (or '34) edition with Scott's latest and copious revisions and annotations. (All the poems were thoroughly
read by me, but the ballads of the Border Minstrelsy over and
over again.)

cles, the old German Nibelungen, the ancient Hindoo
poems, and one or two other masterpieces, Dante's among
them. As it happen'd, I read the latter mostly in an old
wood. The Iliad (Buckley's prose version,) I read first
thoroughly on the peninsula of Orient, northeast end of
Long Island, in a shelter'd hollow of rocks and sand, with
the sea on each side. (I have wonder'd since why I was
not overwhelm'd by those mighty masters. Likely because
I read them, as described, in the full presence of Nature,
under the sun, with the far-spreading landscape and vistas,
or the sea rolling in.)

Toward the last I had among much else look'd over
Edgar Poe's poems—of which I was not an admirer, tho' I
always saw that beyond their limited range of melody (like
perpetual chimes of music bells, ringing from lower *b* flat
up to *g*) they were melodious expressions, and perhaps
never excell'd ones, of certain pronounc'd phases of human
morbidity. (The Poetic area is very spacious—has room for
all—has so many mansions!) But I was repaid in Poe's prose
by the idea that (at any rate for our occasions, our day)
there can be no such thing as a long poem. The same
thought had been haunting my mind before, but Poe's
argument, though short, work'd the sum out and proved
it to me.

Another point had an early settlement, clearing the
ground greatly. I saw, from the time my enterprise and
questionings positively shaped themselves (how best can I
express my own distinctive era and surroundings, America,
Democracy?) that the trunk and centre whence the answer
was to radiate, and to which all should return from straying however far a distance, must be an identical body and
soul, a personality—which personality, after many considerations and ponderings I deliberately settled should be
myself—indeed could not be any other. I also felt strongly
(whether I have shown it or not) that to the true and full
estimate of the Present both the Past and the Future are
main considerations.

These, however, and much more might have gone on
and come to naught (almost positively would have come
to naught,) if a sudden, vast, terrible, direct and indirect

stimulus for new and national declamatory expression had not been given to me. It is certain, I say, that, although I had made a start before, only from the occurrence of the Secession War, and what it show'd me as by flashes of lightning, with the emotional depths it sounded and arous'd (of course, I don't mean in my own heart only, I saw it just as plainly in others, in millions)—that only from the strong flare and provocation of that war's sights and scenes the final reasons-for-being of an autochthonic and passionate song definitely came forth.

I went down to the war fields in Virginia (end of 1862), lived thenceforward in camp—saw great battles and the days and nights afterward—partook of all the fluctuations, gloom, despair, hopes again arous'd, courage evoked— death readily risk'd—*the cause*, too—along and filling those agonistic and lurid following years, 1863–'64–'65—the real parturition years (more than 1776–'83) of this henceforth homogeneous Union. Without those three or four years and the experiences they gave, "Leaves of Grass" would not now be existing.

But I set out with the intention also of indicating or hinting some point-characteristics which I since see (though I did not then, at least not definitely) were bases and object-urgings toward those "Leaves" from the first. The word I myself put primarily for the description of them as they stand at last, is the word Suggestiveness. I round and finish little, if anything; and could not, consistently with my scheme. The reader will always have his or her part to do, just as much as I have had mine. I seek less to state or display any theme or thought, and more to bring you, reader, into the atmosphere of the theme or thought—there to pursue your own flight. Another impetus-word is Comradeship as for all lands, and in a more commanding and acknowledg'd sense than hitherto. Other word-signs would be Good Cheer, Content, and Hope.

The chief trait of any given poet is always the spirit he brings to the observation of Humanity and Nature—the mood out of which he contemplates his subjects. What kind of temper and what amount of faith report these things? Up to how recent a date is the song carried? What the equipment, and special raciness of the singer—what his tinge of coloring? The last value of artistic expressers, past and present—Greek æsthetes, Shakspere—or in our own day Tennyson, Victor Hugo, Carlyle, Emerson—is certainly involv'd in such questions. I say the profoundest service that poems or any other writings can do for their reader is not merely to satisfy the intellect, or supply something polish'd and interesting, nor even to depict great passions, or persons or events, but to fill him with vigorous and clean manliness, religiousness, and give him *good heart* as a radical possession and habit. The educated world seems to have been growing more and more ennuyed for ages, leaving to our time the inheritance of it all. Fortunately there is the original inexhaustible fund of buoyancy, normally resident in the race, forever eligible to be appeal'd to and relied on.

As for native American individuality, though certain to come, and on a large scale, the distinctive and ideal type of Western character (as consistent with the operative political and even money-making features of United States' humanity in the Nineteenth Century as chosen knights, gentlemen and warriors were the ideals of the centuries of European feudalism) it has not yet appear'd. I have allow'd the stress of my poems from beginning to end to bear upon American individuality and assist it—not only because that is a great lesson in Nature, amid all her generalizing laws, but as counterpoise to the leveling tendencies of Democracy—and for other reasons. Defiant of ostensible literary and other conventions, I avowedly chant "the great pride of man in himself," and permit it to be more or less a *motif* of nearly all my verse. I think this pride indispensable to an American. I think it not inconsistent with obedience, humility, deference, and self-questioning.

Democracy has been so retarded and jeopardized by powerful personalities, that its first instincts are fain to clip, conform, bring in stragglers, and reduce everything to a dead level. While the ambitious thought of my song is to help the forming of a great aggregate Nation, it is, perhaps, altogether through the forming of myriads of fully develop'd and enclosing individuals. Welcome as are equality's and fraternity's doctrines and popular education, a certain liability accompanies them all, as we see. That primal and interior something in man, in his soul's abysms, coloring all, and, by exceptional fruitions, giving the last majesty to him—something continually touch'd upon and attain'd by the old poems and ballads of feudalism, and often the principal foundation of them—modern science and democracy appear to be endangering, perhaps eliminating. But that forms an appearance only; the reality is quite different. The new influences, upon the whole, are surely preparing the way for grander individualities than ever. To-day and here personal force is behind everything, just the same. The times and depictions from the Iliad to Shakspere inclusive can happily never again be realized—but the elements of courageous and lofty manhood are unchanged.

Without yielding an inch the working-man and working-woman were to be in my pages from first to last. The ranges of heroism and loftiness with which Greek and feudal poets endow'd their god-like or lordly born characters—indeed prouder and better based and with fuller ranges than those—I was to endow the democratic averages of America. I was to show that we, here and to-day, are eligible to the grandest and the best—more eligible now than any times of old were. I will also want my utterances (I said to myself before beginning) to be in spirit the poems of the morning. (They have been founded and mainly written in the sunny forenoon and early midday of my life.) I will want them to be the poems of women entirely as much as men. I have wish'd to put the complete Union of the States in my songs without any preference or partiality whatever. Henceforth, if they live and are read, it must be just as much South as North—just as much along the Pacific as Atlantic—in the valley of the Mississippi, in Canada, up in Maine, down in Texas, and on the shores of Puget Sound.

From another point of view "Leaves of Grass" is avowedly the song of Sex and Amativeness, and even Animality—though meanings that do not usually go along with those words are behind all, and will duly emerge; and all are sought to be lifted into a different light and atmosphere. Of this feature, intentionally palpable in a few lines, I shall only say the espousing principle of those lines so gives breath of life to my whole scheme that the bulk of the pieces might as well have been left unwritten were those lines omitted. Difficult as it will be, it has become, in my opinion, imperative to achieve a shifted attitude from superior men and women towards the thought and fact of sexuality, as an element in character, personality, the emotions, and a theme in literature. I am not going to argue the question by itself; it does not stand by itself. The vitality of it is altogether in its relations, bearings, significance—like the clef of a symphony. At last analogy the lines I allude to, and the spirit in which they are spoken, permeate all "Leaves of Grass," and the work must stand or fall with them, as the human body and soul must remain as an entirety.

Universal as are certain facts and symptoms of communities or individuals all times, there is nothing so rare in modern conventions and poetry as their normal recognizance. Literature is always calling in the doctor for consultation and confession, and always giving evasions and swathing suppressions in place of that "heroic nudity"* on which only a genuine diagnosis of serious cases can be built. And in respect to editions of "Leaves of Grass" in time to come (if there should be such) I take occasion now to confirm those lines with the settled convictions and deliberate renewals of thirty years, and to hereby prohibit, as far as word of mine can do so, any elision of them.

Then still a purpose enclosing all, and over and beneath all. Ever since what might be call'd thought, or the budding of thought, fairly began in my youthful mind, I had had a desire to attempt some worthy record of that entire faith and acceptance ("to justify the ways of God to man" is Milton's well-known and ambitious phrase) which is the foundation of moral America. I felt it all as positively then in my young days as I do now in my old ones; to

* "Nineteenth Century," July, 1883.

formulate a poem whose every thought or fact should directly or indirectly be or connive at an implicit belief in the wisdom, health, mystery, beauty of every process, every concrete object, every human or other existence, not only consider'd from the point of view of all, but of each.

While I can not understand it or argue it out, I fully believe in a clue and purpose in Nature, entire and several; and that invisible spiritual results, just as real and definite as the visible, eventuate all concrete life and all materialism, through Time. My book ought to emanate buoyancy and gladness legitimately enough, for it was grown out of those elements, and has been the comfort of my life since it was originally commenced.

One main genesis-motive of the "Leaves" was my conviction (just as strong to-day as ever) that the crowning growth of the United States is to be spiritual and heroic. To help start and favor that growth—or even to call attention to it, or the need of it—is the beginning, middle and final purpose of the poems. (In fact, when really cipher'd out and summ'd to the last, plowing up in earnest the interminable average fallows of humanity—not "good government" merely, in the common sense—is the justification and main purpose of these United States.)

Isolated advantages in any rank or grace or fortune—the direct or indirect threads of all the poetry of the past—are in my opinion distasteful to the republican genius, and offer no foundation for its fitting verse. Establish'd poems, I know, have the very great advantage of chanting the already perform'd, so full of glories, reminiscences dear to the minds of men. But my volume is a candidate for the future. "All original art," says Taine, anyhow, "is self-regulated, and no original art can be regulated from without; it carries its own counterpoise, and does not receive it from elsewhere—lives on its own blood"—a solace to my frequent bruises and sulky vanity.

As the present is perhaps mainly an attempt at personal statement or illustration, I will allow myself as further help to extract the following anecdote from a book, "Annals of Old Painters," conn'd by me in youth. Rubens, the Flemish painter, in one of his wanderings through the galleries of old convents, came across a singular work. After looking at it thoughtfully for a good while, and listening to the criticisms of his suite of students, he said to the latter, in answer to their questions (as to what school the work implied or belong'd,) "I do not believe the artist, unknown and perhaps no longer living, who has given the world this legacy, ever belong'd to any school, or ever painted anything but this one picture, which is a personal affair—a piece out of a man's life."

"Leaves of Grass" indeed (I cannot too often reiterate) has mainly been the outcropping of my own emotional and other personal nature—an attempt, from first to last, to put *a Person*, a human being (myself, in the latter half of the Nineteenth Century, in America,) freely, fully and truly on record. I could not find any similar personal record in current literature that satisfied me. But it is not on "Leaves of Grass" distinctively as *literature*, or a specimen thereof, that I feel to dwell, or advance claims. No one will get at my verses who insists upon viewing them as a literary performance, or attempt at such performance, or as aiming mainly toward art or æstheticism.

I say no land or people or circumstances ever existed so needing a race of singers and poems differing from all others, and rigidly their own, as the land and people and circumstances of our United States need such singers and poems to-day, and for the future. Still further, as long as the States continue to absorb and be dominated by the poetry of the Old World, and remain unsupplied with autochthonous song, to express, vitalize and give color to and define their material and political success, and minister to them distinctively, so long will they stop short of first-class Nationality and remain defective.

In the free evening of my day I give to you, reader, the foregoing garrulous talk, thoughts, reminiscences,

> As idly drifting down the ebb,
> Such ripples, half-caught voices, echo from the shore.

Concluding with two items for the imaginative genius of the West, when it worthily rises—First, what Herder taught to the young Goethe, that really great poetry is always (like the Homeric or Biblical canticles) the result of a national spirit, and not the privilege of a polish'd and select few; Second, that the strongest and sweetest songs yet remain to be sung.

THE ADVENT OF EMILY
DICKINSON

Emily Dickinson's poetry became available after her death only bit by bit, as three generations of editors between 1890 and 1955 made selections from hundreds of manuscript poems which they transcribed according to varying ideas of auctorial intent and editorial responsibility. Only within the last few years has the entire body of her work been brought together in Thomas H. Johnson's careful edition of *The Poems of Emily Dickinson.* Her work still seems more enigmatic than that of any other major writer of the last century. One reason for this is that in the privacy of her poetic activity she offers no statement to her readers of the theories of art and life on which her poems were based that could supply the discursive exposition Whitman provided with his "Preface" to the first edition of *Leaves of Grass.* Her readers are required to approach her at first on their own terms, then, ultimately, on hers.

The following selections are the first two significant attempts to understand Emily Dickinson's work. One is the earliest public identification of Dickinson as a poet, written by her literary adviser and first editor, T. W. Higginson. The other is the comment on her first book by the novelist William Dean Howells. The incapacity of the generation which Whitman had assailed as "pistareen, paste-pot" poets to accommodate Emily Dickinson's poems to its bloodless conventions is illustrated, ironically, in the effort which Higginson, her chosen adviser, must make to admit the merit of work so "defiant in form, measure, rhyme, and even grammar." Howells, made more receptive to genius by his own long experience as an author, perspicuously recognizes the poetic necessity of the "harsh" texture in Dickinson's work to the uncompromised intensity of utterance in her poems.

I

THOMAS WENTWORTH HIGGINSON

1823–1911

Colonel of a Negro regiment in the Civil War, editor, and literary critic, Higginson was one of the few persons outside her immediate family to whom Emily Dickinson showed her poems. She wrote to him in 1862, a year of extraordinary poetic achievement for her; Higginson first visited her in Amherst in 1870. It has been suggested that she turned to Higginson rather than, say, to Emerson, because he represented the standards of the literary world from which she had exiled herself. He was certainly a sounding-board of genteel opinion; to the modern reader he seems blandly unperceptive of her merits. Yet he recognized that she had an unusual talent, though to his decorous taste her work was deficient in form and crude in diction, and he advised her not to publish. After her death, with the urging of members of her family, he collaborated with Mabel Loomis Todd in editing the first three volumes of Emily Dickinson's verse (1890, 1891, 1896). His article in *The Christian Union*—a religious journal devoted to good works and liberal causes, though hardly to innovations in literary taste—was intended to publicize the forthcoming first edition of her *Poems*. Higginson's brief preface to that volume, to which Howells alludes, rephrases some of his comments here. From his choices of her poems one can gauge the preference of the time for narrative moralizing poems on such topics as "Life," "Nature," "Love," and "Death." Under such rubrics, and under poem titles of his own composition, Higginson presents his poetess, only by degrees moving the reader toward the disquieting surprises of a poem like "Safe in their alabaster chambers."

TEXT: *The Christian Union*, XLII, (25 September 1890), 392–93. For Higginson's relation to Emily Dickinson and his role in

editing her poems, see: Millicent Todd Bingham, *Ancestors'
Brocades: The Literary Debut of Emily Dickinson* (1945);
Richard Chase, *Emily Dickinson* (1951).

AN OPEN PORTFOLIO

Emerson said, many years since, in the "Dial," that
the most interesting department of poetry would hereafter
be found in what might be called "The Poetry of the
Portfolio"; the work, that is, of persons who wrote for the
relief of their own minds, and without thought of publication. Such poetry, when accumulated for years, will have
at least the merit of perfect freedom; accompanied, of
course, by whatever drawback follows from the habitual
absence of criticism. Thought will have its full strength
and uplifting, but without the proper control and chasten-
ing of literary expression; there will be wonderful strokes
and felicities, and yet an incomplete and unsatisfactory
whole. If we believe, with Ruskin, that "no beauty of
execution can outweigh one grain or fragment of thought,"
then we may often gain by the seclusion of the portfolio,
which rests content with a first stroke and does not over-
refine and prune away afterwards. Such a sheaf of un-
published verse lies before me, the life-work of a woman
so secluded that she lived literally indoors by choice for
many years, and within the limits of her father's estate
for many more—who shrank even from the tranquil society
of a New England college town, and yet loved her few
friends with profound devotedness, and divided her life
between them and her flowers. It absolutely startles one to
find among the memorials of this secluded inland life a
picture so vividly objective as this:

BY THE SEA.

Glee! the great storm is over!
  Four have recovered the land;
Forty gone down together
  Into the boiling sand.

Ring! for the scant salvation!
  Toll! for the bonnie souls,
Neighbor and friend and bridegroom,
  Spinning upon the shoals.

How will they tell the shipwreck
  When winter shakes the door,
Till the children ask, "But the forty?
  Did they come back no more?"

Then a silence suffuses the story
  And a softness the teller's eye,
And the children no further question;
  And only the waves reply.

Celia Thaxter on her rocky island, Jean Ingelow by her
English cliffs, never drew a sea picture in stronger lines
than this secluded woman in her inland village, who writes
elsewhere, as tersely:

I never saw a moor,
  I never saw the sea,
Yet I know how the heather looks
  And what the billows be.

I never spoke with God
  Nor visited in heaven,
Yet certain am I of the spot,
  As if the chart were given.

See now with what corresponding vigor she draws the mightier storms and shipwrecks of the soul; the title being here, as elsewhere, my own, for she herself never prefixes any:

ROUGE ET NOIR.

> Soul, wilt thou toss again?
> By just such a hazard
> Hundreds have lost, indeed,
> But tens have won an all.
>
> Angels' breathless ballot
> Lingers to record thee;
> Imps in eager caucus
> Raffle for my soul!

Was ever the concentrated contest of a lifetime, the very issue between good and evil, put into fewer words? Then comes another, which might fairly be linked with it, and might be called

ROUGE GAGNE!

> 'Tis so much joy! 'Tis so much joy!
> If I should fail, what poverty!
>   And yet as poor as I
> Have ventured all upon a throw;
> Have gained! Yes! Hesitated so
>   This side the victory.
>
> Life is but life, and death but death!
> Bliss is but bliss, and breath but breath!
>   And if indeed I fail,
> At least, to know the worst is sweet!
> Defeat means nothing but defeat,
>   No drearier can prevail.

And if I gain! O sun at sea!
O bells! that in the steeple be,
    At first, repeat it slow!
For heaven is a different thing
Conjectured and worked sudden in,
    And might o'erwhelm me so.

Many of these poems are, as might be expected, drawn
from the aspects of Nature, but always with some insight
or image of their own; as in the following, which might
be called

THE SEA OF SUNSET.

This is the land the sunset washes,
    These are the banks of the yellow sea;
Where it rose, or whither it rushes,
    These are the western mystery.

Night after night, her purple traffic
    Strews the landing with opal bales,
Merchantmen poise upon horizons,
    Dip and vanish with airy sails.

or this:

THE WIND.

Of all the sounds despatched abroad
    There's not a charge to me
Like that old measure in the boughs,
    That phraseless melody
The wind makes, working like a hand
    Whose fingers brush the sky,
Then quiver down, with tufts of tune,
    Permitted gods—and me.

I crave him grace of summer boughs
  If such an outcast be
Who never heard that fleshless chant
  Rise solemn in the tree;
As if some caravan of sound
  On deserts in the sky
Had broken ranks, then knit, and passed
  In seamless company.

This last image needs no praise, and in dealing with Nature she often seems to possess—as was said of her fellow-townswoman, Helen Jackson ("H. H.")—a sixth sense. But most of her poems grapple at first hand—the more audaciously the better—with the very mysteries of life and death, as in the following:

TWO KINSMEN.

I died for Beauty, but was scarce
  Adjusted in the tomb
When one who died for Truth was lain
  In an adjoining room.

He questioned softly, why I failed?
  "For Beauty," I replied;
"And I for Truth—the two are one—
  We brethren are," he said.

And so, as kinsmen, met a night,
  We talked between the rooms
Until the moss had reached our lips
  And covered up our names.

The conception is weird enough for William Blake, and one can no more criticize a faulty rhyme here and there than a defect of drawing in one of Blake's pictures. When a thought takes one's breath away, who cares to count the syllables? The same iron strength shows itself, merging into tenderness, in this brief dirge for one of the nameless Marthas, cumbered about many things:

REQUIESCAT.

How many times these low feet staggered
  Only the soldered month can tell;
Try! can you stir the awful rivet?
  Try! can you lift the hasps of steel?

Stroke the cool forehead, hot so often;
  Lift, if you can, the listless hair;
Handle the adamantine fingers
  Never a thimble more shall wear.

Buzz the dull flies on the chamber window;
  Brave shines the sun through the freckled pane;
Fearless the cobweb swings from the ceiling;
  Indolent housewife! in daisies lain.

The unutterable dignity of death seems to have forced itself again and again upon this lonely woman, and she has several times touched it with her accustomed terse strength, as in these verses:

One dignity delays for all,
  One mitred afternoon.
None can avoid this purple;
  None can evade this crown.

Coach it insures, and footmen,
  Chamber and state and throng,
Bells also, in the village,
  As we ride grand along.

What dignified attendants!
  What service when we pause!
How loyally, at parting,
  Their hundred hats they raise!

What pomp surpassing ermine
When simple you and I
Present our meek escutcheon
And claim the rank to die!

Then, approaching the great change from time to eternity at a different angle, she gives two verses of superb concentration, like the following, which might be christened, after the medieval motto,

ASTRA CASTRA.

Departed to the Judgment
    A mighty afternoon;
Great clouds, like ushers, leaning,
    Creation looking on.

The flesh surrendered, canceled,
    The bodiless begun;
Two worlds, like audiences, disperse,
    And leave the soul alone.

She shrinks from no concomitant of death; all is ennobled in her imagination:

Safe in their alabaster chambers,
    Untouched by morning and untouched by noon,
Sleep the meek members of the resurrection;
    Rafter of satin and roof of stone.

Light laughs the breeze in her castle above them;
    Babbles the bee in a stolid ear;
Pipe the sweet birds in ignorant cadence—
    Ah! what sagacity perished here!

This is the form in which she finally left these lines, but as she sent them to me, years ago, the following took the place of the second verse, and it seems to me that, with all its too daring condensation, it strikes a note too fine to be lost:

> Grand go the years in the crescent above them,
>   Worlds scoop their arcs, and firmaments row;
> Diadems drop, and Doges surrender,
>   Soundless as dots on a disk of snow.

But with these mighty visions of death and eternity, there are such touches of tender individual sympathy as we find in this, which may be called

TOO LATE.

> Delayed till she had ceased to know!
> Delayed till in its vest of snow
>   Her loving bosom lay.
> An hour behind the fleeting breath!
> Later by just an hour than Death!
>   O! lagging yesterday!
>
> Could she have guessed that it would be;
> Could but a crier of the glee
>   Have climbed the distant hill;
> Had not the bliss so slow a pace,
> Who knows but this surrendered face
>   Were undefeated still?
>
> O! if there may departing be
> Any forgot by victory
>   In her imperial sound,
> Show them this meek-appareled thing,
> That could not stop to be a king,
>   Doubtful if it be crowned!

Almost all these poems are strangely impersonal, but here and there we have a glimpse of experiences too intense to be more plainly intimated, as in the following:

I shall know why, when time is over
 And I have ceased to wonder why;
Christ will explain each separate anguish
 In the fair schoolroom of the sky.

He will tell me what Peter promised,
 And I, for wonder at his woe,
I shall forget the drop of anguish
 That scalds me now—that scalds me now!

Surely this is as if woven out of the heart's own atoms, and will endear the name of Emily Dickinson, in some hour of trial, to those who never before encountered that name, and who will seek it vainly in the cyclopædias. Her verses are in most cases like poetry plucked up by the roots; we have them with earth, stones, and dew adhering, and must accept them as they are. Wayward and unconventional in the last degree; defiant of form, measure, rhyme, and even grammar; she yet had an exacting standard of her own, and would wait many days for a word that satisfied. Asked again and again for verses to be published, she scarcely ever yielded, even to a friend so tried and dear as the late Mr. Bowles, of the Springfield "Republican;" but she sent her poems with gifts of flowers or —as in my own case—to correspondents whom she had never seen. It is with some misgiving, and almost with a sense of questionable publicity, that it has at last been decided by her surviving sister and her friends to print a small selection from these poems, which will be issued by Roberts Brothers, Boston. The only hint found among her papers of any possible contact with a wider public is found in these few lines, which—although probably the utterance of a passing mood only—have been selected as the prelude to the forthcoming volume:

This is my letter to the world
 That never wrote to me;
The simple news that nature told
 With tender majesty.

Her message is committed
    To hands I cannot see;
For love of her, sweet countrymen,
    Judge tenderly of me!

II

WILLIAM DEAN HOWELLS

1837–1920

Novelist, editor-in-chief of *The Atlantic Monthly,* and later an editor on *Harper's,* Howells was the most influential reviewer of the time. He was a friend of Higginson's co-editor of the Dickinson poems, Mabel Loomis Todd. She showed him some of Emily Dickinson's work before publication and reported to Higginson that Howells was "immensely enthusiastic." In his notice of the first Dickinson volume in *Harper's* he recognizes the originality and the artistic control which later generations would find in Emily Dickinson's poems. The author of some eighty volumes of fiction, criticism, biography, and plays, Howells was himself writer of occasional and entirely conventional verse.

TEXT: "Editor's Study," *Harper's New Monthly Magazine,* LXXXII (January, 1891), 318–21.

POEMS OF EMILY DICKINSON

The strange *Poems of Emily Dickinson* we think will form something like an intrinsic experience with the understanding reader of them. They have been edited by Mrs. Mabel Loomis Todd, who was a personal friend of the poet, and by Colonel T. W. Higginson, who was long her epistolary and literary acquaintance, but only met her twice. Few people met her so often, as the reader will learn from Colonel Higginson's interesting preface, for her life was mainly spent in her father's house at Amherst, Massachusetts; she seldom passed its doors, and never, for many years, passed the gates of its grounds. There is no hint of what turned her life in upon herself, and probably this was its natural evolution, or involution, from tendencies inherent in the New England, or the Puritan spirit. We are told that once a year she met the local world at a reception in her father's house; we do not know that there is any harm in adding, that she did not always literally meet it, but sometimes sat with her face averted from the company in another room. One of her few friends was Helen Hunt Jackson, whom she suffered to send one of her poems to be included in the volume of anonymous pieces which Messrs. Roberts Brothers once published with the title of *A Masque of Poets*. Whether the anonymity flattered her love of obscurity or not, it is certain that her darkling presence in this book was the occasion of her holding for many years a correspondence with its publishers. She wrote them, as the fancy took her, comments on their new books, and always enclosed a scrap of her verse, though without making any reference to it. She never intended or allowed anything more from her pen to be printed in her lifetime; but it was evident that she wished her poetry finally to meet the eyes of that world which she had herself always shrunk from. She could not have made such poetry without knowing its rarity, its singular worth; and no doubt it was a radiant happiness in the twilight of her hidden, silent life.

The editors have discharged their delicate duty toward it with unimpeachable discretion, and Colonel Higginson has said so many apt things of her work in his introduction, that one who cannot differ with him must be vexed a little to be left so little to say. He speaks of her "curious indifference to all conventional rules of verse," but adds that "when a thought takes one's breath away, a lesson on grammar seems an impertinence." He notes "the quality suggestive of the poetry of William Blake" in her, but he leaves us the chance to say that it is a Blake who has read Emerson who has read Blake. The fantasy is as often

Blakian as the philosophy is Emersonian; but after feeling
this again and again, one is ready to declare that the utterance of this most singular and authentic spirit would
have been the same if there had never been an Emerson
or a Blake in the world. She sometimes suggests Heine as
much as either of these; all three in fact are spiritually
present in some of the pieces; yet it is hardly probable
that she had read Heine, or if she had, would not have
abhorred him.

Here is something that seems compact of both Emerson
and Blake, with a touch of Heine too:

> I taste a liquor never brewed
> From tankards scooped in pearl;
> Not all the vats upon the Rhine
> Yield such an alcohol!
>
> Inebriate of air am I,
> And debauchee of dew,
> Reeling, through endless summer days,
> From inns of molten blue.
>
> When landlords turn the drunken bee
> Out of the foxglove's door,
> When butterflies renounce their drams,
> I shall but drink the more!
>
> Till seraphs swing their snowy hats,
> And saints to windows run,
> To see the little tippler
> Leaning against the sun!

But we believe it is only seeming; we believe these
things are as wholly her own as this:

> The bustle in a house
> The morning after death
> Is solemnest of industries
> Enacted upon earth,—

The sweeping up the heart,
And putting love away
We shall not want to use again
Until eternity.

Such things could have come only from a woman's heart to which the experiences in a New England town have brought more knowledge of death than of life. Terribly unsparing many of these strange poems are, but true as the grave and certain as mortality. The associations of house-keeping in the following poem have a force that drags us almost into the presence of the poor, cold, quiet thing:

"TROUBLED ABOUT MANY THINGS"

How many times these low feet staggered,
Only the soldered mouth can tell;
Try! can you stir the awful rivet?
Try! can you lift the hasps of steel?

Stroke the cool forehead, hot so often,
Lift, if you can, the listless hair;
Handle the adamantine fingers
Never a thimble more shall wear.

Buzz the dull flies on the chamber window;
Brave shines the sun through the freckled pane;
Fearless the cobweb swings from the ceiling—
Indolent housewife, in daisies lain!

[Howells then quotes "I died for beauty," "I like a look of agony," "New feet within my garden go," and "Elysium is as far as to."]

The last poem is from the group which the editors have named "Love"; the other groups from which we have been quoting are "Nature," and "Time and Eternity"; but the love poems are of the same piercingly introspective cast as those differently named. The same force of imagination is in them; in them, as in the rest, touch often becomes clutch. In them love walks on heights he seldom treads, and it is the heart of full womanhood that speaks in the words of this nun-like New England life.

Few of the poems in the book are long, but none of the short, quick impulses of intense feeling or poignant thought can be called fragments. They are each a compassed whole, a sharply finished point, and there is evidence, circumstantial and direct, that the author spared no pains in the perfect expression of her ideals. Nothing, for example, could be added that would say more than she has said in four lines:

> Presentiment is that long shadow on the lawn
> Indicative that suns go down;
> The notice to the startled grass
> That darkness is about to pass.

Occasionally, the outside of the poem, so to speak, is left so rough, so rude, that the art seems to have faltered. But there is apparent to reflection the fact that the artist meant just this harsh exterior to remain, and that no grace of smoothness could have imparted her intention as it does. It is the soul of an abrupt, exalted New England woman that speaks in such brokenness. The range of all the poems is of the loftiest; and sometimes there is a kind of swelling lift, an almost boastful rise of feeling, which is really the spring of faith in them:

> I never saw a moor,
> I never saw the sea;
> Yet I know how the heather looks,
> And what a wave must be.

> I never spoke with God,
> Nor visited in heaven;
> Yet certain am I of the spot
> As if the chart were given.

There is a noble tenderness, too, in some of the pieces; a quaintness that does not discord with the highest solemnity. . . . The companionship of human nature with inanimate nature is very close in certain of the poems; and we have never known the invisible and intangible ties binding all creation in one, so nearly touched as in them.

If nothing else had come out of our life but this strange poetry we should feel that in the work of Emily Dickinson America, or New England rather, had made a distinctive addition to the literature of the world, and could not be left out of any record of it; and the interesting and important thing is that this poetry is as characteristic of our life as our business enterprise, our political turmoil, our demagogism, our millionairism. "Listen!" says Mr. James McNeill Whistler in that "Ten o'Clock" lecture of his which must have made his hearers feel very much lectured indeed, not to say browbeaten,—"Listen! There never was an artistic period. There never was an art-loving nation." But there were moments and there were persons to whom art was dear, and Emily Dickinson was one of those persons, one of these moments in a national life, and she could as well happen in Amherst, Mass., as in Athens, Att.

GEORGE SANTAYANA

1863–1952

Santayana has said that his philosophy is based on his distinction between existence and essence. "It is by its very ideality, non-existence, and eternity . . . that essence is inwardly linked with existence, not by being an extension or a portion of that which exists." His argument for poetry as an autonomous reality "truer to the ultimate possibilities of our soul" than the experiential materials on which it is based leads directly to the Romantic-Symbolist aesthetic.

TEXT: *Interpretations of Poetry and Religion* (1900).

THE ELEMENTS AND FUNCTIONS OF POETRY

Measure is a condition of perfection, for perfection requires that order should be pervasive, that not only the whole before us should have a form, but that every part in turn should have a form of its own, and that those parts should be coördinated among themselves as the whole is coördinated with the other parts of some greater cosmos. . . .

The stuff of language is words, and the sensuous material of words is sound; if language therefore is to be made perfect, its materials must be made beautiful by being themselves subjected to a measure, and endowed with a form. It is true that language is a symbol for intelligence rather than a stimulus to sense, and accordingly the beauties of discourse which commonly attract attention are merely the beauties of the objects and ideas signified; yet the symbols have a sensible reality of their own, a euphony which appeals to our senses if we keep them open. . . .

If poetry in its higher reaches is more philosophical than history, because it presents the memorable types of men and things apart from unmeaning circumstances, so in its primary substance and texture poetry is more philosophical than prose because it is nearer to our immediate experience. Poetry breaks up the trite conceptions designated by current words into the sensuous qualities out of which those conceptions were originally put together. We name what we conceive and believe in, not what we see; things, not images; souls, not voices and silhouettes. This naming, with the whole education of the senses which it accompanies, subserves the uses of life; in order to thread our way through the labyrinth of objects which assault us, we must make a great selection in our sensuous experience; half of what we see and hear we must pass over as insignificant, while we piece out the other half with such an ideal complement as is necessary to turn it into a fixed and well-ordered world. This labour of perception and understanding, this spelling of the material meaning of experience is enshrined in our work-a-day language and ideas; ideas which are literally poetic in the sense that they are "made" (for every conception in an adult mind is a fiction), but which are at the same time prosaic because they are made economically, by abstraction, and for use.

When the child of poetic genius, who has learned this intellectual and utilitarian language in the cradle, goes afield and gathers for himself the aspects of Nature, he begins to encumber his mind with the many living impressions which the intellect rejected, and which the language of the intellect can hardly convey; he labours with his nameless burden of perception, and wastes himself in aimless impulses of emotion and revery, until finally the method of some art offers a vent to his inspiration, or to such part of it as can survive the test of time and the discipline of expression.

The poet retains by nature the innocence of the eye, or recovers it easily; he disintegrates the fictions of common perception into their sensuous elements, gathers these together again into chance groups as the accidents of his environment or the affinities of his temperament may conjoin them; and this wealth of sensation and this freedom of fancy, which make an extraordinary ferment in his ignorant heart, presently bubble over into some kind of utterance. . . .

The first element which the intellect rejects in forming its ideas of things is the emotion which accompanies the perception; and this emotion is the first thing the poet restores. He stops at the image, because he stops to enjoy. He wanders into the by-paths of association because the by-paths are delightful. The love of beauty which made him give measure and cadence to his words, the love of harmony which made him rhyme them, reappear in his imagination and make him select there also the material that is itself beautiful, or capable of assuming beautiful forms. The link that binds together the ideas, sometimes so wide apart, which his wit assimilates, is most often the link of emotion; they have in common some element of beauty or of horror.

The poet's art is to a great extent the art of intensifying emotions by assembling the scattered objects that naturally arouse them. He sees the affinities of things by seeing their common affinities with passion. As the guiding principle of practical thinking is some interest, so that only what is pertinent to that interest is selected by the attention; as the guiding principle of scientific thinking is some connection of things in time or space, or some identity of law; so in poetic thinking the guiding principle is often a mood or a quality of sentiment. By this union of disparate things having a common overtone of feeling, the feeling is itself evoked in all its strength; nay, it is often created for the first time . . . Poets can thus arouse sentiments finer than any which they have known, and in the act of composition become discoverers of new realms of delightfulness and grief. Expression is a misleading term which suggests that something previously known is rendered or imitated; whereas the expression is itself an original fact, the values of which are then referred to the thing expressed. . . .

The outer world bathed in the hues of human feeling, the inner world expressed in the forms of things,—that is the primitive condition of both [perceptive and emotional elements] before intelligence and the prosaic classification of objects have abstracted them and assigned them to their respective spheres. Such identifications, on which a certain kind of metaphysics prides itself also, are not discoveries of profound genius; . . . they are disintegrations of conventional objects, so that the original associates of our perceptions reappear; then the thing and the emotion which chanced to be simultaneous are said to be one, and we return, unless a better principle of organization is substituted for the principle abandoned, to the chaos of a passive animal consciousness, where all is mixed together, and felt as an unutterable whole.

The pathetic fallacy is a return to that early habit of thought by which our ancestors peopled the world with benevolent and malevolent spirits; what they felt in the presence of objects they took to be a part of the objects themselves. In returning to this natural confusion, poetry does us a service in that she recalls and consecrates those phases of our experience which, as useless to the understanding of material reality, we are in danger of forgetting altogether. Therein is her vitality, for she pierces to the quick and shakes us out of our servile speech and imaginative poverty; she reminds us of all we have felt, she invites us even to dream a little, to nurse the wonderful spontaneous creations which at every waking moment we are snuffing out in our brain. . . . When the veil of convention is once removed from our eyes by the poet, we are better able to dominate any particular experience and, as it were, to change its scale, now losing ourselves in its infinitesimal texture, now in its infinite ramifications. . . .

The great function of poetry, which we have not yet directly mentioned, is precisely this: to repair to the material of experience, seizing hold of the reality of sensation and fancy beneath the surface of conventional ideas, and then out of that living but indefinite material to build new structures, richer, finer, fitter to the primary tendencies of our nature, truer to the ultimate possibilities of our soul.

Our descent into the elements of our being is then justified by our subsequent freer ascent toward its goal: we
revert to sense only to find food for reason; we destroy
conventions only to construct ideals.

Such analysis for the sake of creation is the essence of
all great poetry. Science and common sense are themselves
in their way poets of no mean order, since they take the
material of experience and make out of it a clear, symmetrical, and beautiful world; the very propriety of this art,
however, has made it common. Its figures have become
mere rhetoric and its metaphors prose. Yet, even as it is, a
scientific and mathematical vision has a higher beauty than
the irrational poetry of sensation and impulse, which
merely tickles the brain, like liquor, and plays upon our
random, imaginative lusts. The imagination of a great poet,
on the contrary, is as orderly as that of an astronomer, and
as large; he has the naturalist's patience, the naturalist's
love of detail and eye trained to see fine gradations and
essential lines; he knows no hurry; he has no pose, no
sense of originality; he finds his effects in his subject, and
his subject in his inevitable world. Resembling the naturalist in all this, he differs from him in the balance of his
interests; the poet has the concreter mind; his visible world
wears all its colours and retains its indwelling passion and
life. Instead of studying in experience its calculable elements, he studies its moral values, its beauty, the openings
it offers to the soul: and the cosmos he constructs is accordingly an ideal theatre for the spirit in which its noblest
potential drama is enacted and its destiny resolved.

This supreme function of poetry is only the consumma-
tion of the method by which words and imagery are transformed into verse. As verse breaks up the prosaic order of
syllables and subjects them to a recognizable and pleasing
measure, so poetry breaks up the whole prosaic picture of
experience to introduce into it a rhythm more congenial
and intelligible to the mind. And in both these cases the
operation is essentially the same as that by which, in an
intermediate sphere, the images rejected by practical
thought, and the emotions ignored by it, are so marshalled
as to fill the mind with a truer and intenser consciousness

of its memorable experience. The poetry of fancy, of observation, and of passion moves on this intermediate level;
the poetry of mere sound and virtuosity is confined to the
lower sphere; and the highest is reserved for the poetry of
the creative reason. But one principle is present throughout,—the principle of Beauty,—the art of assimilating phenomena, whether words, images, emotions, or systems of
ideas, to the deeper innate cravings of the mind. . . .

The distinction of a poet—the dignity and humanity of
his thought—can be measured by nothing, perhaps, so well
as by the diameter of the world in which he lives; if he is
supreme, his vision, like Dante's, always stretches to the
stars. And Virgil, a supreme poet sometimes unjustly be-
littled, shows us the same thing in another form; his landscape is the Roman universe, his theme the sacred springs
of Roman greatness in piety, constancy, and law. He has
not written a line in forgetfulness that he was a Roman;
he loves country life and its labours because he sees in it
the origin and bulwark of civic greatness; he honours tradition because it gives perspective and momentum to the
history that ensues; he invokes the gods, because they are
symbols of the physical and moral forces by which Rome
struggled to dominion.

Almost every classic poet has the topographical sense;
he swarms with proper names and allusions to history and
fable; if an epithet is to be thrown in anywhere to fill up
the measure of a line, he chooses instinctively an appella-
tion of place or family; his wine is not red, but Samian; his
gorges are not deep, but are the gorges of Haemus; his
songs are not sweet, but Pierian. We may deride their
practice as conventional, but they could far more justly
deride ours as insignificant. Conventions do not arise without some reason, and genius will know how to rise above
them by a fresh appreciation of their rightness, and will
feel no temptation to overturn them in favour of personal
whimsies. The ancients found poetry not so much in sensible accidents as in essential forms and noble associations;
and this fact marks very clearly their superior education.
They dominated the world as we no longer dominate it,

and lived, as we are too distracted to live, in the presence of the rational and the important.

A physical and historical background, however, is of little moment to the poet in comparison with that other environment of his characters,—the dramatic situations in which they are involved. . . . The passions are the chief basis of all interests, even the most ideal, and the passions are seldom brought into play except by contact of man with man. . . .

But the passions are naturally blind, and the poverty of the imagination, when left alone, is absolute. The passions may ferment as they will, they can never breed an idea out of their own energy. This idea must be furnished by the senses, by outward experience, else the hunger of the soul will gnaw its own emptiness for ever. Where the seed of sensation has once fallen, however, the growth, variations, and exuberance of fancy may be left unlimited. Only we still observe (as in the child, in dreams, and in the poetry of ignorant or mystical poets) that the intensity of inwardly generated visions does not involve any real increase in their scope or dignity. . . .

The alleged fertility of the will is, however, disproved by experience, from which metaphysics must in the end draw its analogies and plausibility. The passions discover, they do not create, their occasions; a fact which is patent when we observe how they seize upon what objects they find, and how reversible, contingent, and transferable the emotions are in respect to their objects. A doll will be loved instead of a child, a child instead of a lover, God instead of everything. The differentiation of the passions, as far as consciousness is concerned, depends on the variety of the objects of experience,—that is, on the differentiation of the senses and of the environment which stimulates them. . . .

Hence flows the greatest opportunity of fiction. We have, in a sense, an infinite will; but we have a limited experience, an experience sadly inadequate to exercise that will either in its purity or its strength. To give form to our capacities nothing is required but the appropriate occasion; this the poet, studying the world, will construct for us out of the materials of his observations. . . . The possibilities of love or glory, of intrigue and perplexity, will be opened up before us; if he gives us a good plot, we can readily furnish the characters, because each of them will be the realization of some stunted potential self of our own. . . .

This is the essence of tragedy: the sense of the finished life, of the will fulfilled and enlightened: that purging of the mind so much debated upon, which relieves us of pent-up energies, transfers our feelings to a greater object, and thus justifies and entertains our dumb passions, detaching them at the same time for a moment from their accidental occasions in our earthly life. . . . Without such a glimpse of the goal of a passion the passion has not been adequately read, and the fiction has served to amuse us without really enlarging the frontiers of our ideal experience. . . .

The function of poetry, like that of science, can only be fulfilled by the conception of harmonies that become clearer as they grow richer. . . . The highest ideality is the comprehension of the real. Poetry is not at its best when it depicts a further possible experience, but when it initiates us, by feigning something which as an experience is impossible, into the meaning of the experience which we have actually had.

The highest example of this kind of poetry is religion; and although disfigured and misunderstood by the simplicity of men who believe in it without being capable of that imaginative interpretation of life in which truth consists, yet this religion is even then often beneficent, because it colours life harmoniously with the ideal. . . .

The highest poetry, then, is not that of the versifiers, but that of the prophets, or of such poets as interpret verbally the visions which the prophets have rendered in action and sentiment rather than in adequate words. . . . Where poetry rises from its elementary and detached expressions in rhythm, euphuism, characterization, and story-telling, and comes to the consciousness of its highest function, that of portraying the ideals of experience and destiny, then the poet becomes aware that he is essentially a prophet, and either devotes himself, like Homer or Dante, to the loving expression of the religion that exists, or like Lucretius or Wordsworth, to the heralding of one which he believes to be possible. Such poets are aware of their highest mission; others, whatever the energy of their genius, have not conceived their ultimate functions as poets. . . . The good man is a poet whose syllables are deeds and make a harmony in Nature. The poet is a rebuilder of the imagination, to make a harmony in that. And he is not a complete poet if his whole imagination is not attuned and his whole experience composed into a single symphony.

For his complete equipment, then, it is necessary, in the first place, that he sing; that his voice be pure and well pitched, and that his numbers flow; then, at a higher stage, his images must fit with one another; he must be euphuistic, colouring his thoughts with many reflected lights of memory and suggestion, so that their harmony may be rich and profound; again, at a higher stage, he must be sensuous and free, that is, he must build up his world with the primary elements of experience, not with the conventions of common sense or intelligence; he must draw the whole soul into his harmonies, even if in doing so he disintegrates the partial systematizations of experience made by abstract science in the categories of prose. But finally, this disintegration must not leave the poet weltering in a chaos of sense and passion; it must be merely the ploughing of the ground before a new harvest, the kneading of the clay before the modelling of a more perfect form. The expression of emotion should be rationalized by derivation from character and by reference to the real objects that arouse it—to Nature, to history, and to the universe of truth; the experience imagined should be conceived as a destiny, governed by principles, and issuing in the discipline and enlightenment of the will. In this way alone can poetry become an interpretation of life and not merely an irrelevant excursion into the realm of fancy, multiplying our images without purpose, and distracting us from our business without spiritual gain.

If we may then define poetry, not in the formal sense of giving the minimum of what may be called by that name, but in the ideal sense of determining the goal which it approaches and the achievements in which all its principles would be fulfilled, we may say that poetry is metrical and euphuistic discourse, expressing thought which is both sensuous and ideal.

Such is poetry as a literary form; but if we drop the limitation to verbal expression, and think of poetry as that subtle fire and inward thought which seems at times to shine through the world and to touch the images in our minds with ineffable beauty, then poetry is a momentary harmony in the soul amid stagnation or conflict,—a glimpse of the divine and an incitation to a religious life. . . .

This higher plane is the sphere of significant imagination, of relevant fiction, of idealism become the interpretation of the reality it leaves behind. Poetry raised to its highest power is then identical with religion grasped in its inmost truth; at their point of union both reach their utmost purity and beneficence, for then poetry loses its frivolity and ceases to demoralize, while religion surrenders its illusions and ceases to deceive.

ROBERT FROST

Born 1874

"The Figure a Poem Makes," one of Frost's infrequent essays, stands as the preface to the 1939 edition of *Collected Poems* and to the later *Complete Poems.*

TEXT: *Complete Poems of Robert Frost* (1949).

THE FIGURE A POEM MAKES

Abstraction is an old story with the philosophers, but it has been like a new toy in the hands of the artists of our day. Why can't we have any one quality of poetry we choose by itself? We can have in thought. Then it will go hard if we can't in practice. Our lives for it.

Granted no one but a humanist much cares how sound a poem is if it is only *a* sound. The sound is the gold in the ore. Then we will have the sound out alone and dispense with the inessential. We do till we make the discovery that the object in writing poetry is to make all poems sound as different as possible from each other, and the resources for that of vowels, consonants, punctuation, syntax, words, sentences, meter are not enough. We need the help of context—meaning—subject matter. That is the greatest help towards variety. All that can be done with words is soon told. So also with meters—particularly in our language where there are virtually but two, strict iambic and loose iambic. The ancients with many were still poor if they depended on meters for all tune. It is painful to watch our sprung-rhythmists straining at the point of omitting one short from a foot for relief from monotony. The possibilities for tune from the dramatic tones of meaning struck across the rigidity of a limited meter are endless. And we are back in poetry as merely one more art of having something to say, sound or unsound. Probably better if sound, because deeper and from wider experience.

Then there is this wildness whereof it is spoken. Granted again that it has an equal claim with sound to being a poem's better half. If it is a wild tune, it is a poem. Our problem then is, as modern abstractionists, to have the wildness pure; to be wild with nothing to be wild about. We bring up as aberrationists, giving way to undirected associations and kicking ourselves from one chance suggestion to another in all directions as of a hot afternoon in the life of a grasshopper. Theme alone can steady us down. Just as the first mystery was how a poem could have a tune in such a straightness as meter, so the second mystery is how a poem can have wildness and at the same time a subject that shall be fulfilled.

It should be of the pleasure of a poem itself to tell how it can. The figure a poem makes. It begins in delight and ends in wisdom. The figure is the same as for love. No one can really hold that ecstasy should be static and stand still in one place. It begins in delight, it inclines to the impulse, it assumes direction with the first line laid down, it runs a course of lucky events, and ends in a clarification of life—not necessarily a great clarification, such as sects and cults are founded on, but in a momentary stay against confusion. It has denouement. It has an outcome that though unforeseen was predestined from the first image of the original mood—and indeed from the very mood. It is but a trick poem and no poem at all if the best of it was thought of first and saved for the last. It finds its own name as it goes and discovers the best waiting for it in some final phrase at once wise and sad—the happy-sad blend of the drinking song.

No tears in the writer, no tears in the reader. No surprise for the writer, no surprise for the reader. For me the initial delight is in the surprise of remembering something I didn't know I knew. I am in a place, in a situation, as if I had materialized from cloud or risen out of the ground. There is a glad recognition of the long lost and the rest follows. Step by step the wonder of unexpected supply keeps growing. The impressions most useful to my purpose seem always those I was unaware of and so made no note of at the time when taken, and the conclusion is come to that like giants we are always hurling experience ahead of us to pave the future with against the day when we may want to strike a line of purpose across it for somewhere. The line will have the more charm for not being mechanically straight. We enjoy the straight crookedness of a good walking stick. Modern instruments of precision are being used to make things crooked as if by eye and hand in the old days.

I tell how there may be a better wildness of logic than of inconsequence. But the logic is backward, in retrospect, after the act. It must be more felt than seen ahead like prophecy. It must be a revelation, or a series of revelations, as much for the poet as for the reader. For it to be that there must have been the greatest freedom of the material to move about in it and to establish relations in it regardless of time and space, previous relation, and everything but affinity. We prate of freedom. We call our schools free because we are not free to stay away from them till we are sixteen years of age. I have given up my democratic prejudices and now willingly set the lower classes free to be completely taken care of by the upper classes. Political freedom is nothing to me. I bestow it right and left. All I would keep for myself is the freedom of my material—the condition of body and mind now and then to summon aptly from the vast chaos of all I have lived through.

Scholars and artists thrown together are often annoyed at the puzzle of where they differ. Both work from knowledge; but I suspect they differ most importantly in the way their knowledge is come by. Scholars get theirs with conscientious thoroughness along projected lines of logic; poets theirs cavalierly and as it happens in and out of books. They stick to nothing deliberately, but let what will stick to them like burrs where they walk in the fields. Knowledge of the second kind is much more available in the wild free ways of wit and art. A schoolboy may be defined as one who can tell you what he knows in the order in which he learned it. The artist must value himself as he snatches a thing from some previous order in time and space into a new order with not so much as a ligature clinging to it of the old place where it was organic.

More than once I should have lost my soul to radicalism if it had been the originality it was mistaken for by its young converts. Originality and initiative are what I ask for my country. For myself the originality need be no more than the freshness of a poem run in the way I have described: from delight to wisdom. The figure is the same as for love. Like a piece of ice on a hot stove the poem must ride on its own melting. A poem may be worked over once it is in being, but may not be worried into being. Its most precious quality will remain its having run itself and carried away the poet with it. Read it a hundred times: it will forever keep its freshness as a metal keeps its fragrance. It can never lose its sense of a meaning that once unfolded by surprise as it went.

INDEX

ANCHOR BOOKS

AMERICAN HISTORY AND STUDIES

AMERICAN FICTION

ANCHOR BOOKS

POETRY

ANCHOR BOOKS

FORSTER, E. M.   Alexandria: A History and a Guide, A231

FULLER, MARGARET   Margaret Fuller: American Romantic—A Selection from Her Writings and Correspondence, ed. Miller, A356

GRANVILLE-BARKER, H., & HARRISON, G. B., eds.   A Companion to Shakespeare Studies, A191

HOFFMAN, DANIEL, ed.   American Poetry and Poetics, A304

HOWARD, LEON   Literature and the American Tradition, A329

HYTIER, JEAN   Andre Gide, A307

JAMES, HENRY   The Art of Travel, ed. Zabel, A306

KAUFMANN, WALTER   From Shakespeare to Existentialism, A213

KAZIN, ALFRED   On Native Grounds, A69

KITTO, H. D. F.   Greek Tragedy, A38

KRONENBERGER, LOUIS, ed.   Novelists on Novelists, A293

LAWRENCE, D. H.   Studies in Classic American Literature, A5

MC CORMICK, JOHN, & MAC INNES, MAIRI, eds.   Versions of Censorship, A297

MEREDITH, GEORGE   Essay on Comedy (with Bergson's *Laughter*) in Comedy, A87

MONTAIGNE   Complete Essays of Montaigne, trans. Frame: 3 vols. A227a, A227b, A227c

MOORE, W. G.   Moliere: A New Criticism, A291

MORRIS, WRIGHT, ed.   A Mississippi River Reader, A299

NICOLSON, HAROLD   Tennyson, A284

NIETZSCHE, FRIEDRICH   The Birth of Tragedy *and* The Genealogy of Morals, A81

ORTEGA Y GASSET, JOSE   The Dehumanization of Art and Other Writings on Art and Culture, A72

ORWELL, GEORGE   A Collection of Essays, A29

ROURKE, CONSTANCE   American Humor, A12

SCOTT, A. C.   Literature and the Arts in Twentieth Century China, A343

SHATTUCK, ROGER   The Banquet Years, A238

SHAW, GEORGE BERNARD   Shaw on Music, ed. Bentley, A53

SYPHER, WYLIE   Four Stages of Renaissance Style, A45

TOKLAS, ALICE B.   The Alice B. Toklas Cook Book, A196

TRAVERSI, D. A.   An Approach to Shakespeare, A74

TRILLING, LIONEL   The Liberal Imagination, A13

VAN DOREN, MARK   Shakespeare, A11

WELSFORD, ENID   The Fool: His Social and Literary History, A262

WILLEY, BASIL   The Seventeeth Century Background, A19

WILSON, EDMUND   A Literary Chronicle: 1920–1950, A85

—— A Piece of My Mind, A143

DOLPHIN BOOKS

POETRY AND DRAMA

BYRON, GEORGE GORDON, LORD Don Juan, C64

BROWNING, ELIZABETH BARRETT Sonnets from the Portuguese and Other Poems, C209

BROWNING, ROBERT Men and Women, C136

CERF, BENNETT, & CARTMELL, VAN H., eds. 24 Favorite One-Act Plays, C423

COLERIDGE, SAMUEL TAYLOR, & WORDSWORTH, WILLIAM Lyrical Ballads, C4

FITZGERALD, EDWARD, trans. The Rubáiyát of Omar Khayyám, C28

FRANKENBERG, LLOYD, ed. Invitation to Poetry, C24

—— Pleasure Dome: On Reading Modern Poetry, C190

GILBERT, W. S. H.M.S. Pinafore and Six Other Savoy Operas, C155

—— The Mikado and Five Other Savoy Operas, C158

KEATS, JOHN, & SHELLEY, PERCY BYSSHE Poems of Keats and Shelley (1820), C11

MARQUIS, DON archy and mehitabel, C26

MILTON, JOHN Paradise Lost, C73

OMAR KHAYYAM The Rubáiyát of Omar Khayyám, trans. FitzGerald, C28

SHAKESPEARE, WILLIAM Shakespeare's Sonnets, C33

SHELLEY, PERCY BYSSHE, & KEATS, JOHN Poems of Keats and Shelley, C11

TENNYSON, ALFRED, LORD Idylls of the King, C165

WHITMAN, WALT Leaves of Grass (1855), C3

WILDE, OSCAR The Plays of Oscar Wilde, C137

WORDSWORTH, WILLIAM, & COLERIDGE, SAMUEL TAYLOR Lyrical Ballads, C4

ESSAYS AND LETTERS

BACON, FRANCIS Essays of Francis Bacon, C67

CALDERON DE LA BARCA, FRANCES Life in Mexico, C93

CARLYLE, THOMAS On Heroes and Hero-Worship *and* Representative Men, C83
(THOMAS CARLYLE: On Heroes and Hero-Worship; RALPH WALDO EMERSON: Representative Men)

CREVECOEUR, J. H. ST. JOHN Letters from an American Farmer, C164

DE QUINCEY, THOMAS Confessions of an English Opium-Eater *and* Suspiria de Profundis, C97

DOUGLAS, WILLIAM O. An Almanac of Liberty, C115

EMERSON, RALPH WALDO Conduct of Life, C2

—— On Heroes and Hero-Worship *and* Representative Men, C83
(THOMAS CARLYLE: On Heroes and Hero-Worship; RALPH WALDO EMERSON: Representative Men)

JACOBS, ROBERT D., & RUBIN, LOUIS D., JR., eds. South: Modern Southern Literature in Its Cultural Setting, C316

JAMES, HENRY Hawthorne, C58

LAMB, CHARLES The Essays of Elia *and* The Last Essays of Elia, C6

MAUROIS, ANDRE Seven Faces of Love, C391

RUBIN, LOUIS D., JR., & JACOBS, ROBERT D., eds. South: Modern Southern Literature in Its Cultural Setting, C316

SHAW, G. B., ed. Fabian Essays in Socialism, C170

ANCHOR BOOKS